MANIA

MANIA

*The Story of the Outraged &
Outrageous Lives That Launched
a Cultural Revolution*

RONALD K.L. COLLINS
& DAVID M. SKOVER

Top Five Books
2013

A TOP FIVE BOOK

Published by Top Five Books, LLC
521 Home Avenue, Oak Park, Illinois 60304
www.top-five-books.com

Library of Congress Cataloging-in-Publication Data

Collins, Ronald K.L.
Mania: the story of the outraged and outrageous lives that launched a cultural revolution / Ronald K.L. Collins & David M. Skover.
p. cm.
Includes bibliographical references and index.
ISBN 978-1-938938-02-3
1. Beat generation. 2. Kerouac, Jack, 1922–1969. 3. Ginsberg, Allen, 1926–1997.
4. Burroughs, William S., 1914–1997. 5. Literature and society—United States.
6. American literature—20th century—History and criticism. I. Skover, David M., 1951– II. Title.
PS228.B6C65 2013
810.9'0054—dc23   2012034839

Book design by Top Five Books

Printed in the United States of America

10 9 8 7 6 5 4 3 2 1

To Dyl

I am with you tonight
& in the flight of timeless light
You are my star in a wholly wondrous sky
as I journey beyond the limits of all reasons why
to a place where love lingers & dreams never die
—Ron

To Kellye Testy

Who values the rule of law,
the reason and riches of education,
and the rhythms and rhymes of poetry
—David

The only people for me are the mad ones, the ones who are mad to live, mad to talk, mad to be saved...

—Jack Kerouac

Contents

Note to the Reader

BY ANY MEASURE, they were a bizarre band—at once genius and junkie, cerebral and criminal, innocent and malevolent, lovable and lewd, spiritual and cynical. And they were crazy enough to invite all sorts of trouble, including the kind that produced rebel literature and helped to launch a cultural revolution in America.

Who were they? How did they live? What did they value? And how did their literature reflect all of that? In attempting to answer these questions, we were less concerned with media catchphrases than with what first fueled and then fired the artistic/cultural movement launched by Allen Ginsberg, Jack Kerouac, William S. Burroughs, John Clellon Holmes, and others.

In their lives and literature, they wove fact into fiction and then fiction back into fact—the facts of their lives. Any work that does justice to the heroes, heroines, and rogues of this generation of artists must weave their lives and literature together, if only because they did. The furious, defiant lines in "Howl," the wondrous scenes in *On the Road*, the despair in *Junky*, the unnerving satire of *Naked Lunch*, and the thrill in *Go* simply cannot be divorced from the ways that Ginsberg, Kerouac, Burroughs, Holmes, Neal Cassady, Lucien Carr, Bill Cannastra, and Herbert Huncke, among others, actually lived their lives.

To give the reader a truer *feeling* of their history, we cast our work in narrative form, offering anecdotal slices of their lives (from about

1944 to 1957), and present it as a montage of vivid snapshots. In that sense, portions of *Mania* are necessarily impressionistic. Still, these are impressions based on numerous documented sources. While there are, to be sure, other and more exhaustive ways to tell their story, we find our approach both more natural and contained. The hope is that you can experience something of the remarkable and risky lives these men and women lived...and to experience it all without being overwhelmed by mountains of data.

We seek neither to demonize nor apologize for Ginsberg and his cohorts. While we tell their tales, we do not feel obliged to defend their darker sides. A sobering line by John Leland about this group bears repeating: "[They were] shaped by suicide, depression, psychosis, institutionalization, addiction, alcoholism, jail and early death." Indeed. If their story, as we tell it, seems at times to be cartoonish or unduly dark, that is because that is how they led their lives—not entirely, but quite often. Yes, there was more to the story, and we try to tell that by way of their amazing literary talents.

Still, very much like Kerouac, we admire those "who yearn for the impossible," who crave a life never lived, a reality never recognized, a love never pursued, a faith never finalized, and a world never imagined. Hence, we do not hesitate to fly their flags from time to time—flags of artistic creativity and personal freedom. Or to invoke another metaphor, we echo Douglas Brinkley's "manic desire to find the key to one's life meaning by putting the accelerator through the floorboard." So we are of two minds.

Freedom is always risky business. And once one tastes it, it is all too easy to get drunk under its influence. Those drawn to the free-spirited side of the human equation must be mindful of the ruinous potential in "the cannibalism of a lifeboat," as Kenneth Rexroth so vividly tagged it. And yet, one cannot ignore—and Rexroth could not—the vastness of the creative spirit launched by Ginsberg, Kerouac, Burroughs, Holmes, and their kind.

Whatever one makes of their spirit, its DNA traces can be found in everything from the lyrics of Bob Dylan to the music of Jim Morrison, the vitalizing spirit of the Baltimore folk singer Sonia Rutstein, the theater of Stephen Sondheim, the photography of Annie Leibovitz, the novels of Norman Mailer and Ken Kesey, the short stories of T.C. Boyle, the essays of Susan Sontag, the journalism of Nat Hentoff, and the free-speech jurisprudence of Justice William O. Douglas. If you need more, lend your ears to John Turturro's recitation of "Howl," or Matt Dillon's reading of *On the Road*, or Dennis Hopper's belting out of Burroughs' lines. These experiences will, we think, move the matter of your being.

Our story culminates in a momentous poem—Allen Ginsberg's "Howl." That poem, in turn, is one born and bred in the real-life experiences of young men and women eager to test the limits of life, love, law, language, and every norm of normality. We picture their fast and fantastic stories largely through the filter of the history of "Howl" and those associated with its author.

"Howl" alone did not, of course, launch the revolution in American culture that produced some of the great creative lights of our time. Still, if one looks through the wide lens of its story as set out on our pages, there is much to witness—snapshots of the inexplicable spirit and spontaneity of a group of talented (and troubled) "angelheaded hipsters" who left an indelible mark on the American soul.

This chronicle opens with an unforgiveable killing, continues a few years later with an unusual car crash, and ends with an unexpected court verdict in a free-speech case. In between, the story is even more unbelievable, though all true. The wondrous and tragic stories that follow are their stories; the words are their words; and the mania of it all was their reality. It is, to borrow from the historian James L. Swanson, a story "far too incredible to have ever been made up."

PROLOGUE

Life is a brute creation, beautiful and cruel...
—Jack Kerouac

Previous page: Jack Kerouac (left) and Lucien Carr at Columbia University in 1944

What to do with the body? He gazed over the dark waters of the Hudson River and then looked down.

One hundred and eighty-five pounds of human flesh lay at his feet, stock still. He had to act soon. Panicked, he struggled to roll the warm body down the grassy embankment to the water's edge. The six-foot-long mass wouldn't budge. He pushed again, and then mightily once more. Finally, he succeeded. At the riverbank, he removed the laces from his victim's shoes and used them to tie the hands and feet. But they weren't strong enough. So he tore off the man's shirt, ripped it into strips, and bound the wrists and ankles with the cloth pieces. That would do it. Tightening a belt around the arms for extra measure, he observed thick blots of blood oozing out of the fresh stab wounds.

Had anyone seen him? Time, precious time, was passing. If he didn't take off soon, surely he would be spotted. Hastily, he inspected his surroundings. Rocks. Stones. Yes, he could use them. He frantically gathered them up and shoved them into pockets and inside the clothing of his victim. More rocks, more stones. Now he was ready. He dragged the limp body along the bank's jagged surface, leaving a blood trail in the muddy cracks. He heaved and tugged until the bulk of bound flesh took to the bouncy waters.

But it wouldn't sink; it just floated. Damn!

Impulsively, he stripped to his briefs, ran along the shore, and waded into the waters, up to his chin. The body *had* to sink; the evidence *had* to vanish; gravity *had* to take hold. He threw his arms around it, forced the body down. No luck. He pressed again, down, down. Still no luck. Maybe, he thought, the corpse would sink later. Surely it would; it had to. Meanwhile, the body drifted off, face down, into the void of the dark distance.

It was done. He would vanish before the dawn, allowing him just enough time to get back and continue reading one of his favorite books—Rimbaud's *A Season in Hell.*

———

LUCIEN CARR was a beautiful, bright, privileged, and adventurous boy, charmed by Arthur Rimbaud, the precocious poet obsessed with alienation and symbolism. Lucien (pronounced *Looshun*) enjoyed quoting Rimbaud and the poet Charles Baudelaire. Although Carr had his poetic side, he sported a riotous and bizarre side, as well. A wild partier, the *enfant terrible* had been expelled from Andover prep school. If he was feeling maniacal, he'd chug Canadian Club whiskey, chew shards of a cocktail glass, and pick the sharp slivers from between his bloody teeth. If he was feeling deviant, he would urinate out of windows. Or if he was feeling devilish, he'd rip up a Bible. Once he put his head into an oven and turned on the gas—an art experiment is how he explained it to the doctor who prescribed psychiatric care. Still, this madcap with a fondness for poetry remained the object of much desire.

Lucien was a young man with a very strange take on life…and death. It was that take that made him the center of attraction for those who wished to reinvent their world. Though he appeared demonic to some, in young Allen Ginsberg's eyes he was "the most angelic looking kid…romantically glorious." Born into an aristocratic

St. Louis family, he was five feet, nine inches tall, handsome, fair-haired with almond-shaped green eyes. The young liberal arts student had met Ginsberg in December 1943 at Columbia University when Allen was a seventeen-year-old pre-law student. Together they penned poems—those wondrous manifestos of their New Vision in which they were seers experiencing "drug-induced visions, breakthroughs in consciousness, freedom to experiment sexually, and a total break from the past." That vision was an extension of Lucien's past—a life given over to alcohol, drugs, sex, and trouble.

Jack Kerouac knew Lucien from the time of his merchant-seaman days, when Jack would come back on leave and hang around Columbia University, where he had once been a student. He had a fatal attachment to the "mischievous little prick...prettier than any woman I'd ever seen." In Jack's eyes, they were doomed soulmates. Though Edith ("Edie") Parker was Kerouac's girlfriend (of sorts), her buck-toothed grin could not begin to rival the aura of the strikingly attractive Lucien Carr.

In the summer of 1944 the world was at Lucien Carr's beck and call. The slender nineteen-year-old's popularity at Columbia was everywhere to be seen. He was also one of Lionel Trilling's brightest students at Columbia—a fact not lost on scores of students, including Ginsberg, who adored the famed English professor. Beyond Ginsberg and Kerouac, all sorts of young, male literary types—John Hollander and Herbert Gold, among them—trailed after the dashing sophomore. William Burroughs, though older (he was then thirty), had also fooled around with Lucien, having spent time with him in St. Louis and Chicago, and now in New York. Indeed, Lucien was at the hub of the circle of friends that only later would become known as the Beats. Jack Kerouac's girlfriend, Edie, an art student he had first met while a student at Columbia, introduced him to Carr, who introduced Ginsberg to Burroughs, and then Burroughs to Kerouac, who afterward met Allen at Lucien's urging.

Kerouac was captivated by the boy's literary imagination. He was drawn by Carr's knowledge of the dark side of Nietzsche and the mystical side of Yeats. But Lucien caught more than Jack's mind's eye. Jack looked on with a trace of envy as others trailed "Angel Boy," as Lucien was nicknamed. Admitting his own hounding of Lucien, Jack confessed, "I'm sure I ruined his grades at Columbia. When he wasn't around, I went chasing all over town after him, asking everybody where he was."

One of the many involved in the contest for the boy's attention and affection was David Eames Kammerer. William Burroughs knew Kammerer back from their school days in St. Louis. David was one of Bill's best friends there; the two got along because they both were homosexual and shunned conventional societal norms. In 1933 they cruised Paris's Rue de Lappe "Apaches" neighborhood together.

David was fourteen years older than Lucien. He first met the boy in St. Louis, when he was Lucien's supervisor in various junior high school activities. Clearly, the former English teacher and physical education instructor became emotionally obsessed, pursuing Lucien with a passion. David doggedly chased after Lucien from school to school, from St. Louis to Bowdoin College in Maine to the University of Chicago to New York. Carr didn't seem to mind the attention from his tall, red-haired friend since Kammerer had a good sense of humor. In time, David's infatuation led to a reduced social status, as he took menial jobs to pay the rent. The aim was always the same: to be with or near Lucien. And, if necessary, Kammerer would even occasionally prostitute himself in order to earn more money to lavish on his beloved boy.

As the young Adonis walked across the Columbia quadrangle, it was not uncommon to see poor Kammerer following like a pitiful shadow. There were other times, however, when Lucien took the lead, as when he once asked Professor Lionel Trilling if he could bring his bearded friend to class. In this way and others—as when the two traveled together or when Lucien made a point to save David's many letters to him—Lucien revealed another more accepting side of his feelings toward David.

Kammerer was insanely jealous of anyone who had anything to do with Carr. Predictably, David found himself in amorous competition with Jack and Allen, among others, including Lucien's Marlene Dietrich–like girlfriend Celine Young, the half-French Barnard coed whose mind and flesh charmed the impressionable Lucien.

While Carr was sometimes ambivalent in his reactions toward Kammerer, Kerouac was not; he was open in his disgust of "Mother" Kammerer. Responding to that, the jealous Kammerer once tried to kill Kerouac's cat and would have succeeded were it not for Bill Burroughs' intervention.

Although he continued to send mixed signals, Lucien became increasingly intolerant of David's pestering presence. "Gotta get away" from Kammerer, Carr would say to Kerouac. Jack imagined that he and Lucien eventually might ship off to Paris: "We'll write poetry, paint, drink red wine, wear berets," he mused.

That never happened. But things did get more intense between Jack and Lucien. On the Sunday evening of August 13, 1944, the two were drinking at The West End, a bar on Broadway across from the Columbia campus. They mulled over what to do with their lives…*and* David's. When Lucien got into an intense existential argument with someone else and became testy, Kerouac left. Walking home, Jack passed through the campus. As he did, David approached in the gloom, and asked, "Where's Lucien?"

"In The West End," Kerouac replied.

"Thanks, I'll see ya later," blurted Kammerer, as he headed for the bar.

Finding his precious boy, David sat down to drink and talk. They left in the early morning hours, bought some booze, headed toward the lower levels of Riverside Park, where lovers made out. They strolled along the Hudson and then sat on the grassy bank. Exactly what happened next is uncertain. As Lucien told it, David made "an indecent proposal" to him, became sexually demanding, and even threatened to harm Lucien's girlfriend if he didn't have oral sex with David.

Lucien's frustration—perhaps fueled by fear—took him to the next level. He reached into his pocket and grabbed for his Scout knife. Grasping its brown, jigged Delrin handle, he pulled it out quickly. He opened up its four inches of stainless metal. Would the BSA insignia on the blade remind him of that core tenet of Boy Scout law?—*A Scout is a friend to all. He seeks to understand others.* Would it remind him of that line from the Scout oath?—*To help other people at all times.* Would the Scout slogan—*Do a good turn daily*—stay his hand?

No. Soon enough, the two found themselves in the throes of a Hobbesian struggle, man against man.

There in the dark shortly before 3:30 A.M., Lucien's homicidal blade traveled toward David's chest. The arc of his death swing moved ever closer to its target. He could feel David's gasping breath as the knife's point pierced Kammerer's shirt and then his flesh... and then again, as another furious jab cut its merciless way deep into the heart. David collapsed, his thick red and bloodied hair matting the green earth.

—~~~—

ONCE HE HAD disposed of the body in the river, Lucien quickly put his clothes back on. He had to get away. But traces of David—incriminating traces—remained. For one thing, there were his glasses. They must have fallen off during the fracas. Lucien put them in his pocket. And then there was the blood-stained knife. That, too, went into his pocket. He would deal with both later. Reflexively, he did one more thing—he took David's smokes.

What happened next was a rapid fire of events.

Carr climbed back up to Riverside Park, then out to Riverside Drive to hail a cab. What would he do? What would he say? Ah... Bill Burroughs would know. He'd seek Big Bill's counsel.

The loud knock woke Burroughs. Bill hurried to the door in his bathrobe. Opening it, he saw Lucien, crazy-eyed and upset.

"I just killed the old man."

Burroughs was shocked. "What?" Could it be true? Had Lucien snapped?

Before Bill could say more, Lucien told his story and handed him the blood-stained pack of Lucky Strikes that had been in Kammerer's pocket.

"Have the last cigarette," he said.

Strange. Burroughs paused. Then, with his trademark nasal sneer, he spoke. "So this is how Dave Kammerer ends." He was not, however, so snide as to hold back on giving some street-sage legal advice. "You'd better turn yourself in. You could plead some sort of self-defense."

Lucien feared going to the law. "I'll get the hot seat," he answered.

"Don't be absurd!" Burroughs exclaimed. "Get a good lawyer and do what he tells you to do. Say what he tells you to say. Make a case for self-defense. It's pretty preposterous, but juries have swallowed bigger ones than that."

Still ambivalent over what to do, Lucien headed uptown to Edie's place to get some advice from Jack.

"Well, I disposed of the old man last night," said Lucien as Jack struggled to wake up. Kerouac knew exactly what he meant.

"Why'd ya go and do that?"

"No time for that now," replied Lucien. "I've still got the knife and his glasses covered with blood. Wanna come with me and see what we can do to dump 'em?"

Still confused, Jack paused. "What the hell didja go and do that for?"

There was no time to talk about remorse or to offer explanations. The two fled off to Morningside Park; they could dump the damning stuff in the tall weeds. In the disgusting heat of the early August morning, with Jack pretending to take a leak so as to draw attention away from Lucien, the young man buried Kammerer's rimless glasses, but not the knife.

Clad in khaki pants and white T-shirts, the pair headed toward the bars of Harlem; they stopped when they found one on 125th Street. Before they entered, Kerouac noticed a grate, right at his feet. "There, look, a good subway grate." The wheels turned in his mind. A grate—that's it. That was the key to Lucien's way out.

The grate's steel bars separated the moral world from its immoral counterpart. Between its slats had fallen much evidence of the sins of humankind. Below the grates rested the hitman's Luger, the hooker's used condoms, the junkie's bent needles, the drunkard's empty bottles, and the miles of sewer-soaked gum that held everything in eternal place. It was the perfect resting spot for the bloody Boy Scout knife that had taken David Kammerer's life.

"Drop the knife down there," said Jack.

Lucien complied, but in a curious way. He knelt down as if in prayer and let the evidence of his felonious act drop to the underworld. At first, it struck the grating sideways and wouldn't go in. So Lucien stood up and kicked it. As it fell, so too did David Kammerer's body...into the river's dark domain. It was all subterranean now.

"Let's go in this cool zebra lounge and have a cold beer." Jack was thirsty, but Lucien couldn't clear his mind.

"I stabbed him in the heart."

Jack drank as his buddy rambled.

"I pushed him in the river with all those rocks."

More drinking, more Macbeth-like rambling.

"He went off floating with his feet upside down." He could not stop. "His head's down below."

What to do with Lucien? Jack had an idea.

"Let's take a subway downtown, go to see a movie or something."

No. Now was not the time for that.

"Let's take a cab, go see my psychiatrist," Lucien insisted.

As the day wore on, they rode down Park Avenue to a grand building with an elegant foyer, up the elevator to the office where Lucien's analyst awaited. When the confessional story was told, in whatever form, Lucien was uncertain whether his psychiatrist believed him. But no matter. It was done, and it was all for the best. Time to shift mental gears. Oddly, the shrink loaned him five dollars, just enough for the two to hop over to Third Avenue to catch a matinee of *Four Feathers* (in Technicolor). Afterward, they meandered to Times Square, ate hotdogs, and checked out the paintings at the Museum of Modern Art. His frolicking over, Lucien went to his mom's place and told her about what he had done. Marion Carr was flabbergasted and insisted that they go to the police.

Another maddening swirl of events followed as they all confronted the law:

—A day or so later, Lucien Carr, flanked by his high-priced lawyer, turned himself in to the offices of Frank S. Hogan, the district attorney. When Lucien told his amazing story to the D.A., the boy was "astonishingly calm and self-possessed."

—Later, the police found the glasses, and went to the scene of the crime after the Coast Guard had located the body. They pulled the corpse from the waters. The police were stunned by the gruesome sight before them and by Lucien's aloofness. With no trace of emotion, Carr identified the man he had killed.

—Lucien was taken to the Elizabeth Street station and booked. While incarcerated, he spent his time reading Rimbaud's *A Season in Hell*.

—Kerouac and Burroughs were hauled in as material witnesses shortly thereafter. They faced the possibility of being charged as accessories after-the-fact. Bill made bail, Jack could not. His father refused to post the bond.

—Meanwhile, David Kammerer's bloated and blue body lay tucked away in a human-size file (No. 169) in the stinking basement of the City Morgue at Bellevue Hospital.

The investigation continued. As it did, one thing became clear: the boys' sexual preferences would determine the outcome of the case. If Lucien had dabbled in homosexual antics, he would be doomed, for no one would believe that his acts amounted to an "honor slaying," as the *Daily News* tagged it.

Jack was also in deep trouble. He had helped Lucien dispose of the incriminating evidence. That meant that he, too, could go to jail. As with Lucien, Jack had to establish his heterosexual status. Later, as they waited in the courtroom to be arraigned, Lucien spoke softly to Jack out of the corner of his mouth: "Heterosexuality all the way down the line."

To help spring him from the Bronx Jail, Jack called Edie. "Lissen, my father is mad as hell, won't lend me [the money] for the bond, the hell with him." He then pleaded with her for help: "[Y]ou borrow that money from your aunt, I'll get out of here, we'll get married right now, we'll go to Detroit, and I'll get a job in a war plant and pay her off her hundred dollars."

Forever hoping, Edie replied: "Okay, Jackie."*

---

*According to Edie Parker, Jack's bail bond was paid with money inherited from her grandfather's estate, which was tied up in probate. The probate judge released the sum on condition that Edie and Jack were married.

They were married in the Manhattan City Hall chambers of Judge Manninger Shawl. Their marital moment was surreal. The judge insisted that Jack remain shackled to the wrist of a police detective throughout the ceremony. Soon Jack was out on bail.

Meanwhile Lucien, aided by defense lawyers Vincent J. Malone and Kenneth Spence, copped a manslaughter plea. This guaranteed that there would be no trial replete with incriminating evidence, including testimony that pointed away from heterosexuality all the way down the line. He was sentenced to serve an indefinite term, up to a maximum of ten years, in the Elmira Reformatory in New York.

"It was a year of low, evil decadence," Jack recalled. When it was nearly over—with Lucien in Elmira and Jack breaking up with Edie after a few months of marriage—Kerouac recalled those days when he and Carr ventured off like carefree Symbolist poets to the "dark bridge waters." It was there that they yelled out an infamous passage from Baudelaire, and in their best French:

"Plonger au fond du gouffre...ciel ou enfer, qu'importe?"

Translated: To plunge to the bottom of the abyss, Heaven or Hell, what matter?

Sometime later, Kerouac and Burroughs wrote a mystery thriller, *And the Hippos Were Boiled in Their Tanks*, based on the Kammerer killing. They shopped it around to various publishing houses, but nothing came of their efforts. "It isn't very good, it isn't worth publishing," said Burroughs.*

As for Allen Ginsberg, when he walked past a subway entrance where he once kept David's company, he would stop and weep and

---

*The complete novel was first published in 2008, with a sober and informative afterword by James Grauerholz on the Kammerer killing. Excerpts from the unpublished manuscript appeared earlier in *Word Virus: The William S. Burroughs Reader* (1998). In 2013 a movie based on the Kammerer killing, titled *Kill Your Darlings*, was released. Directed by John Krokidas, the film stars Dane DeHaan (Lucien Carr), Michael C. Hall (David Kammerer), Jack Huston (Jack Kerouac), Ben Foster (William Burroughs), and Daniel Radcliffe (Allen Ginsberg).

then shout above the roar of the passing train: "Kammerer, Kammerer, where are you? Dead? So soon?"

But Allen's feelings were cut from two cloths. Notwithstanding his sentiments about poor David, Allen was unable to fault Lucien: "I can't find it in me to condemn him," he told his dad. Allen had started work on a novel on the Carr-Kammerer affair titled *West End Sunday: A Romanticized Version of a Tragedy.* He even submitted a chapter of it for credit in his Columbia creative writing class. Taken aback, his professor reported the matter to the administration. Associate dean Nicholas McKnight immediately demanded that Allen abandon this project since it clearly contravened school policy. Moreover, the work was smutty insofar as it dwelt on an unacceptable topic like homosexuality and glorified louts like Lucien Carr and Jack Kerouac.

Allen's father agreed with the opinion of the college authorities and had some strong ones of his own. "The homosexual and the insane person is a menace to himself and to society," Louis Ginsberg admonished his son. "Danger and disaster lie that way!" Although Louis knew nothing yet of Allen's own homoerotic urges, he condemned even his son's academic interest in the subject or his friendship with homosexuals like Burroughs. Liberal as Louis was, he would not tolerate senseless nonconformity: "No, pleasure is not the final reference of morality. Were it so, chaos, confusion, anarchy would result, not communism or socialism or a better society or a better man. License is not liberty.... I tell you, Allen, you are living in an Ivory Tower." Literally, his bottom line was: "What about a psychiatrist?"

Ginsberg's journal entry for August 19, 1944, introspectively assessed the significance of what had happened: "And now, this curtain has been rung down! Everything I have loved of the past year has fled into the past. My world is no longer the same."

It was the first tragedy to befall the Beats. For Allen, its meaning was clear: "The libertine circle is destroyed with the death of Kammerer."

—◦◦◦—

THE STORY REALLY began there, back on that dark night in August 1944. What came afterward was generally glorious by comparison. Like Carr's name on the original dedication page of Allen Ginsberg's *Howl* (1957)—which was removed before its mass publication—Lucien's legacy was largely invisible. And yet there was something about Lucien and his world that loomed large, though dimly, in the life and times of Ginsberg and his clan. It took a car chase to bring that world back into bold focus. And, when it did, the libertine circle reopened, and Carr came back into the picture... though appearing altogether different.

PART I THE CHASE

[They] were attracted to "madness" as a sustained presence; a lucid, singular, and obsessive way to illuminate the shadows of the day.... They used "madness"— which they regarded as naturalness—as a break- through to clarity, as a proper perspective from which to see.

—John Tytell

Previous page: Allen Ginsberg (left) and Herbert Huncke

1.

"IT WAS A NICE DAY," Allen Ginsberg recalled. April 22, 1949, was sunny and warm, and the temperature climbed gently to a comfortable 72 degrees. Rain would only come later in the day. Until then, it was a perfect Friday for cruising along Utopia Parkway with the windows down and the radio up. "I liked the idea," he observed, "of a freshening ride in Long Island." So the young man and his two roommates took to the road.

Slightly before noon, the trio left their small cold-water flat at 1401 York Avenue in Manhattan. They climbed into a sedan and pulled away, distancing themselves from the dreary neighborhood of thrift shops, cheap bars, and rows of dingy and dilapidated tenements. Pointed toward Long Island, their car was packed with clothes, journals, and letters, among other things. They had begun to clean out their apartment, which had become unbearably crammed.

Jack Melody—"Little Jack," as his friends called him—was at the wheel; he would drop his stuff off at his mom's home. Allen, who sat in the back, would visit his brother Eugene, a New York University law student, on the return trip. He wanted to deliver some personal papers there. And Vicki, Little Jack's girlfriend, came along for the ride.

While journeying down Northern Boulevard, Allen rambled on and on about a trip he had taken to Dakar years earlier, this as Vicki squawked at Jack nonstop, one "conversational bit" after another. The chatter distracted Little Jack to the point that he mistakenly turned onto 43rd Avenue in Bayside, Queens, and drove the wrong way on a one-way street. To make matters worse, the twenty-six-year-old headed toward trouble. Two officers manning a black-and-white radio squad car observed him driving against traffic. Predictably, they flagged the wayward sedan to a stop. Patrolman George McClancy approached the vehicle.

"Where's the light?" asked Little Jack, figuring he had run a red light. The cop shook his head. No, that wasn't the problem. Driving the wrong way down the street—*that* was the problem—and Little Jack was about to be ticketed. Officer McClancy returned to his car, got his summons book, and prepared to write out a traffic ticket. Suddenly things spun wildly out of control.

Little Jack stretched his short leg and pumped the pedal. The sedan jolted forward. The tires smoked and squealed. "Look out, George!" yelled McClancy's partner, Officer John Colleton. Officer McClancy looked up, barely in time to hurl himself out of the path of the speeding car... saving his life. Little Jack then threw the car in reverse, forward again, and made a hard turn toward Northern Boulevard. "We have to outrun them!" he screamed.

The siren blared, the red light spun; the cops were in hot pursuit. Even though Jack was gunnin' it to the max, Vicki hounded him. *Where* exactly was he going? Little Jack replied that they had to abandon the car. Somewhat testily, Vicki asked if they had to ditch everything else, too. "Fuck the clothes," Jack snapped back, "we have to abandon the whole mess." Meanwhile Allen, the twenty-two-year-old, frightened, Jewish kid in the back seat, begged Jack to slow down, implored Vicki to cool down, and prayed to God to come down and save them.

The carburetor was full throttle. The transmission was well into high gear. The sedan rocketed from zero to sixty-five in a frenzied mile. Jack then made a lightning-flash decision to turn onto a side street at 205th. The suicidal swerve propelled the car against and over a curb, launching it airborne into a telephone pole. Allen felt the car flip over and over. He feared for his life. He sang *sotto voce*, "Lord God of Israel, Isaac, and Abraham." The experience made him feel "slightly mystical." He had "the very distinct sensation…that all my mistakes of the past year…had led in a chain to this one retribution moment where now I was going to have to pay for it."

Perhaps the Lord on High heard Allen's spiritual singing. For when the battered car slid to a rest on its top, with its doors flung open and its contents strewn everywhere, the occupants emerged alive…miraculously.

Jack's leg was severely bruised. Vicki and Allen were shaken up, but they were otherwise fine. Allen's black horn-rimmed glasses had flown off his face during the violent toss and tumble. Seriously nearsighted, he dug around frantically in the debris, searching for his glasses and his private papers. He would long remember "the horror of the scramble after them" and the "sickening feeling of failure when I saw everything upside down and confused, including myself." Nonetheless, the naïve young man was clear-headed enough to understand "that if I didn't beat it I was going to get caught."

Shocked onlookers tried to help Allen. He emerged clumsily with a notebook under his arm. Instinctively, Allen knew what to do. He "refused aid in walking away" and pretended to be "confused when people asked me questions." Cautiously, he faded from the wreck. Slowly, deliberately, and then quickly.

"Turn off the ignition before the car explodes!" a bystander screamed out. Feeling the pain of his injury, Little Jack realized that he could not elude the oncoming "heat." As Vicki and Allen made a run for it, Little Jack remained pressed against the steering wheel, his leg twitching and his mouth ajar. Accepting his felonious fate, he surrendered to an arrest at the scene of the accident.

Like terrified prey scurrying before hounds on a hunt, Vicki and Allen split apart and dashed off in different directions. Vicki had enough money to hail a cab to return to the York Avenue apartment. Allen, however, wandered blindly; with no more than seven cents in his pocket, he didn't have enough fare for the subway. His only option was to find a phone and call for help.

But he couldn't, not yet. In a dizzied stupor, he wandered to and fro like a lost soul searching for Yahweh in an urban desert. The young man felt the "complete, final, and awful" sense of "Divine Wrath." Memories of all sorts rushed through his mind, memories with a moral, as though to torment him. He recalled his ruinous ways, his impotence in dealing with his problems, and felt "twinges of anxiety, muffled visions of what was to come."

The sky darkened. Allen's imagination flashed on images of tragic Shakespearean figures who meandered in storms or defied tempests—the likes of Lear, Macbeth, and Hamlet. His tossing thoughts finally descended back to reality; focusing on Vicki and Little Jack, Allen understood that "their troubles are their own now." Acknowledging his own follies, he "felt thankful and began to pray."

As his mind moved from prayer to the practical, Allen remembered that he had once been told that, if he were ever in trouble, he was to call Little Jack's family. Luckily, he discovered a phone booth, made a nickel call, and left a message with one of Jack's sisters. Learning of Allen's whereabouts through their intermediary, Vicki called him back shortly thereafter at the pay phone. She was upset and concerned about Little Jack. Was he hurt? What happened to him? And she asked Allen if he was okay. Yes, he was safe but extremely distressed. Not to worry; Vicki would rescue Allen in a few minutes.

Thirty minutes passed. Where was she?

Allen's steps were heavy with anxiety. He looked for cigarette butts on the street.

Another thirty minutes passed. What was taking her? He smoked the butts.

Another hour passed. More angst, more smoking.

Finally, Vicki arrived, driven in a car by a guy named Carl. The three headed to Little Jack's family home in Long Island. Allen had nothing much to tell Jack's sisters, except that he and Vicki had left their brother at the scene of the crash and were unsure of what had happened to him.

Finally, Vicki and Allen took a cab to the apartment. It was around four P.M. when they arrived. On the way, Vicki gave Allen $22, so he would have some money. But Little Jack—what was going to happen to him? She wept. Would he go to jail?

Back at the scene of the accident, the patrolmen sifted through the wreckage. They found one clue after another. First, there was the totaled car; it had been stolen a month earlier in Washington, D.C. Then there were its contents: scattered silverware, costly clothes, and an assortment of other things. As they would learn, it was all stolen—some of the loot from a recent $10,000 robbery of jewelry, clothing, and furs. The crime had been committed only two nights earlier at the home of a wealthy contractor living in Garden Bay Manor, Astoria. The police search also turned up one of Vicki's shoes, as though abandoned by a large-slippered Cinderella. Most importantly, they happened upon an envelope with this return address:

1401 York Avenue
New York, N.Y.*

---

*Ironically, the finger of guilt was that of Allen's father, who had penned his son's name and address on one of the envelopes that the police discovered.

After the car and its contents were impounded, Detective Lieutenant James M. Sloan of the Bayside Police Station continued his investigation. Soon enough, he discovered that he was dealing with seasoned lawbreakers. Early inquiries revealed that Little Jack, the son of a small-time Long Island mob family, had been arrested some eighteen times in other cities on charges of safe-cracking, larceny, and related crimes. Vicki Russell, a six-foot redhead—known on the street as the "Detroit Redhead"—was a waitress by day and a hooker by night. She was also the daughter of a Philadelphia judge. Quite a pair they made—a pale-skinned, fiery haired "Amazonian" heroin addict was the romantic companion of a swarthy, elfin-sized, balding, Sicilian-American crook who typically wore huge, widebrimmed hats.

And then there were all the papers, inside and outside of the wrecked car: personal letters and private journals belonging to Allen, laced with line after line of incriminating evidence about the true identities and activities of Little Jack Melody (thirty-four years old, né Jack Melodia), Vicki Russell (twenty-four, née Patricia Arminger), and Allen Ginsberg (twenty-two, né Irwin Allen Ginsberg), among others. Those papers also revealed all sorts of eyeopening facts... about additional crimes and aberrant sex, including homosexual acts. The police would pay Allen a visit.

As Detective Joseph Monaca neared York Avenue, he and his partner were about to hit paydirt. Not only would they find Vicki and Allen there, but they would come upon Herbert E. Huncke. He was a friend of Allen's, Vicki's, and Little Jack's. He was, as well, the biggest criminal and sexual deviant of them all.

It was no longer a beautiful day; a hard rain was now falling.

2.

He had all the habits you could possibly get.
—William S. Burroughs

HERBERT HUNCKE was a junkie. The rhyme rang true. It explained much in the lives of Vicki, Jack, Allen, and many of their friends. His junk entered the bloodstream of their veins or minds or both. Once it did, they and their worlds were radically changed in ways good and evil, beautiful and bizarre, magical and maddening.

Times Square low-lifers tagged Huncke the "Mayor of 42nd Street"; the cops called him "Creep." He used the Angler Bar as his center of operations. Some called the L-shaped room abutting Eighth Avenue and West 43rd Street "the evil bar." Huncke traded there in drugs and flesh. A constant user since the age of twelve, Herbert pumped himself with all manner of mind-altering stuff: pot, bennies, and heroin, too—or "antifreeze," "Bombs Away," "Aunt Hazel," as junk was called in street vernacular. He often traded mental sobriety for a Benzedrine haze.

A hustler since the age of sixteen, Huncke tricked with his male johns whenever and wherever he could, even in toilet stalls. Once a small-time runner for the Capone gang after he dropped out of high school in Chicago, he graduated in time to larceny, burglary, and any other property crime on or off the books.

No home—including those of his dearest friends—was safe from Huncke's thieving ways. One of his standard brand of rip-offs involved Allen, who had first befriended him in 1945. Soon after meeting Herbert, Allen performed a *mitzvah* (a kind act) by inviting the junkie to move into an apartment that Ginsberg sublet from a Columbia University theology student. What followed was case-book Huncke: rare volumes vanished from the shelves, silverware disappeared from the kitchen drawers, and record collections moved from the student's apartment to "fences" throughout New York City.

Ever the street philosopher, the junk-man later observed: "I always followed the road of least resistance. I just continued to do what I wanted. I didn't weigh or balance things. I started out this way and I never really changed."

His lure was not his looks. Huncke was small and skinny; his eyes were hazel, turtle-lidded, and bagged; he had a slightly bulbous nose; his dark, wavy, greasy hair contrasted starkly with pale skin; his lips drew at the corners into a perpetual pout; he had lost some teeth; and the needle tracks and scabs that dotted his skeletal arms and legs were so ugly that pancake makeup was sometimes needed to hide them. His body was a breeding ground for parasites and fungi.

Neither would his nature win him favor. Indeed, Huncke saw himself to be a vile creature. To his friends, Herbert characterized himself as "unscrupulous" and "completely saturated with narcotics." For emphasis, he added, "I believe I am rotten in my entire being."

Huncke's charm was his storytelling, which translated his hard-world experiences into spell-binding yarns. He was the Sartre of the streets, the existential con man who turned hustlers and hipsters into cultural heroes.

Taking a break from tricking or thieving, Huncke often locked himself behind subway toilet doors ("the only place [to] work in peace"). There he scribbled anecdotes into notebooks that became a resource for his oral tales and literary narratives. Even more importantly, his novel influence became so strong in time as to inspire characters and scenes in the writings of William Burroughs, Jack Kerouac, John Clellon Holmes, and Allen Ginsberg. In fact, Huncke's constant use of the word "beat"—meaning down-and-out, deadbeat, or a sad sack—later sparked Kerouac's imagination to give the term a new and popular meaning for rebellious youths soon to be branded "the Beat Generation."

In the early 1940s the young and bright came to study at Herbert's feet. Ivy League students and graduates found their way to him to hear the master's words and experience his seedy world firsthand. "They were all so very, very intellectual," Huncke observed. Among them, William Seward Burroughs II—an Ivy League–educated, three-piece-suited thirty-year-old living off the fat of his inheritance from the Burroughs Adding Machine Corporation—became one of Herbert's premier "mentees."

Burroughs "was definitely 'fruit.'" Though he sometimes kept the company of women (and was involved in a sham marriage in 1937 that went nowhere), he much preferred male flesh. Bill resembled a tall Buster Keaton and usually dressed formally—Brooks Brothers garb or seersucker suits. In Allen's eyes, the "well-traveled ex-Harvard" man looked like one of "the busts of Dante."

Bill Burroughs dabbled in various occupational fields, including medical school in Vienna and graduate school in anthropology at Harvard; he toyed with jobs as an adman, a bartender, and even once as a bug exterminator.* But the straight life was never his; he was fascinated by life's darker sides and saw himself as an adventurer and outlaw. By that measure, Huncke was his man, his

---

*Years later Burroughs published a novel titled *Exterminator!*, though it was not about bugs.

demonic hipster. Burroughs' dry and sardonic wit, slowly brewed and craftily served, was suited to the bizarre life-stories Huncke brought his way. He reveled in a "sort of grifter's realism picked up from a long study of the underworld. Burroughs' only religion was that of 'fact.'" Still, it was more than a tad strange—Huncke and this Harvard man.

Flirting with the venues of the underworld, Bill Burroughs had once offered to solicit buyers for bounty recently stolen from a Navy store—a Thompson submachine gun, a cartridge clip for an automatic pistol, and several boxes of morphine syrettes owned by one of his shadier acquaintances. The very idea of crime was a rush for him. Pursuing a potential lead, Burroughs knocked on the door of a low-rent Henry Street apartment near the Brooklyn Bridge. It was there that he first entered the lives of Herbert Huncke, Little Jack Melody, and Vicki Russell, who all lived together.

Huncke was immediately suspicious of the stranger dressed elegantly in a Chesterfield coat. Bill "didn't know any of the underground language" and "appeared like a fish out of water"; so Herbert warned his roommates, "He's the FBI." Within days, however, Huncke realized that the eager Burroughs had criminal potential. Soon, the well-bred fellow had fallen under the tutelage of "Professor" Huncke, who inured him to hard drugs, to hardened criminals, and to the heinous sagas of the street. When that happened, Burroughs dumped his aristocratic lifestyle—he was "shitting it out," as he put it.

Herbert's association with Bill brought him into the company of young and aspiring writers; he loved to thrill and amuse them with his tawdry tales. "Talk about storytelling," Neal Cassady wrote to Jack Kerouac, "Huncke gabs in my ear all day and night, he relishes bullshitting with me. We sure whip up a breeze, especially when we're high. Bill & Huncke & I get high every night on tea [pot] & lush [liquor]. 'It's out of this world'—to quote Huncke." The formula for Burroughs, Kerouac, Ginsberg, and others was simple: hang with Herbert, hear his stories, heed his world, and then harmonize it all into the texts of their writings. In time, the Huncke-like life would become the stuff of their literary chronicles.

3.

THERE WAS MORE to Herbert Huncke than storytelling, however. He also involved and encouraged his friends, when they were willing, to engage in sex-ploits that otherwise might have passed them by. Ever the erotic tumbler, Huncke would trick with anyone, usually for a price. On a higher plane, however, Huncke hooked up with Alfred Kinsey when the distinguished researcher, who had heard about Herbert from a student, called him and visited him at one of his haunts on Times Square.

"What exactly is it you're interested in?" Huncke had asked when Kinsey phoned.

"All I want you to do," replied Dr. Kinsey, "is tell me about your sex life, what experiences you've had, what your interests are, whether you've masturbated and how often, [and] whether you've had homosexual experiences."

"That all you want?"

"That's all I want."

When Kinsey's cab pulled up at the bar where they were to meet, Huncke stared at the round-faced, gray-haired professor nattily clad in a suit. Spotting Huncke, Kinsey declared, "I'm Kinsey, you're Herbert Huncke. Let's go in. You'd like to have a drink?"

"He showed me a card with a phallus drawn on it," said Huncke. "He said he'd like to know the length of it when erect and when soft." From there, the conversation moved to many topics on life and sex in general, and Huncke's sex life in particular. "I sort of unburdened myself of many things that I'd long been keeping to myself." As if dictating an issue of *True Confessions*, Herbert related one lurid sexual experience after another.

Kinsey paid Huncke $10 for the interview and inquired whether any in his circle might also agree to be interviewed. "Subcontracting" for the Indiana University study that would become *Sexual Behavior in the Human Male*, Huncke recruited Burroughs, Kerouac, and Ginsberg for interviews on their ribald sex practices. Herbert netted two dollars for each referral. "I became a pimp for Kinsey," Huncke mused.

4.

IT WAS HUNCKE'S rare blend of junkie, queer, and underworld bard that made him irresistible to the impressionable Allen Ginsberg, who had an idealized image of him as the dark angel of 42nd Street. To Allen, Herbert was "an actual damned soul living already in hell, aware of it, powerless to help himself and powerless to be aided." Despite this romanticized view, Ginsberg found it hard to forgive Huncke for betraying Allen's kind trust when his fast-fingered friend ransacked the sublet apartment. "Never darken my door again," Allen warned him. But when Herbert returned, like the prodigal son, to test his patron's charity, the *menschkeit* in Allen could not suffer Huncke's hardships.

The winter of 1948 was a bitter one for Herbert. Recently released from jail for possession of pot ("shiazit," in slang), he carved out a meager existence on caffeine, bennies, and doughnuts. "I lived in cafeterias and slept in all-night movie theaters.... I'd walk the underground tunnels down around Penn Station, into the station restrooms, nodding on toilet seats," Huncke recalled. Confused and suicidal, Huncke confessed, "I felt I *was* dying—could observe death feeding on me. I saw it in the pallor of my skin and the patches of oozing sores on my face... in the smell from my crotch and from my dirty bleeding feet.... [Allen] was the only love I knew for a long stretch of time, my only contact with life."

With nowhere-left-to-turn desperation, the ghostly vagabond rapped on Allen's apartment door one snowy February day at eight o'clock in the morning. The spectacle of Herbert's plight was horrifying. His frozen face was icy white; his tattered clothes hardly sheltered his skeletal form; and his soaked socks were bloodied by blisters caused by his badly torn leather shoes.

Compassion replaced anger. Allen first opened his heart, and then his door. The two hadn't seen each other for more than sixty days, but now Huncke was standing in Allen's living room. Herbert was once again in his home...and in his life.

"Did you get my letter on Rikers Island?"

"No," replied Huncke, "thank you for thinking of me, though." He sat down, removed his shoes, and exposed his horrid sores. The vagrant guest told his host how he had not slept in several days, the last time at the 50th Street Greyhound Bus Terminal. What little he ate consisted of Benzedrine doses mixed with coffee and an occasional doughnut.

However pathetic his state, Huncke "discussed these things with some humor," Ginsberg recalled.

Throughout it all, Allen—like the Passover Christ in John 13—took saintly steps: "I boiled up a pot full of hot water and helped him wash his feet," recalled Ginsberg. "I was aware of how little love had been shown him in the last ten days of half hallucinated wandering. Yet I washed with averted eyes."

Allen's compassion provided needed relief. Huncke "went to sleep on the couch and slept for a day and night." In the weeks ahead, Allen nursed the ailing thirty-year-old man back to health. "He lay on my couch," Ginsberg remembered, "sleeping in withdrawal for a month." Even so, Allen didn't want the past to repeat itself: "I hadn't planned to leave him alone in the house without further talk with him, [without some] reassurance that he wouldn't run off with any of my valuables." So a pact was sealed, and Huncke vowed not to steal from his benefactor.

Even if Herbert didn't steal from Allen, there was still the problem of supporting him. "It's about time to tell you, Herbert, that my hospitality can't last forever. I only make $25 a week and I can't put us both up on that very long. I'm already going in debt."

No need to worry. "'Well, I'll be off your hands as soon as'—he dropped his shoulders wearily, 'I can figure up some sort of plan of action.'"

Allen believed him. "Once you have a little money," he responded, "you'll be better off obviously. You'll keep out of trouble, you won't have to worry about jail. You might be able to find yourself a boy and set up a pad of your own." Staying out of trouble with the law was stretching it—even Allen realized that. For, once Huncke had money, he might "invest in some heroin." Better still: "You might even be able to afford a habit if you need it."

Ever optimistic and naïve, Allen sought to convince his friend that life need not be a Nietzschean nightmare; it need not be a dark and dismal series of bad dreams. Huncke warmed up to the promise of a new life. "I'll mull it over. I haven't worked in I don't know how many years, and I don't know if I want to," he told Allen. "But maybe you're right, I really don't have anything else to do."

Herbert Huncke seemed willing to mend his ways and move on with his life. The tables turned enough that, at one point in March, Herbert actually nursed Allen when he experienced a relapse of bronchitis. For once, Allen was on the receiving end of kindness. So maybe Huncke was really on the road to recovery.

But a strange "recovery" it was. Once healthy again, Huncke returned to his old trade with a new vigor. Nevertheless, Allen was excited: "Then one day he finally went out, to my relief, and came back with some money. He'd robbed a car," Allen explained.* "I was overjoyed! He'd come back to life. Like he was back operating again, which meant that he wasn't going to die."

---

*Young Allen Ginsberg was so taken by Huncke's persona that he devoted fifteen or more printed pages to describe him in dreadful detail in his pre-1950 journal entries. Years later Huncke, as others, would assume a role in Ginsberg's poem "Howl."

5.

LIFE FOR HERBERT and Allen was back to "normal" in the early months of 1949. At the time, Allen worked a graveyard shift (midnight to eight) as a copyboy at the Associated Press. His exact pay: $31.75 a week. But while Allen toiled at honest work, Herbert reunited with his criminal comrades, Little Jack and Vicki. They busily took over Ginsberg's apartment and rearranged the furniture. After all, they had to make space for all the booty they stole and stored nightly.

"It was like a whole *Beggar's Opera* scene at my house," Allen recalled. "The three of them were going out on burglary expeditions together and bringing back all the loot." Allen's apartment got smaller as the stash grew larger: "silver sets, all sorts of dreck like radios, phonograph machines. It was getting crowded, actually." Even so, the ever imaginative Ginsberg viewed himself as a vicarious player whose only involvement was observing the fruits of the crimes and listening to thrilling stories about them.

Finally, Allen took it to the next level; he agreed, for the first time, to go along on a caper. One evening in April 1949, he joined the York Avenue gang as they stalked the town in search of unoccupied cars with anything of value in plain view. His fantasies, however, were checked by reality. Allen could not bring himself either to break into cars or even to act as a lookout for Herbert, Little Jack, and Vicki when they did so. "My feelings at the time were mixed," Ginsberg recounted. "I thought, possibly, I might take part in a car haul. But I did not, when the opportunity arose, from a clammy feeling of fear and desire not to get involved in the actual operation." On the return trip, the group worked through Allen's psychological hang-ups. "They (especially Little Jack) were quick to . . . sympathize with my desire to keep my 'cherry,' as we referred to it."

Excited as he was to witness the criminal life in real time, Allen was nonetheless becoming ever more worried about a police raid of his loot-laden apartment. Feeling the need for action, he penned a two-page "manifesto" that ordered the immediate removal of all drugs and stolen property. The headstrong trio ignored Allen's mandate; they persisted in their hot-fingered heists.

"I remonstrated in vain," Allen complained. "Every time I'd put Huncke down he'd say, 'What do you want me to do? What am I *supposed* to do?'" Things only got worse. Without request or shame, Herbert wore Allen's clothes ("suits, socks, shirts"), and Little Jack and Vicki took over Allen's bedroom and moved his few possessions into a living-room bureau. Now, Allen had little choice: he either had to kick them out, move himself out, or push the goods out.

Whereas Ginsberg idealized Huncke, Burroughs long understood who Huncke actually was. Though Bill dabbled in Herbert's world and took chances in it, Burroughs nonetheless understood the dangers of the devil. In the spring of 1949, he wrote Allen twice from New Orleans, where he had moved to take a break from the junk-saturated temptations of New York City. His first letter urged Allen to rid himself of Herbert, who was no more than a "parasite" that would inevitably bleed the hand that fed him. Burroughs recounted Huncke's "vile act" during a recent visit to his home in the neighborhood of Algiers, across the river from the French Quarter; at the end of the trip, Herbert repaid Bill's hospitality by stealing an expensive Oriental rug. Pure Huncke.

Bill's next letter, however, ratcheted up Allen's anxiety. It seems that Burroughs had found the drug-filled environs of New Orleans' French Quarter more difficult to resist than he had imagined. Shortly before Easter, he was arrested for narcotics possession, his home was searched, and letters from Allen proposing pot sales in New York were seized.* However improbable an FBI investigation of Allen's apartment might be, Burroughs now strongly urged Ginsberg to play it safe and eliminate all signs of criminal activity.

Allen took it to heart. He became ever more paranoid. Not knowing quite where to turn, he shared Bill's letter with his buddy, Lucien Carr. After all, Lucien had been tested; he knew about the system and how it worked; hence, he could offer some sage advice.

---

*In fact, approximately two years earlier—in June 1947—Ginsberg had spent most of the month on a farm near New Waverly, Texas. There, Burroughs, Huncke, Ginsberg, and others had set out to grow marijuana.

6.

TIMES AND CIRCUMSTANCES had changed Lucien Carr. The demonic life no longer lured him as it once had. His perspective had become more sober and law-abiding ever since he had been paroled after serving only two years. (While incarcerated, he carved "'KEROUAC' into his cell wall with his fingernail.") Now Lucien had altered his ways and could counsel Allen on what to do with the criminal direction of his wayward life.

In late April 1949, Lucien and Allen took a midnight stroll through the Bowery and Chinatown. Rapping for hours, they meandered here and there and then walked up to 42nd Street and back down to Lucien's house on E Street. Concerned that the police, when investigating the contents of the crashed car, might read Allen's journal references to Lucien and mistakenly link him to the York Avenue heists, the now-reformed Carr rebuked Ginsberg: "[Y]ou better watch yourself, because these are a bunch of thieves you are dealing with here, and when the cops come down on them, they're going to come down on you."

Although Burroughs' earlier warnings and Carr's present ones finally overcame Ginsberg's inertia, the tender-hearted and confrontation-averse young man chose a less intimidating path: he would only ask that Huncke and his cohorts remove all of the stolen property, but they could remain in the apartment. Moreover, he himself now felt pressured to dispose of all his personal papers and journals, some of which included incriminating evidence of his drug habits and passionate letters to the male objects of his amorous affection (including Jack Kerouac).

Ginsberg's journals alone were a treasure trove of guilt and complicated candor. In them, Allen kept detailed accounts of his daily life, all of this to be used someday to assist him in writing "a large autobiographical work of fiction."

Many of the entries would have stunned any straitlaced cop who perused them. For example, in a February 1947 entry, Allen explicitly described his carnal fantasies with his then lover, Neal Cassady (the man who was later to become the hero of Kerouac's *On the Road*). "I want some real hip sex." This is how he tagged it, after depicting a string of homosexual lovemaking positions.

Elsewhere, in recounting a dream, Allen wrote of a "glass room-cage-bathroom" in which he was "masturbating." In another entry from July 1947, Ginsberg recalled a nightmare in which two uniformed cops beat up a big "Irishman," and then pulled "his pants down" and "tortured him (castrating probably)," as young Allen watched in "horror and anger and dread and disgust."

And there were numerous drug-related entries, such as:

—Called up Bill a minute ago, high on a benny to give him
  some uplift with his attempt at kicking habit.
—I am alone in a room in Spanish Harlem high on weed, and
  what a kick...
—Got high...last night with Norman, Jack, Vicki, [and] Huncke...
—Tried tea and junk tonight...

Moreover, there were several letters back and forth between Ginsberg and Burroughs in which the two openly wrote of marijuana deals—with the "tea" being sent by Bill to Allen care of the U.S. mail. As was his practice, Allen saved the letters—he had about a hundred of them that he kept in a manila envelope.

Such hallucinatory frames of reference also inspired dreams like the one Allen had in the summer of 1947. In his journal he wrote: "I met the Mad Hatter walking under the Third Avenue El, talking to himself, mumbling." And then later: "I am walking down the street and there is the Mad Hatter again.... He's mumbling about marihuana, talking too loud." Ginsberg appropriately titled the dream: "White Rabbit. Thoughts last week of Allen in Wonderland."

Such admissions in the late 1940s were enough to make one a social outcast or even land a guy in Rikers. For at that time homosexuality was still viewed as a mental illness by the psychiatric profession, and sodomy was penalized as a criminal offense in many jurisdictions.

Combined with all of the stolen property in his apartment, these journals stoked Allen's anxiety level. He had to take some action. He had to do something to protect himself. But before he did, there was one other pressing matter to attend to . . . a party.

7.

IT WAS A PARTY for Jack.

Ginsberg had been very supportive of Kerouac's efforts to get *The Town and the City* published—the tome that Jack hauled around in a tattered black leather briefcase. Jack had experienced difficulties in placing the work: Little, Brown had rejected the novel, and Alfred Kazin, the noted literary critic, had not even received a response when he sent it to Harcourt, Brace on Jack's behalf. So Allen took the book-to-be to his friend and Columbia University English teacher, Mark Van Doren. Van Doren read it, liked it, and passed it on to his former student, Robert Giroux, who worked as an editor at Harcourt, Brace. The rest was history—a happy history for Jack.

On April 20, 1949, John Holmes threw a party for Kerouac. Harcourt, Brace had just offered to buy *The Town and the City*, Jack's second novel.* This autobiographical work, offered up under the name John Kerouac,† featured characters patterned after Ginsberg,

---

*Kerouac's first novel, *The Sea Is My Brother*, was written in 1943 but never published in his lifetime. It wasn't until 2011 in the UK and 2012 in the U.S. that it was published as his "lost novel."

†Born on March 12, 1922, Kerouac was named Jean-Louis. In his youth, he was sometimes called Ti Jean ("Little Jack"), which later became Jackie and then simply Jack.

Huncke, Burroughs, and Carr, among others.* Jack was elated with the offer. Fate had finally smiled on him; his novel was to be published. And he had one grand in hand thanks to the publisher's advance.

"Mad?—I tell you it's mad. Mad?—me mad? Heh heh heh!" he exclaimed with joy to his friend, Ed White. So "BET-A-THOUSAND KEROUAC" was ready to party! Heh heh heh—the mad party was on.

Party life was a vital part of the on-the-edge existence of Allen, Jack, and their clan. They looked for *any* opportunity to celebrate anything. Allen often threw parties and did bizarre things like lighting firecrackers in ashtrays just to liven things up. Similarly, Bill Cannastra, a young Harvard Law grad with a flair for suicidal stunts, frequently hosted never-ending, outrageous parties in his Chelsea loft where, to outdo all the others, he shocked and amused by extremes. In a typical drunken moment, Cannastra once dashed records against a wall, shouting, "Good-bye, Berlioz...Good-bye, Harry James...Good-bye, you all!" Shortly afterward, he passed out, sprawled on the floor with his jeans off.

Between the fireworks and shattered LPs, the boys' parties encouraged an uncommon mixture of high-brow talk, low-brow action, and just enough drugs, sex (hetero, homo, and bi), and loud bebop music to catch the fancy of this happy band of revelers. And many joined that merry band, sometimes including the likes of Tennessee Williams and W.H. Auden.

But in the quiet of more reclusive moments, away from the gang's madcap antics, Jack Kerouac revealed another side. Time and again in his diaries and notebooks, he wrestled with the angel of God: "And what do I owe You, God, for my gifts: I owe you inspiration and suffering and all the dark night of my life." This man, who hung

---

*"Kerouac kept Kammerer's stabbing out of *The Town and the City*," notes Ann Charters, "romanticizing it as a suicide."

a crucifix over his bed, took strange comfort in his Savior: "Christ's teachings were a turning-to, a confrontation and a *confoundment* of the terrible enigma of human life. What a miraculous thing!" More characteristic of his hipster soul, he mixed the Messiah with the madman: "Didn't Jesus warn against the sin of ignoring the madman, to the most high exalted point of recognizing no madness anywhere?"

While this side of Kerouac, the "holy outcast," was easily missed at Bacchanalian revelries, it would become manifest in time. But that time had not yet arrived.

Perhaps more than the rest, John Clellon Holmes, a fair-haired Columbia student who had served in the Navy, had a sense of both sides of Jack Kerouac. There was "something about Jack," something different that Holmes had always found particularly intriguing. Holmes saw and understood both the rowdy and spiritual sides of the bunch. John was the lone restrained one of the lot. Nonetheless, he considered Allen and his crew the "most interesting people" he had met since the war. And he didn't mind keeping (and chronicling) their company.

Amiably, John and his wife opened the doors of their apartment and let all the gang in to celebrate Jack's newfound success. The guest of honor had invited his pals—Allen, Huncke, Little Jack, and Vicki—but they didn't arrive at the start.

The four would have come sooner, but Huncke and Little Jack had "pulled a caper" earlier that day, and things had gotten a bit complicated. Before they could party, they needed to stash the jewelry, fur coats, guns, suits,* and porn they had just stolen (from a Harlem cop's place, no less!) in Allen's apartment. The sight of more loot only increased Ginsberg's anxiety.

---

*Sometime that same day, the dapper Little Jack tried to sell Kerouac a couple of suits. Kerouac passed.

Allen had to pull himself together. He had to get his mind off his troubles. He had to relax. He had to think about Jack. After all, he was happy for his friend. He was ecstatic (though also envious) that Jack's literary career had finally been launched. This was the beginning of something big, perhaps even the beginning of a movement.

It was an occasion for dancing and drinking and uninhibited fun. Why not party, then, and forget about Herbert, Little Jack, Vicki, and all that material and mental mess back at York Avenue? Have fun! So Allen and his three outlaw friends took off for the event... in a stolen car.

The party was well along when they arrived. Ear-splitting music, lots of "beer for the boys," and plenty of "tea for friends." Some danced, some laughed, and some got mystical and tripped down the labyrinths of their subconscious. Try as he might, Allen could not get into the mood, despite his happiness for Jack's newfound literary success. Instead, he focused on the hot goods back at his apartment, and he *schvitzed* about his journals and letters, filled as they were with incriminating evidence.

Allen asked Jack if he planned to stop by afterward. If so, might he perhaps take Allen's papers with him back to his mother's place in Ozone Park? But Jack had no such plans. The New Orleans police who had arrested Bill Burroughs had also seized Kerouac's letters to Burroughs, letters in which Jack, too, had written of drug-related matters. Thus, his mother's place was not safe, either.

"Yes, it's true," sighed the disheartened Allen. But what was Allen to do with his papers and the criminal trio that had taken over his apartment? Kerouac was stern: "If you really wanted to get them out of the house, you would have done so already yourself." Jack was right, and Allen knew it. Well, he would take action... but later.

As Holmes hosted and Allen toasted, the party improved. Still, it apparently was not quite good enough for Little Jack and his lady. They "became argumentative, and we left Holmes' place," recalled

Huncke. Once in the car, they cursed at each other. When things got really heated, Herbert asked to leave: "Look, let me out of the car. I'll go on about my business. I'll see you back at the apartment in the morning." Huncke hit a couple of bars, downed a couple of drinks, met a couple of friends, and ended up at the old Grover Cleveland Hotel. The next morning, Huncke returned to the York Avenue apartment.

The party was over, and reality was setting in.

Just after returning from work at nine A.M. on Thursday, April 21, Allen finally made his move. He insisted that Little Jack get rid of the hot goods the very next day. And Allen contacted his older brother, Eugene, who agreed to store his cache of documents, including Allen's journals and letters. The plan was then formulated: on Friday afternoon, Jack would deliver some of the stash to his mother's home on Long Island, and on the way back Allen would drop off his collection of papers at Eugene's.

It was simple enough. A car ride, a delivery, the problem fixed, and danger avoided. Then Allen and the boys could get back to their rowdy lives. They could party again and cap things off with an early breakfast at Bickford's Cafeteria.

What had not been anticipated, of course, were the car chase, the crash, and the manhunt that ensued.

8.

DAYS IN THE EARLY A.M. at Bickford's were zany and deliciously decadent. Pimps and hookers hung there; dope dealers and addicts traded there; fags and drag queens rendezvoused there, and Allen Ginsberg once bussed tables there. When he was not working, the spindly, awkward New Jersey kid with large and protruding ears that arched to the sides of his thick, wavy hair savored the world of Bickford's patrons. Kerouac, Burroughs, Holmes, Carr, and Russell joked and jived at the notorious cafeteria. Huncke could blow eighteen hours a day listening to the jukebox and bullshitting with his friends at this all-night food joint on the north side of West 42nd Street. It was the place where the future literati commingled with the present "criminati."

But the wild and wondrous Bickford days were numbered. For the first time in his life, Allen Ginsberg confronted a terrifying reality— the Bickford life was *dangerous*. On April 22, 1949—the afternoon of the car chase—he was now facing the prospect of serious jail time.

As Vicki and Allen rushed back in a cab to York Avenue after the crash, Allen could not ignore the inevitable—the police would arrive soon and encounter Huncke, a career criminal. Moreover, the place was crammed with all kinds of contraband, from illegal drugs to stolen goods. His time to clean house was rapidly running out.

Unknown to Allen and Vicki, Herbert had just settled down there to "cook up" some "stuff." It was time for his fix, the kind that helped him "believe in life again." After all, when junk streamed into his veins, it eased his sickness, extinguished his loneliness, and alleviated all the "tension and anxiety" that plagued him. It showed Huncke a "new concept of reality." And if the mixture was "just right," his cursed existence looked different: "I don't mind being alive."

Herbert was just starting to relax and enjoy his "new concept" when the apartment door flew open. Vicki was in tears as she pulled Allen by the hand into the room behind her. He was "without his glasses," Huncke recalled. "He looked dazed."

Vicki cried, "Man, Jackie's been busted."

"Oh, no. What happened?" Herbert asked.

Vicki recounted the story of their travails—the chase, the crash, and their escape. The cops had to be close behind. So they had to do something.

"Look," said Huncke, "let's get a few things together and get the fuck out of here." But there wasn't time enough for that—there was too much incriminating shit in the place.

Anxious and fearful, Allen and Vicki tried to figure out a plan. They paced back and forth. What to do? What to do!

Meanwhile, Huncke's junk was kicking in; he didn't need to be "harassed by anxiety." No, he could take things in mellow stride now and dwell on the ordinary joys of life—things like a clean house. "I wanted to leave things in order a little bit," Huncke explained, "so I began to sweep the floor."

Allen exploded when he observed the anally compulsive Herbert casually pushing a broom across the kitchen floor. Sweep. Sweep. Sweep. The problem was that Herbert was literally cleaning house rather than cleaning out the telltale signs of crime everywhere in the house.

"My God, Herbert. What are you doing?!" Allen asked in exasperated disbelief. "You don't have to sweep the place. The police will be here any minute now."

Allen decided to take things into his own hands. He dashed down the hallway outside his apartment to the bathroom and flushed their drugs down the toilet. But what about all the rest of the loot stacked here and there? With Vicki crying and Herbert sweeping, Allen was freaking because nobody was doing anything.

Huncke, who had already served time for seven offenses, took it all with ease. Though he hid a few things in drawers and bookcases, he was resigned to what was about to happen. "Why get hung up?" he asked casually. "It's hopeless now. I've been through this so many times. There's nothing you can do."

With those words, Ginsberg knew he was fucked.

The time for consequences had come. Fate was working its way through the dingy hallway that reeked of garbage and up four flights of stairs to the backside of the tenement house where these fugitives from justice hung out in their $15-a-month flat.

BANG! BANG! BANG! Two detectives pounded on the door. "Does Allen Ginsberg live here?" they asked as the door opened. Entering the violet blue–painted apartment, they requested: "May we see some identification, please?" The police inquiry continued: "Is this apartment yours?" "Who else lives here?" Huncke chimed in at that point; he lived there, too. The probing became sharper: "Have you ever been arrested?"

Then came the search of the apartment—a kitchen and a few rooms strewn with empty beer bottles, dirty ashtrays, weird magazines, dirty clothes, and poetry books. Whatever the clutter, the police could not be oblivious to the obvious:

—Two opium pipes sitting atop the baroque mantel of a bricked-up fireplace

—Furs, jewels, and piles of clothes next to books on orange crates

—Stacks of small radios near moldy maroon drapes

—Expensive furniture, everything from a carved foyer cabinet to elegant dining room chairs, placed haphazardly under a high ceiling

Everything had either *drugs* or *stolen* stamped all over it. The police "seemed to assume," Allen felt, that he "kept a regular opium den or house of pleasure." It was a fair assumption. It was also reasonable to believe that much of the expensive stuff scattered around his place could be hot. Soon enough it would be identified as the remainder of the loot from the Garden Bay Manor heist and from break-ins at thirteen or more homes in Queens over the past year.

The detectives had seen enough. Given what they already knew and what they had just discovered, they had sufficient evidence to haul Allen, Vicki, and Huncke away. So it was off with them to the 68th Street precinct. Busted.

For Huncke and Vicki, being cuffed and whisked off to the police station for booking and interrogation may have seemed rather routine. For Ginsberg, however, it was anything but. This was the first time he witnessed the specter of steel slapping his wrists. The entire experience was a surreal, Kafkaesque moment.

But he could not lose hope. Faithful to his spiritual side, Allen carried two books with him—a copy of the Hebrew Bible and the Upanishads.

Vicki was worldlier. She carried a child. She told the officers of her pregnancy, and they treated her gently, holding her arm and helping her down the stairs.

As for Huncke, he carried no spiritual texts, though he had hoped he would remain high when they took him away.

A strange collection of criminals these three were: a strung-out junkie, a pregnant accomplice, and a crazed poet with a spiritual bent.

When the police ran a make on the suspects' rap sheets— "screamers," in cop talk—they were real attention-grabbers. They revealed Huncke's prior sentences for six narcotics violations and one burglar-tool charge; he was also wanted in Detroit for burglary. The records likewise established Little Jack's eighteen former arrests on larceny and safe-cracking charges, among other crimes, and Vicki's three priors for narcotics possession.

The puzzling person was Allen Ginsberg, a recent Columbia University grad. No prior convictions, no prior arrests, no prior tips...nothing. Who was this kid? Why was he consorting with the likes of Herbert, Little Jack, and Vicki? What was his story?

9.

IT WAS INTERROGATION time. The police started with Allen. He was taken aside and questioned.

Had he "been out in a car in Long Island?"

"Yes."

Where, exactly, in Long Island had he been?

He "didn't know."

Who else was in the car?

He could see now that he was about to get in over his head. He had to be careful. "I don't want to speak anymore until I see my brother; he's a lawyer."

They were not about to let him lawyer up. They persisted. He had to answer, they told him.

"No." He continued to insist on seeing his brother Eugene, the lawyer in the family.

No way. They slapped him around. They wanted answers, and now. Next came a question about his sexual life. "Did he like men or women?"

"Mostly men," he replied tentatively.

Such interrogation was tactical; it was meant to humiliate Allen, and it did. But the cops had bigger fish to fry. Vicki had 'fessed up to being in the car, they told him.

So who was this Jack—"Jack de Peretti"?*

Allen got worried. They were closing in.

"Do you use heroin?"

Now they were trying to pin him with a Huncke-like rap.

"No," he replied.

They were unconvinced. He was lying, and they could prove it. They had gone through the papers in the car—his papers. They had seen his correspondence with Dr. A. Allan Cott, his psychiatrist. They had read the letter about his drug problem and his need for medical help.

Allen grew more anxious. He would say no more. He wanted to see a lawyer before saying another word.

In time, in good time. But first Allen had to help them and help himself while he could. After all, they were getting more and more evidence by the moment. For one thing, "they had already [spoken to] Dr. Cott, and he told them that [Allen] was 'probably an incurable heroin addict.'"

Not true. Not at all. And why would Dr. Cott say that, Allen wondered. Was it because Allen once had refused to stop using marijuana while under his care?

The young man barely had time to ponder such things when another bombshell question hit him. It was another gleaned from the papers he had left in the car.

Had he "ever corresponded with anybody in Elmira"?—the locale of a criminal reformatory.

"Yes," he had.

They knew that. They knew that he had corresponded with Lucien Carr. And they had checked Carr's record. He was a killer.

The detectives then returned to interrogating him about the stolen goods.

---

*This reference might have been to Henry Pieretti, the man whose Astoria home Little Jack had burglarized to the tune of $10,000 worth of furs, jewelry, and clothing.

What did he know about the burglaries? How many were there? Where did they occur? Who all was in on them? What exactly was taken? Who was his fence?

Allen stood his ground. He knew nothing and had done nothing.

It was around six in the evening, and things looked bleak for Allen. They could tie him to the stolen car. They might also be able to tie him to a drug rap. And they had all the hot goods in his apartment. Add to that his links to a convicted killer. There was cause for serious concern, and Allen knew it.

After all, the police had questioned Vicki and Herbert separately. Who knew what had happened to Little Jack? Had he coughed up his guts? The cops must have learned something, since two of them were now about to drag Allen back to his apartment for yet more questioning there. Back to York Avenue, back to those piles of guilt-ridden stuff.

The questioning of the suspect resumed: Why were so many people running in and out of his apartment? Why were they there? Why did they come by? Why so often? What kind of house was he running?

Allen answered in his naïve but honest way. He "liked people," "the more the merrier," and he was a writer—he needed lots of people around to provide him with "a great deal of atmosphere and subject matter." But he didn't, as the papers would allege, ride along on a "crime wave" in order to "get material for [his] writings." No. He would not do that. Well, not quite. It was more nuanced than that.

The young man's explanation for his involvement with the Huncke "gang" was unique: he was a copyboy for the Associated Press and a writer, he said, who hung with the criminal element to obtain "realism" for his stories. However implausible or ludicrous such an account may have seemed to the police, in a real sense it was quite true. The allure of the illicit lifestyle for Allen was not in the actual crime. Given his one chance to participate in a caper, he had "preserved his cherry," as it were. Nor was it the profit to be gained by the loot, for he had personally gained little of it.

After the York Avenue interrogation and further searches, the police took their suspect back to the 68th Street station. Once there, Allen, Herbert, and Vicki were rounded up and taken in a paddy wagon to the Bayside stationhouse. More questioning still.

At this stage, Ginsberg's interrogators were losing their patience. They didn't want any more dilly-dallying. They wanted answers. He was in "deep" trouble. He had no choice but to "confess everything" and "tell a straight story." Otherwise, he would not see a lawyer "for a long time." They even threatened to beat him.

Allen would not budge.

Next they were taken to another jailhouse for booking and then skirted off to Queens Prison. It was there that Allen saw Little Jack for the first time since the car crash. Poor Little Jack. He limped as he passed through the room where Allen sat. The cops pushed him, and he winced as he tried to walk. Not only did Jack appear hurt from the crash, he also looked beaten.

When all of them, including Little Jack, finally got a chance to exchange notes, they reassured Allen that none of them had implicated him in the burglaries. They also had told the police that Allen had no knowledge that the items in his apartment were stolen and that he was not dealing in drugs. He needn't worry about anything.

When it was all said and done, Little Jack had confessed, holding nothing back, which meant that he faced a very stiff sentence. Vicki had confessed, too, "with certain withholdings." Herbert had followed Vicki's example, assuming some responsibility while denying some.

And Allen? "[A]ll denied that [he] had any part in it." But would the police believe that? Would they believe that this college kid was totally oblivious to all that was going on in his apartment?

In short time, they were formally charged. Little Jack was tagged with felonious assault against a policeman, and he and his three cohorts with burglary, grand larceny, and receiving stolen goods. On the spiritual side of the ledger, Allen was allowed to keep his Bible, but the sergeant nixed the Upanishads. The explanation given? Hinduism was not a real religion, so the Upanishads could not be a religious book.

When the time for arraignment arrived, Ginsberg fared better than some of his colleagues. He appeared before magistrate David P. McKean in the Ridgewood Felony Court of Queens. Because Herbert and Little Jack were considered hardened criminals, they were held without bail until a hearing scheduled for the following week. In contrast, both Allen and Vicki were given the opportunity for release on $2,500 bail. The three men were then transferred to the Long Island House of Detention, and Vicki sent to the Women's House of Detention in Greenwich Village.

What a pitiful figure Allen cut when his tearful father, accompanied by his brother Eugene (the law student later to become a criminal lawyer), collected him after paying bail. "I remember looking up and seeing him standing at the [jail] bars peering around with a woebegone expression," Huncke poignantly stated. "It was the first time he'd come so close to anything of this nature. He was saying Jewish prayers. I felt so sorry for him."

The path from the booths at Bickford's Cafeteria to the bars at the House of Detention was not a long one. Huncke had always known that. Ginsberg had just discovered it.

10.

Of course, there was always the question, should this
young man be rescued, should he be restored?
—Diana Trilling

ALLEN GINSBERG'S FANTASY had become reality, although a shameful one. The Columbia-educated intellectual/poet, the son of Jewish school teachers, had made it big in the *New York Times*. He was *in*famous now:

WRONG-WAY TURN CLEARS UP ROBBERY

He had made it, as well, in the *New York Herald Tribune*:

ONE-WAY STREET VIOLATION
TRAPS FOUR AS ROBBERS

The *Daily Mirror* put it whimsically:

"CINDERELLA'S SHOE" TRAPS 4 IN THEFTS

There was even a picture in a Brooklyn paper of the "gang" in a patrol wagon.

Thus had Allen Ginsberg's name first been announced to the world. While that news would one day be transformed into "almost literal truth" (as Holmes put it) or "true story novels" (as Jack Kerouac called them), on the morning of April 23, 1949, it had no literary value. It had nothing but shock value for the important people in the young man's life. It was not touting his artistic talents, after all, but rather his criminal savvy.

The tabloid-like accounts had turned Ginsberg and his cadre of quirky friends into a conspiratorial "gang." His bungling naïveté was characterized as methodical scheming. His vicarious adventures were depicted as vile avarice. His pot-smoking and booze-drinking were transformed into a portrait of a mindless puppet controlled by hard-core drug lords. And his literary and life-experiencing curiosity was held out as criminal intent. In reality, however, his "crimes" were far closer to those of Charlie Chaplin than Al Capone. It was all so funny that it could have made for a comedy of errors.

Ginsberg saw things similarly, although he did so with grandiose philosophical flair: "[T]he whole situation was transformed from the hermetic, cosmic, nebulous Dostoevskian thing that it was...into this total stereotype of a giant robbery operation." The script grew ever more surreal: "Yeah, I was advertised as the brilliant student genius who was...plotting out big criminal scenes....I was addicted to drugs, and this gang kept me supplied and forced me to mastermind robberies. It was all a bunch of awful misrepresentations."

When the robbery story broke, the reactions of Ginsberg's friends were mixed. Bill Burroughs was too occupied with his own legal problems in Louisiana to track what was going on in Allen's world. For Lucien Carr, the headlines confirmed his predictions of only a few days earlier—Ginsberg's folly had, indeed, become his misfortune. Jack Kerouac probably shared Lucien's I-told-you-so attitude, for he, too, had warned Allen to rid himself of his incriminating letters and to be careful of Huncke's company. And then there was

Kerouac's fascination with fiction based on real-life adventures—
this news item could well make for part of a chapter in one of his
future novels. The same idea, no doubt, came soon enough to John
Clellon Holmes who, like his colleagues, poached on hipster reality
to produce "Beat" fiction. As for Herbert Huncke, he couldn't give
a fuck.

But when Allen's Columbia University professors first read the
news, their reactions were anything but mixed. The Ginsberg headlines reminded them of the institutional embarrassment that they
had felt when the Lucien Carr story made banner news five years
earlier in the *New York Times*:

COLUMBIA STUDENT KILLS FRIEND

AND SINKS BODY IN HUDSON RIVER

STUDENT IS SILENT ON SLAYING FRIEND

STUDENT SLAYER SENT TO THE REFORMATORY

"Of course," Ginsberg noted, "everybody around Columbia was
aghast. Like, 'You've made scandals before, Ginsberg, but *this*! And
on top of everything, a Columbia student right on the front page
of the *Daily News*!'" This time Ginsberg had taken his mischief to
a new level, beyond even that of his profane 1945 prank, which got
him suspended for a year.*

---

*One night, in mid-March 1945, Kerouac visited Ginsberg in his Columbia University
dorm room to discuss poetry and life in general. Since it was too late for Jack to return
to his mother's home in Ozone Park, he slept over. The next morning, the dean of
students came to Ginsberg's room in response to a complaint by the dormitory's cleaning
woman. Allen had earlier scrawled some profane words ("fuck the Jews" and "[Columbia
University President] Butler has no balls") on a dusty windowpane, and drew a skull and
crossbones and a penis to provoke the cleaning woman, whom Allen believed was both
anti-Semitic and too lazy to clean his windows. Entering the unlocked room, the dean
discovered Jack and Allen together in bed, and may have suspected that the boys were

Aghast as everybody else was, two of the professors Allen most respected—Lionel Trilling and Mark Van Doren—were particularly troubled. They "were talking to me as though I were Lucien," Allen recalled. "'What were you doing with those people?' Van Doren asked. 'What were you doing with simple common criminals?'"

Trilling and Van Doren, both highly distinguished English professors, knew precisely what it took to build and maintain sterling professional and personal reputations. A more radical thinker in the 1930s, Trilling had moderated his views a decade later to become a mandarin intellectual of the first order. As a teacher and scholar, the young Trilling equated civilization itself with the best of the upper-class British thinkers. The more senior Van Doren, then fifty-five—a poet, biographer, novelist, and editor and critic for the *Nation*—had been awarded a Pulitzer Prize in 1940 for his *Collected Poems*. When Allen studied under them with aspirations for a future academic career, Trilling and Van Doren may well have shared his lofty hopes. Any such hopes were now dashed by Allen's criminal capers and the sensationalist news reports about them. Ginsberg expressed his own disappointment and fretfulness in a letter to Trilling:

> I suppose you are aware by this time of "what I have let happen to me" now. I hope the publicity around Columbia is not too widespread. My immediate future is uncertain depending on how my case goes but things do not look too favorable. I have been exposed to considerable horror and stock taking and feel myself more clearly. What remains is a restless anxiety about my family.

Finding himself in a bind with the law, Allen's natural instinct was to turn not to lawyers, but to professors—English professors,

---

"fooling around." When both incidents came under disciplinary review, Ginsberg was suspended. A year later, thanks to the help of Lionel Trilling and a letter from a bona fide psychiatrist, Allen was readmitted.

no less. What he first sought was less legal counsel than life counsel. Ginsberg prevailed on Van Doren for his professional advice and assistance. The legendary poet, who had inspired generations of Columbia University students, was willing to go the extra mile for Ginsberg, if only because he feared that a prison sentence might unbalance Allen's all-too-delicate psyche.

When the young graduate and his father visited Van Doren in his office (No. 306 Hamilton Hall), his lesson for the day was one of tough love. "A lot of us around here have been thinking maybe you'd better hear the clank of iron, Ginsberg," he chastised his former student. "You don't seem to realize what you're doing. If you want my help, you've got to promise never to break the law again." Van Doren didn't mince words. The message was clear: Allen had better change his wild ways.

Moving from Van Doren to Trilling, whose office was situated only one door down, Allen sought help from yet another Columbia father figure. He had often gone to Trilling's home on West 116th Street for guidance of all sorts. He sometimes even called him very late in the evening to discuss his poetry. When Trilling heard the news, the professor was horrified. Still, he saw the need for immediate, pragmatic action. It was time to bring in the big guns, a top-notch lawyer. And he did just that when he directed Allen to one of the best minds in American law—Herbert Wechsler of the Columbia University Law School.

His Brooks Brothers suits bespoke his status. The very man who would now advise Allen was the same man who, a few years earlier, had been the chief adviser to American judges at the Nuremberg Trials. Years later, Professor Wechsler would be the central architect of a renowned legal work—the Model Penal Code. (Later still, his remarkable résumé would list his successful Supreme Court argument in a landmark First Amendment case, *New York Times v. Sullivan*.) In his wisdom, the esteemed professor developed a legal strategy ideally suited for this madcap kid. "The thing Wechsler said," Allen recalled, "was that what I had to do was put myself into a bughouse. Plead insanity and go to a bughouse and get out of all this. So my father got me a lawyer who was an old friend of the family and who was like a real middle-class cat."

At this point, Ilo Orleans, a poet/lawyer who did not wear conservative suits, entered into the picture. Not only was the London-born, Columbia University–educated attorney a partner in the Manhattan law firm of Falk & Orleans, Ilo was also a member in good standing of the American Poetry Society. When this former editor of the *Columbia Law Review* was not writing legal memoranda, he penned books of verse for children, including the somewhat celebrated *Father Gander* (1933).

To buttress Ginsberg's plea of mental illness, Orleans instructed him to write an autobiographical essay about his maniacal life experiences, ranging from his troubled family life to his turbulent drug life to his aberrant sex life. Titled "The Fall," Allen's essay foreshadowed by some six years Albert Camus' great novel of the same name. Ironically, the two shared some common psychological themes: self-loathing and personal judgment by way of confession. Ginsberg's long self-portrait depicted the sincere struggle of a young man who craved to move from deviancy to normalcy. "I am sick," Allen asserted. He professed a heartfelt desire "to be cured" and "stable, serene, secure, happy, working...and married." In this endeavor, the young man may have been trying merely to preserve his liberty or save his sanity, or both.

Whatever Ginsberg's true intentions, his Columbia faculty friends were determined to keep one of their young protégés out of Rikers.* Trilling and Van Doren appealed to Dean Harry Corman for help on

---

*Meanwhile, Huncke was hospitalized in the prison ward of Bellevue with blood poisoning. Ginsberg described him as "alone, sad, weary, beat, ended." Allen even thought Herbert might die soon.

Allen's behalf. The dean, tall and heavyset with reddish-brown hair and a friendly disposition, was quite amenable to calling on one of Columbia's more loyal and influential graduates, Manhattan district attorney Frank S. Hogan.

A man wed to civility, Hogan's office plaque read: COURTESY IS THE GOLDEN KEY THAT UNLOCKS ALL DOORS. Had the Irish-Catholic prosecutor known more about Ginsberg and his friends, he no doubt would have loathed them the same way that he despised the "filthy" comedian Lenny Bruce, whom he would prosecute years later in 1964. Given the state's somewhat weak case against Ginsberg, Hogan was predictably more willing to extend a courtesy to the dean of his alma mater. Mindful of Wechsler's counsel, Hogan proposed that all criminal charges against Ginsberg be dropped on the condition that Allen plead psychological disability and undergo psychiatric treatment in an asylum. Dean Corman closed the deal by arranging an opportunity for Allen's voluntary commitment, free of charge, at the Columbia Presbyterian Psychiatric Institute (later renamed New York State Psychiatric Institute) on West 168th Street in Manhattan.

Lionel Trilling and Mark Van Doren did not let Ginsberg down. They went the extra mile and testified for Allen at the plea hearing that the accused did not attend. Their colleague, Jacques Barzun, the forty-two-year-old Frenchman who had made a name for himself at Columbia University for founding the discipline of cultural history and co-teaching a popular Great Books course with Trilling, wrote a letter of support on behalf of his former student. In essence, the letter characterized Allen as a budding intellectual who only needed to rein in his unruly behavior. Unknown to Ginsberg, Columbia's powerhouse faculty had lined up, one after another, in a phalanx of defense at the hearing. It was "mighty cricket" of them all, Allen later wrote to Kerouac.

Nonetheless, if Allen were to avoid jail time, he needed more than professorial character witnesses. He needed someone with psychiatric credentials. Dr. A. Allan Cott of Newark, New Jersey, was that person. Cott had come into Ginsberg's life two years earlier by way of a recommendation from the world-famous psychoanalyst Wilhelm Reich.

Ginsberg had written to the Austrian-born Reich, who was then practicing in the United States. "My main psychic difficulty," Allen wrote, "is the usual oedipal entanglement. I have been a homosexual for as long as I can remember, and have a limited number of homosexual affairs, both temporary and protracted. They have been unsatisfactory to me, and I have always approached love affairs with a sort of self-contradictory, conscious masochism." Attempting to build his case for Reichian therapy, Allen added: "I have long periods of depression, guilt feelings—disguised mostly as a sort of Kafkian sordidness of sense of self—melancholy, and the whole gamut I suppose."

Allen's three months of therapy with Cott ended abruptly when he ignored the doctor's order that he quit smoking pot. Hence, Dr. Cott may have been hesitant to help his former patient when the police first approached him. But, when push came to psychological shove, Dr. Cott returned to Ginsberg's rescue and testified to the young man's need for psychiatric care.

On the strength of the defense's evidence, the court accepted the plea arrangement first offered by District Attorney Hogan—no jail time, just asylum time. Lionel Trilling, however, would not rest with the fact that Allen had narrowly escaped jail; his young charge needed to appreciate just how mentally ill he was. Trilling took Ginsberg to a psychiatrist, one Dr. Fagin, who confirmed that he was, indeed, badly off. Dr. Fagin assured them, however, that at Columbia Presbyterian Allen would "'be given the works psychoanalytically.'"

"The punishment literally fitted the crime," Ginsberg wrote in his journal. His crazy life would now be treated for what it was.

Although relieved that he would be wearing hospital whites instead of jail stripes, his Jewish guilt pricked him. After all, Vicki was saddled with a five-year probation sentence, and Huncke with a five-year prison sentence. "Somebody had to do [the time]," Herbert quipped sarcastically. But Little Jack followed in Allen's footsteps— "he avoided jail by getting himself committed to Pilgrim State Hospital."

Burroughs, still in Louisiana, took a dim view of Ginsberg's plea arrangement. True to his rebel creed, Bill was convinced that Trilling and Van Doren had pointed Allen to a prescription-induced future of boot-licking conformity, all made possible by shock therapy, straitjackets, and incontinence pants. Ginsberg should take it as a man, as Huncke did. "If I was in Al's place," Burroughs wrote to Kerouac, "I would say 'Go ahead and place your charges, if any.' His present position is insufferable. Imagine being herded around by a lot of old women like [his father] and Van Doren.... Sniveling old Liberal Fruit." Although Burroughs feared the worst, Kerouac was more optimistic: his April 29, 1949, journal entry read, "Allen will be alright."

Days before committing himself to the psychiatric institute, Allen Ginsberg was psychologically self-absorbed. In a humble and castigating moment, he turned to therapy for salvation. Writing to John Clellon Holmes, he bared his soul: "[I]t would be quite a miraculous and wonderful surprise if one day as the result of analysis I should have my eyes open and see that *I* am what is troubling me in the world at large, and in other people's conduct, ideas, etc. That, like Oedipus, I am the criminal that has been bringing on all the plague."

Allen's journal entry for his birthday (June 3, 1949) was bleaker yet. Without a stroke of mercy, he mentally flagellated himself. "What a terrible future," he penned. "I am 23.... I am ill. I have become spiritually or practically impotent in my madness..."

His madcap life had collapsed into a mad life. The "psychological portrait" of his being "caught for robbery by the police" did not blossom into a carefree, fictionalized story, the one he had imagined when he penned it in his journal several months earlier. No. Fiction had become fact—a frightening fact.

Yesterday's exhilaration had become today's alienation. Once he frolicked all night with Huncke and the boys; now he faced mind-ordering days with doctors. Once he got high in his apartment while playing Billie Holiday* records on his Victrola; now he would live the blues. Once he planned to spend the summer of '49 outside with Kerouac on the banks of the Mississippi River; now he would pass the summertime inside, on beds in psychiatric wards. Once he thought of teaching English at Cooper Union College or working as a reporter for the *New York Times*; now he was unemployed, having lost his job at the Associated Press. And once he hoped to leave town with his pals for life on the road; now he could not go along for the ride.

When the car chase *finally* ended, it took Allen Ginsberg straight to the doors of an asylum. Little did he know then that the mania in his life (and in the lives of his wild friends) was about to escalate further...beyond all imagination.

---

*Apparently, Little Jack and Vicki knew the famed blues singer and promised to introduce her to Allen. It never happened.

PART II THE ASYLUM

Of course, everyone has his monster, the personification of everything he really fears. A sort of Dracula in the daylight! And what is analysis but the patient coming to that moment of self-truth where he can embrace his monster? And kiss the hairy cheeks without a shudder.

—David Stofsky

(Stofsky is the fictional Allen Ginsberg character in John Clellon Holmes' 1952 reality-based novel, *Go.*)

Previous page (from left to right): Carl Solomon posing on his bed in a shirt and tie; William Burroughs, with right hand extended, offering advice to Jack Kerouac (right), "But Jack I've told you before, if you continue your present pattern living with Mémêre you'll be wound closer & closer round her apron-strings till you're an old man . . ." (this according to photographer Allen Ginsberg's handwritten caption).

11.

TOWNSEND HARRIS was an Enlightenment man. He believed in the power of reason, the progress of knowledge, and the potential for freedom and happiness that education could foster. Although he was renowned as the first United States Consul General to Japan who opened the Japanese Empire to foreign commerce, the successful New York City merchant was just as proud of his efforts to champion the life of the mind. He joined the New York City Board of Education in 1846 and then founded the Free Academy, later known as the City College of New York, to provide excellent public education to the working classes. A high school bearing his name, Townsend Harris High School, eventually emerged out of the Free Academy's secondary-level curriculum.

"Open the doors to all," Harris proclaimed as the mission of the Free Academy. "Let the children of the rich and the poor take their seats together and know of no distinction save that of industry, good conduct, and intellect."

The doors of Townsend Harris High were not, however, really thrown open to all. Only males were admitted to the original school; and a highly competitive admissions process, including a personal interview and a challenging written examination, ensured that "the Harrisites," as the students called themselves, were the best and the brightest of the poor. Located on three floors of what is now Baruch College, the school offered a curriculum styled on a classical education, emphasizing the learning of Latin and Greek, as well as courses in the liberal arts and sciences. Fitting the classical standard of education, all new students were required to recite the Ephebic Oath during the fall Founder's Day ceremony. They pledged: "I shall willingly pay heed to whomever renders judgment with wisdom" and "I shall not leave my city any less but rather greater than I found it."

Many of the students who honored those promises became celebrated alumni. Chemist Herbert Hauptman and economist Kenneth Arrow, both Nobel laureates, were counted in the ranks of the school's most distinguished graduates. Along with them were Pulitzer Prize–winning songwriters Ira Gershwin and Richard Rogers, novelist Herman Wouk, and playwright Sidney Kingsley. There were famous actors, such as Edward G. Robinson and Clifton Webb, and controversial politicians, such as Adam Clayton Powell Jr. The Townsend Harris literati ran the gamut from the weighty philosopher Irwin Edman to the wondrous cartoonist William Steig and windy gossip columnist Army Archerd.

Far less prominent than other Harrisites, but perhaps no less brilliant, was the son of a fishmonger, Carl Wolfe Solomon. Born on March 30, 1928, Carl had been raised by his patriotic Jewish immigrant father to salute the American flag, love the country's cultural traditions, and excel at his studies. He did that and more. Carl adored the all-American sport of baseball; he could recite the names and key stats of all the players in baseball history. And he was a scholastic star; he skipped four grades and graduated from the prestigious Townsend Harris High School not long after he turned fifteen. In many ways, the underprivileged and bright Carl Solomon was the very kind of student Townsend Harris aimed to promote.

In 1943 Carl entered the City College of New York, then located at the edge of Harlem, and declared himself a social science major because of his deep-founded compassion for "the plight of the Negro" and the concerns of the poor. Young Carl was also impressionable and easily seduced by the fantasy of cinema and literature. Charmed by films such as Humphrey Bogart's *Action in the North Atlantic*, Carl got caught up in the romantic swirl of it all and set out to sea—he joined the U.S. Maritime Service at the age of seventeen. During the next two years, he alternated terms at college with times at sea.

For all his high marks, Carl Solomon had an eccentric streak in him, which often ran contrary to social conventions. He dabbled in radical politics at college, such as when he joined the American Youth for Democracy, an arm of the American Communist Party. He dabbled in the avant-garde lifestyle, as when he jumped ship in France in 1947, became a member of the French Communist Party, and lived with a Pigalle prostitute named Odette Belmaure. And, when in Paris, he dabbled in philosophy; he searched the streets "looking for existentialists," as he put it. Soon enough, he found them.

One evening, Solomon came upon a crowd gathered around a young man with shoulder-length black hair and a thin face; the man trembled and screamed out lines from Antonin Artaud's surrealist poem "Ci-Gît." The bizarre street scene fascinated Carl, and he quickly became obsessed with the works of the French dramatist, who died in a madhouse only one year later. Artaud's *Van Gogh, the Man Suicided by Society*, convinced Carl that the true existentialist hero was a madman. In Artaud's words, "a lunatic is a man who prefers to become what is socially understood as mad rather than forfeit a certain superior idea of human honor." That maxim became the measure of Carl's own existence when he returned to the States, transferred to Brooklyn College, and became a part of the Greenwich Village scene.

Still very much under Artaud's sway, Carl hooked up with two of his friends, Leni Gruber and Ronnie Gold,* at a delicatessen near the college. They chatted about Wallace Markfield, an NYU graduate student who would speak that evening on "Stéphane Mallermé and Alienation." Time was running short, so they ordered a potato salad to go and rushed to the hall to hear the lecture on the French symbolist poet. Markfield was well into his remarks on the aesthetics of Mallermé's poetry. Suddenly, a projectile of food flew his way. Then another and another. Pieces of potato scattered, bits of celery sailed, and egged mayonnaise stuck everywhere on and around him. What was going on? The shocked audience gasped and grumbled, no doubt failing to understand the deeper philosophical meaning of such sophomoric antics.

"We staged a dadaist demonstration," Solomon explained, "and threw potato salad at Markfield.... I was in a very negative, nihilistic mood."

At that time, Solomon and his friends were pouring over the works of André Gide, the French humanist and moralist who received the Nobel Prize for Literature in 1947. "I was also influenced by the famous gratuitous crime in André Gide's *Les Caves du Vatican*." Indeed, committing *le crime gratuit*—a criminal act taken for its own sake and without purpose—intrigued Carl. Although Ronnie had told him that "the only legitimate acts of free will are suicide and psychosis," he was not about to succumb to anything so dire as suicide. Rather, the pudgy and bespectacled college student had used food to practice his anti-rationalistic philosophy. And he would do it again shortly thereafter, this time with clear criminal

---

*Years earlier, beginning at the age of thirteen, Ronnie Gold had been sent by his parents to various psychiatrists to cure his homosexuality. He eventually became a reporter for *Variety* magazine and one of the five original founders of the National Gay and Lesbian Task Force. Gold spearheaded the movement that succeeded in convincing the American Psychiatric Association, in 1973, to take homosexuality off of its list of mental illnesses.

intent. Or, as he later quipped, "The tendency toward crime among the young men of my generation is impossible to surmount. We are all guttersnipes. Gratuitousness is the spirit of the age."

Sometime later, as he strolled casually into the Brooklyn College cafeteria and noticed a uniformed guard monitoring the doors, Carl lit upon another idea of gratuitous crime. "I picked up a peanut butter sandwich without paying for it," he described. He brandished it for the guard to see, "hoping to be fired upon and executed summarily by the huge cop on duty." When the beefy guard arrested him, the municipal authorities handled him in an appropriate Artaudian fashion. Similar to Allen Ginsberg, Solomon's charges were dropped on the condition that he submit to psychiatric treatment. "What happened was no execution," he explained, "but an introduction to the head nurse at Manhattan's Psychiatric Institute."

On his twenty-first birthday in 1949, the day he attained legal majority, Carl found himself flailing hopelessly in Artaud's void. "Things seemed so sick to me, and I wanted a lobotomy, or to be suicided," Carl remarked. "I thought I was a madman." So he checked himself into the Columbia Presbyterian Psychiatric Institute. It became readily apparent that the whiz-kid graduate of Townsend Harris High School was in dire psychological straits—not enough for a lobotomy, but sufficient for therapeutic care.

The state psychiatric institute was a model of scientific progress. As opposed to the nineteenth century, when lunatics were warehoused in cold and crowded asylums, locked up and beaten, the mental hospital devoted itself to innovative treatment methods, including neurochemical, genetic, psychoanalytic, and psychopharmacological research. Under the directorship of Dr. Nolan Lewis, electroshock and insulin shock therapies were also developed as treatments for a variety of psychological disorders.

Solomon was diagnosed as a fitting candidate for insulin shock treatment. Although seen as appropriate (if not advanced) in those days, he viewed the procedure as nightmarish. An orderly would come to his room in the wee hours, tear back the sheet from his bed, and haul him away into an elevator as he screamed. On another floor, he was strapped into a bed awaiting an insulin injection. He felt as though they were about to amputate his brain. "I would at once break off my usual stream of puns and hysterical chatter." While confined, awaiting an enormous hypodermic needle, "I would stare at the bulge I made beneath the canvas restraining sheet." After the hypodermic was emptied, the insulin created acute sugar withdrawal (or hypoglycemia), which caused convulsions and comas.

"I was revived from my coma intravenously by an Egyptian resident psychiatrist, who then, very brusquely, ordered the nurses to wrap the sheets around me a bit tighter," as if Carl were a mummy. "Help! Help! Help!" he screamed as he awoke from his comas. "The nurses and doctors would ignore me," he complained, "letting me flap about until my whole aching body and my aching mind … pulled themselves by their bootstraps out of the void of terror and, suddenly, attained a perfectly disciplined silence." Thereafter, when wheeled back to his room, he would be given his "breakfast tray and a glucose apéritif." His resultant amnesia was diagnosed as a symptom of deeper psychological problems, and his doctors continued to administer insulin shock treatments. During his nine months at the institute, he was subjected to fifty such episodes.

On June 29, 1949, Carl struggled to emerge from one of his comas. Bloated with insulin, he shook and tried to regain his composure as he squirmed around in his bulky bathrobe. An orderly wheeled him onto the sixth-floor ward. Peering through his thick lenses, Carl noticed a figure sitting on a chair against the wall. As he focused in, he spied a thin young man with thick, wavy, dark hair. He blinked, cleared his vision, and saw that the man clasped a small book (a copy of the sacred Hindu text Bhagavad-Gita). Laboring to stand up, Carl shuffled over to him.

"Who are you?" the insulin patient asked, his head wrapped turban-style in a towel.

"I'm Myshkin," the man answered, thinking of the saintly but simple-minded prince in Dostoyevsky's *The Idiot*.

Carl was ready for the retort. "I'm Kirilov," he responded, calling to mind the suicidal atheist from Dostoyevsky's *The Possessed*.

This Dostoyevskian dialogue between Carl Solomon and Allen Ginsberg set into motion a friendship that would span more than four decades. The opening spark brought these two impressionable Jewish minds together in a bond forged by the Russian writer famous for his "psychological penetration into the darkest recesses of the human heart." In this "real madhouse," as Allen tagged it, he had found a kindred soul.

"There is a boy here named Karl Solomon," Allen wrote to Jack Kerouac, "who is the most interesting of all—I spend many hours conversing with him.... He is a big queer from Greenwich Village, formerly from Brooklyn—a 'swish' (he used to be he says)... but big and fat, and interested in surrealistic literature." During one of their early conversations, Ginsberg continued, "I gave way to the temptation of telling him about my mystical experiences—it was very embarrassing, in a madhouse, to do this. He accepted me as if I were another nutty ignu." And then Carl responded with conspiratorial flair: "Oh well, you're new here. Just wait awhile and you'll meet some of the other repentant mystics."

Absorbed as Ginsberg was with his experiences—"I take my madhouses seriously," he confessed—Kerouac was concerned that his friend might fall in love with his mania. "Be careful while convincing the docs you're nuts not to convince yourself," Jack cautioned. But he showed Allen some *simpatico*, as well: "Be smart, now, and don't shit in your pants. The world is only waiting for you to pitch sad silent love in the place of excrement. Okay?"* For his part, Bill Burroughs, ever skeptical of institutional authorities, was much more caustic: "I wouldn't let them croakers up there treat my corn let alone my psyche."

The "croakers," of course, had a different view of things. The Psychiatric Institute's clinical summary of Allen's condition suggested that his psyche needed mending:

THE PROBLEM

The problem is that of a 23-year-old, single, white, American Hebrew man with a long history of psychopathic behavior culminating in a recent arrest the charges of which were dropped providing he seek psychiatric care.

Dated: June 29, 1949

Allen's daily routine was much regimented. Time to get up...time to shave (the razors were locked up)...time for breakfast...time for psychotherapy (two or three times a week)...time for activities...time for lunch...time for afternoon naps...release time (four P.M. to seven P.M. daily, and from four P.M. on Friday until Sunday night, when he sometimes met up with Kerouac and Cassady)...time for dinner...time for recreation...time for bed. His four rotating doctors (Allen called them "ghouls of mediocrity") pelted him with queries—"Do you still think you are superior to other people and different?" The patient paused, and then lied: "No." His strategy was to please and thereby avoid "a lot of trouble." They

---

*Late in 1942 or thereafter, while Kerouac was in the Navy, he was sent off for insubordination to the base's psychiatric ward. While there, he told the "examining psychiatrist...that his name was Samuel Johnson, and asked to be executed by firing squad. During his incarceration in the psychiatric ward, he seems to have seriously wondered if he might in fact be mentally disturbed."

also asked him repeatedly about his homosexuality and his cadre of criminal colleagues. Here again, Allen prevaricated. "I am torn between putting aside my loyalty and love directed to the past (the underworld, the mythical symbols of tragedy, suffering and solitary grandeur)," he penned in his journal, "and the prosaic community of feeling which I might enter by affirming my own allegiance to those bourgeois standards which I had rejected."

When Allen was not lying to his psychiatrists, he was lying on the rooftop sunning himself. He spent much time there, gazing out at the Lower Hudson River across to New Jersey. The George Washington Bridge, then a one-level suspended structure, was prominent in his vision; the sun glistened off its silver cross-girders and magnificent inverted arches that stretched between its east and west towers. "As I look out the Washington Bridge stands as if eternally, a monument to the vast illusions of time, floating across the river, looking so fragile," Allen wrote in his journal. "Why is the bridge always a challenge to my own sense of reality? It stands as a symbol of all that is permanent and real, although man-made and a vast machine, but so huge and airy that it seems to be a part of nature."

Ginsberg spent hours daily with his journals, sketching his thoughts and feelings in long prose sentences that were free from the more formal strictures of his early poetry. "I was just writing prose and not thinking of it as poetry," he recounted. In time, however, many of those entries would be folded into poems. "I didn't understand the literary value of the prose when I was writing it. It was accidental." Meanwhile, he continued to craft and clean up poems to be included in a book that he hoped some day to publish.

Many of Allen's days were spent in conversation with his new-found friend. They introduced one another to unfamiliar literature. Carl acquainted Allen with the works of Jean Genet, Henri Michaux, Antonin Artaud, and an assortment of other French existentialists.

Allen, in turn, read Yeats and Melville to Carl and told him of the creative aspirations of Kerouac and Burroughs. The pair passed the time away in the day room, often discussing their writings, debating politics and psychiatry, and disputing the nature of poetry. They fought over Whitman: Who was he as a poet? What did his words mean? Why was his message important? Was he a sexual revolutionary, as Allen maintained? Or was he a political revolutionary, as Carl held? Furthermore, in Allen's eyes, the true poet was a "sensitive soul." For Carl, the advocate of Artaud, the real poet was a brute. By that standard, Ginsberg was, as Solomon branded him, a "dopey daffodil."

But life between the two wasn't all conversation and clash. They sometimes pulled pranks to get the goat of the staff. Once they pounded on a piano and wailed as if insane. The discordant noise caused pandemonium in the otherwise controlled environment. Panicky doctors and nurses rushed to the surreal scene. To Carl and Allen, it was a big joke; to their doctors, however, playing mad in a madhouse was itself a sign of madness.

At other times they joined together to draft imaginary letters to famous people. In one such fictional missive—dated December 19, 1949—the devious duo wrote some 1,200 mocking words to T.S. Eliot, a suspected anti-Semite, whose politics and poetry they scorned. "To the Most distinguished Number 1 poet of 1949," they began playfully, "The year is fast running out.... Does this not frighten you?" Pretending to be members of a political phalanx defending Eliot's literary reputation, they promised: "We'll make riots for you. We'll make bonfires for you." They chastised the "literary dirigibles" who "claim that you are a dictator," calling them "stinkers." Yet, they sent "regards and highest genuflections to Mrs. Literary Dictator and all the little literary dictators.... [W]e know that your family is really mongoloid." Playing on the Jewish Question, they wrote: "Some of our younger legislators are Jews (you don't know their names).... They think they are all budding young Clemenceaus.* Perhaps there is a place for them in France." The letter concluded: "We are waiting for marching orders.... We take our leave by asking us to kiss you goodbye." They signed off with yet more mockery:

> Your 44 favorite legislators,
> (one dissenting vote)
> who are your brightest acolytes,
> Yisraeli Soccer Team.

But it was not all play. By stark contrast, in his somber moments Allen used his psychotherapy to reveal the subconscious phantoms that tormented him. Striving to be normal, he soon discovered a disturbing fact: "I am beginning to hate my mother."

---

*Georges Clemenceau (1841–1929), a French statesman, was the leader of the extreme left in the National Assembly and premier around the time of World War I. He was known for his intransigent hatred of the German State.

12.

LIFE AT CAMP NITGEDAYGET was good. Its name promised as much: the loosely translated Yiddish meant "no worries." In this land of bliss, on the lush banks of Monroe Lake in Upstate New York, the Ginsberg family found peace in the summer months of the mid-1930s. It was an escape from the travails of life back in Paterson. Naomi Levi Ginsberg, Allen's mother, sat outside her cabin in the shade of the woods as the sun gently filtered through the green canopy of trees. She was calm and content as she listened to the melodious chirping of birds, occasionally punctuated by the percussive chattering of her children, Eugene and Allen, as they frolicked with their friends. How much she enjoyed the evening sing-a-longs when all the campers raised their voices in unison. They sang songs such as "On the Line" or "The Red Flag" to extol the values of the working class. How greatly she delighted in the banter of adult conversation that contrasted the evils of capitalism or socialism to the virtues of communism. How thrilled she was that her children attended camp-sponsored classes where communist ideology was the thread that ran through the curriculum. At this communist-run resort, Naomi, an ardent Marxist, was among her own.

The short woman, whose large and animated dark eyes were framed by long black hair, had revolutionary blood running in her veins. As a ten-year-old girl in 1905, she immigrated to the United States from western Russia with her parents, who opposed czarist rule. Moving from the tenements of Manhattan's Lower East Side to Newark, New Jersey, she met her future husband, Louis Ginsberg, in 1912 at Barringer High School. Louis was drawn to the exceptionally bright, attractive, and charismatic Naomi and married her in an elegant Woodbine mansion in 1919. His family was not enthusiastic over the match: as socialists, they were uncomfortable with her strident communist beliefs; as middle-class businesspeople, they were suspicious of her disdain for the bourgeoisie; and, even more importantly, they were troubled by signs of her mental instability.

The idyllic life of Camp Nitgedayget (chasing salamanders in the streams, picnicking in the meadows, huddling around a campfire beneath a spiral of stars) was a respite for Allen and Eugene from the tensions of their family life—those ferocious fights between their parents over politics and finances. Naomi regularly ridiculed Louis, an English high school teacher, for being no more than a "bourgeois lackey." She lashed out at him for his milquetoast socialist views and for his cowardliness in refusing to embrace stalwart communist tenets. Louis grew furious and responded in kind, calling her a "stinking Red." Meanwhile, as the epithets flew wildly, the children cowered in fear.

Louis Ginsberg was forced to stay in Paterson during the week to teach summer-school in order to make money; his absence ensured tranquility during the vacation period. The family always had to tighten its financial belt, but now even more so to pay Naomi's expensive medical bills. Louis's salary as a teacher and his paltry earnings as an aspiring poet were nowhere enough to cover the costs of the Bloomingdale Sanatorium, a private asylum near Tarrytown, New York, where Naomi had been sent for a severe nervous breakdown in the early 1930s. She had experienced hypersensitivity to light and sound, confusion and disorientation, and by 1932 was diagnosed with what was then called "dementia praecox"—paranoid schizophrenia. While she found temporary relief from her symptoms, by 1935 her condition seriously worsened and became irreversible.

As an advocate of nudism, Naomi regularly walked about the house without clothes. Sometimes, she wore only a belt and bloody menstrual pad while doing her chores. The specter of their mother schlepping down the halls in a Kotex belt with her bare breasts sagging disgusted the boys. At other times, she rambled on and on about Rebecca Ginsberg, Louis's mother, whom she accused of wanting to kill her, and screamed at Louis for conspiring with "Buba" in these designs. Naomi also heard voices in her head and was convinced they were caused by hospital-implanted wires in her brain; she likewise suspected that the government monitored her conversations by means of bugs planted in her ceiling. Because Louis could no longer afford private care, he had no choice but to place his wife in Greystone, a huge state asylum near Morristown, New Jersey.

Life at Greystone was anything but pleasant. "It stank, sour smell of wards, disinfectant, vomit, piss, people incontinent," Allen recalled. "I remember walking down the wards, there were all these old people, and middle-aged people lined up, crooning to themselves, singing, talking to themselves.... Some of them had been left there for years by their families." The facility offered little but insulin shock and electroshock therapies; over the year of her stay, Naomi was subjected to forty insulin shock treatments and Metrazol, a drug that lowered her metabolism and ruined her figure.

Naomi Ginsberg was back at the family's apartment in time to celebrate Eugene's graduation from high school. He intended to go to New York University Law School. His family was proud of him, so Louis threw a party for Eugene on the evening of June 23, 1937. It was a joyous occasion for the Ginsberg family. At least, it started out that way. By the next day's dawn, their happiness turned to horror.

"I have it," Naomi muttered, "I have it."

Hearing this, Louis turned in his bed and noticed Naomi was gone.

"I have it."

He could hear her, but where was she? Something was wrong. Louis jumped up and rushed to the bathroom. The door was locked. He panicked. He feared that Naomi had found his razor, the one which he had hidden.

"Open the door!" he yelled. Louis pleaded with Naomi to come out. They could fix this. Fearing the worst, he pleaded again, this time more loudly. It woke the boys. Unsure of what was happening, they hurried to the hallway, standing witness, shivering in their nightclothes.

"Open the door or I'll smash in the glass panel!" Louis yelled. Naomi choked on her tears, coughing, but would not respond. There was no more time to wait. He broke the glass. *Cccrrraaassshhh!* Slivers of green glass spewed everywhere as Naomi's pathetic plight came into plain view.

There she stood, naked, in the pool of broken glass strewn across the floor. Her eyes were reddened with grief. Louis looked down; he saw blood oozing from her wrists. Nothing serious, mere surface cuts that could be bandaged, but more than enough to terrify Allen and Eugene. Their mother had tried to kill herself. Louis thought of the boys. "What traumas," he wondered, "might sink into them and burrow into their psyches?"

Back to Greystone* for Naomi, this time for more than two years.

In the winter of 1941, another psychotic episode emblazoned itself in Allen's memory. His mother was once again in a crazed

---

*At this time, the Ginsberg family had financial problems, though they were not due entirely to the costs of Naomi's treatment. In 1937 Louis spent $2,000 to subsidize a printing of a book of his poems, *The Everlasting Minute* (Liveright Publishing Co.). The book was dedicated to Naomi.

state, complaining of Greystone-implanted sticks in her back and assassins hired by "Buba" to kill her. The fifteen-year-old boy had no choice; he needed to stay home from school in order to watch over her. And what a manic day it turned out to be for Allen.

"They're listening to everything we say," Naomi whispered. "I don't want to put you in danger."

Now a familiar routine, Allen challenged her: "Who?" But when Naomi would not speak, Allen handed her a pad and pencil. She secretly penned "Buba"—his grandmother was the evil mastermind behind all of these machinations.

Leaning toward him, she spoke softly: "The wires are in this ceiling. I could hear the crackling when you gave me the pencil. They knew it."

Allen would have none of it. To prove his point, he got up on a chair and poked at the ceiling with the end of a broom. "There's no place for wires," he said.

Naomi was unconvinced: "They're smarter than you are."

And then more voices. She could hear them talking about her. They called her a whore; they even conspired with one of their agents to murder her. Frightened, she dashed toward the window. Allen followed. Looking across the street, they saw a group waiting on the corner for a bus. Among them was a well-dressed man sporting a hat.

"That's him! He's the one!" She shoved the window up, leaned out, and yelled, "Go away, you rotten thing!"

As the psychological drama escalated that day, Naomi pleaded with Allen to get her out of the house and into a safe place, like a rest home in Lakewood, New Jersey. Without asking Louis, Allen called Dr. Hans Wassing, Naomi's therapist, and arranged for her stay. He packed Naomi's suitcase, and the two headed to the bus depot.

Once there, and wishing to take no chances, Naomi scrutinized the bus. What she saw troubled her: "We can't go on this bus. He's not going to Newark, can't you see? The bus is empty. He's going to kidnap us." To avoid her cerebral captors, Naomi demanded that they take a circuitous route to New York and then over to Lakewood. For three hours, Allen was forced to listen to his mother ramble on "about poison germs, the sticks in her back, Louis, and a recent day in which she claimed to have seen Buba, dressed like a man, climbing up the apartment building with a sack on her back."

They reached the Lakewood rest home by dusk. "I'm weak, my blood spoiled by electricity," Naomi complained to the admissions desk clerk. "Can you give me a blood transfusion?"

Taken aback, the woman answered firmly, to Allen: "I'm sorry. This place is a rest home for elder people or people with mild nervous conditions. We haven't the facilities to handle your mother's case. This is not an insane asylum." She immediately showed them the door.

Allen found another nearby rest home to admit Naomi. He paid a week's rent for the cheapest room in the place and accompanied her to a small chamber in the attic. She would be safe, for the time being. And a catastrophe had been avoided for now.

The ride back to Paterson was a long and depressing one. But that was topped by Louis's irritation when he first learned of what Allen had done. After all that they had experienced, didn't Allen know that Naomi would become hysterical once left alone in Lakewood? Didn't he already know that?

It was predictable: a two A.M. phone call from the rest home. There was no escaping it, one horror story after another. Naomi had knocked and knocked on doors in the middle of the night and had frightened the elderly residents. The attendants attempted to pacify her to no avail. When they pursued her, she scuttled under her bed and blocked herself off with her suitcase. She screeched out a litany of her torturers: "Mussolini! Hitler! Buba! Fascists! Death!" Throughout, she interjected screams of "Help! Help!"

Several things were becoming apparent. Painful as it was for the Ginsbergs, Naomi had to return to Greystone, which she did within a week. Hard as it was for Louis and his family, he had to divorce Naomi, which he did in 1944. And Naomi could not live by herself or with others outside of an asylum; she alienated Eugene, her sister Eleanor, and her cousins Max and Edie Frohman when she stayed with them temporarily after leaving Greystone. With Naomi's options exhausted, Allen—who at the age of eighteen now had to assume the role of legal guardian for his own mother—had no other option: he reluctantly committed her to Pilgrim State Hospital, at that time the largest asylum in the world. Now Naomi Ginsberg would be one of its 25,000 patients.

Finally, the worst became apparent. Naomi's mental health had deteriorated to the point that, in mid-November 1947, the senior director at Pilgrim State recommended to Allen that she undergo a pre-frontal lobotomy. She had been doing all sorts of self-destructive things: pounding her head against a wall, lathering herself into a fearful frenzy, and tempting fate in ways that could kill her. Once again, Allen felt that he had no option: he authorized the lobotomy.

Unlike all of the other things Allen had done, this last desperate act was irreversible. Neither Naomi nor he would ever be the same afterward. About that time, the guilt-ridden son penned a three-word injunction in his journal: "Allen, don't die."

13.

HOW DOES A DOCTOR at the Columbia Presbyterian Psychiatric Institute repair the mind of a man who was damaged by a deranged mother?

Who grew to hate his father?

Who was insecure, yet had an inflated sense of self?

Who abused drugs?

Who lusted for fanatical men?

Who cavorted with junkies, criminals, and whores?

Who had mystical experiences?

Who confused fact with fiction?

Who in the asylum befriended its craziest patient?

Who loved life's darkest sides?

And who wasn't quite sure if he preferred normalcy to madness?

Those were the questions that Allen's doctors had to answer before they could release him back into the world of the sane and sensible. Their answer, in short, was normalcy. If Allen's life were to be repaired, he would have to embrace conformity in work, in play, in relationships, and in sex. In other words, the wild night life with Huncke, Kerouac, Cassady, Burroughs, and others had to stop.

Convinced that Allen was not a danger to himself or others and that he was willing to conform to societal norms, his doctor told him that he would soon be released from the institute. Before doing so, however, the psychiatrist had a private office consultation with Louis and his new wife, Edith. "He is partly homosexual," he informed them. "If you really want to have a close relationship with your son, you have to accept that, even to the point of receiving his lovers in your home, and if you really want a close relation, of allowing them to stay over." Edith, an intelligent and tolerant soul, was ready to accept Allen as he was. The news fell much harder, however, on Louis, who had hoped that the hospital would cure Allen of his homosexuality, which he considered a form of insanity and a menace to society.

With that, Allen Ginsberg was formally discharged on February 27, 1950. To make it official, he was given "a certificate stating that he wasn't mad, merely run-of-the-mill neurotic." On the day of his release, Allen wrote to Jack Kerouac of his serious intention to go straight: "A turning point has been reached in that I am not going to have anymore homosexual affairs: my free will is enough now to put this in writing as a final statement." Allen knew, however, that the road to heterosexual love would not run smoothly: "I wish that I could meet a really gone sweet girl who could love me," he pondered, but that could be "too much to expect."

At first blush, Helen Parker seemed to be that sweet girl. Allen had earlier been furloughed from the institute for the December holidays when he met Helen, a slightly older woman with two children. For Allen, Helen was "an interesting doll who dug painters and was smart as a whip," and had a "beautiful generous nature." But nothing much came of it that night. He wrote to Helen several weeks later, suggesting that she might be "a compatible woman" for him and encouraged her to respond. Though it was a step in the right psychological direction, it didn't look promising until much later.

"There *is* something new under the sun," Allen told Jack, "I have started into a new season, choosing women as my theme. I love

Helen Parker, and she loves me." He was referring to the Fourth of July weekend he had just spent with Helen at her cottage in Provincetown. "Many of my fears and dun rags fell from me after the first night I slept with her, when we understood that we wanted each other and began a love affair." Pleased by his heterosexual progress, he confessed: "All my queerness was camp, unnecessary, morbid, so lacking in completion and sharing of love as to be almost as bad as impotence and celibacy, which it practically was anyway.... Ah, Jack, I always said that I would be a great lover some day. I am. I am." Crowing with male pride, Allen declared: "I'm a man, I'm a man, I've got a cock."

Bill Burroughs, the King of Queers, was unimpressed. It was no more than a case of wishful thinking brought on by Allen's need to please authority figures. "I am more than a little dubious of a program to overcome queerness." When Ginsberg accused Burroughs of not wanting him to be cured, Bill replied in his characteristically wry way: "Laying one woman or a thousand merely *emphasizes* the fact that a woman is not what I want." To drive his point home, he quipped: "Better than nothing, of course, like a tortilla is better than no food. But no matter how many tortillas I eat I still want a steak." As it turned out, Allen savored Helen's tortilla for only three nights. When he returned to Paterson after the holiday weekend, the affair ended.

Allen's success on the job front wasn't much better. Thanks to his Uncle Leo, the twenty-three-year-old landed a reporting job at the *Labor Herald*, this after being turned down at the *Paterson Morning Call* and the *Passaic Evening News*. The New Jersey AFL paper, published in Newark, was fifteen miles away from Louis and Edith's new home in Paterson, where Allen now resided. He rose early to leave for his job, which combined his love of labor advocacy and writing. But it was an unrequited love: at the end of September 1950, the Columbia grad who majored in English was fired for incompetence.

True to his proletariat aspirations, Allen next tried his hand at factory work. Awkward as he was when it came to anything manual, he nevertheless grabbed a job at a Paterson ribbon factory. There he was paid $1.25 hourly and expected to "pick up all the broken threads and tie them back into the loom." Though it was not the kind of work for daydreaming, Allen did so nonetheless: "I would daydream, I lost track of how to do the simplest things and wandered around embarrassedly trying to fit in." But fit in he didn't. After two and a half weeks of daydreaming, he was fired again. Now he had failed at both mental and manual labor. "Truly the real world is my downfall," he sighed.

It was depressing the way failure tracked Ginsberg. Even on the poetry front, things looked bleak. Harcourt, Brace & Company had just rejected *A Book of Doldrums*, his collection of poems. "I think that your very personal idiom needs some channel of contact with the reading public before book publication is possible," editor Robert Giroux wrote to him. It was but another example of Allen's inability to connect with conventional minds.

In all of this, there were two signs of hope. One was Ginsberg's budding relationship with the famous poet William Carlos Williams. A medical doctor working the local rounds in his home town of Rutherford, New Jersey, Williams had published poetry, essays, plays, and novels since 1913. He wrote a five-volume philosophical epic in verse called *Paterson*, the first three volumes of which had been published by 1950. And in that same year, his *Collected Later Poems* was released. A friend of Ezra Pound, Williams had abandoned traditional rhyme and meter in his poetry and opted instead to experiment with an imagism that advocated a "controlled free verse."

After hearing him read at the Guggenheim Museum in New York, Allen took the initiative to introduce himself and his poetry to Williams by way of a bold letter. "I would like to make my presence in Paterson known to you, and I hope you will welcome this from me, an unknown young poet, to you, an unknown old poet, who live in the same rusty county of the world." The sixty-six-year-old poet was charmed by the comic and quasi-neurotic letter from the young man. Allen's poetry, however, was less fetching. Williams replied to him that his poems were not that great. Their formality was at odds with "rhythmical construction"—a poem must reflect the way language is commonly spoken, rather than the way it is typically written. It was an idea that would soon transform Allen's work. And though he had yet to gain the great poet's professional respect, he had gained his personal friendship, which would one day prove important.

The other sign of hope was that Ginsberg had freed himself from his Benzedrine habit, for now, anyway. "I refuse to use Benny anymore," he bragged to Neal Cassady, who downed the drug recklessly.

Try as he might, Allen could not entirely resist many of the same temptations that had first landed him in the asylum. While he no longer hung with Huncke and Little Jack, that was due to the simple fact that they were unavailable. And Vicki Russell seemed to have vanished after her last run-in with the law. Nonetheless, even before he checked out of the bughouse, Allen still reveled in the delights of his old gang's wild and wondrous company.

A few months before his discharge from the institute, Ginsberg got a pass to attend a New Year's Eve party Carl Solomon was hosting. (The idea for the party was Allen's.) Carl had been released just before Christmas and had moved into a low-rent apartment near the headquarters of the National Maritime Union. Many of Allen's pals were there, including Jack and Neal. Anatole Broyard, a literary critic who taught fiction writing at Columbia, was also partying along with a group of students from Brooklyn College. Other literary types dropped in, as well, including Jay Landesman, the editor of the magazine *Neurotica*, whom Solomon first met when Allen introduced the two. It was the old formula all over again: literati, liquor, and liveliness.

Always the showman, a pumped-up Cassady mesmerized the group with his frenetic and high-blown word flow. He bounced energetically from person to person, talking up a storm. To keep spirits high, he jauntily played an ocarina (a sort of bulbous flute) and performed "Amos 'n' Andy" bits, imitating the slow-paced, gravelly bass and rapid-fire tenor voices of the comic radio characters. He echoed lines such as Kingfish's famous catchphrase "Holy Mackerel, Andy!" and "Ah, ah, Sapphire!" Everybody in the room laughed and drank more. It was a sight, with Neal doing his shtick in front of friends decked out in plastic noses, the ones with bebop glasses attached.

But Carl Solomon's apartment was not in the same league as the notorious San Remo bar or the veterans of temptation who haunted it. Located at the northeast corner of Bleecker and MacDougal streets in the Village, the San Remo was a bohemian hangout like no other. It served "the strongest espresso this side of Sicily." For a cheap high, there were fifteen-cent beers; and for those willing to spend a buck, potent Martinis were poured by bartenders tagged "the Minor Mafia." In its wooden booths and below its pressed-tin ceiling, "subterraneans" of all types (as Allen called them) joined in the revelries; everyone from the young Miles Davis and Gore Vidal to Tennessee Williams could be found among the disaffected. Particularly on Thursday nights, things took off as the joint transformed into a homosexual pickup place. But all week long, "amid the discussion of Reich and existentialism, jazz and marijuana, a comfortable *maudit* atmosphere reigned, causing some to refer to the bar as the San Remorse."

Not long after Ginsberg walked out through the arched doors of the Columbia Presbyterian Psychiatric Institute, his shoe soles made contact with the black-and-white-tiled floor of the San Remo. Allen was unable to suppress the spirit of nonconformity that was the bar's trademark. Time and again, he trekked from Paterson to the Village, leading a double existence: "For all his apparent attempts at living a more ordered, even if mundane, life, Allen never strayed far from the New York bohemian life that he found so compelling." Allen became a regular face at the San Remo, making new friends and hanging out with old ones.

Bill Cannastra was one of those friends. He was also one of the most infamous and uninhibited habitués of the San Remo.

14.

Drinking was his vocation, brutal sarcasm his métier,
self-abuse his element.
—William Plummer

BILL CANNASTRA looked debonair one October night in 1950 when Allen Ginsberg and Carl Solomon spotted him in the San Remo. Dressed in a black suit and designer tie, he looked like a Harvard lawyer, which he was. His dark garb perfectly matched his thick black eyebrows, curly black hair, and onyx eyes, set off by a fair complexion. There was an air of refinement, even dignity, about him. It was all very impressive; it was also very atypical.

The young man of Italian ancestry looked nowhere as dignified when he danced barefoot on broken glass to the tune of Bach fugues, teetered on the thin outside ledges of seventy-foot buildings, or lay in front of oncoming traffic, all as gags for his buddies. Or when he threw a jungle party and dressed as a palm tree, with only a jock strap and leafy headdress to cover him. Or when he urged Jack Kerouac to strip and streak down 16th Street with him at three o'clock on a rainy morning (Jack kept his shorts on). Or when he peaked through windows or peepholes (he had one in his bathroom) for voyeuristic kicks. And he certainly didn't look dignified when he'd "guzzle liquor so fast" that the change from dapper to drunk was "like the swoosh when you light a gas stove."

Strange as Cannastra's appearance was that evening at the San Remo, it was not the thing that most captivated Allen. What really caught his eye was the sight of Bill standing in the middle of the floor with the celebrated playwright Tennessee Williams. "I was gnawed by envy," Allen admitted, "and a desire to seize an opportunity to involve myself with Williams through Cannastra." But at first Bill didn't seem to notice Allen. He was just "jiggling and swaying side to side, from foot to foot, slowly and weavingly" while chatting with the thirty-nine-year-old dramatist who had recently won fame for *The Glass Menagerie* (1944) and *A Streetcar Named Desire* (1947). Try as he may, Allen couldn't pick up their conversation, and wondered what the bisexual Cannastra and the "queer playwright" might be saying: "What could Cannastra have to say to him? What relationship had they to each other?"

Allen wasn't the only person who was puzzled at Tennessee Williams's interest in Cannastra. Tennessee himself found the relationship an odd one. Cannastra's piercing eyes and attractive face, resembling Botticelli's *Saint Sebastian*, were alluring enough to bring Williams to Cambridge in pursuit of the then twenty-two-year-old Harvard law student, who also kept the company of another famous literary figure, W.H. Auden. But Bill's charm could not camouflage the eccentricity of his unappealing clique: "This boy had a group of friends at Harvard, and they were all sort of freaked out, in varying degrees," as Williams described it. "One had attempted to slash his wrists a few days before." Williams also recalled "how this attempt on his life had made him a celebrity in the group and the shy pride he took in exhibiting the scars when the wrists were unbandaged." One night, years earlier, this "very mad crowd of young professors and students" drove Williams away as quickly as he had arrived; in the rush, he left his briefcase there with the latest draft of his nearly completed *Menagerie*.

Cannastra's high life with the literati was short-lived. Soon enough, Auden tired of him, as did the celebrated editors and critics who earlier had frequented the trendsetting parties held at his huge, U-shaped loft at 121 West 21st Street. The likes of dance critic Edwin Denby, *New Yorker* poetry editor Howard Moss, and Random House editor William Frankel once mingled with painters, writers, opera devotees, and aspiring artists (like Allen, Jack, and their gang) who admired the eighty feet of classical, jazz, and bluegrass records that lined his walls. But Bill's near-suicidal antics and uncontrolled drinking had alienated his more distinguished friends one by one, and those who stuck around did so primarily to be amused by their maniacal clown. "Cannastra continues to be kept," his Harvard friend John Snow explained, "on the condition that he remains . . . intelligently desperate."

Bill's life in the law had also been short-lived. To begin with, he had only attended law school at the insistence of his aristocratic mother; he wanted to be an artist and *bon vivant* instead. True to his self-destructive nature, Cannastra was unprepared and intoxicated when he sat for the New York State bar exam, which he passed nonetheless. He practiced law for a short time, but when he regularly arrived late to the office and drunk, he was fired from the firm. Afterward, he flea-skipped from job to job, leaving either for lack of success or for lack of interest. There was Bill's brief position at Random House as a dictionary compilation consultant; then his work as a baker; then his seasonal stint as a fisherman. Anything to pay the rent for his warehouse-district loft over a lampshade factory and to pay for liquor at his neighborhood bar or the San Remo.

Cannastra was sufficiently liquored up that October night in 1950 at the San Remo to fuel his crass, and often cruel, sense of humor. Allen noticed that Bill had deserted Tennessee Williams and was now involved in conversation "with some of the lesser luminaries of the bar." Within seconds, Cannastra raised the temperature of the room some forty degrees. Standing directly in the faces of a middle-aged Italian and his *amici*, Bill shouted: "I hate wops! I hate wops! I hate wops and Irishmen!" Faces reddened, backs straightened, and fists tightened. At the very last moment, Cannastra brought the temperature back down to a comfortable level. He showed the Italian his business card, WM. CANNASTRA, COUNSELOR AT LAW, to prove that he was a "wop," as well. Characteristic Cannastra.

This wasn't the first time that Allen and his friends had witnessed Bill's reckless, raunchy, or ruthless pranks. What about the time he walked into a joint filled with roughnecks, yelling, "Up your ass with Mobilgas"? That wisecrack got Jack Kerouac into trouble, when he took a fist in the eye trying to defend Cannastra from the descending horde. And how about the time Bill strolled into a bar near the docks, took a tough longshoreman unawares, gave him a big wet French kiss, and then said, "Buy me a drink?" One would think that he'd not live to see another day. But that stranger ended up buying, because Bill convinced him he wasn't a "pansy." Cannastra's girlfriend, Joan Haverty, understood precisely what these jokes signified: "Bill was of more value as a novelty, a conversation piece. I'd overhear [his friends] discussing his flirtations with death as if it were all some zany game for their benefit."

After his shouting bout with the Italian, Cannastra wandered over to Ginsberg's table and took a seat with Allen's friends. They spoke a bit, and then Bill focused on the woman sitting next to Bob Steen, a brilliant physician and fellow "subterranean." Steen had been flirting with her all night long, but she was playing hard to get. Bill decided to help Bob out.

"Why don't you fuck s-s-somebody?!" he yelled at her. "Why don't you fuck Steen?" He slipped in and out of the stutter that sometimes impeded his *s*'s and *b*'s. Silence at the table. The woman was stunned, speechless. "Cunt is the greatest! Cunt is b-b-better than anything!" Silence of all within earshot. Amazement. "Why don't you fuck s-s-somebody?! I don't mean fuck me! I don't want woman! I wouldn't fuck you in a thousand years! I wouldn't fuck you for all the money in the world! I mean, why don't you fuck *somebody*?"

There was truth in his barbs; he probably wouldn't have fucked her. Not because he wasn't sexual. Quite to the contrary. Almost every party at his loft ended with sex—sometimes with men, sometimes with women, sometimes with both. In Tennessee Williams's eyes, Bill's libido loved men first: "Bill was way out of his closet and he was always drunk, but a good drunk, I mean a wildly exuberant drunk, and he was a good lay." Williams should have known—he "had been carrying on a running affair with Cannastra since 1944."

In Joan Haverty's eyes, however, Bill's heart loved her. She was his playmate, his soulmate, and his anchor. When Joan moved from Upstate New York to escape the strictures of her mother, she soon fell under the spell of Cannastra, who acted as her mentor in most matters. While she spent most of her time at Bill's loft, theirs was a relationship of affection, rather than sexual passion. Though he had a temper and could be abusive at times, he respected her for her innocence and encouraged her to get married for protection. "When women are protected, they are respected," Cannastra once told her. He hoped to play the role of matchmaker, hooking her up with Jack Kerouac. "He's a writer, and *mensch* in his own way," Bill told her. "He has s-s-some middle-class ideas about marriage and he's very s-serious about settling down and having a family." Joan laughed incredulously: "And you want to introduce him to *me*?"

Homosexual as he was, Allen never felt threatened by women, including Joan Haverty. He even had an eye pealed for the glamorous starlet-looking young woman, whose thin brows arched above expressive eyes and sensuous lips. But that night at the San Remo, Allen didn't want to talk about women; he wanted to talk about Tennessee Williams.

Cannastra obliged, telling Allen that Tennessee had said that "he would give me all of his legal b-b-business if I would 'come off the party.'" Allen stared at him. He didn't understand what he meant by the phrase. Was this some sexual allusion? But no. Bill held his arms high in the air, as though he were holding two whiskey bottles. Allen then appreciated what Bill meant: that Williams's offer turned on Cannastra's sobering up.

"What are you going to do? Why don't you accept?" Allen asked.

"I don't know," he responded dismissively. "But the party's coming to an end."

And it did, the very next day, October 12, 1950.

The No. 6 subway train, the Uptown IRT, stopped at the Bleecker Street platform. Bill Cannastra and his raucous friends were on it. He was sauced. They all had been partying at Ann Adams' place and were now on their way to Lucien Carr's apartment to get some money so that they could party more. Someone mentioned the Bleecker Street Tavern and their favorite black barmaid, Winnie, who worked there. Cannastra made noises about returning to the tavern just as the subway car doors closed. Bill dashed to an open window and thrust his head and torso out, as if to leap back onto the platform. It was meant to be just another death-defying prank.

Suddenly, the train lurched away from the station. Bill lost his balance and became stuck as the train accelerated. He screamed. His friends rushed to pull him back in, but they couldn't get a grip on him. They yanked furiously on his coat; it tore. More screaming. Louder screaming. The car rolled faster. Soot blew into his nostrils and flew into his eyes as the train began to speed through the tunnel. He saw pillars. He tried to duck. He panicked. He let out a blood-curdling scream. It was too late.

THUD! His head cracked against the iron pillar. The immense force ripped his body out of the window and sucked it down to the cold ground. Someone pulled the emergency cord, and the train slammed to a halt. Terrified, Ann Adams ran to the last car to look out its window. The battered body had been dragged for fifty feet or more. It was a ghastly sight. Cannastra's head had been cracked open. Brains oozed out of his bloody temple.*

Later that day, Joan Haverty was at the San Remo when Bob Steen told her that Bill was dead. *"What!?"* she cried.

"It was a subway accident. Oh, Joan, he tried to climb out the window of a moving train."

Shocked, she sat still, pondering for a few seconds. "Then he finally killed himself," she uttered softly.†

Rising without another word, she hastened out the door and ran down the street. "I rushed to my room and secluded myself there, locked myself in, turned my mind inward, grieving," Joan recalled. "I stayed in the room after that for days. . . . I thought maybe I'd never come out."

It was not long, however, before Joan helped Fred Cannastra, Bill's brother, cart away his clothes, records, books, and papers. But she couldn't bear the notion that someone else would change the colors of the walls, mount different pictures, or replace the furniture. So she decided to rent the loft herself and preserve its appearance as a memorial to Bill.

Cannastra's death, Lucien Carr told Allen Ginsberg, was the tragic consequence of a joke, a dare. But such an unabashed love of the

---

*Bill Cannastra's life and his freakish death were immortalized in Jack Kerouac's *Visions of Cody* and *Book of Dreams* (as Finistra in both books), in John Clellon Holmes's *Go* (as Agatson), in Alan Harrington's *The Secret Swinger* (as Genovese), and in Allen Ginsberg's "Howl" and *Empty Mirror*.

†Allen Ginsberg deliberated over the issue of Cannastra's suicide: "The great question on everybody's soul, was, was it an accident or did he do it on purpose?" The question was never resolved conclusively. Notably, Bill's mother had attempted suicide by swallowing lye.

"chaotic element," Allen thought, was "ultimately death-dealing." And it taught him a lesson that he hadn't learned in the asylum: "You can't play around with non-existence...there is no life after death." What Cannastra never appreciated was "what it really meant to die, and that it was really possible for him to die." W.H. Auden's reported response was far less philosophical or sensitive: "The most tragic thing about it was that it had caused a three-hour delay in the New York subways."

15.

For me, Jack's appeal lay more in what he was not
than in what he was.
—Joan Haverty

"**HELLOOOOOOO!** Helloooooo!"

Joan Haverty opened her loft window and peered at the stranger standing in the dimly lit street below. Even in that light, she could see his athletic figure: a V-shaped muscular body with wide shoulders atop his five-foot, nine-inch frame. "Who is it?"

"Kerouac!" he yelled.

Aaah, she thought, this was the friend that Bill had always wanted her to meet. "I'll throw you the keys. Come on up!" She tossed the key chain. Her aim was off, but he caught them easily. It was almost as though the former high school football star were intercepting a pass.

"Who's that?" asked Herb Lashinsky, a young Columbia grad student in physics with whom Joan had once had a passionate affair. He had come over that evening for conversation and a cup of chocolate and now wondered at Joan's invitation to this stranger. "Why are you letting him up?"

"Friend of Lucien Carr's and Allen Ginsberg's . . . and Bill's. Bill spoke of him," she answered cautiously.

With athletic vigor and obvious enthusiasm, Jack sprinted up the stairs, carrying a briefcase. In seconds, he walked into the loft. Joan's eyes lit upon the full vision. She was struck by his arresting look—his full, black hair carefully combed to the side, dreamy blue eyes, beautifully shaped lips, and strong chin. And he was dressed conservatively in a neatly pressed shirt and pants, not the style she was accustomed to seeing in Bill's gang.

"Somebody told me there was a party here tonight." He was trying to explain his presence, why he yelled out when he saw a light in the loft.

Joan was puzzled. She wasn't having a party. Jack must have been thinking of Lucien's, the place next door at 149 West 21st Street. In fact, his loft was accessible from hers by use of a fire escape.

"Probably at Lucien's," Joan suggested. "But we can have a hot chocolate party. I was just making some." Her invitation was pregnant with possibilities. She left the room and went to the kitchen to brew up some cocoa.

Jack turned to Herb: "Your girl?"

"Nope," he answered.

From the kitchen area, Joan overheard Herb's abrupt and casual reply. It stung her. But it seemed to please Jack: she was fair game.

"What do you do?" Herb asked.

Jack reacted with some humility, bashfully gesturing and looking at his feet: "Oh, well, I . . ." He paused. "I wrote a book." With a shy grin, he added: "I'm writing another one." More excitedly, he went on: "This one's about my travels. All over the country. And Mexico, too!"

"Sounds interesting," Herb replied with courteous dismissal, as he resumed reading a magazine.

Unaffected, the scorned writer opened his briefcase, pulled out one of a half-dozen copies of his book, and handed it to Joan.

While Herb's face was buried in his magazine, Joan read the title aloud: "*The Town and the City.*" She glanced at the photo on the back cover. "It doesn't look like you."

"Nah!" Kerouac growled. Taking a macho swipe at the photographer, he continued: "Guy was a faggot. Made me look like one, too."

"You'll have to autograph it for me," Joan stated, as she opened the thick book and handed it to him.

He pulled a pen from his pocket, signed the bottom of the flyleaf, and inscribed the following at the top of the page: "For Joan." Handing the book back to her, he said, "When I know you better, I'll add something to that."

"Thanks. I'll start reading it tonight."

Now Jack was ready to make his move: "No, don't do that. I've got a better idea. Let's all go over to Lucien's party.... I'm inviting you.... Whadaya say?... Hey! We don't even have to go downstairs! We can go right across the fire escape."

Their lives moved at a fast-forward pace afterward. Jack and Joan saw much of one another in a short time. By November 5, 1950, only two days after they met in her loft, Jack was getting quite romantic, or as romantic as he could be: "Listen, I got to thinking about you last night when I got home, and I thought about you all day today. I even told my mom about you. I want to marry you."

"What?" Joan gasped. "What... what on earth for?"

"What does anyone get married for? To have a home together. To have children. To grow old."

Incredulous, Joan persisted in questioning him, trying to understand the meaning of this drop-from-the-sky proposal: "But why me? We just met! We don't even know each other."

Jack was undeterred: "We have the rest of our lives to get to know each other. And I want you to be my wife.... Bill told me a lot about you."

"What did Bill tell you about me?"

"I told him what kind of girl I was looking for, and he said I had described you perfectly," Jack asserted. Then he really laid on the charm, in his inimitable way: "A sweet little, nice little home-type girl, just like you. Not clever or witty, not worldly or jaded, and ... not forward, you know? Not a man-chaser." He continued to laud her virtues: "He said you were a great cook! I'd be home with you."

"Why?" Joan asked.

After all that, the words finally rolled off his lips: "Because I love you!" Then, accelerating like a rocket-fueled joyride, he urged, "There's no time to waste. You quit your job and we'll get the license tomorrow. You know ... someday I'm going to be a big author. I'll make lots of money.... Now just be a sweet girl and tell me you'll marry me."

Joan surprised even herself when she accepted the proposal. She wasn't, however, under any illusions about Jack's real reasons: "I was being wooed because our meeting coincided with Jack's decision to marry, because Bill, before his death, had expected our relationship to be propitious, and because I was acceptable to his mother." And then there were other reasons: "It helped that I could cook and that I was no threat to him, would not upstage him."

Joan, too, had her reasons. This accomplished dressmaker wanted dearly to remain in New York to build a career. There simply was no real opportunity for that back in Albany with her family. And then there was her mother, whom she never seemed able to please. All in all, so the rationalization went, Jack Kerouac wasn't a bad catch. He was strong, handsome, smart, and appeared to care about her and having children.* More importantly, he wasn't sexually aggressive; he wasn't critical; and he wasn't demanding (not usually). Marrying Jack, she thought, "was the least of a number of evils."

---

*Joyce Johnson (née Glassman), one of Kerouac's subsequent girlfriends, wrote: "I think the idea of having children was very frightening to him."

Twelve days after Jack proposed, he and Joan married on the Friday evening of November 17, 1950. It didn't prove to be easy. For one thing, he had to confirm that his previous marriage with Edie Parker had, in fact, been annulled. For another, at the time that city hall closed, the couple was thirty-four minutes shy of the three-day waiting period required by law. Jack had to prevail on a relative, Judge Vincent Lupiano, to marry them at his residence on Abingdon Square, with his wife and secretary serving as witnesses. "Do you want hearts and flowers," Judge Lupiano asked, "or shall we just get it over with?" The ceremony had all the charm of a Tijuana wedding.

Jack insisted on a quickie marriage because the reception had been planned for that night, and the carousers—some two hundred of them—were all ready at play. When the bride and groom arrived on the scene, the party was well along and the beer kegs were flowing freely.

The gang was there. Allen Ginsberg, Lucien Carr, John Holmes, and Carl Solomon were among them. Even Winnie from the Bleecker Street Tavern came. Only a little more than a month earlier, Bill Cannastra had slept in this loft; and only a few weeks earlier, this loft had been preserved to commemorate Cannastra. Now, a raucous celebration was once again underway. The deafening noise, the nonstop drinking, the overflowing keg, the clouds of cigarette smoke, the clogged toilet, the coffeepot hurled out the window, the sausage platter that fell behind the icebox, and the copulating in closets—it all befitted the absent reveler.

As the newlyweds stood in the breakfast nook, a toast was about to be made in their honor. With friends all around (except for any of Joan's friends), Holmes looked into their eyes and said, "I believe in you, Jack and Joan. I believe in you." Heartfelt as his sentiment was, it was still ironic for Joan: "We had made a commitment to the marriage, but none to each other.... The whole thing had been

Jack's idea, and I had seen it as his party, and his wedding, for that matter." Cynically, she felt that "none of it seemed to have anything to do with the rest of my life."

In the early hours toward the end of the party, a boisterous trio came together to do a boozy rendition of the 1929 classic, "Wedding Bells Are Breaking Up That Old Gang of Mine." In rough variation on a three-part harmony, Allen, John, and Lucien gave it their drunken best:

> *There goes Jack, there goes Jim,*
> *Down to lover's lane.*
> *Now and then we meet again,*
> *But they don't seem the same.*
> *Gee, I get a lonesome feeling*
> *When I hear the church bells chime.*
> *Those wedding bells are breaking up that old gang of mine.*

The party wound down, and the couple prepared for their wedding night. "Whesher nightie?" Jack asked. Turning off the bedside lamp, Joan went to the bathroom to slip into her diaphanous gown. "By the time I got into bed," Joan remarked, "he was completely out." Sarcastically, she added, "So far, the marriage had lived up to my expectations."

Several hours later, Lucien and Allen turned up. They pounded on the door, eager to share in the bubble of the champagne that John Holmes had presented as a wedding gift. Jack awoke and was more than happy to oblige. As they drank and spoke, Joan could hear them through the thin bathroom wall. Jack was bragging: "Man, we wailed all night! Sweetest little girl in the world!" It was, of course, a lie.

With the wedding now behind him, Jack returned to his first love—writing.

16.

> *My heart resides in a typewriter, and I don't have a*
> *heart unless there's a typewriter somewhere nearby, with*
> *a chair in front of it and some blank sheets of paper.*
> —Jack Kerouac

CLACK, CLACK, CLACK, *clack, clack, clackclackclackclack, clack-clackclackclack. Ding. Zzzziiiipppp.*

I first met Neal not long after my father died . . . I had just gotten over a

Click, click, clack, clack, clack, clack, clackclackclackclackclackclack-clack. Ding. Zzzziiiipppp.

serious illness that I won't bother to talk about except that it really had some

Clack, clack, clack, clack, clack, clackclackclackclack, clackclackclack-clack. Ding. Zzzziiiipppp.
Click, click, clack, clack, clack, clackclackclackclackclackclackclack-clack, clackclackclackclack. Ding. Zzzziiiipppp.

thing to do with my father's death and my awful feeling that everything was dead.

His fingers raced over the antique L.C. Smith typewriter, pounding down on the four rows of round, white-topped keys that floated above the oak wood visible through the key bars. With machine-gun rapidity, the steel arms of the typebar slammed their raised metal letters against the ribbon's black-inked fabric, steadily striking onto the smooth surface of the translucent paper wrapped around the cylindrical black platen. The ceaseless clacking echoed off the walls of the tiny studio apartment at 454 West 20th Street in Chelsea, to which Jack and Joan had recently moved.

The carriage quickly traveled to the left as he neared the end of a line of type. *Ding.* At the high-pitched sound of the tiny bell, his left hand flew up to the silver carriage lever at the end of the platen and shoved it to the right. *Zzzziiipppp.* The platen rotated to expose the empty space on which he hammered out the next line of slightly uneven type.

Clack, clack, clack, clack, clack, clackclackclackclack, clackclackclackclack.

Jack Kerouac hunched over his old typewriter atop the desk that his sister, Nin, and brother-in-law had recently given to him as a birthday present. That rainy Monday morning, April 2, 1951, the twenty-nine-year-old was comfortable in his fresh T-shirt. From time to time, he interrupted his typing to flip through the spiraled pocket notebooks with eighteen lines of scribbled writings. Or through his journals containing detailed travelogue descriptions of his cross-country journeys. Or through letters that Neal Cassady, his adventurous friend, had sent him. Or, at times, he consulted the various one-page plot lines he had developed earlier. And just as often, he relied on his remarkable memory. So close was his story to reality that he regularly used real names for his fictional characters.

It was old hat for Jack. Between 1943 and 1945, he had "produced thousands of pages of fiction, poetry, and essays on literary, philosophical, and, to a lesser extent, sociopolitical subjects." Later, he would type, "NIGHT NOTES & DIAGRAMS for ON THE ROAD." And now he was doing it once again: writing...remembering...rewriting...recreating...reconfiguring. He tumbled fact with fiction, noun with verb, and typed everything down at breakneck speed. Solitude, scribblings, and memories were his main companions.

Joan was off to her waitressing job at Stouffer's, having made Jack a big pot of coffee before she left. As he shuffled in his sheepskin slippers to the kitchen for another cup of joe, he could not erase from his mind the discussion he had just had with her about the writer's block that plagued him. And then they spoke about his travels with Neal Cassady.

"What was it like, Jack?"

"To be on the road with Neal?"

"Yes," Joan replied. "What happened, what really happened?"

The questions broke a dam in his mind. Jack's remarkable memory (his boyhood friends tagged him "Memory Babe") released a flood of images: people, places, conversations, and countless colorful experiences that shaped his life and those around him. At long last, after all of his aborted starts,* he finally had begun the work that he described in a journal entry on July 28, 1948: "I have another novel in mind—'On the Road'—which I keep thinking about;—About two guys hitch-hiking to California in search of something they don't really find, and losing themselves on the road, and coming all the way back hopeful of something else."

_____

*This was the fourth of five attempts, as Tim Hunt first established. The final attempt came by way of an expanded, reworked, and far more uninhibited text titled *Visions of Cody* (1973), published years after *On the Road*.

Clackclackclackclack, clackclackclackclack, clackclackclacklack, clack-clackclack. Ding. Zip.

> With the coming of Neal there really began for me that part of
> my life that you could call my life on the road.

In a trance-like state, Kerouac fashioned fact into fiction at an amazing clip. He "just flung it down. He could dissociate himself from his fingers, and he was simply following the movie in his head. Jack was a lightning typist." Even on an old manual typewriter, he could beat out one hundred words or so per minute. Faster and faster, he typed away as if he were a junkie jazz man "drawing a breath, and blowing a phrase on his saxophone, till he runs out of breath." Or as Jack once put it in a journal entry: "IT'S NOT THE WORDS THAT COUNT, BUT THE RUSH OF TRUTH WHICH USES WORDS FOR ITS PURPOSES."

As he rushed along, Jack noticed that the architectural drafting paper began to slide to the right. So he adjusted it, trying not to smudge the fresh ink. But this slowed him down a bit, which was contrary to his purpose for using that paper at all. Ironically, the whole idea traced back to Cannastra.

Before Jack and Joan moved out of Bill's loft, Kerouac accidentally found a big roll of paper in a cabinet. It sparked an imaginative idea: if he could feed that paper into the typewriter, he could save all the wasteful time and trouble of constantly inserting new pages into the roller every so many minutes. That process would enable him to type as fast as he thought. Jack soon discovered, however, that the full roll was unmanageable; so he cut it up into eight pieces of different lengths. Moreover, the pieces were too wide for the typewriter carriage. To remedy that problem, Jack pencil-marked a side of each piece and cut it along the edge. He intended to tape the long, crinkly sheets back together again, once he finished typing on them, so as to transform them into a hefty scroll.

Clackclackclackclack, clackclackclackclack, clackclackclacklack, clackclackclack. Ding. Zip.

> ...they danced down the street like dingle-dodoies and I shambled after as usual as I've been doing all my life after people that interest me, because the only people that interest me are the mad ones, the ones who are mad to live, mad to talk, desirous of everything at the same time, the ones that never yawn or say a commonplace thing...but burn, burn, burn like roman candles across the night.

It was a draft, but it was a great start. There would be time enough later to polish it. To make it more poetic. To make it sparkle. To add colorful adjectives and wondrous metaphors until finally the long sentence ended: "burn, burn, burn like fabulous yellow roman candles exploding like spiders across the stars and in the middle you see the blue centerlight pop and everybody goes 'Awww!'"

Even on day one, Jack Kerouac had managed to fuse speed with his own unique style. Now he was actualizing what Neal Cassady had advised him to do three years earlier: "When one writes, one should forget all rules, literary styles, and other such pretensions as large words, lordly clauses and other phrases...rolling the words around in the mouth as one would wine.... [O]ne should write, as nearly as possible, as if he were the first person on earth and was humbly and sincerely putting on paper that which he saw and experienced, loved and lost; what his passing thoughts were, and his sorrows and desires." Awww! He was writing his world.

Key to that world was the man whom he had just described several hundred words earlier:

> My first impression of Neal was of a young Gene Autry—trim, thin hipped, blue eyes, with a real Oklahoma accent.

Neal. Neal. Neal. Without him and his story, Jack could not have been the same man, and *On the Road* could not have been written. As he turned time back—picking this from letters, picking that from journals—he recreated the Neal who had ruled one side of his soul.

From the moment they met, Kerouac fell under Cassady's spell. To Jack, Neal was a fascinating study in contradictions. On the one hand, he was a fallen angel, a car thief, a conman, and a sex maniac. Born on February 8, 1926, in a Salt Lake City charity hospital as his parents traveled from Iowa to California, Neal lived in Denver flophouses with his divorced alcoholic father and ate breakfast alone at the Citizen's Mission before walking to kindergarten. At the age of fourteen,* he stole his first car; he lifted some five hundred over the next seven years. Generally, Neal hoisted a car from a parking lot, took a joy ride for a few hours, and returned it before the owner noticed it missing. Fortune did not always run his way, however; he was arrested ten times for grand larceny by 1946, was convicted on six occasions, and served a total of over a year in jail. And Neal's reputation as a "cocksman" was legendary in Denver. He could masturbate half a dozen times and have enough remaining desire to seduce a woman or two on the same day with his "big huge crown," as Jack depicted it. Cassady was "a walking, breathing hard-on." Kerouac captured the spirit of Cassady's sexual drive in a single telling sentence that he typed on his scroll:

[T]o him, sex was the only holy and important thing in life.

On the other hand, Neal did demonstrate a cerebral side. When he was not committing felonies or fucking, he haunted the Denver public library to skim the likes of Dostoyevsky, Kant, Nietzsche,

---

*A vivid portrayal of the young Cassady (aka Cody Pomeray) appears in part 2 of Jack Kerouac's *Visions of Cody* and later, some sixty pages into the "Joan Rawshanks in the Fog" section of that book.

Proust, Schopenhauer, and Shakespeare. The "Nietzschean hero of the pure snow wild West" sprinkled his conversations with morsel-references to such great authors, leading sometimes to greater understanding and other times to confusion brought on by gibberish. Even so, Kerouac was impressed that Cassady was self-educated and that he always showed a deep interest in Jack's writings (and those of other friends like Ginsberg and Holmes).

And then there was Neal's mesmerizing way of meshing his body language and verbal language. With boundless energy, Neal moved constantly as he talked rapidly. He swayed to and fro or bobbed up and down like a boxer; his hands gestured here and there, and his animated eyes expressed this and that. All this frenzied motion jibed perfectly with his frenetic speech, monologues delivered at triple-speed and sentences frequently interrupted by "you see," "that's right," or a string of "yeahs." Neal was a natural showman, whose stories were a collage of his eccentric life experiences mixed with traces of philosophy, history, spirituality, or pure bullshit. "Sounds, sights, personalities came to life as he talked, assuming monumental proportion," Joan Haverty Kerouac observed. "Text could never capture the vitality and intensity" of his unique perspective and voice. Even so, that was exactly what Jack had recorded in the literary account of his first meeting with Neal:

> In the bar I told Neal, "For krissakes man I know very well you didn't come to me only to want to become a writer and after all what do I really know about it except you've got to stick to it with the energy of a benny addict," and he said, "Yes of course, I know exactly what you mean and in fact those problems have occurred to me but the thing that I want is the realization of those factors that should one depend on Schopenhauer's dichotomy for any inwardly realized..." and on and on in that way, things I understood not a bit and he himself didn't... that

is to say, he was a young jailkid all hung up on the wonderful possibilities of becoming a real intellectual and he liked to talk in the tone and using the words but in a jumbled way that he had heard "real intellectuals" talk altho mind you he wasn't so naïve as that in all other things.

When the twenty-year-old Cassady stormed into New York City in 1946 and into Kerouac's life, he embodied Jack's notions of the American West hero, a "siren singing freedom, excitement, kicks... enthusiastically flying after food and sex like a holy primitive." And it was Neal's siren song that pulled Jack onto the road time and again, providing the journeys of self-discovery that he would describe in kaleidoscopic detail in his latest novel.

The stories of those journeys were soon to come. But first Jack needed more coffee. Was it his third or fifth cup? He wasn't counting. And now, with his eyes and mind wide open, he wrote about the irrepressible erotic attraction that his friend Allen immediately felt toward Neal upon meeting him, and the beginning of their on-again, off-again sexual relationship.

Clackclackclackclack, clackclackclackclack, clackclackclackclack, clackclackclack. Ding. Zip.

Allen was queer in those days, experimenting with himself to the hilt, and Neal saw that, and a former boyhood hustler himself in the Denver night, and wanting dearly to learn how to write poetry like Allen, the first thing you know he was attacking Allen with a great amorous soul such as only a conman can have. I was in the same room, I heard them across the darkness and I mused and said to myself "Hmm, now something's started, but I don't want anything to do with it." So I didn't see them for about two weeks during which time they cemented their relationship to mad proportions.

Jack recalled that, before Allen's "straightening-out" at the asylum, he yearned for homosexual bliss, and Neal's insatiable sexual appetite tantalized him. From their first night together on January 10, 1947, Allen obsessed about Neal with a mix of elation and desolation: "Having spent a wild weekend in sexual drama with Cassady," Ginsberg wrote in his journal, "I am left washed up on the shore of my 'despair' again. It is after such pleasure that I get full knowledge of what I have slowly closed myself off from. . . . I could be satisfied, if at all . . . by a physical union (intermittent) with Cassady." With wild abandon, Allen fantasized about all of the sexual experimentation that he aimed to undertake with Neal: "Try him laying me again; try breast to breast position. Try 69 again, coming both at once. . . . Make him give me a trip around the world. Try (and this requires real passion) browning him. . . . Wrestling—whipping? Have I guts? . . . I want some real hip sex, what is it?"

But Neal was too heterosexual, and actively so, for Allen's needs. Soon after stoking Allen's sexual flames, Neal reached for the fire extinguisher. Back in Denver, Cassady cautioned Ginsberg not to count on him for anything much in the long term: "I *really don't* know how much I can be satisfied to love you, I mean bodily, you know," Neal wrote Allen. "This is a sad state and upsets me for I want to become nearer to you than any one & still I don't want to be unconsciously insincere by passing over my un-queerness to please you." (That sentence sparked an angry response from Allen: "dirty, double crossing, faithless bitch.") Yet Neal was intrigued with Allen's mind, and could not suffer the thought of losing him completely; Neal's words and actions sent enough mixed messages to keep the embers of Ginsberg's love blazing for quite a while. "I can't promise a darn thing, I know I'm bisexual, but prefer women," Neal stressed, but "there's a slimmer line than you think between my attitude toward love and yours, don't be so concerned, it'll fall into line. Beyond that—who knows? Let's try it & see, huh?"

Even after Neal met Carolyn Robinson (the beautiful blonde Bennington alumna and graduate student in the University of Denver's Theater and Fine Arts department who eventually became his second wife), he had enough spare libido to share with Ginsberg if Allen made himself available and insisted upon sex. Ever the Don Juan, Cassady accommodated Ginsberg—on Neal's own terms, of course—when Allen came to Denver in June 1947 to revive his flagging relationship. During this period, in fact, Cassady triple-dipped with Carolyn, Allen, and Neal's first wife, Lu Anne Henderson, who still had the hots for him. Following a stupefying sexual schedule that only the Fastestmanalive could execute, Neal satisfied Carolyn in the daytime and early evening hours, satiated Lu Anne later the same evening, resumed with Carolyn at night, and then hooked up for occasional sex with Allen at six in the morning, when Ginsberg returned to his apartment after his graveyard shift as a janitor at the downtown May Company department store.

Jack intended to write about that mind-boggling schedule, about Neal and Allen's trip in August 1947 from Denver to New Waverly, Texas, to visit Bill Burroughs, and about the demise of Neal and Allen's sexual affair there. But not now. Jack's T-shirt clung to him, soaked with sweat; he took it off, wrung it out, and hung it up alongside the others that he had dampened during this first full day of athletic typing. He was exhausted and needed a few hours of shut-eye, if all the caffeine in his body would allow it. But before climbing into bed with Joan, Jack rolled up the long page that he had been working on, roughly estimating the number of words that he had written. As he walked around the screen that separated his desk from their bed, he thought to himself with satisfaction: *Twelve thousand words the first day!*

17.

OVER THE NEXT nineteen days, as Jack isolated himself before his typewriter, he plowed further into his memories. He recalled a time in 1948, not long after Neal and Carolyn Cassady's first daughter, Cathy, was born.* It was a wild time, when Neal bought that beautiful, full-throttled Hudson.

Clackclackclackclack, clackclackclackclack, clackclackclackclack, clackclackclack. Ding. Zip.

> He had lived happily with Carolyn in San Francisco ever since that Fall in 1947; he got a job on the railroad and made a lot of money. He became the father of a cute little girl, Cathy Jo Ann Cassady. Then suddenly he blew his top and while walking down the street one day he saw a '49 Hudson for sale and rushed to the bank for his entire roll. He bought the car on the spot.

Far away, in distance and mind, from the imaginary world Jack Kerouac was creating, there was the reality of the harsh world Carolyn Cassady faced. In her world, the hero of Jack's novel was a

---

*As Gerald Nicosia and Anne-Marie Santos tell it: "Neal was in a state of near panic and great confusion when he learned ... that Carolyn was pregnant. He sought and failed to arrange an abortion for her."

demon oblivious to the financial misery his squandering inflicted on his family. Although Carolyn strove to save what income they had, Neal was hell-bent on blowing it. So Carolyn never forgot the day that Neal burst into their San Francisco apartment in wild excitement.*

"Come with me baby...I've got a surprise for you. Come on, now...I'll show you...just wait till you see..."

"Now what?" Carolyn asked, as she stopped folding diapers to follow Neal outside, barely having time to throw on something as they rushed down the stairs.

"Where are you taking me?" she complained. Neal tugged on her arm.

"Nowhere, my baby, we're *here*....Right here, my dear! Now, look at *that*, woodja?"

Neal waved, and then he pointed to a shiny new Hudson, a two-toned one. Carolyn watched with a blank expression—what was he doing? She focused on that thought as Neal rambled on and on about the metallic maroon–and-gray Hudson.

"Just look at this, honey, see? The floor is sunk below the door frame...it's a step-down living...I mean...*driving* room, how about that?" He became increasingly excited as he spoke: "And look at that dash—like an airplane, eh? See? Radio...oh, and baby, it drives like a dreeeeeam, smooth as silk. Just wait till you ride in it. Come on, I'll take you for a spin."

Carolyn could not believe her eyes or her ears. "Each word was like a giant demolition ball, crushing all my hopes," she recalled. Oblivious to her feelings, Neal reached for her elbow; he wanted to show her the other side of the car. She would have none of it; she bolted back to the apartment, crying as she scaled the stairs.

---

*Carolyn's account of this event, upon which we drew for our narrative, was written years after Kerouac's *On the Road* and cast Neal in a far less flattering light than Jack's did.

"Now, now, Carolyn, look here, you don't understand," he said as he chased after her. Carolyn demanded to know how it was that he got this new car.

"Why, I bought it, naturally, my dear...or the down payment, of course. It's for you, you and Cathy, so you can take her to the doctor and the store and—"

Carolyn was furious: "You mean...you used our savings?"

"Well, our savings, yes, but look, I can make that much back in two months when I'm on the railroad next spring...easy."

As if that were not enough, Neal had one other surprise in his bag of heartless news. He was about to leave tomorrow, for a few weeks or more, to race up to New York to get Jack and "break in the new car."

This was for real; he was serious. "But, Neal," Carolyn protested, "what about *us*? How will we live with no money?"

"Now, honey," he was making it up as he went along, "don't you worry. I've thought of that, of course. I have it all arranged, so don't fret."

As he spoke, Carolyn thought: "Here we [are] living in a cardboard dump with orange-crate bookcases, yet we [have] a brand new car, no savings, no income, a new baby," and he's blabbing on about leaving and driving across country.

But Neal, silent now, was indifferent to her tears. He went to the closet, pulled out his suitcase and began to pack.

"Oh, Neal, don't, please don't leave us!"

"Now, Carolyn, I'm not leaving *you*. I'll be right back." He continued to pack.

With that, her pain turned to anger: "How can you, how *can* you? Have you no heart at all? How could you lie about loving me...use me...make me bear your child? All you do is take advantage of people....You'd just walk out with all our money? Leave a *baby*?

Oh, you bastard, you lousy *bastard....* You don't care for us.... *My* car! What a riot *that* is."

Not knowing quite what to say, Neal played a wild card...the victim card: "I have feelings, too, you know."

When the commotion woke up the baby, Carolyn went for her and then held Cathy in her arms, just as Neal walked by with his suitcase. He extended his hand. But it was a one-way gesture. Carolyn backed off and yelled, "Just go, if you're going. Get out, now! I never want to see you again—not ever!"

Neal walked on, Carolyn cried on, and Cathy began to scream.

That portrayal of Neal Cassady never found its way to the translucent text of Jack Kerouac's *Road* story.* Then again, Jack and Neal's world was never the world of Joan and Carolyn's—the creed of the "fraternity of undesirables" was seldom, if ever, a compassionate or committed one.† It was a world where, by and large, men were verbs and women objects.

---

*In the scroll version of *On the Road*, Kerouac devoted 191 words to this episode. He wrote that after Neal bought the car, when "they were broke," and then decided to go to New York, Carolyn "wasn't too pleased." "Why are you doing this to me?" Jack had Carolyn asking. To which Neal responded, "It's nothing, it's nothing darling." Finally, Kerouac had Cassady giving some half-answer and then added, "of course it made no sense." The final version of *On the Road* contains nearly identical passages. Kerouac did, however, write the following: "The truth of the matter is that we don't understand our women; we blame all of them and it's our fault."

†As John Leland put it: Kerouac's "female characters, swiftly drawn, and often as swiftly discarded, act on men like bumpers in a pinball machine, popping up suddenly and speeding the balls on their way. Their role is not to move, but to propel the men even faster" down the road.

18.

Neal is, of course, the very soul of the voyage into
pure, abstract, meaningless motion. He is The Mover,
compulsive, dedicated, ready to sacrifice family, friends,
even his very car itself to the necessity of moving from
one place to another. Wife and child may starve, friends
exist only to exploit for gas money....Neal must move.
—William Burroughs

FOR NEAL, driving was not a way of life, it was life itself. To be "gone on the road" (the original title of Jack's novel) was to be gone from the demands of work and family and responsibility and anything else that might slow down the mad driving force within him. The rule of the road, its ethic, was eternal motion...ceaseless momentum, spontaneous movement. The thrill was in the journey, not in the destination—blowin' out four thousand miles in four frenzy-filled days. Life was overdrive, revving it up until one redlined on the tachometer of risk. That thrill, that spontaneity, that freedom was what Neal Cassady was all about. That is what Jack toiled away to capture—the spirit of Neal, The Mover.

Kerouac sipped the split-pea soup that Joan had just brought home from Stouffer's. It gave him the energy he needed to continue typing the story of Christmas 1948—the time when Neal and his friends drove cross-country to meet Jack at his sister's place in Rocky Mount, North Carolina. Jack aimed to capture the zig-zag-zonk of Neal's spontaneous mind and actions.

Clackclackclackclackclackclackclackclack, clackclackclacklackclack-clackclack. Ding. Zip.

He was roaring through Las Cruces New Mexico when he suddenly had an explosive yen to see his sweet first wife Louanne [sic] again. She was up in Denver. He swung the car North...and zoomed into Denver in the evening. He ran and found Louanne in a hotel. They had ten hours of wild lovemaking.

Here, as elsewhere, Jack's fiction tracked reality. Once Neal had left Carolyn in San Francisco, he needed a little nookie for the cross-country road trip. He told his pal, Al Hinkle, who was in the car with him, that a detour to Denver to find Lu Anne Henderson, who was visiting friends, would not take long. Al didn't object. Of course, he never did when it came to Neal. A fellow brakeman on the Southern Pacific Railroad who had been laid off like Neal, the jolly and gullible six-foot muscle-man was Cassady's stooge. Al followed Neal's every suggestion without much independent thought.

In fact, Hinkle was on the road with Cassady only because Neal needed Al to provide gas and food money. And to ensure that Al could foot that bill, Neal urged him to marry his fiancée, a stolid half-Greek, half-Portuguese woman named Helen Argee, whom Neal wrongly believed was well-heeled. Cassady proposed that the newlyweds might then take the trip with him and celebrate their honeymoon in New York City. Naturally, Al agreed and married Helen the day before hauling off for the East Coast.

Not surprisingly, Neal's idea of great livin'—driving like a devil nonstop for days on end—was not Helen's. When she wanted a bathroom break, Neal responded, "Piss out the window." When she wanted a romantic evening with her hubby in a hotel, Neal replied, "Bang in the back." By the time they got to Tucson, Helen had enough and wanted out. Persuaded by Neal to abandon his wife, Al gave her his railroad pass and told her to find her way to the Louisiana home of Bill Burroughs, a total stranger to her, where she would be picked up on the return trip.

With uncooperative Helen out of his hair, Neal couldn't wait to get his hands on the compliant Lu Anne. Orgasmically sexy, the ripe eighteen-year-old was as available to him as ever, even though she was currently fiancéed to Ray Murphy, a San Francisco–based sailor then at sea. Neal wooed her, whispering "honeycunt" and other such sweet nothings; and he convinced her that having kicks in New York on New Year's Eve would beat waiting around for an absent husband-to-be in a Denver hotel. Lu Anne conceded, but conditionally: although she would diddle with Neal, she insisted on being free to sleep with any other man of her choice.

Clackclackclackclack, clackclackclackclack, clackclackclackclackclack-clackclack. Ding. Zip.

Neal, Louanne, and Al Hinkle roared east along Colfax and out to the Kansas plains. Great snowstorms overtook them. In Missouri, at night, Neal had to drive with his scarf-wrapped head stuck out the window with snowglasses that made him look like a monk peering into the manuscripts of the snow because the windshield was covered with an inch of ice. He drove by the birth county of his forebears without a thought. In the morning the car skidded on an icy hill and flapped into a ditch. A farmer offered to help them out.

The actual trip through the Great Plains was all of that and more. Without a working heater and defroster, the Hudson roadster was not suited to the Midwest blizzard conditions that they faced.

Cassady would not be deterred, however. With near-zero visibility out of a windshield caked with ice, Neal put on a pair of goggles, rolled down the window, craned his neck and head outside, and barreled down the road as fast as he could muster—only seventy miles per hour now. Al and Lu Anne huddled together in the front bench seat, trying to keep warm, as a relentless stream of freezing air and snowflakes flowed into the cabin. Meanwhile, the radio blared on and Neal yakked on at high-decibel levels. Hinkle was grateful for Lu Anne's presence, no doubt, as he rubbed his hands back and forth between her legs . . . for warmth.

Though an expert driver, Neal was no match for the icy roads in Kansas at the speed he was going. Early in the morning, he hit a patch of ice; the low-slung Hudson swerved and slid, flew off the road, and nosed into a deep snow-filled ditch. Only real horsepower—two horses hitched to the car by a farmer who braved the cold to help them out—put them back on the road again. Neal was forced to drive more slowly now, however, because the car's bearings had been damaged in the accident. Only halfway to their Rocky Mount destination, the trio faced the prospect of an even longer and much more frigid trip than they had anticipated. With no more money for food or gas, they chewed on candy, cheese crackers, and rotten potatoes. As Lu Anne tells it: "The only way we could make it across the country was to keep picking up people, hitchhikers, and getting a couple of bucks from them. Or sometimes we pulled into a gas station, and Neal knew how to run the pump. He'd put in some gas and run it back to zero, put in some more and run it back to zero again, quick before the guy got out and could see what we were doing."

Clackclackclackclackclackclackclackclackclackclackclacklackclackclackclack. Ding. Zip.

[A] mud-splattered '49 Hudson drew up in front of the house on
the dirt road. I had no idea who it was. A weary young fellow,

muscular and ragged in a T-shirt, unshaven, red-eyed came to
the porch and rang the bell. I opened the door and suddenly
realized it was Neal.

Before their traditional turkey dinner, Kerouac and his southern in-laws sat gossiping in the parlor when the doorbell rang. The
sedate southern folk raised their eyebrows at the sight of the three
cold, dirty, starving, and exhausted vagabonds, looking all the part
of impoverished beggars at their feast. At first, Jack did not even
recognize Neal, the ragtag at the door. And he was shocked to see
the grimy appearance of Neal's brand new car and its occupants.
Still, it was great to have Neal there at his sister Nin's home.

In fact, Jack was quite relieved, for now he had a buffer. He
did not get along well with his brother-in-law, Paul Blake Jr., and
the tension between the two increased during the Christmas visit
because the clacking of Jack's typewriter kept Paul awake at night.
Their strained relationship did ease a bit, however, when Nin and
Paul delighted Jack with their gift of an antique oak rolltop desk—
the very one at which he was now sitting in 1951 to type out his
recollections of that Christmas holiday in 1948.

Cassady's ingratiating personality won them all over, particularly
Mémère. (Jack's mother, Gabrielle, had been tagged "Mémère"—
grandma in Quebécois—by Nin's baby son, and now the entire family
called her that.) She quickly warmed up to Neal when he offered to
haul back to New York a set of parlor furniture and boxes with smaller
effects, which Nin had given her for her Richmond Hill apartment.

"Dog-tired" as he claimed to be, Neal would not rest; he wanted
to get moving once again. After the group cleaned up and ate dinner,
the men packed the roadster with chairs and boxes, and the four
friends—Neal, Lu Anne, Al, and now Jack—headed out at nightfall.
For Jack, this began the first of three major road trips that he would
take with Neal over the next two years.

Clackclackclackclackclackclackclackclackclackclackclackclack, clack-clackclack. Ding. Zip.

We packed my sister's boxes of clothes and dishes and a few chairs in back of the car and took off at dark, promising to be back in thirty hours. Thirty hours for a thousand miles North and South. But that's the way Neal wanted it.... the heater was not working and consequently the windshield developed fog and ice. Neal kept reaching out while driving seventy to wipe it with a rag and make a hole to see the road. In the spacious Hudson we had plenty room all four of us to sit up front. A blanket covered our laps. The radio was not working.

Clackclackclack,clackclackclackclackclack,clackclackclackclack,clack-clackclack. Ding. Zip.

It was a brand new car bought five days ago and already it was broken. There was only one installment paid on it too.... And Neal talked, no one else talked. He gestured furiously... sometimes he had no hands on the wheel and yet the car went as straight as an arrow, not for once deviating the slightest bit from the white line in the middle of the road that unwound kissing our left front tire.

Reality matched fiction when it came to Cassady's travel plan. Neal and Jack drove one thousand miles at seventy miles per hour in a winter storm, Neal jaw-boning all the way, to deposit Al, Lu Anne, some chairs, and the boxes at Mémêre's place; then, after resting there briefly, they drove back to North Carolina, only to return the same night with Mémêre and the rest of her furniture. Such a travel plan was unimaginable—at least, to anyone but Neal.

As they charged up and down the highways, Cassady had the opportunity to share his latest philosophical observations with

Kerouac. The linear thinking of the West was completely false: "Everything since the Greeks has been predicated wrong," Jack recorded Neal as saying. "You can't make it with geometry and geometrical systems of thinking. It's all THIS!" Shoving a single finger into his wrapped fist, as though a penis sticking into a vagina or anus were the icon of perfect unity, Neal proclaimed, "This is what *it's* about, man."

Clackclackclackclackclackclackclackclackclackclackclackclack-clackclack. Ding. Zip.

> So now Neal had come about four thousand miles from Frisco, via Arizona and up to Denver, inside four days with innumerable adventures sandwiched in and it was only the beginning.

Indeed, it was only the beginning. Some of Neal and Jack's highest highs and lowest lows came during other cross-country trips. There was the time in the spring of 1949 when Jack tried to relocate to Denver, but instead hooked up with Neal in San Francisco and hit the black jazz clubs; then Cassady, hell-bent for New York, trashed a travel-bureau car as he grounded it into the highway. There also was the time the following spring when Jack bussed his way to Denver and later joined Neal and Frank Jeffries to coax an old Ford to carry them to Mexico City for the tortillas, tequila, and señoritas; when Jack fell sick with dysentery, Neal split.

But those were other stories, episodes yet to be written. Cassady never had the skill or will to put those stories on paper. He lived most fully during his journeys, and his life on the road was his literature. Kerouac, however, lived his writing. It was left to Jack, then, who had both the needed ability and ambition, to write Neal into a literary legend.

19.

IMPORTANT AS NEAL CASSADY was, he represented only a part of the story of *On the Road*, a story about how to live. There were, to be sure, other characters, who brought to the story their own takes on life—characters such as Bill ("Bull") Burroughs and Kerouac himself.

Clack, clack, clackclackclack, clackclack, clack, clackclackclackclack-clack. Ding. Zip.

> Bill had a sentimental streak about the old days in America, especially in 1910 when you could get morphine in a drugstore without prescription and Chinamen smoked opium in their evening windows and the country was wild and brawling and free with abundance and any kind of freedom for everyone. His chief hate was Washington bureaucracy; second to that, Liberals; also cops.

The lines were vintage Burroughs, the man who hated paternalism with every ounce of blood in his junkie veins. This freedom to be left alone, however, didn't depend on suicidal bursts onto the dark highways of a snowy night. Bill Burroughs was not Neal Cassady, whom he loathed. Then again, neither was Jack Kerouac, the narrator and other key character in *On the Road*.

In many ways, the narrator (later named Sal Paradise*) was Neal's opposite. For him, *On the Road*'s five journeys were more than joy rides interrupted by hitchhikers, hookers, and hobos lingering in the dank armpits of existence. They were searches for paradise, for meaning, for purpose, for knowledge, and even for God. "Whoever strives in ceaseless toil," as Goethe put it, "him we may grant redemption." That was his narrator's creed. By that measure, Kerouac's Catholicism—as earnest as it was convoluted—very much influenced the vision of his narrator as he journeyed across America in search of his Holy Grail, his Christ in a cafeteria.

There was the time, for example, when Jack hooked up with some Okie cotton pickers and an old "Negro couple" to pick cotton in a small Northern California town. Strange as it seemed, it was in this calm field, and not on the cavorting road, where Jack (the narrator) found his peace.

Clackclackclackclackclack, clack, clackclackclackclackclackclack, clackclackclack. Ding. Zip.

> We bent down and began picking cotton. It was beautiful. Across the field were tents, and beyond them the sere brown cotton fields that stretched out of sight, and over that the snowcapped Sierras in the blue morning air.... There was an old Negro couple in the field with us. They picked cotton with the same Godblessed patience their grandfathers had practiced in prewar Alabama: they moved right along their rows, bent and blue, and their bags increased. My back began to ache. But it was beautiful kneeling and hiding in that earth: if I felt like resting I did, with my face on the pillow of brown moist earth. Birds sang an accompaniment. I thought I had found my life's work.

---

*When the scroll version was edited and became the popular book version of *On the Road*, the narrator's name was changed to "Sal Paradise." That name traced back to a 1947 Ginsberg poem.

Something of that same otherworld concern found its way into Jack's vision when his narrator spoke of the dream of the "Shrouded Stranger" (later named "Traveler"), the strange Arabic figure who pursued him across the desert.

Clackclackclackclackclackclack,clackclackclack,clackclackclack,clack-clackclack. Ding. Zip.

> The one thing we yearn for in all our living days, that makes us sigh and groan and undergo sweet nauseas of all kinds, is the remembrance of some lost bliss that was probably experienced in the womb and can only be reproduced—tho we hate to admit it—in death. But who wants to die?

Jack tumbled his vision of *On the Road* between Neal's quest for fast rides and the narrator's quest for answers to life's big questions. In the process, the divide between the narrator and Neal grew.

When Jack got toward the end of scroll on April 22, 1951, he had typed 125,000 or so words. Once there, he closed with the man with whom he began, Neal Cassady. It was the end of the road for Cassady and his narrator; it was a time for farewells. That time came, as he told it, when Neal happened upon Joan and Jack as they prepared to go to a Duke Ellington concert one cold January night in 1951. Henri Cru, a wealthy childhood friend, had picked up the tab for the tickets to the Metropolitan Opera performance of Ellington and his orchestra. He had also arranged for a chauffeur to take the four of them (Cru's girlfriend also came along) to the concert in a big black Cadillac. They were all dressed up and ready to go, when Neal appeared.

Clackclackclack,clack,clackclackclackclackclackclackclackclack,clack-clackclack. Ding. Zip.

> Neal stood outside the windows with his big bag ready to go to Penn Station and on across the land. "Goodbye Neal," I said. "I

sure wish I didn't have to go to the concert." "D'you think I can ride to 40th St. with you?" he whispered. "Want to be with you as much as possible, m'boy and besides it's so durned cold in this here New Yawk." I whispered to Henri. No, he wouldn't have it.... "Absolutely out of the question Jack!" ... So Neal couldn't ride uptown with us and the only thing I could do was sit in the back of the Cadillac and wave at him.... Neal, ragged in a motheaten overcoat he bought specially for the freezing temperature of the East, walked off alone and the last I saw him he rounded the corner of 7th Ave., eyes on the street ahead, and bent to it again.

That story was pretty close to the mark of what really happened when Jack Kerouac and Neal Cassady actually parted company that freezing winter night. Joan, who was there, felt that Jack had betrayed Neal: "That's a lousy way to say goodbye to a friend," she scolded. And the more Joan thought about it—about the image of Neal "hurling himself down a Manhattan street alone"—"the more the episode took on an air of finality for me as well."

But Jack, beat after days of intense typing, would have the last word ... in the manuscript that was final, for now. The poetic beauty of the passage would have made even Allen Ginsberg envious.

Clackclack, clackclackclackclack, clackclackclackclackclackclack, clackclackclack. Ding. Zip.

So in America when the sun goes down and I sit on the old brokendown river pier watching the long, long skies over New Jersey and sense all that raw land that rolls in one unbelievable huge bulge over to the West Coast, all that road going, all the people dreaming in the immensity of it, and in Iowa I know by now* the

---

*In the final version, the following words were inserted at this point in the text: "the children must be crying in the land where children cry, and tonight the stars will be out, and don't you know that God is Pooh Bear?"

evening-star must be drooping and shedding her sparkler dims on the prairie, which is just before the coming of complete night that blesses the earth, darkens all rivers, cups the peaks in the west and

Clackclackclackclackclackclackclackclackclack, clacklackclack, clack-clackclack. Ding. Zip.

folds the last and final shore in, and nobody, just nobody knows what's going to happen to anybody besides the forlorn rags of growing old, I think of Neal Cassady, I even think of Old Neal Cassady the father we never found, I think of Neal Cassady, I think of Neal Cassady.

Memories. Memories. After it all, even as the novel tilted to tomorrow, the narrator turned back in time and thought of the beginning: "I first met ... Neal not long after my father died." While the Great Father had not been found, the journey had been traveled. And that seemed to be the point. Or to put it differently: "Still we travel, and still we live, because what else can we do?"

It was a triumphant moment. The marathon was over. Jack Kerouac, beat,* had finally crossed the narrative finish line. The scroll was a testament to his victory. Its twelve (or so) foot-long strips (nine inches wide) had been taped together. When done, they stretched out for 119 feet and eight inches. On his old L.C. Smith typewriter, Jack had punched out a novel, 125,000 words of single-spaced text without any paragraphs or chapter divides. Some mistakes or corrections were xxxxx'd out, some deletions or additions

---

*While the words "BEAT—the root, the soul of Beatific" appeared in the final published version, they did not appear in the scroll version of the manuscript. As early as 1948, Kerouac had paired the term "beatific" to the word "beat" in one of his journals, giving the latter a spiritual connotation.

penciled in, and some occasional notes placed in the margins of the semi-translucent paper. On its backside, he penciled in the following: "John Kerouac, 94-21 134th Street, Richmond Hill, NY" (his mother's address).

His brain buzzed from coffee; his taste buds tired of split-pea soup; his back ached from bending over; his typing fingers were swollen; his pores were open; and his apartment was strewn with soiled T-shirts. Jack had done it again; he had finished another book. With the joy that comes from hard work, Jack Kerouac thought of Robert Giroux—the man who was his editor at Harcourt, Brace, who had first published him with *The Town and the City*. It was time to pay him a visit.

20.

I don't know how it will be received....
I've telled all the road now. Went fast because road is
fast ... rolled it out on floor and it looks like a road.
—Jack Kerouac to Neal Cassady
May 22, 1951

IN LATE APRIL 1951, Robert Giroux sat at his desk high atop 46th Street and Madison Avenue. There had seldom been a quiet day in his life at Harcourt, Brace since the 1948 publication of the best-selling book by Thomas Merton, *The Seven Storey Mountain.* That autobiography, written by a Trappist monk who had been a fellow student with Giroux at Columbia, sold 600,000 hardback copies and over one million copies in paperback. The success of that book, which Giroux had edited, propelled him to the position of editor-in-chief.*

Giroux's secretary buzzed him. There was a call from one of his authors, Jack Kerouac. Would he take it?

"Hello? Hi, Bob. . . . I've finished it!" Jack was referring to his latest novel. His voice was filled with enthusiasm. After Giroux had edited

---

*Giroux earlier had edited several other notable books, including William Saroyan's best-selling *The Human Comedy* (1943) and Edmund Wilson's much acclaimed *To the Finland Station: A Study in the Writing and Acting of History* (1940). Giroux was also the editor for other literary stars such as T.S. Eliot, Ezra Pound, and Robert Lowell.

The Town and the City and Harcourt, Brace had published it, Jack now thought that Bob would be eager to see his new experimental work.

"Oh, great, Jack, that's wonderful news."

Unable to contain himself, Jack blurted, "I want to come over."

"What, right now?" Giroux asked.

"Yeah. I have to see you, I *have* to show you—"

Yielding, Giroux replied, "Okay, come on, come over to the office."

Busy as he was, Giroux would see the young author...even though his first book was hardly a financial boon. Still, his connection with Kerouac traced back to the time when Mark Van Doren, one of Bob's favorite Columbia University professors, directed Jack to him with *The Town and the City* manuscript. Moreover, Bob and Jack were two French-speaking Catholics with a passionate interest in literature. The genteel Giroux, eight years older than Kerouac, had a fondness for him. Bob had been to Mémêre's home for dinner; he'd taken his young author to the Metropolitan Opera, where they mingled with the likes of Gore Vidal. And Giroux often introduced Kerouac as a rising star in the literary sphere. So, naturally, Bob stole some time from his calendar for this unexpected visit.

The day that Kerouac headed over to Giroux's office was not too long after he had penciled in some edits on the scroll. Jack was so proud of it—a "complete departure from *Town & City* and in fact from previous American Lit," he bragged to Neal, with whom he continued to communicate as if the slight of the Henri Cru incident meant nothing. After all, the *Road* book's style and substance were rebellious, and its scrolled form was revolutionary. This could be the book that would make him another one of Giroux's success stories.

When Jack entered Bob's office, beaming like a kid with a straight-A report card, he was a curious sight. His manner led Giroux to believe that he had been drinking. It wasn't just Jack's swaggering way—that Giroux had seen before. It was also that Jack was cradling some bizarre roll under his left arm. But where was the manuscript, the 8½ x 11 typed pages of bulky text?

Before Bob could make sense of it, Jack took an end of the typescript scroll and unrolled it. Was this the manuscript? Bob was taken aback. For a few seconds he said nothing. Looking down, his eyes scanned the solid body of text—with no paragraphs or page numbers or chapter headings—imprinted on what looked like onion-skin paper. It had a medieval, monastic character to it. "This is a strange manuscript," Giroux thought. "I've never seen a manuscript like this before."

Oblivious to Kerouac's enthusiasm, Giroux could not get past the practical problems. For one thing, how would he edit such an unwieldy document? How could a printer work from it? And how could the average reader tolerate this uncontrolled barrage of text?

"Jack, you know you have to cut this up." Giroux was trying to be reasonable: "It has to be edited."

Caught off guard, Kerouac immediately became defensive and then emphatic: "There'll be no editing on this manuscript."

"Why not, Jack?"

"This manuscript has been dictated by the Holy Ghost."

Reeling the dialogue back to reality, Giroux quipped, "Even after you have been inspired by the Holy Ghost, you have to sit down and read your manuscript."

Crushed, Jack would have none of this. He threw down the gauntlet: "Everything's down there just the way I want it. That's the way it is. That's the way it will be." His heart broken, he stormed out like a rejected lover.

Giroux strove to make sense of what had happened. Was it stupid of him to be so candid with Jack? So indifferent to his feelings? Could he have handled the situation more diplomatically? Say something like: "My God, you've just finished a book! This is a great occasion! Put the MS. on my desk and let's go have a drink to celebrate." When Jack was flying so high, would that not have been a better approach than an ego-deflating ultimatum?

When he finally calmed down, Kerouac knew what he had to do. He got to work as soon as he got home. He had to undertake another marathon, a full thirty days of "typing and revising," as he informed Cassady. On April 22, he began the work in his loft. Pumped, he pushed on to the typographic end, all 297 typed pages of it. Incredibly, it took Jack longer to rework and retype his manuscript—this time on paper resembling unlined legal-pad sheets with edits in black crayon and pencil—than it did to compose his original draft. But all of this was necessary to make a proper submission to Giroux in the hope that Harcourt, Brace would make him an offer. That done, he anxiously awaited Giroux's final word. For his literary fate hung in the balance: he always dreamed of being a famous writer, and to do that, he had to publish a book that would have wide appeal.

Meanwhile, life at home spun out of control. It had only been two hundred and some days since Joan and Jack had taken their quickie vows before Judge Lupiano, and it now looked like his marriage was spiraling down a vortex. In early June, Joan informed him that she was pregnant. Jack was stunned. Almost reflexively, he blamed her.

"The preparation should have been before the fact. Where was your diaphragm?"

Incredulously, she snapped back, "It was the night you wouldn't let me get up."

"That's no excuse," he replied. "A woman should always be prepared."

She was boiling mad. "That would be ridiculous, Jack, considering how seldom there's a need."

There was no reason to be mad; there was an alternative. "We can get something done.... Look, this isn't the dark ages. What are you afraid of? The legality? The morality?"

It was amazing. He was a Catholic. He was the one who spoke of a family with children when he first proposed to her. Now Jack was urging her to have an abortion. And, yes, it was illegal and immoral. Joan shook her head and then in a devilishly flip way said, "I'm going to name this kid 'Spontaneity.'"

"That's not very funny." In a more serious vein, Jack threatened her with what he meant to be a Hobson's choice: "Do you want a husband or do you want a baby?"

She chuckled, "You mean, which baby do I want?... There is no choice. Jack, this is too easy. This baby is mine. It's the only thing in life that belongs to me. If you want to move out, move out." And he did. On June 11 he left for Lucien's loft and continued his work there.*

Jack's second marriage was over. Now, like Carolyn Cassady in San Francisco, Joan Kerouac was with child and abandoned.† As for Jack, things went from bad to worse.

"I'm completely fucked," he wrote to Neal Cassady on June 24, 1951. "Giroux didn't take my book. Harcourt won't publish it." Although he claimed that Giroux himself liked the book, the guys in the sales department didn't—too much like Dostoyevsky. How would they know? After all, "they don't even read Dosty and don't care about all that shit."

---

*Reportedly, at some point in Lucien's loft, Jack's original scroll was nearly destroyed: "a little cocker spaniel," named Potchky, "that Lucien had at the loft chewed up the last few feet of the manuscript and Jack retyped it, but it was the only part of *On the Road* that he rewrote there." Toward the end of the scroll, Jack documented the incident with a penciled note reading: "—DOG ATE (Potchky—a dog)." Some authorities are skeptical of this shaggy-dog tale, however, asserting that Kerouac had rejected his original ending and was searching for a stronger one.

†On February 16, 1952, Joan gave birth to Janet ("Jan") Michele. From the start, Jack publicly maintained that Joan had become pregnant by sleeping with a Puerto Rican restaurant coworker, an affair that she squarely denied. Years later, in a journal entry, he wrote: "Janet is NOT my daughter." Joan brought a paternity action, and it was ultimately resolved against Jack. Although he was ordered to pay only the minimum of $52 a month, he complained that the $2,500 of legal fees impoverished him.

Now, Kerouac was forced to do what all aspiring writers have to do: find an agent and hope to secure a publishing contract. Thanks to John Holmes, who urged his own agent to take Jack on as a client, Rae Everitt of MCA Management agreed to represent him. Admire him as she did, Rae had reservations about working professionally with Jack since the two had flirted with one another at a couple of parties. Although Everitt found moments of "sheer magic poetry" in *On the Road*, she felt that Kerouac's "extremely specialized style of writing" made the novel much too long. She conveyed that message through Allen Ginsberg, who acted as an intermediary. He told Jack that Rae had some reservations about his manuscript but was hesitant to tell him for fear of his hostile reactions. Ultimately, she delivered her honest assessment.

With Rae as an official agent and Allen as an *ex officio* one, a portion of the manuscript found itself in the hands—of all people—of Carl Solomon. Ginsberg's psychiatric-ward pal had left the asylum, married, and was living a relatively stable life. Carl worked as an editor for his uncle, A.A. Wyn, the publisher of Wyn Books and Ace paperbacks. Ace was known in the trade for specializing in comics, Gothic romances, sci-fi, and other pop literature. Allen used his connection with Carl to promote his friends' works. About this time, he was pushing a book by Bill Burroughs; and now, with Rae Everitt taking the lead, Allen brought *On the Road* to Carl's attention.

When Carl got back to Jack, he proposed a three-book contract with Ace Books for a $250 advance. Kerouac was scornful; this was a paltry sum, compared to the $20,000 paperback reprint rights that John Holmes, a lesser light in his view, had received for his first novel, *Go*. To keep negotiations on track, Rae insisted on a $1,000 advance, with $250 to be paid upon signing and $100 per month thereafter while Jack made revisions. A.A. Wyn finally agreed; once the contract was signed, Kerouac was required to submit his latest draft. What he sent, however, was not remotely like the novel that he originally had written.

During this time, Jack Kerouac was working on a yet even more uninhibited and unconventional form of writing. "Prose sketching" or "spontaneous prose," as he tagged his new style, brought to his literature what abstract painting brought to art and bebop jazz brought to music. Using free-association, which linked the subconscious and the conscious, he gave vent to a wild form of writing that captured unrepressed impressions—of B movies, men's bathrooms, the sense of spring, a man reading a paper, bums in subways, and poor lonely old ladies in Lowell—or of any image or memory that he could conjure up. By blowing mad poetic literature—juxtaposing image upon image in long metaphorical lines—he offered a totally new vision of narrative. Radically reconstructing *On the Road*, Jack transformed his journey stories of Cassady into a raw phenomenological portrait of Neal's character and his world. At a time when editors and friends urged him to make his prose more mainstream, Jack moved more and more against the stream.

When Kerouac submitted his "spontaneous prose" manuscript to Solomon, Carl might have been reminded of his insulin-induced hazes. He read passages—very, very long passages:

> The wainscot effect of dark then yellow up to ceiling is also to be found in the clock-tocking reading rooms of flophouses like the Skylark in Denver where Cody and his father stayed where bums sit on creaky chairs and with their cloth caps settin straight on their heads and still covered with grease spots probably from Montana they grimly read the papers to show that tonight they are not goofing in no alleys with rotgut and in fact they've just eaten supper in the restaurant with all the cheap prices soaped-in on the plate glass . . .

On and on for some 250 words before taking a brief rest at a period.

This was insanity, pure insanity. Even Carl's manic mind was not ready for such experimental prose. For all his surrealist tendencies, he could not imagine Ace Books publishing such a meandering work.* On April 13, 1952, Carl called Allen to say that Jack's draft was "incoherent." Solomon feared that the whole publishing deal might go down. Allen was "scared, since he roped Jack into the company at my pushing and advice," as he recorded in his journal. Carl was now "afraid of making a wrong move, losing prestige and power at his office." While Allen thought Kerouac to be the "greatest writer alive in America," this new experimental work was judged by Carl to be "a garble of unrelated free associations." Be that as it may, Allen would be faithful to his friend: "I think I will stick by Jack, though I haven't seen the pages yet, only snatches in his letters. He understands me—so he must be great."

At this point in his life, Jack Kerouac needed a lift, some sign that his literary career had a future. When he opened Allen's latest letter, he hoped it carried good news about *On the Road*. His heart dropped three lines into the letter: "I don't see how it will ever be published, it's so personal, it's so full of sex language, so full of our local mythological references. I don't know if it would make sense to any publisher." Once he read that, it was hard to accept any praise from Allen. No matter that he wrote, "The language is great, the blowing is mostly great, the inventions have fullblown ecstatic style," or that he found the sketching, at times, to be "the best that is written in America."

The bottom line for Jack was that his friend hated his work— "It's crazy.... Sounds like you were just blowing and tacking things

---

*On April 7, 1952, Jack wrote to Solomon offering a "sensational 200-page novel about Lucien Murder." This work, titled *And the Hippos Were Boiled in Their Tanks*, was written with Bill Burroughs. Nothing came of the offer, however. It remained unpublished until Grove Press issued it in 2008.

together...just for madness sake, or despair." Kerouac felt the dag-
ger go deeper into his heart when he read on: "I can't see anyone...
putting it out as it is." That was it. Never mind all the words about
salvaging the work, making sense of it, or taking "ACTION."* Fuck
that. Fuck Allen. Soon enough, that sentiment would extend to Carl.

"We've had a reading of ON THE ROAD and...we are thoroughly bewildered by almost everything you've done," Solomon
wrote to Jack on July 30, 1952. "At present, some ninety-five percent
of what follows page 23 seems to us a thoroughly incoherent mess."
More bad news, the last thing Jack needed. It angered him even
more—fuck that hysterical little bastard, too.

Livid as he was, Kerouac struck back in a letter to Solomon: "I
believe 'On the Road' because its new vision roughs against the
grain of established ideas is going to be considered unprintable for
awhile to come." Comparing himself to Hemingway and Joyce, he
predicted that his *Road* book would be published one day and would
"gain its due recognition, in time, as the first or one of the first modern prose books in America." Sarcastically, Jack asserted, "[A]ll you
will have succeeded in doing is putting another cookbook on your
list to fill the gap I leave." This nothing editor and this nothing publishing house had no idea of the "thousands of hours of anxiety and
hard work" that he had poured into everything since Ace Books
had first contacted him. Kerouac closed with two poignant words:
"Yours bitterly."

But he wasn't done venting. He saved his sharpest words for his
close friend. "This is to notify you and the rest of the whole lot
what I think of you," he began his October 8, 1952, letter to Allen.
"Do you think I don't realize how jealous you are and how you and

---

*Allen was even more forthright in a July 3, 1952, letter to Neal Cassady: Jack's book
was "a holy mess," and he had done "everything he could to fuck it up with a lot of
meaningless bullshit...page after page of surrealist free association that don't make sense
to anybody except someone who has blown Jack."

Holmes and Solomon all would give your right arm to be able to write like the writing in *On the Road*?" Slamming down the insults, one by one, he added, "Why you goddamn cheap little shits are all the same and always were and why did I ever listen and fawn and fart with you—15 years of my life wasted.... Parasites every one of you." Not yet done with his ranting, he ratcheted it up with a threat: "Beware of meeting me on the street in New York."

Bitter to the typographic end, Jack savaged Allen and the gang whom he had once loved: "[S]o I say to you, never speak to me again or try to write or have anything to do with me ... besides you will never probably see me again ... and that is good ... the time has come for all you frivolous fools to realize what the subject of poetry is ... death ... so die ... and die like men ... and shut up ... and above all ... leave me alone ... & don't ever darken me again."

Remarkably, only four days after that, Kerouac wrote Holmes from a San Francisco skid-row flophouse. He needed to thank him for the $50 that John had sent. That gift took some venom out of Jack's soul. Down and out, he confessed: "I feel like an Indian, a North American Exile in North America.... I [will] never make a cent off the huge productivity of my crazy pen." At thirty, his world was collapsing all around him: he hated his friends, he couldn't get published, he fended off bouts of thrombophlebitis, his wife was trying to jail him, his mother was still slaving away in a shoe shop, and he didn't even have cash for a whore. Jack ended on a desperate and touching note: "Please stay my friend thru life, it'll be long & hard."

Meanwhile, the dark shadow of hard times hovered over Carl Solomon, as well. After the Kerouac deal failed, Carl worried that his uncle was disappointed in him. And Solomon's marriage was falling apart. It got to be too much; in time, he began to demonstrate spectacular signs of a total relapse into madness. No object was safe in his presence: he knifed books, flung shoes and a briefcase at cars, and streaked paint across his apartment walls and flooded the place. Soon he was back on the psychiatric gurneys at Bellevue Hospital.

While Jack kept his sanity, depression was taking hold of him. With each turn of the calendar page, Kerouac's prospects as a writer grew dimmer. Harcourt, Brace and Ace Books had rejected *On the Road*—so did Criterion; Bobbs, Merrill; Scribner's; Ballantine; Little, Brown; Dutton; Knopf; and Dodd, Mead. And Allen Ginsberg, whose forgiving friendship returned, continued to have trouble landing a contract for Jack. As Kerouac's star fell, those of his friends had risen, however. Scribner's had recently published the paperback version of John Holmes's *Go*, and the *New York Times Magazine* had just invited John to write an article on the Beat generation. And Ace Books had contracted with Bill Burroughs to publish his manuscript, *Junk*. So everybody, Jack thought, was getting on the Beat bandwagon *except* him, the guy who started it all.

21.

I have not only the right but the duty to carry a gun.
—William Burroughs

A **.22 SWIFT,** with the right velocity, can hit its mark at close to 4,000 feet per second. A .38 Special, by contrast, is much slower. Bill Burroughs would have understood that. He was a gun nut. "He is exceedingly interested in guns." That fact, reported by Herbert Huncke, was known by everyone acquainted with Burroughs.

"I always carry a gun," Bill once declared, "I don't figure to take any shit off anybody." A shoulder holster was a normal part of his attire, and he'd often don one with a suit, tie, and hat when going out to the races or to the bars. At bedtime, he kept his favorite "house gun" close at hand. But his devotion to guns was not monogamous; he had a reserve of firearms that would make any proud member of the National Rifle Association jealous. "I've got enough guns," he once quipped, "to stand off a siege." At various times, his private arsenal included a .22 pistol, a cap and ball revolver, an old Colt .45 automatic, a Webley .38 revolver, a hammerless Charter Arms Undercover .38 Special with two-inch barrel, a Diana air pistol with a gas cylinder, shotguns, tear gas guns, and air rifles. When he worked as a bug-exterminator, he had a spray gun, which he wielded with deadly precision: "I could adjust it from a fine spray to a stream and go in a room and get a bug, 'Phatt!' from across the room, just like that."

"Shooting is my principal pastime," Burroughs put it bluntly. That hobby stretched back to his adolescence, when he would go out duck-hunting with his father. But it was not always an idyllic pastime. One day during his sophomore year at Harvard, he almost shot a friend while goofing around with a .32 caliber revolver he believed to be empty. To Bill's good fortune, nothing came of it but a hole in the wall. His luck turned sour one night, years later in New Orleans, when a police prowl car pulled him over in a seedy, drug-infested neighborhood. He was arrested for possession of an unregistered gun and narcotics—an event that would prove fateful.

Of course, for Bill Burroughs, guns had their therapeutic side. When he was down in the dumps, he told Ginsberg, he would look to his weapons for emotional release: "Maybe I will feel a little better when I get my shotgun and kill something." In a yet more flip moment, Burroughs asserted that he would never use a gun on himself: "All my life I've never considered committing suicide; I'd rather make a list of people to kill than go out and shoot myself." In Bill's later years, shotguns became his paint brushes for art therapy: stapling tubes of oil and acrylic paints to plywood sheets hung by ropes from ladders, he blasted the paints into random patterns. If it weren't for guns, this modernist "Van Gogh" conceded, "I wouldn't have started painting."*

---

*Burroughs' connection to Van Gogh is not entirely facetious. Around 1940 in New York City, he lopped off the tip of a finger with poultry shears as a dramatic gesture of alienation and depression brought on by the rejection of a lover, a male hustler. When Bill presented the bloody stub to his psychoanalyst, the doctor convinced him to go to Bellevue Hospital. Thereafter, his father arranged for treatment in a private asylum where he stayed for a month. Burroughs summarized it all thus: "I once got on a Van Gogh kick and cut off a finger joint to impress someone who interested me at the time. The nut house doctors had never heard of Van Gogh. They put me down for schizophrenia, adding paranoid type to explain the upsetting fact that I knew where I was and who was President of the United States."

Between the summer of 1946 and the fall of 1951, as Burroughs migrated from Texas to Louisiana to Mexico, guns remained a constant source of pleasure and protection, and sometimes led to pranks. There were days when he sat stoned on the porch of his dilapidated Tobacco Road house in East Texas bayou country and passed the time away shooting at trees while listening to Viennese waltzes on an old wind-up phonograph. On other days, he fired rounds off at creepy crawlers—gigantic scorpions and tarantulas—and rats the size of opossums. The battle never ended: "I shot [a rat] who was too fat and got wedged in his hole, but the survivors are legion and gun shy." The gunfire was so frequent and thunderous that neighbors believed that gangsters were holed up in his clapboard cabin. In the 15th Ward neighborhood of Algiers, across the Mississippi from the more desirable real estate in New Orleans, Bill would police the property around his rickety house, taking potshots at loads of lizards scampering up trees in the yard. And in a Mexico City bar, a notorious hangout for American students at the Mexico City College (MCC), Burroughs playfully took aim at a mouse that a drinking buddy dangled by the tail. The bullet whizzed inches below the man's hand, ripped through the rodent, lodged in the wall, and became a popular fixture in the nautical décor of the Bounty Bar & Grill.

There was, however, one gun in Bill's collection that didn't shoot true. It was a cheap Czech-made .380 Star single-action automatic pistol with a faded blue-gray phosphate finish. Short of cash, Bill opted to sell the gun; Robert Addison, a twenty-six-year-old MCC student, expressed some interest in buying it.* Unwilling to invite

---

*Suggesting skepticism on this point, Burroughs scholar James Grauerholz carefully worded his statement: "The story goes that he made an appointment with an M.C.C. student..." John Healy himself shed some doubt on the Robert Addison connection, remembering that, in Mexico City, Bob "couldn't buy a water pistol. Never had enough money."

a virtual stranger into his home, Bill arranged for a meeting at the apartment of John Healy, the Bounty bartender who lived three floors above the bar. The deal would go down on the night of Thursday, September 6, 1951.

Earlier that day, a squealing sound of steel grinding against gritty stone carried above the street noise through the open windows of Apartment 5 of 210 Orizaba in the center of Mexico City. The whistle reminded Bill that he had some dull knives, so he hustled out of his apartment and down to the knife-sharpener. All of a sudden and for no apparent reason, tears poured down his face. "What the hell is the matter?" he asked himself. "What the hell is the matter [with me]?" Before he knew it, the air became unbearably thin. He gasped for breath. And a cloud of depression lowered over him, darkening his spirit. His nerves seriously rattled, Bill struggled back to his apartment—and drank and drank through the afternoon, until the curious cloud lifted.

With his mind recalibrated, Bill packed the .380 Star into a small overnight bag. It was a short stroll to the Bounty, located in the Colonia Roma part of town near to Chapultepec Park, the spacious nature reserve in Mexico City. Healy's place at 122 Monterrey showed signs of an all-afternoon party, the kind that occurred regularly in his apartment and at the Bounty, especially when G.I. checks arrived at the beginning of the month. Four Oso Negro bottles sat on a dining room table, next to twelve dirty glasses partially filled with liquor; cigarette butts lay in ashtrays placed here and there; and a closet was stocked with empty liquor bottles. When Bill arrived, he was ready for whatever alcoholic merriment might be offered; of course, he was already quite merry. And so was Joan Vollmer, Bill's common-law wife, who held a *limonada* spiked with Ginebra, a cheap gin, which she brought upstairs from the bar.

Joan had known Bill for some six years and lived with him since early 1946. What was most striking about the five-foot-six Barnard

College journalism student was her "quick-silver intellect." Daily, she read as many as six newspapers, including the *New York Times* and the *Daily Worker*. She was a woman drawn to café talk about Plato and Kant, and to bubble baths while reading Marcel Proust. Born of a privileged family in Loudonville, New York, Joan was also intensely nonconformist, scorning anything that smacked of bourgeois values. With her heart-shaped face, Joan spent many nights in Manhattan bars searching for company in the arms of strangers. Her mind and her manner attracted many to her roomy West 115th Street apartment, which quickly became a home for some Beats and a mecca for others. At various times, Jack Kerouac and his first wife Edie Parker, Herbert Huncke, Vicki Russell, Allen Ginsberg, and Hal Chase* shared the apartment as roommates, while Lucien Carr, his girlfriend Celine Young, and a host of other hipsters dropped in unannounced on Joan and her infant daughter.† One of those early visitors was William Burroughs—who, notwithstanding his homosexuality, was drawn to her keen wit and free spirit.

What attracted Joan, in part, was Burroughs' book-smart wisdom. Bill's esoteric taste in literature ran the gamut from Blake, Rimbaud, and Proust, to Spengler, Kafka, and Korzbyski. He could quote Shakespeare to drive home a point: reacting to the story of a Greenwich Village bar fight in which a patron's ear had been bitten off, he deadpanned: "'Tis too starved a subject for my sword." Burroughs and Vollmer were so intellectually compatible that Ginsberg, like a scheming *Yenta*, worked to hook them up: "Jack and I

---

*An anthropology student at Columbia University, Chase was from Denver, Colorado, and became particularly significant to the Beats as the man who introduced them to Neal Cassady.

†Joan's daughter, Julie, was conceived during a brief affair with a Columbia University undergraduate while her law-student husband, Paul Adams, served in the military and was stationed in Tennessee. By the summer of 1945, the couple separated permanently.

decided that Joan and Bill would make a great couple. They were a match for each other, fit for each other, equally tuned and equally witty and funny and intelligent and equally well read, equally refined."

What also appealed to Joan was Bill's sex-smart wildness. When he finally decided to move into Joan's apartment in early 1946, they became lovers, even though he was an unabashed misogynist fond of quoting Joseph Conrad's line that "Women are a perfect curse." Neither his homosexuality nor his misogyny, however, prevented Joan from desiring him: "You're supposed to be a faggot [but] you're as good as a pimp in bed."

And it was Burroughs' street-smart familiarity with life's darker sides that intrigued Joan. She was taken in by the criminal element with which he consorted. Studying at the feet of the infamous Vicki Russell, the hooker with a drug habit, Joan joined the ranks of Jack Kerouac and Bill Burroughs, among others, in learning how to extract Benzedrine from inhalers sold in drug stores. "Blasting benny" with her pals in her apartment, Vollmer consumed more and more Benzedrine-soaked strips until she felt that she had been fired out of an atomic cannon. Always a brother in arms, Bill developed a growing morphine and heroin addiction, and his needles, bands, and other paraphernalia strewn here and there gave 419 West 115th the authentic look of a real-life drug den.

As their lives sped up euphorically, they talked all night, partied on and on, balled for hours on end, and even hallucinated until their phantoms became reality. Joan frequently imagined terrifying voices—sometimes branding her a whore or a junkie, other times threatening murder. The more bennies she used, the paler, uglier, sicklier, and crazier she became. When Benzedrine warred with her circulation, she was left limping. "I got way off the beam," Joan admitted, "with the result that I finally landed in Bellevue Psycho Ward." At the hospital, Joan Vollmer was the first woman to be diagnosed with acute amphetamine psychosis. Though ten days were not enough to cure her, it was all the time she allowed before Bill whisked her out of New York.

In the years that followed, Bill's and Joan's problems worsened, as they moved from cotton farming in Pharr, Texas, to pot growing in New Waverly, Texas, to drug pushing in New Orleans, to heavy drinking in Mexico City, where Bill strove to get off junk and Joan tried hopelessly to score bennies.* Their constant use of drugs and alcohol took its toll on their bodies. Joan became "a large, shapeless woman, with a doughy face and the kind of eyes that used to be placed in antique dolls, made of blue glass and quite vacant." And Bill became "cadaverous-looking—thin lips, bad teeth, yellow fingers, and eyes like death."

What drove them from place to place was the law. When Bill was busted in New York for writing phony drug prescriptions, they moved to Texas. When he was busted in Texas for drunk driving and public indecency,† they moved to Louisiana. When he was busted in New Orleans for heroin possession, they moved to Mexico. "My case in New Orleans looked so unpromising that I decided not to show," Burroughs wrote Kerouac. "So I figure to be in Mexico quite some while." To remain in Mexico City long enough to establish citizenship and thereby avoid extradition to Louisiana, Bill enrolled in the School of Higher Studies at Mexico City College. That enabled him to get an annually renewable student immigrant visa. "I am

---

*By the time Joan left New York, she was pregnant with her second child, William Burroughs III, who was born on July 21, 1947. Because she continued using Benzedrine, she chose not to breast feed her infant.

†In May 1948 Bill and Joan were caught by a Beeville, Texas, sheriff in an inebriated state, fornicating on the side of the road while their two children waited in the car. In early 1949, when Helen Hinkle stayed with them in New Orleans, she observed: "The children were allowed to go potty wherever they liked, whether it was on the dining room floor" or elsewhere. Free of adult supervision, young Julie "had formed the habit of chewing her left arm, in the crook of which there was a large scar."

going to Mexico City College on the G.I. Bill," he explained to Jack. "I always say keep your snout in the public trough."

Life in Mexico City was tough for Joan. Unable to obtain bennies, she resorted to drinking tequila, literally from morning to night. Her limp worsened, and she needed a cane to walk; her teeth blackened; her brown hair thinned out; and unsightly sores scarred her arms. Crisis moments with Bill became more frequent, and the couple fought bitterly. There were times like the one in January 1950 when, in a fit of exasperation over Bill's renewed heroin use, Joan grabbed his cooking spoon and tossed the junk on the floor; he slapped her violently across the face and then went out to score some more. And tolerant as Joan generally was of Bill's homosexuality, she could not ignore his regular visits to the boy bars, his separate apartment for sexual flings, and his devastating obsession over the twenty-one-year-old American MCC student Lewis Marker. It was too much for Vollmer; she filed for divorce in Cuernavaca. But it didn't seem to faze Burroughs, who several months later skipped off to Ecuador, taking Marker with him, in search of the hallucinatory drug, *yagé*. That left Joan alone with her children and her misery.

Allen Ginsberg and Lucien Carr showed up in Mexico City while Bill was away playing with his new boy toy. Disappointed to have missed him, Allen and Lucien nevertheless went sightseeing with Joan and the kids. Wasted on Ginebra gin, Lucien drove his old Chevrolet like a maniac on the mountain roads, while Joan yelled over the noise, "How fast can this heap go?" Not done throwing caution to the wind, she insisted on seeing Parícutin, an active volcano, and demanded that Lucien drive the car across the cracked lava fields to within one mile of the inferno's edge. With molten rocks spewing all around, Joan screamed ecstatically: "Go on! Go on!" For Allen, those experiences were so terrifying that he suspected Joan had a death wish.

At this time, her own mortality was not an unfamiliar thought to Joan. In August 1951 she accidentally bumped into her old roommate, Hal Chase, on the streets of Mexico City. Looking beat down to her bones, she sighed: "I'm not going to make it."

———✦———

IT HAPPENED the evening Bill and Joan went to John Healy's apartment to sell Robert Addison the .380 Star pistol.

The living-room alcove was relatively quiet compared to the reveling going on in other rooms of the apartment. There were a few people in that alcove, but no sign of Addison. Joan relaxed in an easy chair, her cane lying along the side. Sipping on her *limonada*, she rested her arm on the pink cloth that covered the chair. Lewis Marker and his boyhood friend, Eddie Woods, sat next to each other on a living room sofa across from Joan. And Burroughs was perched nearby, making small talk.

Reminiscing on his recent trip to Ecuador with Lewis, Bill fantasized about moving to South America, getting clean, and living off the fat of the land with his trusty guns. Chuckling at the preposterousness of the image, Joan took a playful potshot at Bill: "You—we'll starve to death if we go up there…because you won't be able to shoot, you'd be so shaky if you try to come off [junk]…you'll shake, you won't be able to shoot anything."

Burroughs was not about to be emasculated: "Nonsense." Reaching into his overnight bag, he fumbled around for the Czech pistol. "I guess it's about time for our William Tell act. Put that glass on your head, Joanie, let me show the boys what a great shot old Bill is."

Their "William Tell" bit was nothing new. Bill and Joan had performed this trick before, in front of friends, back in their Texas Valley days. In an orchard, Bill occasionally picked up a big orange or grapefruit, called out to Joan, and tossed it to her. She knew the routine; she placed the fruit on her head, as he took aim. *Bam!* Perfect shot. The fruit exploded, Joan laughed, and Old Bull puffed up with pride. It was quite an act.

Even so, seeing it in closed quarters was something else altogether. The specter of splintering glass, the burst of exploding gunfire, the resulting damage to the bullet-ridden wall, and the possibility of missing—all that, and no one said, "What are you doing, Bill? Don't be ridiculous."

Joan was predictably compliant. Turning her head slightly to the right, she balanced the *limonada* glass atop it, closed her eyes, and then jested with a giggle: "I can't watch this, you know I can't stand the sight of blood." She held her pose as Bill took aim some six feet away. He raised his arm to shoulder height and then extended it. Channeling his eye through the small fixed sight, he focused on the contrast between the starkness of Joan's hairline and the muted colors of the backdrop visible through the transparent glass. He tightened his grip, squeezed the trigger, and released the force that propelled the .38 caliber bullet through the barrel.

Bwreow! At close range, the sound cracked the ear drums. The bullet ripped a seven-millimeter entry hole through the flesh and bone of Joan's forehead, one and three-quarter inches to the left of its midline, and lodged there. The impact pounded her head to the right against her shoulder, as the intact glass fell to the floor and spiraled in concentric circles near her feet.

Nobody moved. Silence. All eyes locked on Joan. Silence. A red trickle of blood oozed from the head wound. Lewis's voice finally broke the stillness: "Bill, I think you hit her."

Stunned, Burroughs screamed, "No!" Lewis and Eddie jumped up and bolted to Joan's side, as she slumped down into the pink of the chair. "I saw the hole in her temple, a little blue hole," Woods recalled. Bill lunged forward and fell into her lap as he grabbed her. "Joan! Joan! Joan!" Frantically, he shook her, trying to find a trace of life. But as he did, all that the three heard was the throated gurgle of her "death rattle"—"*harrrrrrrrhhh.*"

After that, it was all rapid-fire, fast-forward. Panicked, Lewis dashed upstairs to find a medical student living in a rooftop hut; no luck. Worried, he and Eddie ran to the landlady's apartment and told Juanita Penaloza about the shooting. Cautious, she called Burroughs' lawyer, Bernabé Jurado... then called Cruz Roja (Red Cross) Hospital and the police at the nearest headquarters, Octava Delegacíon. Medics, police, and reporters (tipped off by *policía*) converged on the apartment about a half-hour later. When the ambulance sped off, Joan was still breathing, although barely. The medics began life-saving measures—blood transfusion, oxygen, serum—but she was slipping away. Within one hour, Joan Vollmer was dead.

Burroughs arrived at Cruz Roja shortly after the ambulance. In the courtyard, he was confronted by Luis Hurtado, a police investigator, and answered questions in front of reporters. After he gave his first statement, an incriminating one,* his lawyer Jurado came on the scene and quickly and artfully rearranged the facts, telling reporters (and his client) that the pistol had fired accidentally. "The point is," Jurado explained, "William has not testified before the authorities yet, and before he does, he will know perfectly what he has to say." While being questioned outside, Bill received word that Joan had died; he "cried bitterly, tearing out his hair in desperation," the *Excelsior* reported. Investigator Hurtado had heard and seen enough; Bill was arrested and carted off to a cell at police headquarters for further interrogation.

The reality was hard to fathom as Bill Burroughs peered down through his glasses, staring at the front page of next day's issue of

---

*Reported by *El Nacional* on September 8, 1951, Burroughs claimed that "there had been a great consumption of gin" and that "he tried to demonstrate his magnificent marksmanship, emulating William Tell," but as a result "of the state of drunkenness in which he found himself, he missed the shot lamentably."

La Prensa newspaper. It was so sensational, so tacky, so tabloid. A macabre photograph of Joan's bloated and lifeless face nestled below hollering headlines. True to its morbid character, the picture revealed the contrived work of some unknown handler—her hands were prayerfully folded across her midriff. A dark dot of blood stained the collar of her blouse.

For all Bill's recent run-ins with her, Joan's eternal absence was a bitter pill. The absurdity and anguish of it all wracked him. It was worse than the sweating torment of a junkie going cold turkey. He looked down again at the headline:

QUISO DEMONSTRAR

SU PUNTERIA Y

MATÓ A SU MUJER

Loosely translated: "He wanted to demonstrate his marksmanship and killed his wife." It was another incident about Bill Burroughs and his guns. This time it had turned deadly—and led to his present incarceration in a Mexico City jail.

By Saturday, September 8, the date of Burroughs' first formal hearing (similar to an American preliminary hearing), Jurado had done his lawyerly best to straighten out his client's story. Standing behind a wired prison cage, Bill faced the judge of instruction, Eduardo Urzaiz Jiménez ("a bastard, but he's fair, and he cannot be bought," Jurado informed Bill) and his prosecutor, Rogelio Barriga Rivas (the Mexican novelist, who occasionally did legal contract work for Jurado). As though reciting a prepared script in the confined quarters, Burroughs told his side of the story: "The pistol slipped and fell, striking itself on a table, and discharged. . . . I did not put any glass on her head." The bottom line: "All was purely accidental." Bill's account varied so substantially from that of two days prior that it sounded like he was another man discussing another case.* It was to no avail: Judge Urzaiz Jiménez determined that he be held for further hearings, this time with witnesses. Afterward, prisoner Burroughs returned to cell block H of the "Black Palace of Lecumberri," the federal penitentiary built on the panoptican design invented by the philosopher Jeremy Bentham, where he was protected from abuse by the infamous underworld inmate Miguel Yancovich.

Mexican criminal justice had its complex side: the *formal prisión* (like a preliminary hearing), where it was determined that there were "enough facts to make possible the legal guilt of the detainee"; the bail procedure, where Burroughs was released after posting a bond of $2,312; and the *amparo* (like a *habeas corpus* hearing), where the earlier ruling was sustained, thereby permitting the case to go to trial. The good news was that Bill was temporarily out of prison; the bad news was that, if he were later found guilty, he would serve up to five years for the crime of *imprudencia criminal*.

For the thirteen days that Burroughs was held in the Black Palace before release on bail, it fell to his long-suffering and financially indulgent family to take care of pressing matters. Sending Bill's brother Mortimer to Mexico City, they footed the bail bond and the bill for Joan's interment. Mort paid 320 pesos for grave 1018 in section A of Panteón Americano, the American cemetery—seven years "advance rent" for the burial plot. Because Bill never picked up the tab for the following years, her casket was eventually removed and her skeleton tossed on the bone-heap.

---

*Almost fourteen years later, in a 1965 interview, Burroughs held to his fictitious narrative: "I had a revolver that I was planning to sell to a friend. I was checking it over and it went off—killed her. A rumor started that I was trying to shoot a glass of champagne from her head William Tell style. Absurd and false." Ten years earlier, in a letter to Allen Ginsberg, Burroughs told a different story: "I aimed *carefully at [a] distance of 6 feet for the very top of the glass....* The idea of shooting a glass off her head had *never entered my mind*, consciously, until, out of the blue so far as I can recall—I was very drunk, of course—I said: 'It's about time for our William Tell act.... Put a glass on your head, Joan.'... From then on I was concentrating on aiming *for the very top of the glass.*"

Joan Vollmer was the third Beat tragedy, following the deaths of David Kammerer and Bill Cannastra. Similar to them, she was immortalized in Beat literature—in Kerouac's novels (*The Town and the City*, *On the Road*, *The Subterraneans*, *Vanity of Duluoz*, and *Visions of Cody*) and in Ginsberg's poems ("The Names" and "Dream Record: June 8, 1955"). And Burroughs drew on her memory, too, in *Junky* and in his introduction to *Queer*.

Julie, Joan's daughter, was brought to Albany to live with Vollmer's parents, while Billy Jr. was taken to Saint Louis to be raised by Burroughs' parents. As for Old Bull, he fled Mexico in mid-November 1952 and headed for Panama via Florida. He might have stayed in Mexico City to defend himself at trial if it were not for an incident involving a gun.

Bernabé Jurado loved his new sporty Buick Roadmaster, with its chrome shark-tooth front grill, shiny side arc design, and eye-catching whitewall tires. It was the symbol of his success as an attorney. When that symbol was sideswiped outside his home by a carload of drunken teenagers, Jurado saw red and reached for his gun. He fired a round into their car and killed a seventeen-year-old passenger. As Bernabé's fate had it, the boy's family was well connected, and the demands for swift justice reached the ears of Avila Camacho, Mexico's new president. So Jurado took the advice he sometimes gave to his clients—he left the country, which meant that Bill Burroughs had no lawyer and no choice but to do likewise.

22.

John Holmes is really riding our wagon without
knowing where actually it's headed.
—Jack Kerouac

SELF-PRESERVATION. Thomas Hobbes, the noted seventeenth-century English thinker, wove an entire political philosophy out of those two words. Above all else, the brutish forces of nature—"the war of all against all"—had to be harnessed if self-preservation were to be actualized. The highest aim of civil society, then, was to do all in its power to protect mankind against violent death.

That message was not lost on the twenty-five-year-old John Clellon Holmes as he sat, in the fall of 1951, surrounded by books in his fourth-floor apartment. His father had instilled in him an almost obsessive love of literature, and his mother, a pianist and a direct descendant of Benjamin Franklin, had cultivated his passion for music. In ways that would have made his parents proud, John had already published short stories, essays, and poetry in such publications as the *Chicago Review* and the *Saturday Review of Literature*. The Massachusetts-born writer had just completed a draft of his first novel, then titled *The Beat Generation.** The narrator of that

---

*At first conception, this novel was titled *The Daybreak Boys*, referencing an 1840s river

novel was named Paul Hobbes—a conscious choice to link that fictional character with the famous Enlightenment philosopher. Paul Hobbes was also linked to his real-life persona, John Holmes.

The novel was "almost literal truth"—the truth, as John perceived it, about himself and his new circle of friends. Ever since July 3, 1948, the night he met Jack Kerouac and Allen Ginsberg at a Spanish Harlem party, John was intrigued by these fellow literati with maverick lifestyles. In Kerouac, who shared with him *The Town and the City* manuscript, Holmes found a literary ally. And in Ginsberg, Holmes discovered an "excitable, infectious, direct" character who "said whatever came into his head," bringing "himself frankly out before you." That combination of Jack's wild and inspired genius and Allen's charismatic and uninhibited candor opened up new vistas to John—some that he favored and others that he feared. They introduced him, at one and the same time, to the cerebral excitement of a new form of writing and to the dangerous lure of "drugs, madness, visions, booze, jazz and unconventional sexual mores." The underbelly of Times Square and the night-life of dissolute parties in squalid flats fired his imagination.

Jack Kerouac appreciated Holmes' artistic potential and encouraged him to exploit his talents in the telling of his new life experiences. That was the focus of countless conversations that Jack had with John when he visited Holmes and his wife, Marian, at their Lexington Avenue apartment. Jack felt strongly that John "should write immense novels about everybody, using the New York scene and the New York types (that is, us). But on a more social plane." Even while Jack was charting out the contours of *On the Road* in his own mind, he encouraged his friend to map similar literary territories. "I should like to see you invent a potpourri," Kerouac

---

gang that Holmes considered an apt analogy. Ultimately, however, the book came to be titled *Go*, and in England *The Beat Boys*.

advised him, including, "Cannastra, Allen G., the people who come to your parties, the San Remo, the bars, the mad parties...painting a large impassioned portrait like Dickens, only about the crazy generation. Because this is the *Crazy Gen*." Kerouac was confident that Holmes could pull it off, owing to his objective and detached frame of mind: "This I believe to be your special genius: to see everybody as a whole."

Jack had pegged John right. Compared to his rowdy friends, the young writer with black, horn-rimmed glasses was more risk-averse than risk-prone, more guarded than impulsive, more an observer than a participant.* Tall and angular, John Holmes was a mind-man who was often on the scene but mentally outside of it. "John was reserved, his radar dishes were up, his eyes were watching in the night, his brain might be engaged with yours during party small-talk or it might be secretly off on a thousand-mile scouting mission of its own." Ginsberg very much liked the "sweet and generous" sandy-haired Holmes but considered him "a little too calm and sensible, a bit too rational."

The Huncke-Cannastra-Carr-Cassady spectacle was one that Holmes reveled in but primarily as a chronicler. He "had been keeping exhaustive work-journals for the two previous years" of escapades with his friends, Holmes recalled, and his novel "was more or less a transcription of these day-to-day jottings." Like Kerouac and Ginsberg, Holmes was busy spinning fact into fiction.

As he moved his ideas from handwritten journals to typewritten pages, John depicted the plight of Paul Hobbes, an industrious writer striving to save his conventional marriage while succumbing to the thrills of the subterranean life. The stifling norms of his marital

---

*Years later, Holmes contrasted himself with Kerouac: "He is freely contradictory, I tend to be trapped by my own consistencies; he absorbs, I analyze; he is intuitive, I am still mostly cerebral; he muses, I worry; he looks for the perfection in others and finds existence flawed; I am drawn *toward* the flaw and believe in life's perfectibility."

relationship battled constantly against the devil-may-care demands of the guys—Albert Ancke (Huncke), Bill Agatson (Cannastra), Hart Kennedy (Cassady), David Stofsky (Ginsberg), and Gene Pasternak (Kerouac), among others. Their bohemian ways beckoned Hobbes night after night to shun responsibility, avoid commitment, and forsake moderation. Even as he got high at "tea" parties or wasted at dead-end bars or revved by joy rides or rowdy at jazz joints, Hobbes sensed that he was putting his fate in jeopardy.

Like a "tourist in the underworld," Hobbes wandered down the dark and foreboding alleys of drug addiction, alcoholism, criminality, prostitution, and alienation. In those seedy locales, his characters came alive. Stofsky was so blinded by Blakean-like visions that he became a pathetic clown who frolicked among the black flowers of deathly decadence. Meanwhile, Pasternak lost himself in the lager of red-and-white bottles of Rheingold beer, hoping to find salvation there. Ancke, the junkie, searched endlessly for his next fix until his swollen feet bled through his life-worn soles. And con man Kennedy, always on the run, drove madly across America, seldom even glancing in his rearview mirror at the lonely women he abandoned at the crossroads. Finally, there was Agatson, the craziest "goddamn fool" of them all, who in a senseless moment of bravado was sucked from this life and dragged into the abyss under the El. It was an excess of tension, edginess, and downtrodden beatness.

Drawn as he was to the existential antics of the "beat generation," in the end Hobbes walked away from its madness. He was "more interested in self-preservation than in the *dérèglement de tous les sens* [derangement of all the senses] . . . taken up with such ardor by the Beats." Or as Hobbes put it toward the novel's end, he "suddenly knew" that someone who yields to mania "is outraged, violated, raped in his soul, and suffers the most unbearable of all losses: the death of hope." Rejecting that despair, he walked back into the loving arms of his wife, and "he held her closer."

John Holmes had taken Jack Kerouac's advice and hammered out a panoramic novel of their world. Unlike Jack, who had not yet found a publisher for *On the Road*, however, John met with relatively rapid success. Although A.A. Wyn, with whom Carl Solomon was affiliated, rejected the book, Charles Scribner's Sons made an offer conditioned on editorial revisions to avoid being censored. "With considerable reluctance," Holmes agreed to tone down the sex scenes, but he "balked" when he was "asked to cut to *three* Agatson's *six* desperate 'Fuck Yous' in the latter part of the book." In protest, he asked, "What's the difference between three and six?" The point did not remain one of lasting contention, because Scribner's decided to forego paperback publication, which was far more likely to provoke a prosecutor's ire.

When Scribner's demanded that the novel be renamed, Holmes turned to his editor, Burroughs Mitchell, for assistance. It was Mitchell's wife who came up with the title *Go*—evoking an audience's cries of approval as a horn-man flies off on uninhibited jazz riffs. Released in the fall of 1952, the $3.50 hardback sported a cover that was its own artistic riff—a collage of traffic signs and signals, set against a blue background, with "GO" boldly projected above the words "a modern novel of the search for experience and for love." The author's byline read simply "clellon holmes."

The reviews of *Go* were descriptive at best and dour at worst. The *New York Herald Tribune* tagged Holmes' writing style as "slack and erratic," offering "cramped lyricism" and "a bare transcription of happenings." On a pejorative note, it concluded: "This is a beat novel." Likewise, the *Saturday Review* had nothing positive to say about the book. In contrast, Gilbert Millstein's three paragraphs for the *New York Times Book Review* refrained from critical comment, merely summarizing the novel's themes. Whatever their impact, the reviews were enough to sell 2,500 copies of the first book on the Beat Generation . . . but no more.

Go looked like it was heading for oblivion until Burroughs Mitchell managed to sell the paperback rights to Bantam for $20,000 (a figure that conservatively would be seven times greater today). And then, with cash in hand, Holmes watched *Go* drop into oblivion. Having the very same censorship concerns as Scribner's, Bantam never printed the book it had purchased.*

In the eyes of some, that was all well and fine. As it turned out, the harshest criticisms leveled against *Go* came from John Holmes' closest friends, the very people whom he featured as lead characters in his book. "John Holmes' Novel is No good," Allen wrote to Neal and Jack. "I was shocked when I got his eyedea of me. But maybe I'm so prejudiced." Jack Kerouac felt no need to qualify his condemnation, however. To think that Holmes was the *first* to publish a book about the Beats and their adventures! To think that Holmes had made $20,000 on the sale of *Go* when Kerouac couldn't make a cent for *On the Road*! It was all intolerable. In a venomous three-page rant to Allen, Jack complained: "John Holmes, who as everybody knows lives in complete illusion about everything, writes about things he doesn't know about....Everybody knows he has no talent....His book stinks...and you all know it, and my book is great and will never be published....My heart bleeds every time I look at *On the Road*."

No doubt, Jack's heart bled even more when he turned to the spread on page 10 of the November 16 issue of the *New York Times Magazine*. His eyes fell on bold black print:

'This Is the Beat Generation'
Despite its excesses, a contemporary insists, it is moved
by a desperate craving for affirmative beliefs.
By CLELLON HOLMES

---

*In the wake of *On the Road*'s popularity in 1957, Ace Books published an abridged edition of *Go*. "That edition, cut by almost a third, was published in England and Italy, and the original book vanished into the rare-book market."

Underneath the flush-left banner was an abstract tri-toned black, white, and gray image of a solitary man pressed against a wall with arms outstretched above his head. The caption below the artwork, taken from the article, read "beat means being undramatically pushed up against the wall of oneself."

As if it weren't enough that *Go* introduced the Beat life to American literature, now John Holmes was being featured as the spokesman for the Beat Generation. Here was a "latecomer," Jack fumed, a "pryer-intoer" capitalizing on the very literary movement that he and Allen had begun! And all of this at a time when *On the Road* and his more recent manuscripts, like *Doctor Sax* or *Maggie Cassidy*, were going nowhere! But his anger was tempered a tad when he read the third paragraph in the Holmes essay: "It was Jack Kerouac, the author of a fine, neglected novel 'The Town and the City,' who finally came up with [the generational label]. It was several years ago, when the face was harder to recognize, but he has a sharp, sympathetic eye, and one day he said, 'You know, this is really a *beat* generation.'"

Still, opportunity knocked on John's door, not on Jack's. Holmes was invited to submit his essay to the magazine by Gilbert Millstein, the reviewer of *Go*. Millstein was intrigued by Holmes' reference to a "beat generation" in the novel, and asked him to elaborate in an article on the meaning of that phrase.* It fell, then, to Holmes to define the essence of "beatness" and the generation that experienced it.

"The origins of the word 'beat' are obscure," Holmes began, "but the meaning is only too clear to most Americans. More than mere weariness, it implies the feeling of having been used, of being raw. It involves a sort of nakedness of mind, and, ultimately, of soul; a feeling of being reduced to the bedrock of consciousness.... A man is

---

*About this time, Kerouac sent his own article, "The History of Bop," to Millstein, who passed on it.

beat whenever he goes for broke and wagers the sum of his resources on a single number; and the young generation has done that continually from early youth." The members of this postwar generation "have an instinctive individuality"; "they distrust collectivity"; they "lust for freedom, and the ability to live at a pace that kills"; "their excursions into drugs or promiscuity come out of curiosity, not disillusionment." And it is a generation mad about risk-taking: "the hotrod driver invites death only to outwit it. He is affirming the life within him in the only way he knows how, at the extreme."

When the "wildest hipster" makes "a mystique of bop, drugs, and the night life," Holmes explained, he does not "desire to shatter the 'square' society in which he lives, only to elude it." For he is convinced that "the valueless abyss of modern life is unbearable" and has "had enough of homelessness, valuelessness, faithlessness." At the core of its soul, the Beat Generation is "driven by a desperate craving for belief," by "an ever-increasing conviction that the problem of modern life is essentially a spiritual problem," and by a "capacity for sudden wisdom which people who live hard and go far possess." These, Holmes concluded, "are assets" for the American society; they "bear watching. And, anyway, the clear, challenging faces are worth it."

This portrait of the Beat Generation was far more upbeat than the picture painted by John Clellon Holmes in his novel. "Your *Beat Generation* article [is] liked by everyone," Kerouac wrote to Holmes from Mexico City on December 9, 1952. "I see you have considerable journalistic talent, like Lucien—something Allen & I don't have, from secret wildness. You have voice of authority." Sensitive to being ignored, Jack added: "Thank you for mentioning me." But ever contradictory, Kerouac felt the need to distance himself from the "journalist" and the mainstream popularity of the "Beat Generation" he had glorified. The youth of 1952, Jack snapped, were "sleek beasts and middleclass subterraneans," not the real thing.

The real Beats, by contrast, were anything but mainstream popular. Herbert Huncke was serving time, Bill Burroughs was holing up in a male whorehouse in Tangier, Carl Solomon was still fighting his psychotic demons, Neal Cassady was humping paramours in the garage of his home, Jack Kerouac was begging Carolyn Cassady to live with him as a lover in Mexico City, and Bill Cannastra was decaying in his grave. As for Allen Ginsberg, he was striving for normalcy in Paterson and New York, even as he strayed little from the Beat life that he found so alluring.

23.

It was Kerouac who kept telling me I should write.

—Bill Burroughs

IF JACK KEROUAC inspired Bill Burroughs to write, Allen Ginsberg made it possible for him to get published. Ever the literary agent
for his Beat friends, Allen tried to do for Bill what he had yet been
unable to accomplish for Jack—namely, landing a book-publishing
deal. Allen finally succeeded when, on July 5, 1952, Bill signed a contract to publish his novel with the working title *Junk*. A.A. Wyn's
paperback division, Ace Books, agreed to print the book after Doubleday and Bobbs-Merrill passed on it. When Allen secured an $800
advance for Bill, Burroughs was ecstatic: "You really are a sweetheart. I could kiss you on both cheeks."

By the summer of 1952, Bill Burroughs had been off junk for
over a year, although he drank quite heavily now. His junk world
seemed behind him, except for his photographic memory of it. And
that memory was put to good use throughout 1950 and 1951, when
he wrote the bulk of an autobiographical novel about the drug-
and-crime-infested underworlds of New York, New Orleans, and
Mexico City. *Junk* was a chilling anthropological field report on the
drug subculture—its vernacular, habits, economics, criminal and
civil regulation, and medical and psychiatric dynamics. Burroughs'

firsthand account of the drug netherworld (that of marijuana, peyote, Benzedrine, cocaine, opium, etc.) offered up a raw account of
the "real horror of junk," as Bill put it. "When I wrote the original
MS I was on junk," he recalled. But afterward, much of the book
was done "off junk."

The novel was a painfully candid, often confessional, and never
sentimental account of the indignities and sufferings endured by
those who came in contact with a way of life captured in a single
word—*junk*. True to that account, Herbert Huncke appeared as one
of the novel's characters, "Herman." Absent, however, was any reference to characters patterned after Kerouac or Ginsberg or Carr.
And when the publisher urged Burroughs to include something on
the Vollmer incident, he declined: "About the death of Joan, I do
not see how that can be worked in." Even so, the Vollmer tragedy
moved Bill to write as he had never been motivated to do before.
He once admitted that he was "forced to the appalling conclusion"
that he would never have finished *Junk* or pursued life as a writer
"but for Joan's death." Her demise brought him in "contact with the
invader, the Ugly Spirit, and maneuvered me into a lifelong struggle, in which I had no choice except to write my way out." And so
he finished his novel about those beaten by the brutality of their
existence.

Burroughs' book was no generational manifesto; it was a detached
narrative of a sordid, nightmarish world where unrepentant addicts
brushed elbows with unredeemable cops and unpardonable busi-
nessmen while worshipping at the altar of JUNK. Not fanciful, not
romantic, and never, never apologetic, *Junk* was simply factual—like
a man in a radiation field recording the results of a Geiger counter
with complete indifference.

Such indifference, however, did not sit well with Bill's new publisher. For one thing, all sorts of changes needed to be made and
disclaimers added before the manuscript was published lest readers

get the impression that Wyn endorsed the drug lifestyle depicted in *Junk*, whose title would also be changed to *Junkie: Confessions of an Unredeemed Drug Addict*.* More than that, the novel sorely needed "balance," an "opposing view" of the drug life. So it was decided, over Bill's objection, to publish another work in the same volume, this one with a different title on the back cover—*Narcotics Agent* by Maurice Helbrant, a former Federal Bureau of Narcotics agent.

Junkie was so honest that it created another problem. Burroughs did not want to publish it under his real name, since doing so could anger his wealthy parents who might then promptly cut off his monthly allowances. At first, he chose the pseudonym William Dennison, the name of his character in Kerouac's *The Town and the City*. Later, however, he changed it to William Lee, using his mother's maiden name. As *Junkie* moved closer and closer to its pub date, Wyn made more and more editorial demands on Burroughs. All of this infuriated him, if only because he needed to get beyond this novel so he could finish his next one, titled *Queer*.

For his part, Allen Ginsberg thrived more as an agent for his friends than as a promoter of his own poetic works. Ever since making a personal connection to William Carlos Williams in Paterson, Allen yearned to write poetry that his role model would appreciate. "Get form without deforming the language," Williams advised, and Ginsberg aimed to use the "actual talk rhythms" of ordinary life in his poems, rather than the mannered or artificial styles of the academy. In early 1952 Allen scoured his notebooks for ideas and lines—any fragment that might be reshaped into a poetically compelling form. He divided the lines, rearranged and revised them, adding and subtracting until he had a sheaf of ten new poems to send to Williams. Ginsberg was careful not to get his hopes too high, however, portraying them to Jack and Neal as "a bunch of short crappy scraps

---

*A quarter-century later, the title changed to *Junky*.

I picked out of my journals and fixed up like poems, the like of which I could write 10 a day to order."

How surprised and delighted Ginsberg was, then, to discover that Williams enthusiastically approved. "How many such poems do you own?" Carlos inquired. "You *must* have a book. I shall see to it that you get it. Don't throw anything away. These are *it*." Relief mixed with elation as Allen realized that he finally was on to something big—a style that was truly his, definitely authentic, and really hip—and with a distinguished and well-connected mentor willing to advance his literary fortunes, and maybe even those of his Beat pals. Bubbling over with exuberance and plans for the future, Ginsberg wrote to Kerouac and Cassady: "Now you realize you old bonepoles, the two of you, whuzzat means? I can get a book out if I want.... We'll have a huge collected anthology of American Kicks and Mental Muse-eries. The American Spiritual Museum. A gorgeous gallery of Hip American devises."

Collecting eighty-nine notebook-derived poems into a cycle that he named *Empty Mirror*, Ginsberg showed them to his friends. "Blow, baby, blow!" Jack Kerouac howled. "When you 'open yr. mouth to sing,' you are the end...the greatest living poet in America." Recognizing that Allen was striving now to surf the brainwaves of spontaneous writing, Jack affirmed: "The value of yr. mind is its spontaneity."

Shortening his collection to forty-seven poems at the recommendation of William Carlos Williams, Allen prepared *Empty Mirror* for submission to commercial publishers. The cycle was dedicated to Herbert Huncke, the quintessential antihero. It was a tribute to the deviant of Times Square who first inspired Allen to understand the essence of beatness. The manuscript also contained an introduction by Williams, declaring: "This young Jewish boy, already not so young any more, has recognized something that has escaped most of the modern age, he has found that man is lost in the world of his own head." The author of these poems, Williams maintained, was like a modern-day "Jeremiah" screaming at the crowd. Ginsberg's words, he predicted, would "one day rouse the sleeping world."

At long last, Allen would join the publishing ranks of his fellow Beats—Kerouac, Holmes, and Burroughs. He could see his name on the cover now, along with blurbs from the gang and others. The editors at Random House, however, could not: "In these days of exceedingly low sales of books of poetry we did not feel that publishing EMPTY MIRROR was a feasible venture for us." If these uptight, uptown types could not appreciate the path-breaking character of his poems, surely literary journals would. So he sent the manuscript off to the *Partisan Review*, *Hudson Review*, *Commentary*, and *Poetry* magazine. He even mailed one to the celebrated San Francisco poet and literary figure, Kenneth Rexroth, who then reviewed proposals for New Directions publishing house. The answer was always the same: Rejected.

As Allen's literary stock plummeted, Bill's rose. On April 15, 1953, Ace Books finally released *Junkie: The Confessions of an Unredeemed Drug Addict*. Its racy cover was pulp fiction—the title in neon yellow loomed above a colorful scene of a beautiful blonde fighting for her heroin needle as a handsome hero struggled to save her. A full-page *New York Times* ad ran four days later. It proclaimed: "There is no other book remotely like it.... The startling revelations, written under a pen name, of an intelligent, university-bred American, scion of a well-known family." The ad featured two promotional blurbs:

> **Clellon Holmes**, author of GO: "These are the facts and fantasies of drug addiction, written with the dry passion and candid exactitude of a man through whose veins the truth of his life runs like acid. Though this is not its intention, it accomplishes what all the investigations and all the medical reports concerning narcotics have failed to do."

John Kerouac, author of THE TOWN AND THE CITY: "A learned sophisticate makes the first intelligent modern confession on drugs. Stands classic and alone."*

Junkie took off. Within eight months, the thirty-five-cent book sold 113,170 copies, though royalty conflicts prevented Burroughs from making any real money on the deal.

How ironic. The very man who blurbed a best-selling book could not get his own "classic," *On the Road*, or any of his newer novels published. It was only when the kind John Holmes intervened by recommending yet another agent to Jack—this one, the powerfully connected MCA wonder woman, Phyllis Jackson—that his career began to pull out of its tailspin. For all the cruel words that he had written to and about them, Jack owed his literary future to devoted old friends...and to savvy new allies.

Among the names in Phyllis Jackson's black book, one was the hugely influential Malcolm Cowley. In 1929 the Harvard-educated writer replaced Edmund Wilson as the literary editor of the *New Republic*. That same year, Cowley published a book of poetry, entitled *Blue Juanita*, and not long afterward *Exile's Return: A Literary Odyssey of the 1920s*; with the latter book, he became known as the Boswell of the Lost Generation. And as an advisor to Viking Press, he played a significant role in the lives of twentieth-century American literary giants, editing the works of Ernest Hemingway and William Faulkner. Now, at age fifty-five, he was about to discover Jack Kerouac.

When Phyllis Jackson urged Cowley to take Kerouac to lunch, he obliged. Malcolm's closely clipped moustache, tweed sport coat, and

---

*Kerouac's endorsement was most surprising since he had earlier refused to promote the book: "I do not want my real name used in conjunction with habit forming drugs while a pseudonym conceals the real name of the author thus protecting him from prosecution but not myself." Moreover, he did not even want his novel "mentioned in juxtaposition to *Go*."

preppy tie made Jack feel uneasy. What were the chances that this stuffy man would have any appreciation for his prose experiment? Still, since Cowley seemed interested in him, Jack gave him the 297 pages of *On the Road*. The manuscript sparked Malcolm's imagination; the more he read, the more enthusiastic he became. This book had real possibilities, even a publishing contract with Viking. Cowley predicted that the novel might reap $50,000 or more for Jack, but it needed revisions. That was a fly in the ointment: Jack was adamant, no changes! He was feeling low and mighty, and was willing to make concessions to no one except God.

The other fly was that Jack had completed newer works—experimental ones like *The Subterraneans*, a philosophical take on a doomed affair, and *Maggie Cassidy*, a story of an adolescent love. In both, his style became more unorthodox, his sentences grew longer, and his outlook leaned ever more toward a curious kind of Buddhism. He had been reading Ashvaghosha's *Life of the Buddha* and was increasingly enchanted with Eastern thought. Certain key precepts rang true to him: "All life is sorrowful" and "The Cause of Suffering is ignorant desire." He read works such as the *Diamond Sutra* and compiled "Some of the Dharma," a compendium of Buddhist prayers. Even while his *Road* novel searched for a publishing home, Jack Kerouac found himself moving away from it, down new roads of consciousness.

Meanwhile, *On the Road* was still on Cowley's mind. He was not about to abandon this project even if Jack had his mind elsewhere. From time to time, he called Phyllis to ask: "How's your fellow, Kerouac? What's he up to now?" When the response came, it was bleak: Jack was "muttering" things like "he didn't want to be published by anyone." Jackson advised him: "There is nothing to do at this point but wait."

Bill Burroughs, however, wasn't waiting. Riding the crest of *Junkie*'s dime-store success, he blew into town to shack up with Ginsberg for a while before setting sail to Tangier. He wanted to work with

Allen on the manuscript of *The Yagé Letters*, a book of their correspondence penned during his South American quest for the psychedelic plant *yagé*. When not writing, he wanted to "schlup" with Ginsberg—merging their bodies sexually and their souls telepathically in "a kind of monstrous junkie-organic-protoplasmic schlup of two beings," as Allen described it. What Bill readily discovered, however, was that a younger and much more attractive man stood in the way of their schlupping.

Allen had found a new "beat" friend, a new Neal Cassady. This time, it was Gregory Corso, a darkly handsome twenty-three-year-old Italian boy with sparkling eyes and wavy, jet-black hair, who had spent much of his youth in and out of foster homes and jails. When Allen first met him at the Pony Stable bar, he was certainly not turned off by the facts that Corso had spent time in the Bellevue asylum and had served a sentence for robbery at the Clinton State Prison near the Canadian border. More exciting still, this ex-con had read Shelley's poetry, Hugo's *Les Miserables*, and Dostoyevsky's *Brothers Karamazov*, in addition to works on Greek and Roman history. He even wrote his own poetry, which Allen read and liked. Happy as Allen was with Gregory, Old Bull didn't like him. Burroughs gave him menacing looks while wielding his machete to cut all the Peruvian dried *yagé* he had brought with him. Greg got the message and kept his distance until Bill left New York for Tangier at the end of 1953 with *The Yagé Letters* going nowhere.*

In the interim, Allen worried about the publishing future of his friend Jack Kerouac. Would *On the Road* ever see the light of day? Was it destined to the same fate as his *Empty Mirror*, with nothing to show for it save a stack of rejection letters? If not, how would it be saved? Could Jack's next agent do any better than he and Phyllis Jackson had done?

---

*The Yagé Letters would not be published until 1963.

Sterling Lord was that agent. Hailing from the Midwest, the fair-complexioned and dark-haired man with an athletic build was a tennis champion in college; as an adult, he became a connoisseur of fine wines and great literature. Lord met Kerouac when he "first rang the bell and walked through the door of my office, a below-ground-level room...just off Park Avenue. Through our windows, we could see the knees and lower legs of people passing on the 36th Street sidewalk." Dressed in a "light-colored weather-resistant jacket with a lightweight checkered shirt underneath," the handsome thirty-two-year-old struck Lord as a "diamond in the rough."

Jack pulled out a thick package, wrapped in newspaper, from his "weather-beaten rucksack." It was a typed copy of his *Road* manuscript. He hoped that the recommendation from Lord's friend, Robert Giroux, would encourage Sterling to act as his agent even in the face of so many publisher rejections. Because "Giroux thought I would be the right man" to represent Kerouac, Lord agreed to read the work. "I felt that his was a fresh, distinctive voice that should be heard," Sterling concluded. He would represent this young author with a "commitment to serious writing."

Jack and his mother Gabrielle were both taken by the fact that the charming and suave Sterling Lord had married a French woman. They often punned: "Trust in the Lord." Now, the lead partner of the Lord and Colbert Agency was expected to be Jack's savior. Throughout many submissions, Sterling remained hopeful even in the face of failure. *On the Road*, then retitled "The Beat Generation" to appeal to the youth market, "was sent out again and again," Lord recalled. "So many editors saw it, realized immediately that it was like no other book they had ever seen, much less published, and would simply turn it down because of its strangeness."

Malcolm Cowley, a reader for Viking, was another whose faith in Jack's novel remained unshaken. Convinced that mainstream publishers might be more interested if Kerouac's reputation were touted by distinguished literary quarterlies, Cowley promoted excerpts from the *Road* novel to editors at various periodicals. The first bite came from Arabelle Porter, who accepted "Jazz of the Beat Generation" for publication in *New World Writing*; the article contained selections from the book on Jack's and Neal's discovery of the San Francisco and Chicago jazz scenes. Kerouac received $108 dollars after agent's fees of $12 for the piece. Another excerpt, "The Mexican Girl," was accepted by *Paris Review*, and "A Billowy Trip in the World" was slated to appear in *New Directions*.

The bio-statement for the *New World Writing* piece read: "This selection is from a novel in progress, *The Beat Generation*." It also noted that the author used a pen name: "Jean-Louis is the pseudonym of a young American writer of French-Canadian parentage. He is the author of one published novel." Kerouac insisted on the pseudonym because he feared that his ex-wife, Joan Haverty, might claim support money from any income he received. The pen name didn't sit well with Cowley: "I did think it was wrong of you to change your name," he complained, "because John Kerouac is a good name for literary purposes, and by signing your work Jean-Louis you miss the reputation that you have already built up." In the future, the scofflaw agreed to return to "Kerouac," but this time with "Jack" as his first name. That "Jack," however, was still no more than a future prospect, as was *On the Road*.

By this time, Kerouac's car karma had taken him to California, where he visited with Neal and Carolyn Cassady. He had hoped to rendezvous with Ginsberg there. But Allen's journeys—to Washington, D.C.; Florida; Cuba; and an extended tour of Mexico—prevented him from arriving before Jack headed back East. Still, the twenty-eight-year-old Ginsberg was excited about experiencing the thrills of the West Coast. After all, in New York, he had suffered the flames of hell—Naomi's agonizing days at the Greystone asylum; his frightening 1949 arrest; his maddening time at the bughouse with Carl Solomon; the senseless deaths of Kammerer, Cannastra, and Vollmer; his fruitless quest for love; and his depressing career as an unpublished poet. Perhaps his prospects, like those of the miners of old, would improve in the Golden State.

24.

*I had a balanced heterosexual life, to the point where I
really wanted to get married and have kids and settle
down to a life in advertising.*
—Allen Ginsberg

THE JOYS OF the American middle-class life were his. He had
a well-paying job at the Towne-Oller market research firm. He had
two secretaries. He wore a tie and tweed coat, and his hair was
neatly cropped and combed. He lived in a stylish Nob Hill apartment. And when he came home in the evenings, he had a pretty
blonde woman, a loving young child, and a cuddly cat awaiting him.
The Allen Ginsberg of New York days would not have recognized the
Allen Ginsberg of his current San Francisco days. The doctors at the
Columbia Presbyterian Psychiatric Institute would have approved:
their eccentric homosexual patient was finally cured.

True to that spirit, Allen had fantasized about marriage and a
normal life. "When I get married," he once told Neal Cassady, "I
want everybody I know to be there and watch including all regi-
ments of family, in synagogue, where will be great groaning choirs
of weepers, sacraments, everybody in flowers and dress clothes,
slightly awed by the presence of eternal vows, chastened by tradition and individuality of marriage." All he needed was a woman.

"What a doll," Allen boasted to Jack Kerouac about Sheila Williams, his new twenty-two-year-old girlfriend, "finer than *any* girl I met." The new lovers were inseparable, "living in splendor." They talked incessantly; they strolled the romantic streets and rode the enchanting streetcars of San Francisco; they read poetry aloud to one another; they sipped fine coffee in Sheila's apartment and necked after her young son went to bed. Allen "really fell in love"; theirs was a "deep affair." So great was his heterosexual love that Allen "wanted to fuck and could get hardons." But while she told him of being separated from her husband, he was quiet about his secret past, including the time a few months earlier when Carolyn Cassady caught him in bed with her husband Neal.*

Hip as Sheila was—"ex-singer, big buddy of Brubeck, knows all the colored cats"—Allen could not count on her to be as tolerant as Joan Vollmer. He was not confident that Sheila could handle knowing that her man had shared his body with other men. And she was unlikely to appreciate Jack Kerouac's snide humor about Allen's heterosexual conversion; when hearing of his friend's inflated passion, Jack pricked his balloon: "The queers of Remo as you know are in the Black Cat there, on Columbus at Montgomery." What would Sheila think if one of Allen's old flames turned up on her doorstep, hungry for male love?

And that was precisely what William Burroughs, the cheatin' queer home-wrecker, planned to do. He intended to leave Tangier, Morocco, and join Allen in San Francisco. "I did not think that I was hooked on him like this," Bill confessed to Jack. "I love him and nothing cancels love." In a desperately jealous state, he added: "Now Allen is talking about making it with a chick, and I am really upset and worried.... You know how U.S. chicks are. They want it all. It

---

*In a September 5, 1954, letter to Jack Kerouac, Allen wrote about Carolyn's discovery: "Carolyn caught me and Neal—screamed...yelled...but it was not comic, the intensity of insult and horror and even I think spite, indignation, etc."

would be the end of my relation with Allen." Like Burroughs, Ginsberg dumped his anxiety on Kerouac, fretting over the impossible sexual demands that Bill would make if he came to San Francisco: "[H]e is going to be frantic and possessive you know.... The situation with Sheila will be a madhouse. I don't know how to manage it.... It's a real bitch, man." When he mustered the courage, Allen finally wrote Bill a stern letter. His life had jelled and he wasn't about to break it apart. "I think I'm responsible for single-handedly destroying Bill's belief in love," Allen later conceded.

So life was back on track with the beautiful Sheila Williams in beautiful San Francisco. There were so many places to go and so much to do. The more Allen saw of the bohemian quarters of North Beach and elsewhere, the more he liked them. He loved the restless feel, creative spirit, progressive politics, hipster cafés, cool jazz clubs, experimental theaters, street performers, and libraries filled with volumes of new poetry. He could spend hours schmoozing in Vesuvio's bar or paging through poetry journals in the next-door City Lights Bookstore, both havens for leftist literati. He could hang all night drinking and smoking at clubs like The Cellar or The Place. He could down French fries and chili at Foster's Cafeteria or delight in Jewish deli food at the Co-Existence Bagel Shop. He could drop in on the Friday evening soirées hosted by Kenneth Rexroth, the forty-eight-year-old grand poobah of the San Francisco literary scene, where Allen mingled with Bay Area poets such as Robert Duncan, Michael McClure, Ruth Witt-Diamant, and Philip Lamantia from New York. And, of course, he could always find temptation, which was never farther than around the next corner.

By October 1954, little more than a month after Allen bragged about erotic love with Sheila, their budding relationship showed signs of withering. "Depression now," Allen wrote in his journal on October 12, "realizing after moving into this great Nob Hill Apt with Sheila that I 'don't love her' as 'she loves me' thus starving & killing her heart for my 'casual' pleasure." The young woman's "girlish psychological self-dramatizations" irritated him from time to time, but what really took the bloom off the rose was his candor, his true confession about his love affair with a man, Neal Cassady. It repulsed her. This was not the kind of information that the young straight woman, separated with a child, wanted to hear when she dreamed of a future with a respectable man, a real man. They bickered and agonized over what to do with their relationship. Was it best to call it off and part? Was it better to work it out, if that could be done? What would her friends think? Though things were quite tense, the two decided nonetheless to weather the storm and see what happened.

What happened was Peter Orlovsky. At twenty-one, he was a model of Slavic male beauty. The streaks in his thick sandy-brown hair glistened gold when light reflected off them. His swept-back hair rose from a high forehead; intense and dark shooter-marble eyes sat evenly between his gently flared nose; his lips were full, with a trace of a pout; and his skin was fair and unblemished. Orlovsky's outer beauty hinted at an inner fragility, a vulnerability lying just below the surface. His placid manner and quiet way evoked a protective sentiment in some and an exploitative sense in others. Peter was soft on the outside and soft on the inside.

The New York–born young man was emotionally delicate, someone prone to severe bouts of depression. A harsh comment or a callous act, no matter how intentioned, could send him into such melancholic torment that he would weep for days locked in his room. This mental misery stemmed from his family tree—his abusive father, alcoholic mother, schizophrenic oldest brother, severely retarded older brother, and his sporadically institutionalized younger twin siblings. Though Peter was no picture of mental health, it was amazing that he was as sane as he was when Robert LaVigne painted an imposing four-by-six-foot portrait of his face and an alluring five-foot-square nude of him reclining on a settee with onions strewn at his feet.

Allen Ginsberg first met Peter Orlovsky when he was hanging on the canvas of *Nude with Onions* inside Robert LaVigne's apartment at 1403 Gough. It was love at first sight, a sight he would never have seen but for the chance occurrence of meeting LaVigne one evening in early December at Foster's Cafeteria on Polk Street. After another bitter fight with Sheila, Allen dropped into Foster's looking for more amiable company; striking up a conversation about art with an attractive stranger, he learned that the bearded twenty-six-year-old LaVigne was an artist.* He had paintings of his own on display at his nearby apartment. Soon enough, Allen found himself there, taking in the art.

Allen could not believe his eyes. Enthralled by the painting, he asked LaVigne, "Who is that?" Robert smiled teasingly: "Oh, that's Peter." Much to his delight, Allen learned that the stunning model was Robert's roommate. "He's here. He's home," LaVigne continued, "I'll get him." As if stepping down from the canvas, the young man stepped through the doorway and into Allen's vision. Ginsberg's blood rushed as he set eyes on the Adonis. Through all the casual chatter, Allen envied Robert's amorous tie to Peter. He was excited, nonetheless, to be invited back. At least, he'd have a chance to see this boy-god again soon.

On his next visit, Allen brought his pal, Neal Cassady, to meet his new friends and see LaVigne's art. Whatever Neal thought of "Nude with Onions," what really bugged out his eyes was the naked portrait of a sensuous young redhead that Robert was in the course of painting. Now *Fortuna* smiled on Neal the same way she smiled on Allen. It was another case of art merging with reality, as Neal discovered that the model, Natalie Jackson, was also LaVigne's

---

*Allen Ginsberg dubbed Robert LaVigne "the Court painter" who sketched and painted many of the Beat figures, including Corso, Burroughs, Huncke, Robert Creeley, and Ginsberg himself. They were featured at the New York's Whitney Museum of Art in a 1996 exhibit.

roommate and available to meet him. Within days, the duo—she notorious for climactic blow jobs and he for piston-fast fucking—tempered the chill of San Francisco's December air with the heat of their own passion. More astonishing yet was the fact that the two-timing Neal, who was still living with his wife Carolyn in San Jose, brought her to LaVigne's studio; she saw Robert painting the oil Natalie but never met the flesh Natalie, with whom Neal had already fallen deeply in love.*

Peter "needed a sweet companion," Robert one day told Allen. LaVigne had an exhibition in San Diego and was concerned about the dependent Orlovsky being left alone until he returned. Moreover, Robert's affair with Peter—who was less attracted to men than women, although sexually inexperienced with them—was losing traction. When LaVigne suggested, somewhat obliquely, that Ginsberg stay at his apartment and care for Peter while he was away, Allen suspected that Robert was matchmaking: "Ooh, don't mock me," he moaned. His head reeled at the prospect. "[W]hat are you asking *me* for?" He was so conflicted. On the one hand, there were all of his mighty efforts since 1949—at the asylum and in Paterson, New York, and San Francisco—to straighten up and fly right. On the other hand, here was a real chance for soulful love with a stunning man, offered up in such a casual manner. His heart melted at the prospect of having Peter as his own. "Oh God, not again!" he thought, knowing that his homosexual dark angels had returned.

Before Allen flew to New York on December 14 for his brother's wedding, he spent the night with Peter. Eager to please, Peter admitted that he had dreamed about embracing Allen and waking up with him. It was a tender and moving moment. At that, Peter untied the sash of his loose-fitting Japanese robe. He was naked

---

*An iconic Beat photograph, taken in March of 1955 by Allen Ginsberg, captures Neal Cassady and Natalie Jackson hugging beneath a movie marquee advertising Marlon Brando's *The Wild One*.

underneath. He put his arms around Allen's torso, peered into his eyes, and gently drew him into the warmth of his robe, toward his lean and smooth body. Face-to-face, heart-to-heart, and soul-to-soul, the couple folded together into a loneliness-defeating sweetness. Allen carried that fond memory with him as he boarded a plane for the East Coast.

Back in New York, Allen celebrated the joy of Eugene's wedding and suffered the sorrow of his mother's plight when he traveled to Pilgrim State Hospital to visit her. His spirit dropped at how irreversibly insane she had become. In a heart-rending state of confusion, she rattled on and on about the wires in her head. She pleaded with Allen to rescue her and return her home. The situation was hopeless; worse still, it was the last time that Allen saw Naomi.

Upon his return to San Francisco, Robert and Peter invited Allen to move in with them. Confronted with the bitter news, Sheila snapped, "Good, that's what you deserve. Get out of here!" With that ultimatum, Allen's high-flying experiment with heterosexuality took a nosedive. His bourgeois credentials, however, had not yet lapsed, since he continued to punch a nine-to-five clock at the Towne-Oller market research firm.

As the days passed, the complexity of their lives became dizzying. Robert thought that he might make up with Peter; Allen's love for Peter grew obsessive; Robert and Allen quarreled over Peter; trapped in a love triangle, Peter moved out, and into the Hotel Wentley; Allen rented a room across the street in the Hotel Young; and Neal moved into Robert's apartment with Natalie. Every day they were apart, Allen yearned for Peter's love. "I sit up looking out [my] window...[at] Foster's corner as if I might see him crossing [the] street, entering Foster's looking for me," he wrote in his journal. "When will he come? Does he want to see me? Why am I waiting monomaniacally?...How [could] he not come soon, knowing I wait?"

Doctor Philip Hicks at Langley Porter Clinic had an answer for Allen's puzzling predicament. Hicks was a psychiatrist at the public clinic, and had seen Allen already for two months at $1 an hour. He encouraged Allen to speak openly.

"You know," Allen told him, "I'm very hesitant to get into a deep thing with Peter because where can it ever lead?" With emphasis, he asked almost rhetorically: "Besides, shouldn't I be heterosexual?"

Allen was taken aback by Dr. Hicks's answer: "Why don't you do what you want? What would you like to do?"

In a moment of sincere truth, Allen shared his formula for happiness: "Well, I really would just love to get an apartment on Montgomery Street, stop working, and live with Peter and write poems!"

Dr. Hicks's next comment was even more surprising than the former one: "So why don't you do that?"

Incredible. Here was a shrink who didn't castigate him, who didn't treat his homosexuality as a mental illness, who didn't scoff at his dream of being a poet—who gave him full permission to be the man he yearned to be.

Allen heeded the good doctor's advice and took an apartment at 1010 Montgomery Street. Shortly thereafter, on February 11, 1955, Peter Orlovsky moved in. Two of his four wishes had come to fruition. Another wish came true, though it was not one that he told Dr. Hicks—to tie the knot, the one he never tied with Sheila Williams.

Their "wedding chapel" was located at 235 Montgomery near Bush. It wasn't terribly fancy, though it offered services any time of day or night to accommodate couples. It did catering of sorts, and there was a large staff to wait on guests. In 1955 the idea of two men exchanging vows, as Allen and Peter did, was as strange as being wed in Foster's Cafeteria at three A.M., as Allen and Peter did. Sitting below the glare of neon and holding hands above the wipe-clean plasticity of formica, they sacredly sealed their commitment to one another:

Allen: I promise my "two special talents—my creative sense of literary craft kicks, and my insight into mystical Sanctity union with God."

Peter: I promise my physical and emotional love.

Allen: I promise "to stay with you to whatever eternal consciousness," and not enter heaven until I can get you in.

Peter: I promise to do likewise.

There were other promises jointly pledged. "We vowed to each other that he could own me, my mind and everything I knew, and my body, and I could own him, and all he knew, and his body," Allen recalled. "And that we would give each other ourselves, so that we possessed each other as property, to do everything we wanted to, sexually or intellectually, and in a sense explore each other until we reached the mystical 'X' together, emerging two merged souls."

Allen: Do you promise these things?

Peter: "I do." Do you promise these things?

Allen: "I do."

Their vows spoken, they "looked into each other's eyes" and beheld "a kind of celestial cold fire that crept" over them and "blazed up and illuminated the entire cafeteria and made it an eternal place.... It was really a fulfillment of a fantasy." All that remained to complete Allen's fantasy was to give up his job, which he did soon,* and to write poems. In a journal entry from the time, Allen penned: "Peter, I feel as if I'm in heaven." And then this: "I'm on the verge of a great discovery. And the poems to write..."

---

*Towne-Oller closed its San Francisco office on May 1, 1955. Supported by six months of unemployment compensation, Allen now looked forward to writing.

PART III THE POEM & PROSECUTION

There was something wonderfully subversive about "Howl," something the poet had hidden in the body of the poem because it was too dangerous to say openly, something we had to uncover and decode.

—Jonah Raskin

Previous page: Allen Ginsberg typing "Howl" in 1955.

25.

I thought I [would] just write what I wanted to
without fear, let my imagination go, open secrecy,
and scribble magic lines from my real mind.
—Allen Ginsberg

MADNESS WAS ON his mind. There had been so much of it in his past and present. Would it ever end? Would his life dreams simply disintegrate into nothingness? At age twenty-nine, Allen Ginsberg sat on the precipice of dark despair. "I am no closer to the end of the line...than I was ten years ago and more removed from the innocence that then gave promise of sweetness thru experience," he wrote shortly after his birthday in 1955.

He had money problems: with a meager $30 a week in unemployment checks, Allen denied himself and Peter anything but the essentials. "Money problems of reality are not ghostly at all, they're solid as a rock I keep hitting my head on," he moaned. He had "spousal" problems: much as he adored him, Peter's seesaw mood swings—forlornly weeping at one moment and blithely chattering at the next—exhausted and depressed him.* He had girlfriend problems: his ex-lover, Sheila, arrived in a drunken fury one night

---

*"Allen was at a sexual dead end with Peter and he had even begun to sleep with a young woman downstairs, a certain Ms. Philips, whom he considered a pesky neurotic in spite of her professed love for him."

and screamed at him, "You can fuck *me* in the ass if *that's* what you want!" He had sleeping problems: he dreamed of Joan Vollmer forgotten in a foreign grave. And even more disturbing, he had writer's block: though he had studied Jack Kerouac's "Rules for Spontaneous Writing" and tacked them onto his wall, he couldn't get the right focus, muster enough energy, or tap the inspiration to follow them. It all weighed heavily on his mind, leaving him helpless to do much more than "trouble deaf heaven with...bootless cries."

Mottled sunshine filtered through the window facing Montgomery Street in the room that Allen used as his study and bedroom. Narrow dappled rays fell across a simple wooden table on which his typewriter rested amid journals, papers, and Kerouac's and Burroughs' manuscripts that he had yet to place with publishers. A slat of soft afternoon sun illuminated the plywood shelves hinged along the wall, where his books and records were haphazardly stacked. The early August light brought the lines of the roomy and plush armchair into sharp contrast. What radiant sound there was came from a three-speed Webcor monaural phonograph, on which Bach's intense but jubilant Mass in B Minor often played.

Ginsberg was alone in his room, sitting at his typing table. Since Peter had hitchhiked to New York in late July to bring his brother Lafcadio back to San Francisco, Allen now had uninterrupted time to confront his desolation and to jumpstart his writing. But how could he do that? The answer was in front of him, right there on the wall. Like chlorophyll that transforms light to life energy, Kerouac's "rules" for spontaneous writing finally worked to free his inhibitions. When Allen turned his inner madness outward, he released decades of demons that had haunted him.

> *I saw the best minds of my generation*
> *generation destroyed by madness*
> *starving, mystical, naked,*

who dragged themselves thru the angry streets at
   *dawn looking for a negro fix**

With those words, Allen aligned his life with his poetry. True to what Kerouac had advised—*"come* from within, out"—Ginsberg allowed his "subconscious to admit" its "own uninhibited" message. Typing away as if he were in a trance, he was *blowing* it out of his system like a crazy jazzman hopped up on pure, uncut spontaneity.

who poverty and tatters and fantastic minds
   sat up all night in lofts
      contemplating jazz,

Allen was on to something new. With rebel flair, he broke away from the short, pretty, rhyming lines typical of mainstream poetry. Echoing Whitman, he hollered out long lines that spoke to the ear— but his were harsh and angry lines. He latched onto the word *who* as the base to begin each furious strophe, often dividing his thought into the triadic structure that he had learned from the poet Williams Carlos Williams.

who bared their brains to heaven under the El
   and saw Mohammedan angels staggering
      on tenement roofs illuminated,

---

*These opening lines from Allen's first typewritten draft, which repeated the word "generation," derived from an earlier journal entry: "I saw the best mind angel-headed hipsters damned." When finally published, the opening lines of "Howl" read: "I saw the best minds of my generation destroyed by madness, starving hysterical naked, / dragging themselves through the negro streets at dawn looking for an angry fix, / angelheaded hipsters burning for the ancient heavenly connection to the starry dynamo in the machinery of night."

Here was Bill Cannastra, one of the best of those minds. His flesh became words, agonizing words, in a line that harkened back to his tragic subway death. Now Allen built momentum with each repetitive and rhythmic *who*. His subconscious spit out another anguished memory—this one of Carl Solomon, a prisoner of the asylum who, like others, screamed when his brain made contact with burning electrodes.

> *who sat in rooms naked and unshaven*
> *listening to the Terror through the wall,*

Poor Naomi was never freed from her own madness. In his mind's eye, Allen saw the unbearable lunacy that he had witnessed only weeks earlier at Pilgrim State Hospital.

> *who demanded sanity trials accusing the radio of hypnotism,*
> *& were left with their insanity*
> *and their hands and a hung jury,*

Nothing, however, quite rivaled the craziness that sucked the life out of David Kammerer the night that Lucien Carr stabbed his friend again and again and again. The specter of that horrifying 1944 killing struck Allen's psyche as he typed away.

> *who cut out each others hearts on the banks of the Hudson*
> *lifes a drama on a great lost stage*
> *under the crimson streetlamp of the moon,*

And then there was the memory of Herbert Huncke, the friend who first taught Allen what it truly meant to be "beat." Herbert revealed to him unforgettable physical and mental suffering when he showed up on his doorstep in the bitter winter of 1948.

> *who wandered all night with their shoes full of blood*
> *on the snowbanks of East River looking for the door*
> *to open on a roomful of steamheat and opium,*
> *picking his scabs and saying who is my friend?*

There were more *who's*—seventy-eight of them in total in the first draft of the poem. They ran the gamut from the gang's 1945 antics in Joan Vollmer's upper West Side apartment ("who purgatoried their bodies night after night with dreams, with drugs, with waking nightmares, alcohol and cock and endless balls"); to the infamous 1949 car chase ("who flew on out of cars in one shoe upside down on Utopia Boulevard with the hyena sirens of eternity wailing in the void"); to the notorious sexploits of Neal Cassady ("who copulated all weekend ecstatic and insatiate").

Allen used sex slang ("ultimate cunt and come") to sharpen his images of promiscuity. And unconcerned about the popularity of his message or the vulgarity of his words, he defied cultural conventions and legal taboos by flying the banner of homosexual freedom, a freedom born out of his experiences and fantasies.

> *who let themselves be fucked in the ass*
> *by saintly motorcyclists, and screamed with joy,*
> *who were blown by those human angels, the sailors,*
> *caresses of Atlantic and Caribbean love,*

With nocturnal energy, Allen typed as light sunk into darkness. His acute concentration blocked out whatever discomfort he felt from the hardness of his high-backed wooden chair. The pulse of his "bardic breath" rhythms propelled him; the flow of his foot-long free-verse lines sustained him; and the power of his compassion for human affliction emboldened him. He interjected literary devices—repeating words to suggest sounds ("who lit cigarettes in boxcars

boxcars boxcars racketing through snow") and juxtaposing inapposite images to give new impressions ("who listened to the crack of doom on the hydrogen jukebox")—and was energized by the special effects they created.

Allen *typed typed typed typed typed*. He filled seven pages of single-spaced strophes, rejecting inapt words or inferior phrases with "xxxx" strikeouts. Winding down to the end, he knew that he had done it. He had breached the dam that obstructed his poetic imagination. And with the fury of a Hebraic prophet, he had railed on behalf of the madmen and madwomen in his life.* The poem was a "gesture of wild solidarity, a message into the asylum, a sort of heart's trumpet call," he later recalled.

Low on adrenaline, Allen put a final sheet of paper into his manual typewriter. He needed to declare explicitly his sympathetic identification with Carl Solomon, whom he treated as the poetic symbol of mad victimization in a cruel and loveless world. Eking out his last bit of energy, he typed a few lines more, addressing the friend who had recently been committed in Pilgrim State Hospital:

> *Carl Solomon!*
> *I am with you in Rockland*
>   *where you're madder than I am*
> *I am with you in Rockland*
>   *where you stay for the rest of your life*

Finally, exhilaration gave way to exhaustion. Rising slowly from his writing table, Allen collapsed into the sofa bed across the room and drifted into a peaceful sleep.

---

*But for a few oblique references, Kerouac and Burroughs were missing from the poem, perhaps because Ginsberg did not consider their minds to have been destroyed by madness.

—◈◈◈—

"**YOUR HOWL** FOR CARL SOLOMON is very powerful," Jack Kerouac wrote to Allen from Mexico City. Ginsberg had sent the original draft of the poem to him shortly after he had composed it. Jack's words meant a lot to Allen, coming as they did from the man who had tutored him in spontaneous writing. In a reply letter, Allen acknowledged the debt to his friend: "I realize how right you are, that was the first time I sat down to blow, it came out in your method, sounding like you, an imitation practically. How far advanced you are on this."

The manuscript contained, however, numerous strikeouts and initial revisions marked in pink pencil. Immediately, they caught the critical eye of the master of spontaneous prose. "I don't want," Kerouac added, "[the poem to be] arbitrarily negated by secondary emendations.... I want your lingual SPONTANEITY or nothing... the first spout is the only spout." Such spontaneity was the fuel that was igniting Kerouac's own burst of poetic energy. In the same letter to Allen, Jack bragged of completing "150 bloody poetic masterpieces in MEXICO CITY BLUES," his first full collection of poetry.* And on that very day, Kerouac also wrote to Sterling Lord: "MEXICO CITY BLUES... will do for poetry what my prose has done, eventually change it into a medium for *Lingual Spontaneity*." Allen Ginsberg's "Howl for Carl Solomon" was a sign that Jack Kerouac was right.

This avant-garde writing style much appealed to the avant-garde Lawrence Ferlinghetti, now the sole owner of the celebrated City Lights Books and publisher of a Pocket Poets Series. He knew Ginsberg from his frequent visits to City Lights. Ferlinghetti "saw him as another of those far-out poets and wandering intellectuals who had

---

Mexico City Blues was not published until 1959, when it received a savage review in the *New York Times* by Kenneth Rexroth.

started hanging out" in the three-year-old North Beach bookstore. They occasionally strolled together, taking Lawrence's dog, Homer, for a walk and ended up at Mike's, a pool hall, for beers and burgers. Ferlinghetti also knew Allen's work, having recently rejected *Empty Mirror*. But "Howl for Carl Solomon" was different. It was, in Lawrence's estimation, "the most significant single long poem" written "since World War II." So he offered to publish the work, when completed, as the fourth volume of "Pocket Poets." Allen was ecstatic. Finally, he would join the publishing ranks of his fellow Beats— Kerouac, Holmes, and Burroughs. "City Lights Bookstore here . . . will put out 'Howl' (under that title) next year," he boasted to Jack.

With the return of Peter and his teenage brother, some of the madness of "Howl" hit home. Lafcadio spent up to six hours a day in the bathroom and squawked tirelessly about making millions of dollars on schemes like inventing a rocket ship to go to the moon. It drove Allen nuts, and at a time when he needed all his concentration to complete his poem. Since Peter worked at the post office and Allen took part-time odd jobs, there was enough money for him to rent a hideaway. He did just that on September 1, 1955, when he moved to 1624 Milvia Street in Berkeley. Allen adored his respite from the madness on Montgomery Street; he described it as a "35 per mo. ivy-covered one room (plus kitchen & bath) cottage on side street, garden and apricot tree around, private and Shakespearean." Its backyard was "filled with vegetables and flowers." It was a place where he could "write a lot."

26.

JACK KEROUAC was fixated on the death of Jesus Christ. His diaries and journals were filled with entries about and drawings of the crucifixion. In his Columbia University days, he sat in his dorm room and listened to the *St. Matthew Passion* by Johann Sebastian Bach; he considered it to be divinely inspired. That work about Good Friday, one of the greatest choral compositions ever created, was a favorite of Jack's.

Now the magnificent first chorus of the *Passion* played at full volume. Its slow, heavy, and rhythmic pulse beat on and on, as though capturing the sounds of Christ's footsteps as he dragged the cross on his whip-torn shoulder to Golgatha. The tension of the orchestral opening pulled on Jack's God-loving soul as he listened to it on the Webcor phonograph at Allen's Milvia Street cottage. Lost in his reveries, assorted images flitted through his mind: like those of the dusty roads on which he bummed rides out of El Paso after leaving Mexico...like those of the star-filled evening when he slept on a Santa Barbara beach a couple of days before...like those of the sexy blonde in a strapless bathing suit who gave him a lift in her Mercury convertible...like those of the tender night that he spent sleeping with Carolyn Cassady...and like those of the joyful reunion that he had just experienced with his old friend Ginsberg.

Allen was excited when he first told Jack about an upcoming poetry event at a hip, artsy hangout called 6 Gallery, with an illuminated 6 floating above its windowed entry doors. He had talked about the place with Michael McClure, a twenty-three-year-old poet whom he had met a year earlier at a San Francisco writing workshop. Michael had told Allen that Wally Hedrick, one of the owners of 6 Gallery, was willing to host a poetry bash. Since McClure himself lacked the time to do it, he suggested that Ginsberg organize it, although he promised to read a few poems. Thrilled to do so, Allen now asked Jack to join the event he was planning. Perhaps Jack could recite something from *Mexico City Blues*. Kerouac declined; he didn't like performing before strange crowds. He agreed to come, however, being especially eager to witness Allen's first public reading of his spontaneous "Howl."

Jack knew some of the people who were slated to participate in the 6 Gallery happening. In fact, he had been with three of them, only a week or so earlier, at one of Kenneth Rexroth's Friday evening literary soirées. Gary Snyder and Philip Whalen, former roommates at Reed College who were both poets and serious students of Buddhism, were there. Gary and Philip planned to recite some of their recent works, and Rexroth accepted an invitation to give a few remarks to kick things off.

Kerouac thought well of Snyder. Gary was a "lumberjack" he-man, "wiry and fast and muscular," but with a sensitive spiritual side. There was "something earnest and strong and human hopeful" that Jack appreciated in Gary. Whalen struck a slightly different chord in Jack. The "big fat bespectacled quiet" Philip came across to him as a goofy "booboo," though "goodhearted." Nonetheless, what tickled Kerouac about both of them was that they were familiar with his recently published *New World Writing* article, and liked it.

Rexroth, too, had complimented the piece in a recent KPFA-FM radio broadcast. Yet that was not enough to win Kerouac's friendship. He was uncomfortable around the "bow-tied wild-haired old anarchist fud" who held himself out as the *eminence grise* of the San Francisco literary scene. And he particularly disliked Rexroth's arrogance, as when Kenneth put people down with "his snide funny voice." That Friday night at the soirée, Kerouac was the brunt of Rexroth's sarcasm. It happened when the evening's discussion turned to Buddhism. Jack was going on about the *Pure Land Sutra*, one of several spiritual works he had read. Gary and Philip, familiar with the meditation manual, joined in. Jack was jubilant: "Why, there are other people who have read these texts!" The haughty Rexroth, unwilling to yield the limelight to this dilettante, brought him down a notch: "Everybody in San Francisco is a Buddhist, Kerouac! Didn't you know that?"

The other poet to appear at 6 Gallery was Philip Lamantia. Jack had known Philip as a friend years earlier in New York, where they used to bop back and forth from Latin dance halls to Black jazz clubs. And they shared similar outlooks on life, poetry, and spirituality. To Kerouac, Lamantia was an "out-of-this-world genteel-looking Renaissance Italian" type, with a priestly air.

Describing the 6 Gallery program, Allen told Jack about the advertising campaign that he had orchestrated. One hundred printed postcards were mailed, and handbills hung in numerous North Beach bars to publicize the event. The postcards read:

6 POETS AT 6 GALLERY

Philip Lamantia reading mss. of late John Hoffman—Mike McClure, Allen Ginsberg, Gary Snyder & Phil Whalen—all sharp new straightforward writing—remarkable collection of angels on one stage reading their poetry. No charge, small collection for wine and postcards. Charming event.

Kenneth Rexroth, M.C.

8 PM Friday Night October 7, 1955
6 Gallery 3119 Fillmore St.
San Fran

Jack looked forward to that special Friday night. Would listening to the poets be nearly as glorious as listening to Bach? Would experiencing "Howl for Carl Solomon" be like experiencing the *St. Matthew Passion*? He hoped so.

———

"Howl" marked a return of poetry
to the art of vocalization.
—Mikal Gilmore

KENNETH REXROTH was eager to get things started. Kerouac and the boys rolled in a bit late, coming from Vesuvio's bar with Lawrence and Kirby Ferlinghetti in an old model Austin. Jack saw that Allen's postcards and promo had worked. The gallery was jam-packed. Some 150 Bohemians, anarchists, musicians, poets, painters, professors, visionaries, and cynics had journeyed to the "Negro section" of the city to hear six poets at 6 Gallery. Clad in "various costumes, worn-at-the-sleeves corduroy jackets, scuffy shoes," and "books sticking out of their pockets," the nonconformists crammed into the old converted auto-repair shop*—two adjoining rooms with dirt floors and a bathroom door that would not lock. They stood under a big-beamed ceiling and mingled alongside seven pillars that ran up and down the center of the space. Seizing the

---

*6 Gallery was originally a carriage house built in 1906. A station for stage coaches, it was reworked in the 1950s into an automobile repair shop, which was thereafter converted into a cooperative art gallery founded by six artists (Wally Hedrick, Hayward King, Deborah Remington, John Allen Ryan, David Simpson, and Jack Spicer).

opportunity, the already lubed Kerouac and his Boston Irish friend, Bob Donlin, worked the crowd for a booze collection.

Jack took in the first half of the event sitting at the edge of the platform, guzzling from his jug and noting the madcap drift of things. The poets sat in large chairs, arranged in a semicircle on a small low platform at the back end of the place. A surrealist sculpture—splintered pieces of orange crate floating in Plaster of Paris—hovered behind them. Rows of folding chairs were filled with countercultural types; the overflow crowd squeezed into every inch of space left in the smoke-clouded environment.

Sporting a bow tie and a pinstripe cutaway, Rexroth stood before a makeshift podium. He began by joking, "This is a lectern for a midget who is going to recite the *Iliad* in haiku form." He then commented seriously on San Francisco as a unique island of bohemian culture, like Barcelona of the Spanish Anarchists. Rexroth handed the program over to Lamantia, who read John Hoffman's surrealist poetry and turned to McClure, who recited his "Point Lobos Animism" poem before yielding the spotlight to Whalen, who delivered two poems—"Plus Ça Change" and "The Martyrdom of Two Pagans." With his eyes closed and his back to the poets, Kerouac nodded at the lines he liked, sometimes shouting out "wow"s and "yes"es of approval between swigs from his gallon of Thunderbird.

After the intermission, Rexroth took to the orange-crate podium once again to silence the audience. Jack and his buddy Bob stumbled back into the room, hauling more jugs of cheap California burgundy to pass around during the second half of the night's program. It was around eleven P.M.

"Hey, Natalie," Jack yelled, as his eyes caught Natalie Jackson's red hair. Neal, dressed in his railroad brakeman's uniform with watch and vest, stood behind her, his arms encircling her waist. She took a "big slug" from the jug and so did her man. Jack hoped to loosen things up. Too many of these so-called "hip" types had just sat and stood there lifelessly during the first half.

As Kerouac moved in their midst, he eyed his former girlfriend, Jinny Baker, a twenty-three-year-old Japanese woman. Jack was taken aback: she was "beautifuller than ever." "Jinny," he called out. Theirs was a love that had gone sour, and she apologized for her role in that: "I was wrong." It didn't matter now. He was there to hear Allen, so he appeased her with a convenient, "I am madly in love with you," and walked on. When the houselights dimmed, Neal Cassady looked over to Peter Orlovsky, with whom he had spoken earlier. The two of them waited for their poet-hero to begin. Kerouac, Ferlinghetti, Snyder, and Whalen—all of whom already had read the first part of "Howl"*—were also eager to hear the bard vocalize his clarion call.

Slightly intoxicated, the young man with the curly, black hair nervously strode from the back of the gallery to take the stage. Clean-shaven and wearing a charcoal-gray suit, white shirt, and tie, he cut a formal figure—as if he were about to give a funeral oration. Uneasily shifting his feet, Allen Ginsberg found his center of balance and announced the title of his new poem:

Howl for Carl Solomon

Glancing at his manuscript through black, horn-rimmed glasses, he began in a calm, quiet, but pointed tone:

> *I saw the best minds of my generation destroyed by madness,*
> *starving, hysterical, naked,*
> *dragging themselves through the negro streets at dawn looking*
> *for an angry fix,*

---

*Ginsberg chose to read only part I of "Howl" at the 6 Gallery, since it was the only section that he considered complete enough to be performed in public.

angelheaded hipsters exploring for the ancient shuddering
connection between the wires and the wheels of the dynamo
of night,

Allen started slowly, pausing at each comma, punctuating adjectives with staccato force. His words bespoke the craving in the hungry soul for a bond to the heavenly force that governs the constellations.

who got busted in their beards returning through Laredo with
a belt of marijuana for New York,
who passed through universities with radiant cool eyes
hallucinating Arkansas and Blake-light tragedy among the
scholars of war,

With every "who," he breathed deeply and propelled his voice forward to build rhythmic pulse. The base word *who* grounded him. He gained more confidence as he launched defiant images with each new strophe.

who burned cigarette holes in their arms protesting the
narcotic tobacco haze of capitalism,
who passed out supercommunist leaflets in Union Square
weeping and undressing, while the sirens of Los Alamos
wailed them down....
who screamed on all fours in the subway, and were dragged off
the roof waving genitals and manuscripts,

All this talk of genitals made Ruth Witt-Diamant very uncomfortable. It was not so much that the founder of the San Francisco Poetry Center and a sponsor of poetry readings at 6 Gallery was a bluenosed prude. Hardly. But Allen's sexually explicit language—the *cock*'s and *cunt*'s, the getting "blown" and "fucked in the ass"—was a bit too scandalous for her tastes. Such "obscene" words at a general public performance, not to mention the open drinking, all in the presence of minors, could well bring down the law. Gesturing frantically at Rexroth, she signaled that Ginsberg must moderate his expletives. Kenneth, by contrast, appreciated the significance of the poetic breakthrough that he heard; he would not raise a finger to curtail it. There was nothing for Ruth to do except tolerate Allen's uninhibited vernacular.

> who copulated ecstatic and insatiate with a bottle of beer a
> sweetheart a package of cigarettes a candle and fell off the
> bed, and continued along the floor and down the hall and
> ended fainting on the wall with a vision of ultimate cunt
> and come eluding the last gyzym of consciousness,

Through the fog of his alcoholic stupor, Jack Kerouac heard the human horn of Allen's voice blowing long and powerful phrases, exhaling his pent-up fury like a jazzman wailing on an atomic saxophone. It was spontaneous poetry in action. He heard it beat down to his soul; he felt it shake down to his bones. Jack wanted Allen to take it to the next exhilarating level. Caught up like a brother-in-arms, he shouted out his support: "Go! Go! Go!" And go Allen did... all the way back to a place in time and a place in Jack's mind.

> who journeyed to Denver, who died in Denver, who came back
> and waited in Denver, watched and went away finally to
> find out the future,
> who fell on their knees in hopeless cathedrals praying for each
> others' salvation...

The words rang in Neal's ears. Denver... the slums of Denver, the bums of Denver, the altars of Denver, the joyrides of Denver, the jails of Denver, the whores of Denver. Pavlovian Denver. He responded, "Go! Go! Go!"

Allen now came to the strophes in his poem that were the most personal and poignant for him, those dedicated to his mother and to his friend Carl Solomon. His voice deepened with a tenderness born in empathy, as he pledged solidarity to the madman he met in an asylum.

> *ah, Carl, while you're not safe I am not safe, and now you're in*
> *the total soup of Time—*

The crowd could not contain itself. His listeners joined in a thunderous cadence: "Go! Go! Go!" They stomped their feet; they snapped their fingers; they clapped their hands. "Go! Go! Go!" Feeding on their life force, Allen now increased his speed, raised his pitch, and amplified his volume, as he pushed his voice to its maximum power. Swaying with the rhythm of his lines, he chanted his ending with hypnotic rabbinical passion.

> *the madman bum and angel beat in time, unknown, yet putting*
> *down what might be left to say in Time come after death,*
> *and rose reincarnate in the clothes of ghostly jazz in the*
> *goldhorn shadow of the band and blew the suffering of*
> *America's naked mind for love into an eli eli lamma lamma*
> *sabacthani saxophone cry that shivered the cities down to*
> *the last radio*
> *with the absolute heart of the poem of life butchered out of*
> *their own bodies good to eat a thousand years.*

Relentless. Merciless. Wondrous. The unspoken had been spoken...for some fourteen metaphoric minutes. Madness had been outed. It was a howling manifesto that transcended logic and embraced mysticism. Every woman, man, and minor there experienced it. Rexroth cried.

Neal rushed up to the stage. He grabbed Ginsberg's hand, shook it heartily, and said, "Allen, my boy, I'm proud of you." Allen was touched. As he looked around, he saw Jack. Did he appreciate the subterranean meaning and the inspired sound of the poem? Indeed, he did. Kerouac had heard the future, and he told Allen that "Howl" would make him famous in San Francisco. Not to be outdone, Rexroth demurred: "This poem will make you famous from bridge to bridge."

After Gary Snyder concluded the program with his reading of "A Berry Feast," the poets went out to celebrate. They ate at Sam Wo's Chinese restaurant, where Jack first learned to eat with chopsticks, and then resorted to a favorite hangout, The Place, for yet more drink...cocksure that a corner to the counterculture had been rounded. "We had gone beyond a point of no return," Michael McClure recalled, "and we were ready for it, for a point of no return....[We knew] at the deepest level that a barrier had been broken."

Lawrence Ferlinghetti was similarly confident, though he did not join his friends. Rather, he and his wife returned to their top-floor apartment at 339 Chestnut Street. And, as the story goes, he proceeded straight to his study where he composed a telegram to Ginsberg.* In the historical shadow of Emerson's celebrated response to Whitman's *Leaves of Grass*, the telegram read: "I greet you at the beginning of a great career. When do I get the manuscript?"

---

*Ginsberg's archivist and biographer, Bill Morgan, wrote in 2006: "The following day Ferlinghetti supposedly sent him a telegram paraphrasing Emerson's letter to Whitman....Later, in 1964, Allen couldn't remember if Ferlinghetti had really sent a telegram or not. In some ways it seems unlikely, since even short telegrams were expensive, but Lawrence distinctly remembers sending it via Western Union. A twenty-year search of Ginsberg's archive has failed to turn up the telegram, but in sentiment, it certainly happened, if not in fact." Morgan's reference to Ginsberg's recollection is based on a 1964 letter that Allen wrote to his Italian translator, Fernanda Pivano: "Ferl[inghetti] sent telegram only ironically, I don't remember if he really did that." In contrast, Michael Schumacher, another Ginsberg biographer, maintains that both Allen and Lawrence Ferlinghetti confirmed in interviews that such a telegram was sent and received, though no other evidence of it exists. Whatever the fact of the matter, the significance of such a telegram would have been readily understood by Ginsberg, an avid reader of Whitman. Almost exactly one hundred years before the 6 Gallery reading, on July 21, 1855, Ralph Waldo Emerson wrote to Walt Whitman to thank him for the gift of a copy of *Leaves of Grass*. Emerson considered it "the most extraordinary piece of wit and wisdom that America has yet contributed." And he continued: "I greet you at the beginning of a great career, which yet must have had a long foreground somewhere, for such a start."

27.

HE COULD NOT PURGE the name from his mind...

Moloch. *Ba'al* Moloch. The Sacred Bull. The Canaanites, Ammo-
nites, Moabites, and other Punic cultures in the ancient Near East
feared Moloch's fury. To appease him, they offered up their first-
born children to be burned or slaughtered. This pagan figure, however, was an enemy of the Hebrew God. "You shall not give any
of your offspring to sacrifice them to Molech," Leviticus sternly
instructed the Jews, "and so profane the name of your God: I am
the LORD."

Allen Ginsberg came face to face with Moloch one evening in
late August 1955. It happened after he and Peter had taken peyote. Strolling the streets of San Francisco, he was overcome by a
demonic presence. The piercing eyes of a monster startled him. As
they approached Powell and Sutter Streets, the sinister face of a
Death Head loomed ever larger. It stared down at them, as if eager
to seize their souls. Allen had seen this mask of Moloch before, ten
months earlier at Sheila Williams' apartment. Then, too, peyote had
expanded his visionary perception. When he looked out her open
window, he spied the image of Moloch through the wisps of night
fog. It was the silhouette of the tall tower of the Sir Francis Drake
Hotel, with three lit windows that he imagined to be the eyes and

nose of this King of Evil. Writing to Jack Kerouac, Allen recounted his foreboding encounters with Moloch: "We wandered on Peyote all downtown," and saw the "Moloch-smoking building in red glare downtown St. Francis Hotel, with robot upstairs eye & skullface, in smoke, again."

Now, weeks after the 6 Gallery triumph, Allen sat in a cafeteria at the base of the Drake Hotel. He muttered "Moloch," "Moloch," "Moloch" to himself. Sipping coffee, he penned that mantra into snippets for the second part of "Howl." Those same words had rung in his ears earlier when he rode the Powell Street cable car. With each *clang, clang, clang* of the trolley, his mind chanted in rhythm with the sound: *Moloch, Moloch, Moloch.*

Ginsberg then revised that text over and over at his Milvia Street cottage, much to Jack Kerouac's dismay. While he was staying with Allen in the fall of 1955, Jack acted as his writing coach, counseling him to stick to the principles of spontaneous composition. But "no 'spontaneous' poem was more thoroughly rewritten" than "Howl." For months after debuting part I of "Howl," Allen typed one draft after another of part II—some seventeen typewritten drafts followed the handwritten original. As the manuscript evolved, "Moloch" took on more ominous tones.

> *What sphinx of cement and aluminum bashed open their*
> *skulls and ate up their brains and imagination?*
> *Moloch! Solitude! Filth! Ugliness! Ashcans and unobtainable*
> *dollars! Children screaming under the stairways! Boys*
> *sobbing in armies! Old men weeping in the parks!*

Hunched at his typewriter for hours on end, Allen elaborated on the characteristics of the pagan god. As he added, deleted, and modified again and again, he murmured aloud, "Moloch," "Moloch," "Moloch." Gary Snyder, who shared the tiny one-room cottage with him, was flabbergasted by Allen's trance-like trope. Sitting cross-legged, Japanese-style, on the floor rug, Gary struggled to concentrate through the background muttering, as he translated Han Shan from the Chinese. Finally, he called out in jest: "Moloch who reaches up at night thru the bottom of the toilet bowl and grabs my pecker everytime I try to take a crap!" Laughing at Gary and himself, Allen was not deterred. He worked on, using "Moloch" as his poetic base, to rail against the demon who infiltrated men's minds, implanted his evils there, and condemned all who opposed him.

Moloch! Moloch! Nightmare of Moloch! Moloch the loveless!
Mental Moloch! Moloch the heavy judger of men!

Fine-tuning his lines, Allen read aloud to correct the rhythm and to build rhetorical power. His recitation at 6 Gallery convinced him that "Howl" must be crafted for the ear, so dramatic flourish became his tuning fork. With metaphorical momentum, Allen denounced the forces of military-industrial capitalism that, like Moloch, devoured children.

Moloch whose mind is pure machinery! Moloch whose blood
is running money! Moloch whose fingers are ten armies!
Moloch whose breast is a cannibal dynamo! Moloch whose
ear is a smoking tomb!

Having spewed his fury against modern society for the massacre and maddening of its innocent youth, Ginsberg switched gears in the third part of his poem. His theme turned personal, to memories of his days in an asylum. Mercy and compassion animated his sentiments for those who, like Carl Solomon, rebelled against Moloch. What few lines Allen had first typed and then recited at 6 Gallery about Solomon now multiplied into a repeating refrain of solidarity,

"I am with you in Rockland," that united him with Carl's plight. While Ginsberg took some license with the facts—Solomon was never in Rockland, he was in Pilgrim State Hospital*—he nonetheless sympathetically identified with a madness that ate away at the best minds of Allen's generation.

> *I'm with you in Rockland*
> > *where you imitate the shade of my mother . . .*
> *I'm with you in Rockland*
> > *where we are great writers on the same dreadful typewriter*

Ginsberg memorialized the pranks and predicaments of his months with Solomon at the Psychiatric Institute. How comic the time that he and Carl hysterically pounded on the piano in the common room, as the ward nurses and doctors scrambled in to control the madmen! How tragic the fifty insulin shock treatments that Carl suffered there and the electroshock therapy he was currently undergoing at the Pilgrim State Hospital!

> *I'm with you in Rockland*
> > *where you bang on the catatonic piano the soul is innocent*
> > *and immortal it should never die ungodly in an armed*
> > *madhouse*
> *I'm with you in Rockland*
> > *where fifty more shocks will never return your soul to its*
> > *body again from its pilgrimage to a cross in the void*

---

*Solomon later took exception to yet other inaccuracies in the poem and to the very use of his name. Decades later, Ginsberg described such use as "sympathetic attentiveness." Nonetheless, this invasion of Solomon's privacy happened at a time when Allen held back on his own secrets. As he explained in 1986: "I used Mr. Solomon's return to the asylum as an occasion for a masque of my feelings toward my mother . . ."

Allen ended part III with its most tender and blissful strophe. He loved his idyllic retreat at 1624 Milvia Street, the place that Jack Kerouac romantically described as a "little rose-covered cottage" with "a perfect little kitchen," "a perfect little bathroom," and "one fine old tree that I loved to sit under and meditate on those cool perfect starry California October nights." The last image of Allen's poem invoked that sanctuary, far from Moloch and madness, where he might reunite with Carl and comfort his sorrows.

> I'm with you in Rockland
>> in my dreams you walk dripping from a sea-journey on the
>> highway across America in tears to the door of my cottage
>> in the Western night

Although his "Howl for Carl Solomon" was already lengthy, Allen felt that the poem lacked balance. Its tone was negative and disheartening—too much so, in his opinion—and he searched his imagination for some way to end on a more positive note. It finally came to him one afternoon when he was riding the Kearny Street bus in San Francisco. Allen grabbed his notebook and ballpoint pen and scribbled furiously, his eyes streaming with tears of joy. He filled an entire page with lines inspired by the prophet Isaiah's vision of seraphim singing their praise to God with "Holy, holy, holy is the Lord of hosts; the whole earth is full of his glory." Echoing the seraphim in his own uninhibited style, Allen completed the fourth part of his poem, which needed fewer revisions before it reached final form. In doing so, he sanctified his band of friends, outsiders every one of them.

> Holy! Holy! Holy! Holy!...
> The world is holy! The soul is holy! The skin is holy! The nose is
>> holy! The tongue and cock and hand and asshole holy!...

Holy Peter holy Allen holy Solomon holy Lucien holy Kerouac
holy Huncke holy Burroughs holy Cassady holy the
unknown buggered and suffering beggars holy the hideous
human angels!

The prophetic voice that Allen now echoed, informed by his Buddhist learning, culminated in an uplifting exclamation. He carried the poem to a height of majesty that offset the depth of misery he recounted.

Holy the supernatural extra brilliant intelligent kindness of
the soul!

BEFORE DELIVERING his manuscript to Ferlinghetti, Ginsberg wanted the reactions of friends and family to his poem. "Look what I have done with the long line," Allen wrote to William Carlos Williams, sending "Howl" along with "A Strange New Cottage in Berkeley," "A Supermarket in California," and "Sunflower Sutra." These poems, he continued, answered "your demand for a relatively absolute line with a fixed base" and relied "on spontaneity & expressiveness which long line encourages." Focusing his critical eye on "Howl," the seventy-two-year-old Williams wrote back, identifying "a weak spot toward the end of the first part....It wouldn't be harmed by a little pruning at that point." Generally, however, Williams was admiring: these were "the most successful poems" of Allen's that he had yet seen. "You have something to say and say it supremely well. Congratulations. Best luck."

When Louis Ginsberg read his son's drafts, he responded with welcome insight and unwelcome reproach. "Howl" was "a wild, rhapsodic, explosive outpouring with good figures of speech flashing by in its volcanic rushing," Louis wrote. "It's a hot geyser of emotion suddenly released in wild abandon from the subterranean depths of your being." Allen was delighted that his father understood so much of the poem's purpose and spirit. Then came Louis's reservations: "I did not like the dirty words dragged in." Allen's father ended his letter, however, with a big pat on the back: "Bet you're making a literary reputation! Keep it up! You'll land somewhere in time!"

Allen hadn't landed yet. But with the publication of *Howl*, he hoped to do just that... and to leave behind the madness and misfortune that had long haunted him.

28.

Bless those who despitefully use you.
—Variation of Gospel teachings

CAROLYN CASSADY LIVED her faith. The thirty-two-year-old woman was an avid follower of Edgar Cayce, a clairvoyant of Presbyterian background. She believed in his Christianized version of Buddhist thought. His ideas on reincarnation, karma, holistic medicine, and the purpose of life appealed to her. Carolyn was taken by the insights Cayce gleaned through his psychic "readings" of the secrets of the universe, this when he lay in a self-induced meditative sleep state. His philosophy of positive thinking, a precursor to New Age consciousness, particularly struck her. She was convinced that, by focusing on the wrongs that she had done, or that Neal had done to her, she would only attract more of the same. "Cayce had said that no one meets a circumstance he hasn't the power to overcome—if he will," Carolyn explained. "This was welcome news, but then he also said, 'The stronger you are, the tougher the tests.'"

Neal, too, was charmed by Edgar Cayce. He was the first to introduce Carolyn to the spiritualist's teachings, asking her to read Gina Cerminara's *Many Mansions*, an account of Cayce's faith healings and his views on reincarnation. The couple discussed and debated Cayce's thinking, attended annual conferences in San Jose to hear lectures by his son, Hugh Lynn, and sought spiritual guidance from Lynn's associate, Elsie Sechrist, during those programs and afterward by mail. For Neal, Cayce's philosophy proved a convenient and comforting salve for his errant ways. Exploring the connection between reincarnation and his abusive treatment of Carolyn, Neal suggested to her that "it could be that I did something awful to you [in another life] and you didn't forgive me, so now I have to do more stuff so you'll learn forgiveness. I can't make it up to you if you still hold a grudge, see?"

Neal sorely tested Carolyn's faith the day she discovered two love notes in the pocket of his jeans, which she was about to launder. The first, dated April 12, 1955, was written to Neal from Natalie Jackson. She was the red-haired nude model in LaVigne's painting that Neal had shown Carolyn. Jackson's letter, penned at 11:10 P.M., was intimate: "I love you more now, but better.... I know your body—It's a mystery to me." And so on. The letter was signed "N." Had Carolyn immediately linked the signature with the nude portrait, she would have been even more furious. The second was a note to Natalie from Neal. "I dreamed of you last night.... The main part of the dream [was] the desire to find you again." This letter to his "perfect lover" was evidence of the latest in a long line of extramarital affairs, including the one with Allen, but this one apparently more serious.

Red-eyed and dispirited, Carolyn confronted Neal and asked him if he wanted a divorce; he told her he didn't. "But Neal—I just can't take anymore, *please*," she pleaded. "You don't love me at all, what could be more obvious? Why on earth must we stay married? This is no marriage." When Neal stressed that Natalie was no threat to their relationship, Carolyn retorted, "What relationship?"

Shortly thereafter, Neal moved into a San Francisco apartment with Natalie, returning to his San Jose family every two weeks on payday. What little comfort Carolyn received came from writing to her Caycean advisor, Elsie Sechrist, who responded that "'God will make the separation' if a spiritual state is endangered. Otherwise, love and patience would overcome." Trusting Elsie's counsel, Carolyn meditated and prayed for the strength to bear up under Neal's emotionally cruel antics. But there were even tougher tests of Carolyn's faith and fortitude to come.

One morning in the fall of 1955, Carolyn received a telephone call from Mr. Scoville, her investment banker in Cupertino. Neal and she had opened an account at Scoville's bank one year before, and their initial deposit had grown rapidly to $10,000. "Mrs. Cassady? I'm sorry to bother you again," Mr. Scoville apologized, "but when you and your husband were in the other day to withdraw your money, I forgot one paper for you to sign."

Carolyn was confused. "Oh, you must have the wrong Cassady," she replied. "I haven't been in your bank since last year."

When Scoville explained that a red-headed woman, claiming to be Carolyn Cassady, and her husband, Neal, had closed the joint investment account, Carolyn pieced the puzzle together. Impersonating Carolyn, Natalie Jackson had forged her name on the papers necessary to enable Neal to withdraw all $10,000. And Neal had talked his gullible lover into this felonious act!

Indignant at the fraud perpetrated on Mrs. Cassady and the bank, Mr. Scoville was ready to go to the police. "It took every ounce of grit [she] had not to let fly all the vindictiveness" she felt against Neal. She would "never have believed he'd go so far." But the spiritual path that had been laid out before Carolyn was one of silent long-suffering. No, she told Scoville, no need to press charges. Immediately, she rushed to her children's schools, removed them for the rest of the day, and drove to Cupertino to countersign the papers that Natalie had forged. Infuriated as Carolyn was, she would not allow her husband and his mistress to go to jail. It would not be the Caycean thing to do.

Expecting Neal to arrive home that night, Carolyn was uncertain whether, in a face-to-face encounter with her betrayer, she could hold it together. Repeating to herself the Christian maxims that strengthened her resolve—"'Judge not that ye be not judged,' 'Love your enemies,' 'Vengeance is mine, saith the Lord'"—she penned a bedside note for Neal. She wrote and rewrote until the message's tone was as dispassionate as she could muster.

"What did we say about getting greater tests as we grow stronger? It sure happens fast," the note began. "The good Lord decided I should know about your deal in Cupertino, too." Informing Neal that she took this blow as one more "opportunity to overcome rather than one to get even," Carolyn described her conversation with Mr. Scoville and the things she had done to let Natalie and him off the hook. There was nothing for her to do at this point, she figured, other than "hope the horses come in." With a stiff upper lip, Carolyn found the reserve to jest about Jackson's forgery: Natalie "could use a bit more practice on the C's."

It did not take Edgar Cayce's clairvoyance for Carolyn to predict the news that she learned from Neal the next morning. He took the money to bankroll his newfound obsession, "scientific" gambling at the Bay Meadows racetrack. Having invented a cock-eyed betting system—"always bet on the third-choice horses on the grounds that the odds are better and the first two choices are often overrated"—Neal wanted to wager enough to make them all sinfully rich. "I know what you're thinking, but this one really works. I'll show you—prove it to you," he had bragged to Carolyn earlier about his secret system. In the weeks following his bank caper, however, Neal's science experiment failed him. He squandered almost all of the $10,000.

Matters only got worse. Christmas was a little more than three weeks away, and Neal was still living with Natalie. Carolyn didn't like it, but didn't dwell on it. She had other things to think about, such as her three children, Cathy, Jami, and John, and what to do for them during the holidays. But those thoughts were interrupted as she sat down with a cup of coffee to read the morning paper. Her eyes scanned the headline on page two of the December 1, 1955, issue:

WOMAN FIGHTS OFF RESCUE, LEAPS 3 STORIES TO DEATH

A photograph of a building, with a dotted line drawn from roof to sidewalk, caught her attention. Then she saw it. A Packard parked in the street. A car just like Neal's. Her hands trembled. Her stomach turned with fear. With a sense of dread, she read on:

> An unidentified woman about 35 years old slashed her throat on a roof top at 1041 Franklin Street yesterday, then kicked free from the grip of a husky policeman and jumped to her death from a third-story fire escape.
>
> Wearing only a bathrobe and T-shirt, she stood poised outside the railing of the narrow fire escape walkway as Officer O'Rourke lunged through a window to grab her. "All I could do was dive through and grab," he said. "I got a grip on one arm and her robe just as she tried to kick loose. But I couldn't hold her. All at once I was just holding the robe, and she had fallen." His partner said she might have slashed herself with fragments from a broken skylight.

Was this Natalie? No, the dead woman was too old. Natalie was younger; Neal had told her she was twenty-four. And there were other Packards in San Francisco, after all. No, this tragedy didn't involve Neal. At least, Carolyn hoped so, though her doubts lingered.

The phone rang one hour later. She picked up the black receiver. "Carolyn," Neal's voice quivered. "Natalie...Natalie's dead."

"I saw the paper, Neal. I'm so sorry. Do you want to come home for a while?"

"Oh, could I?"

"Of course, Neal. This is your home still, like it or not. I know you loved her. It must be awful for you."

Neal poured himself into his big Packard. During the forty-five-mile trip southeast on Highway 101, his mind raced back to the hysteria that took Natalie over in the past few weeks. All of that speed she did—it just made her more anxious about being busted for her forgery. Images of her, pale and strung-out with terror-struck eyes, haunted him. He should have known once she tried to slit her wrists that something awful was about to happen. But Kerouac was there to comfort her the night before she died, the night Neal was out at work. Jack gave her a big dose of his Buddhist therapy. A lot of good that did. As Neal drove down the dark highway past Mountain View, he cursed himself for sleeping so soundly that he couldn't stop Natalie from going up to the roof and jumping. He was back home now; he needed Carolyn's comfort.

"I saw your car in the photograph. Where were you?" she asked.

"I was asleep, see? She got up and went out. I'd no idea, but when I heard the sirens, I thought of you and the kids getting involved and just grabbed my stuff and ran out the back way."

Sensitive to the situation, she replied, "I certainly thank you for that! What made her do it? Was it suicide, do you think?"

He moaned. "I don't know. Partially—no, I don't want to believe that." She felt "so guilty about forging your signature. . . . I kept telling her it was all right and that you weren't mad, but it didn't help." It was hard for him to continue. "She got so bad, she talked about nothing but sin and guilt and how we were going to be arrested for our sins." Recalling her self-destructive acts, Neal explained: "Last week she tried to cut her wrists, but with a dull knife, and I told her about suicide and not to think of it again. I thought she was better."

With Caycean reflection, Carolyn placed Natalie's death in a positive light. "Maybe it was a chance for her to change her course—start over. She seemed to have boxed herself in. It could be a merciful release, couldn't it?"

The thought consoled him. "Yeah, I suppose it really is better for her. She was insane—I couldn't help her." Neal moved back in the next day.

It was the fourth Beat death. Allen Ginsberg grieved and dealt with it as he had with the deaths of David Kammerer, Bill Cannastra, and Joan Vollmer Burroughs. He turned his pain into poetry:

> *Your truthful eyes troubling me too late.*
> *In the car coming over for Thanksgiving*
> *You gave me look so tearful I knew it was death,*
>   *or thought so . . .*

29.

DRAMA WAS NOT a word one would associate with Lawrence Ferlinghetti. He was not a jumper or junker. While news of Natalie Jackson's suicide sped through the back streets of North Beach and elsewhere, he never became personally involved in the mania that pointed down that path. He was no car-crazed Neal Cassady, no booze-broken Jack Kerouac, no gun-packin' Bill Burroughs, and no madness-prone Allen Ginsberg. Sure he knew them, liked them even, but their madcap ways were not his. Much of the passion that Ferlinghetti had, he poured into his work: selling and printing books.

City Lights Books. The name evoked "the head, heart, and undersoul" of the political, artistic, and literary communities of San Francisco in the 1950s. America's first all-paperback bookstore, named after Charlie Chaplin's famous 1931 movie, *City Lights*, opened in June 1953 in the Classical Revival–styled building at 261 Columbus Avenue. The pie-shaped one-room storefront featured classic and modern literary works, art and pop culture books, leftist and progressive political tracts, and uncommon newspapers and magazines. From late morning until midnight during the week and two A.M. on weekends, the store was a beacon for bohemians who dropped in to browse the stacks or hang in the basement where they read quietly or rapped coolly. The atmosphere was, in short, alternative.

To know City Lights Books was to know Lawrence Ferlinghetti. He was a man of many dimensions. He had his intellectual side: an M.A. from Columbia University and a Ph.D. from the University of Paris, Sorbonne, in literary studies; he taught college-level literature courses in San Francisco for a brief time and kept the close company of avant-garde literary minds such as Kenneth Rexroth and Kenneth Patchen. He had his artistic side: he painted, wrote poems and novels, and published his first collection of poetry, *Pictures of the Gone World*, in 1955. He had his political side: he was committed to a "left-leaning, libertarian, anarchistic political philosophy" and railed against artistic or literary censorship. Lawrence Ferlinghetti was also a savvy businessman. He cofounded City Lights with Peter Martin and then bought him out eighteen months later; shortly afterward, he launched City Lights Publishing and started the Pocket Poets Series. Inspired by the bookstore-publisher combo prevalent in Paris, he replicated the business strategy: "It seemed like a logical thing to do. I never understood why bookstores here didn't do it. The bookstore's a natural source of publicity for the press, and a place to sell the books."

Another thing Ferlinghetti was not was a Beat. "I was the last of the Bohemian generation when I arrived from Paris in San Francisco," Lawrence explained. "I arrived in San Francisco four years before Allen Ginsberg and the Beats did. I was still wearing my French beret." Older than most of the key Beat figures, the tall, slim, clean-cut man with translucent light-blue eyes, strong jaw, and receding dark hair presented more the image of a respectable small businessman than a beatnik, even though he seldom wore a tie and jacket. Moreover, neither his personality nor his poetry shared the feverish mania of Beat lifestyles or the frenetic energy of their writing styles. Ferlinghetti knew talent when he saw it, however, and was willing to make the literary and monetary most of it. He found that talent in Allen Ginsberg.

Nevertheless Lawrence was concerned. Three or so months after he offered to publish "Howl for Carl Solomon," he faced the specter of censorship.* He suspected that he "would be busted, not only for four-letter words," but also for the poem's "frank sexual, especially homosexual content." How could he bring this great Whitman-esque work to life if the government might abort it at the outset? Unless he could solve that riddle, he stood to lose not only the poem but all that he had created to make his bookselling and publishing dreams a reality.

It wasn't merely a matter of winning a censorship case; it was also a matter of affording to stay in the game. "We were just a little, unknown bookstore. We didn't have any resources for hiring law-yers," Ferlinghetti realized. So he contacted the Northern Califor-nia chapter of the American Civil Liberties Union. Good news. The ACLU agreed to defend him if anything came up. The prospect also pleased Allen. "Civil Liberties Union here was consulted and said they'd defend it if it got into trouble, which I almost hope it does," Allen told his father. "I am almost ready to tackle the U.S. Govt out of sheer self delight. There is really a great stupid conspiracy of unconscious negative inertia to keep people from 'expressing' themselves."

Before Allen could fight the good fight, however, he needed to finish revising "Howl for Carl Solomon" and selecting other poems for the book. Ginsberg made the final modifications to "Howl" by the end of April 1956; and Ferlinghetti and he went back and forth until they decided on nine additional poems, including "A Supermar-ket in California," "Sunflower Sutra," and "America." There was also the matter of the title: Lawrence persuaded Allen to "call it simply 'Howl,' making 'for Carl Solomon' a dedication, and thus implying

---

*Legally speaking, there were also possible issues of defamation and invasion of privacy relating to statements published about Carl Solomon. Fortunately for Ginsberg and Ferlinghetti, Solomon never filed any such actions.

a more universal significance." The contents of "Howl" likewise changed: the original part IV was taken out, renamed "Footnote to Howl," and inserted after the title poem.*

Because William Carlos Williams had responded so favorably to an earlier draft of "Howl," Allen urged that he be invited to write an introduction to the book. Williams penned more than five hundred words that spoke eloquently to the poem's compelling meaning and emotional force:

> He proves to us, in spite of the most debasing experiences that life can offer a man, the spirit of love survives to ennoble our lives if we have the wit and the courage and the faith—and the art! to persist.... Hold back the edges of your gowns, Ladies, we are going through hell.

Before the manuscript was ready to send to the printers, two other items needed attention. Allen inserted an epigraph quote by Walt Whitman for the book; the two unattributed lines that he chose from "Song of Myself" captured perfectly the essence of "Howl."

> *Unscrew the locks from the doors!*
> *Unscrew the doors themselves from their jambs!*

Similar to the unpublished *Empty Mirror*, Allen dedicated *Howl and Other Poems* to his Beat pals. Unlike the earlier dedication to Herbert Huncke, however, this one was to three friends—Jack Kerouac, William Seward Burroughs, and Neal Cassady—and to their

---

*In a 1998 interview, Ferlinghetti stated that he had persuaded Ginsberg to "leave out a whole section of 'Howl,' one whole, single-spaced page with a roman numeral at the top. I don't know what happened to that page," he noted. "There's no trace of that page anywhere."

writings. The dedication referred, in all, to thirteen unpublished manuscripts and concluded whimsically: "All of these books are published in Heaven." The fourth friend to be acknowledged was Lucien Carr; he was recognized for being "recently promoted to Night Bureau Manager of New York United Press."*

One of the things Lawrence Ferlinghetti liked about young Allen Ginsberg was his ability to promote himself and others. Part of the success of 6 Gallery was due to the publicity campaign that Allen orchestrated before the event. Now he did much the same for the forthcoming publication of *Howl and Other Poems*. Kenneth Rexroth's wife, Martha, cranked the ditto master at San Francisco State College to make the first copies of the manuscript, and Ginsberg sent out more than one hundred aniline-purpled ditto copies to family, friends, and literary mentors such as Professors Mark Van Doren and Lionel Trilling.

John Clellon Holmes liked the "beautiful gentleness" of the poems, the "real tenderness . . . the sweet humors, the wise giggles. . . . You make me love a world whose punished children still can love it so." Lucien Carr was upbeat: "Thought your *Howl* very good indeed. . . . A considerable departure and improvement over earlier stuff. Keep it up, as we of the petit Bourgeoisie say." And Van Doren had a few nice things to say, as well.

Positive vibes were everywhere. The momentum for *Howl* was building. Allen got a rush when he read the full "Howl" at a Berkeley theater in May 1956. The rapt crowd booed and hissed as Allen repeated "Moloch!" "Moloch!" Moloch!" The evening was a replay of 6 Gallery, with the same participants reading the same

---

*Although the first printing of *Howl and Other Poems* mentioned Lucien Carr in the dedication, subsequent printings did not. Lucien objected strongly to the use of his name. "I value a certain anonymity in life," he wrote Allen. "I hope that you bear that idiosyncrasy in mind in your next book—'Moan.'" Allen saw to it that his friend would not grumble again on this score.

poems. This time, however, Allen saw to it that press and photographers were there. Better still, his poem was being recorded for posterity—Fantasy Records planned to capture the fury of his voice on vinyl. He was on a roll, big-time. "You have no idea what a storm of lunatic-fringe activity I have stirred up," Allen boasted to his father.

To maintain that momentum, Allen took steps to ensure that publicity about the Berkeley reading and "Howl" remained positive. He knew that the young, bright poet and critic Richard Eberhart was writing a piece for the *New York Times* on the San Francisco Poetry Renaissance, and Ginsberg was anxious that the critic not put "Howl" in a false light. To prevent that, Allen wrote Richard a letter of some 4,500 words to describe the themes, technique, and values behind the poem. Now all that remained was to reap the benefits of his cautionary efforts on the glorious pages of America's great newspaper.

Coming from recent and expected highs, Allen hoped for more of the same. More electricity, more publicity, more praise. So he was excited when the mailman delivered a letter that bore the return address of Lionel Trilling. Here was the endorsement, the personal approval, that mattered to him. His heart sank, however, when his eyes fell on the first line from his admired mentor: "I'm afraid I have to tell you that I don't like the poems at all." The more Allen read, the more depressed he became. "I am being sincere when I say they are dull." Dull? How could "Howl" be dull? And even worse, Trilling denied that this poem's long lines could lay any claim to being Whitmanesque. "They are not like Whitman—they are all prose, all rhetoric, without any music.... There is no real voice here." It was a hard pill for Allen to swallow.

It was the story of Allen's life. One moment ascending, the next crashing. And when things got bad, they got real bad. This time the horrible news came by telegram delivered by Peter Orlovsky:

WESTERN UNION

TELEGRAM

MR ALLEN GINSBERG=

CARE ORLOVSKY=

5 TURNER TERRACE

SAN FRAN=

NAOMI GINSBERG DIED SUDDENLY SATURDAY AFTERNOON WOULD
APPRECIATE YOUR COMMUNICATING THIS TO ALLEN GINSBERG
HE MAY CALL ME AT HOTEL REGENT

EUGENE BROOKS=

Only three weeks earlier, Allen had tried to move Naomi from
Greystone to Northport, Long Island, to live with Orlovsky's
mother. But it didn't happen, and now Peter was on his Milvia
Street doorstep with news of her death by cerebral hemorrhaging.
Not finding Allen home, Peter scribbled on the back of the telegram:
"I got this at 7:30 pm, and here at 10:45 pm. Out to find you. Be back
soon. She's in the sunshine now. Love Peter." It was, nonetheless,
a dark moment. "Everything changes toward death. My mother.
Myself," Allen wrote in his journal. "My childhood is gone with my
mother.... Naomi is a memory. My 30 years is a memory to me."
This was the unsung hero of "Howl." Now she, too, was destroyed.*
Ready to ship out as a yeoman storekeeper on the USNS *Sgt. Jack J.
Pendleton* because he desperately needed to make some quick money,

---

*Allen later received Naomi's last letter to him, written two days before her death. After
congratulating him on reaching his thirtieth birthday, she commented on "Howl." "It
seems to me your wording was a little too hard. Do tell me what your father thinks of
it." Ever the protective mother, Naomi concluded: "I hope you are not taking drugs as
suggested by your poetry. That would hurt me. Don't go in for ridiculous things. With
love and good news. (mother) Naomi."

Allen did not attend Naomi's funeral. Instead, he boarded the vessel shouldering a satchel with his journal, some poetry books, and the printer's galleys of *Howl and Other Poems*.

Lawrence Ferlinghetti arranged with Villiers Publishers in London, a small poetry printer and vanity press, to print the first run (1,500 copies) of the fourth volume of his Pocket Poets Series. As he knew, Villiers was a reliable house that charged reasonable prices for its saddle-stitched letterpress work. The printer insisted, however, on the substitution of asterisks for "four-letter" words. Villiers was sensitive to this since *Miscellaneous Man*, one of its earlier projects, ran into censorial trouble in San Francisco because of "obscene" language. It did not want to repeat that scenario. Reluctantly, Ferlinghetti agreed, as did an equally unenthusiastic Ginsberg.

Bound for the Arctic Circle on the *Pendleton*, Allen scanned the galleys of his book. They were a complete mess. His carefully divided long lines were haphazardly broken on the printed page. Because detailed instructions had not been given to the printer, the stylistic integrity of his poems was seriously compromised. "This being my first book I want it right if can," Ginsberg wrote to Ferlinghetti. The "poems are actually sloppy enough written, without sloppiness made worse by typographic arrangement.... It looks like the whole book will have to be reset practically.... I will pay that no matter how much up to $200, which I guess it may well cost." Allen could not fathom the thought that his poetic debut would be marred by such a jumble. "I mean you can't tell *what* I am doing," he continued, "it looks like just primitive random scribbling in pages. I had not intended the prosody to be *that* arbitrary." Ferlinghetti was not about to leave Ginsberg in his distraught state; he ordered a new printing, but this time with precise guidelines.

When Allen received the corrected galleys in August, he sighed in deep relief. His long lines had been restored properly and for a fraction of what he had been willing to pay. "Everything worked out fine with the typography—it looks much better this way and it seems to have been real cheap to do—$20 is nuthin," Ginsberg told Ferlinghetti. In a moment of insecure humility, he admitted: "I shuddered when I read the poetry tho, it looks so jerry-built sloppy and egocentric most of it.... Reading it through I'm not sure it deserves all the care and work you've put into it and the encouragement you've given me." Still, Allen showed his gratitude for Lawrence's efforts to bring his "Howl" to light: "But what the hell, thank you anyway for all your courtesy and I hope few people will see it with such jaded eyes as I do.... I wonder if we will actually sell the thousand copies."

To ensure the sale of those copies, Ginsberg aimed to increase the buzz about *Howl and Other Poems* in literary circles. He provided Ferlinghetti with a list of some hundred luminaries to receive complimentary copies, including Kenneth Rexroth, Kenneth Patchen, W.H. Auden, T.S. Eliot, and Ezra Pound. Books were even mailed off to Charlie Chaplin and Marlon Brando.

Allen didn't learn what his cinematic heroes thought of his poems, but he found out how little Ezra Pound thought of them. William Carlos Williams forwarded Pound's response to him. Writing from St. Elizabeth's mental hospital in Washington, D.C., Pound told his friend, Williams, in verse: "If he's yours why dont yu teach him the valu of time to those who want to / read something that wil tell 'em wot they dont know." Pound's poetic poison was irritating. Here was one of the most talented and revolutionary poets—one of the best minds of his generation—sitting in a bughouse and saying that *Howl* was a waste of his time. He, like Lionel Trilling, found it uninspiring.

Allen's apprehension over sales was relieved when Richard Eberhart's piece, "West Coast Rhythms," appeared in the *New York Times Book Review*. The essay was a godsend. "The West Coast is the liveliest spot in the country in poetry today," it began. The story mentioned the Poetry Center at San Francisco State College, Kenneth Rexroth, Kenneth Patchen, Gary Snyder, Philip Whalen, and Michael McClure, too. But the lion's share of its attention was devoted to a "remarkable Poem" that had created "a furor of praise or abuse whenever read or heard. It is a powerful work, cutting through to dynamic meaning." This compelling work—"profoundly Jewish in temper"—was portrayed as a "howl against everything in our mechanistic civilization which kills the spirit.... It lays bare the nerves of suffering and spiritual struggle." And finally, in words that delighted the Buddhist poet, Eberhart added: "Its positive force and energy come from a redemptive quality of love, although it destructively catalogues evils of our time from physical deprivation to madness."

All this good ink came just as *Howl and Other Poems* worked its way through U.S. customs without incident, ready for distribution to bookstores everywhere. Allen Ginsberg was ecstatic, Louis Ginsberg proud, Lionel Trilling surprised, Ezra Pound dumbfounded, and the radical French-educated Lawrence Ferlinghetti happy as a Jacobin on Bastille Day.

Eberhart's article propelled Ginsberg and *Howl* into the limelight. *Life* magazine and *Mademoiselle* planned to cover the budding poetry movement and its star. Literary journals that had spurned him before now did everything to entice him to publish with them. It was a bright new day. "Beginning to get long admiring letters from starry-eyed Parkinson & N.Y. types about Howl," Allen wrote. "Agh! I'm sick of the whole thing, that's all I think about, famous authorhood, like a happy empty dream.... How beautiful tho. I guess I feel really good about it."

Languishing in Mexico City, with still no book contract for *On the Road*, Kerouac read those self-promoting words in the letter Ginsberg had sent to him. Bright as the day was for Allen, it was still a gloomy one for Jack.

30.

I just keep turning out manuscripts like a machine and they
just keep flying away into the void . . . what other writer can
keep this up and not go crazy like I'm about to do?
—Jack Kerouac

THERE IS SOMETIMES a fine line between fact and fiction. Jack Kerouac understood that and hoped to erase that line, or much of it. His *Road* manuscript, as Malcolm Cowley realized, "was not a work of fiction, but a documentary journal." Kerouac's candor, his real-life fiction, was key to his "theory of writing." In a letter to Cowley, Jack said as much: "The requirements for prose & verse are the same, i.e. *blow*—What a man most wishes to hide, revise, and un-say, is precisely what Literature is waiting and bleeding for—Every doctor knows, every Prophet knows the convulsion of truth.—Let the writer open his mouth & yap it." Such truth-telling was one of his manuscript's greatest strengths; it was also one of its greatest problems.

Kerouac's no-holds-barred writing style demanded that he use real names, revealing situations, and racy scandals. The manuscript was peppered with references to the Beat gang—Allen Ginsberg, Bill Burroughs, Lucien Carr, Neal and Carolyn Cassady, Herbert Huncke, and Joan Vollmer, among others. Its storyline recounted anecdotes like those from Neal's ribald life: "I saw the little midget newspaperselling woman with the short legs, on the corner of Curtis and Fifteenth. 'Man,' Neal told me, 'think of lifting her in the air and fucking her!'" There were other episodes in which real names were used in contexts rife with libelous innuendo: "Justin W. Brierly ... now a lawyer, a realtor, director of the Central City Opera Festival and also an English teacher in a Denver high school ... was purely and simply interested in young people, especially boys." And then there were those lines in which discretion about secret lives was abandoned: "Allen was queer in those days, experimenting with himself to the hilt, and Neal saw that, and a former boyhood hustler himself in the Denver night ... the first thing you know he was attacking Allen with a great amorous soul such as only a conman can have."

Such literary license made Malcolm Cowley anxious, and he told Kerouac so. Although Jack's narrative was compelling, how likely was it that his novel would get past a publisher's lawyers? They would pick its passages apart for fear of libel, obscenity, invasion of privacy, false light, and who knows what other abstruse legal claims?* Cowley was particularly sensitive to these issues now that a window of opportunity had opened for *On the Road*, and he didn't want any obstacles in its way. That window bore the name of Keith W. Jennison.

A new acquisitions editor at Viking, Jennison was exactly the kind of receptive and influential powerhouse that might rescue Kerouac. Only one year earlier in 1954, Jennison had written a novella about "a young man at the crossroads of life," titled *The Green Place*; the year before that, Doubleday had issued his amusing satire about America's

---

*At some point, of course, time trumps the limits of the law. Hence the legal problems that faced Kerouac and his publishers a half-century ago were of little or no concern in 2007 when Viking published *On the Road: The Original Scroll*, this after almost all of the characters portrayed in the work were dead.

car culture, called *The Half-Open Road*. Not only did Cowley admire Jennison's book-selling skills, but he also believed that Keith and Jack were fellow travelers down the same literary highway. So Malcolm prepared to submit the manuscript to Viking for a second time.

Kerouac desperately needed something positive to come of Cowley's connection to Jennison. Jack was stuck at his sister's home in Rocky Mount, North Carolina, with a bout of phlebitis; unable to hold a steady job, he couldn't even afford penicillin to fight off the illness. "[I] hope and pray that you and Keith will take and publish *Beat Generation*...and save me," Jack wrote Malcolm. "I'm about ready not only to stop writing, but jump off a bridge." Things were so bad, he complained, that he couldn't buy a beer or pay for long-distance calls to Sterling Lord's office.*

Much to Kerouac's relief, Cowley had accurately predicted Jennison's reactions. "Keith read the manuscript with great enthusiasm," Malcolm recalled, "and he had great force and conviction in presenting his case." At long last, the publishing gods smiled on poor Jack Kerouac. The good news circulated in the form of an internal memorandum from Evelyn Levine, one of Viking's staff editors. She summarized her evaluation concisely, in four points: "(1) The novel must and will be published eventually. (2) Jack Kerouac is a fresh, new (and fascinating) talent. (3) The manuscript still needs a lot of work. (4) The novel must be published even if it is a literary and financial failure." While Levine had reservations, particularly about the novel's treatment of female characters ("almost none of them are real"), she saw Kerouac through a larger literary lens: he's a "jived up Walt Whitman."

Viking was interested, not yet enough to offer Jack a formal contract but enough to invite him to revise the book with an eye

---

*At this time, Lord was trying to place some of Kerouac's many manuscripts, including the novel *Doctor Sax* and one of his religious writings, "Buddha Tells Us."

toward publication. Excited by the prospect of a contract for a book that had lingered for some six years, Jack now sang a humbler tune about revisions to his spontaneous prose. "Any changes you want to make okay with me," he conceded to Cowley. "I'm available to assist you in any re-arranging matters of course." Kerouac also agreed to change the title back from *The Beat Generation* to *On the Road*. Now Jack could daydream about his future. In drunken high spirits, he fantasized to Sterling Lord: "I can see it now, Marlon Brando (as Neal Cassady) and Montgomery Clift (as Jack Kerouac), in ON THE ROAD. $150,000 . . . 15 percent for you, oops, I mean 10."

Jack's euphoria was tempered soon enough by the unique realities of his publishing situation. For starters, Viking gave him no money for months on end, this while making numerous editing requests of him. There were also geographical problems: Cowley and Kerouac couldn't get together to revise the manuscript, which resulted in more confusion and delay. Furthermore, he "was constantly falling between the cracks at Viking. Neither Keith Jennison, an acquisitions editor, nor Cowley, a consultant, fulfilled the role of a 'working' or 'line' editor, and Kerouac became an orphan at Viking." More aggravating yet was the litany of demands from Viking's lawyer, Nathaniel Whitehorn. He wanted name changes, scene deletions, textual rewrites, and libel-clearing statement forms. True to his trade, Whitehorn presented a nine-page report that detailed the many modifications still recommended, even after initial revisions to avoid defamation and obscenity problems had been made. It seemed to Jack that his publishing Shangri-La was imploding into the Inferno.

Cowley and Kerouac had no alternative but to forge ahead. Jack created fictional names ("Dean Moriarty" for Neal Cassady, "Carlo Marx" for Allen Ginsberg, and "Sal Paradise" as Kerouac's alter ego), reworked passages to obscure real identities, consolidated cross-country trips into one another, and secured releases from Cassady and Ginsberg. Allen playfully signed his form in the name of his character in the novel: "for the benefit of American literature. X. Carlo Marx, as it were."

Although Kerouac boasted to his close friends that his "pure shining original" novel survived the revision process, Cowley knew otherwise: "Well, Jack did something that he would never admit to.... He did a good deal of revision, and it was very good revision." There were adventures extraneous to the novel's central structure that fell to the cutting-room floor; among them were a humorous account of Allen and Neal's 1947 visit with Bill Burroughs and Joan Vollmer, and a raucous party scene that highlighted Neal's manic sex drive. More significantly, the manuscript was massaged to eliminate objectionable passages, such as Ginsberg and Cassady's homosexual tryst and Brierly's fascination with boys. As various changes were made and the draft became "more of a continuous narrative," Jack eagerly awaited word from Cowley about a contract.

February 24, 1956 (Rocky Mount, North Carolina): "Dear Sterling, Haven't heard from Cowley yet. I feel something's wrong somewhere."

May 9, 1956 (Mill Valley, California): "Dear Malcolm...I'm in real straits now, my jeans are all torn, I'm living in a shack with a woodstove, rent free, have no money whatever, dont care (much), and am waiting day after day for word from you concerning...the recommended libel changes for *On the Road*.... It breaks my heart to be neglected so."

September 17, 1956 (San Francisco): "Dear Sterling...Cowley told his son Bob (who told Corso) Viking would publish *On the Road*— what's happening now?"

October 7, 1956 (Mexico City): "Dear Sterling...Please call Mr. Cowley and tell him my deadline has fallen and I want *Beat Generation* back. Tell him I respect his sincerity, but I'm not too sure about the others at Viking and tell him *I don't care*. Sterling, why dont you sell *Beat Generation* to soft cover people.... I want that book sold on street stalls, it is a book *about* the streets.... P.S. On the other hand, I dont feel like hurting Mr. Cowley.... so please just call him... & tell him to write me a letter fixing the date if any of Viking's acceptance—It's obviously not *his* fault."

December 26, 1956 (New York): "Dear John [Holmes]...have much work to do on *On the Road* ms. which Viking is finally taking, option all set, planned for the Fall List."

January 5, 1957 (Orlando, Florida): "Dear Sterling...I will be in to see you Tuesday to...discuss Viking contract with you."

Having completed his final draft of the *Road* book at his sister's new home in Orlando, Kerouac boarded a Greyhound bus with the manuscript in hand and rolled out for New York City. On January 8, 1957, after he arrived and got settled at his friend Helen Weaver's apartment, Jack headed for 625 Madison Avenue. Entering the building, he took the elevator up to the Viking offices. As the car passed one floor after another, he guzzled a full pint of bourbon; this was a day to celebrate.

At long last, he now stood in the same room with Malcolm Cowley. Kerouac handed him his masterpiece, his precious bundle. They exchanged greetings, chatted, and then got around to discussing the terms of his forthcoming contract. Jack would not, however, sign his name to any legal document that day. Three more days would pass before things became official. Kerouac signed the agreement on January 11, although the document was dated one day earlier. At that point, he received his first advance check of $250 (with $150 more to come upon the publisher's final acceptance of the book, and the remainder to be paid in six allotments of $100 per month).

That evening, back at Helen Weaver's place, Kerouac and his pals, Allen, Peter, and Gregory among them, partied nonstop into the early hours. Jack chugged "prodigious amounts" of booze while

Gregory Corso, the poetic tough from the Lower East Side, reveled in his victory. Score another one for the Beats!

Jack was elated and relieved. Apart from the money that he so badly needed, his name finally would return to a book cover. The man who had christened "the Beat Generation" would now rejoin the ranks of its published authors, alongside John Clellon Holmes, Bill Burroughs, and Allen Ginsberg. It had been a long time coming. But soon his *Road*-writing journey would end and his *Road*-publicity journey would begin. In the interim, once the book galleys were sent to him, he would set his mind on the minutiae of proofreading and correcting. Or so he thought.

Jack waited to receive the proofs. Meanwhile, without his knowledge, Viking's copyediting department normalized the style of this most abnormal text. By this late date, the book, unlike the original scroll, had chapter divisions and paragraph breaks; the editors added punctuation to fit the house-style rules but did not tell Kerouac beforehand.

And Jack waited to receive the proofs. Again, without his knowledge, Viking's lawyer approved the manuscript for printing on February 8, 1957, and reexamined the galleys on March 22.

And Jack waited to receive the proofs. Finally, without his knowledge, Malcolm Cowley and Keith Jennison prepared the "Manuscript Acceptance Report," dated April 8, 1957, for the editorial board's regular Wednesday meeting. The document briefly recounted the history of *On the Road* as it traveled twice through Viking's offices, summarized its plot line, and assessed its prospective market potential.

Cowley and Jennison did not heap unqualified praise on Kerouac's "narrative of life among the wild bohemians." In some respects, they declared, *Road* was not "a great or even a likable book"; the characters came across too much like "machines gone haywire, always wound to the last pitch, always nervously moving, drinking, making love, with hardly any emotions except a determination to say Yes to any new experience." Nevertheless, they found the story to be "real, honest, fascinating, everything for kicks, the voice of a new age"; and "at its best," the writing was "deeply felt, poetic, and extremely moving."

In their cost-benefit analysis, the Viking acquisitions editor and its consultant were measured, but ultimately positive. The book "will get mixed but *interested* reviews, it will have a good sale (perhaps a very good one)," and there was little doubt "that it will be reprinted as a paperback." They concluded, moreover, that "it will stand for a long time as the honest record of another way of life." The merits of such a recommendation spoke forcefully: *On the Road* was to be published and announced for release in the fall of 1957.

Having waited long enough, Jack's patience wore down and his anxiety built up. Writing to Sterling Lord on June 26, 1957, from the Berkeley apartment that he had shared with Mémère during her unsuccessful two-month experiment in California living, Jack complained about being left out of the loop. "Sterl, I'm real worried because you never write any more, as tho something was wrong," he explained. "I wrote a long letter to Keith Jennison, also no answer. Is ON THE ROAD going to be published? And if so, what about the final galleys I have to see..." Afraid of the silence, he begged for a response: "[S]ettle my mind and let me write my new book without this eerie silence from everybody."

Yes, Jack realized, he had good reason to fret. It had been seventy-four months since he had first unrolled the typescript scroll of *On the Road* before a befuddled Robert Giroux. Over those six-plus years, he had written a dozen more manuscripts, and not a one had yet been accepted for publication. Without the public spotlight that his *Road* book might shed on him, he had little hope that *Doctor Sax, Maggie Cassidy, Visions of Gerard, Visions of Cody, Subterraneans, Tristessa, Desolation Angels, Dharma Bums,* or his other works would ever emerge from the darkness. No wonder, then, that he believed any writer who cranked out manuscripts like a machine, as he did, eventually would go crazy.

Even worse, Jack pondered, should he be concerned about the recent fracas at City Lights Bookstore? The censorship bust involving Allen's "obscene" poem? "I wouldn't be surprised," he told Gary Snyder, "if Viking Press got chickenshit about HOWL being banned and put off the publication of my book and leave me flat bum broke again." Just as *On the Road* hoped to make its debut, *Howl* was facing a crisis, which could detour the success of Jack's road novel.

31.

GREGORY CORSO couldn't believe it. To think that something as ridiculous as this could happen to Allen Ginsberg's poetic stroke of genius! In San Francisco, no less—the Bohemian city, the West Coast home of the Beats, and the site of the path-shifting 6 Gallery reading, where he had witnessed Allen's howling. And imagine this censorship scam happening on March 25, 1957, only one day before Greg's twenty-seventh birthday. Reading Ginsberg's letter from Tangier, Corso first learned of the U.S. Customs' seizure of a British shipment of *Howl and Other Poems*. The olive-skinned ex-con shook his shaggy hair in amazement. Greg replied to Allen from Barcelona: "[H]ow absurd of that man to seize the books." What was this dumb-ass official thinking? Why would this fool get bent out of shape over *fuck*'s, *cunt*'s, and *cocksucker*'s? Words, words, words— they were just words—so what was the big fuckin' deal? The whole thing irked him. *fuck*'s, *cunt*'s, and *cocksucker*'s?

Back in the Bay Area, the *San Francisco Chronicle* columnist Abe Melinkoff held a similar opinion, though he was far more erudite. The headline of his March 28, 1957, "Morning Report" read: IRON CURTAIN ON THE EMBARCADERO. The forty-four-year-old city editor knew the Collector of Customs, Chester MacPhee, and considered him to be "a nice guy and a good public servant." But his kind words ended there. With a dollop of sarcasm, Melinkoff stated: "[H]e knows no more about modern poetry than I do. What I mean [is that] he is ignorant on the subject. That's why I think he has a lot of nerve in confiscating 520 copies of a book" by Allen Ginsberg. Melinkoff's column explained that *Howl and Other Poems* "was printed in England and picked up on the local docks as being too dirty for Americans to read." And for what compelling purpose? "The words and the sense of the writing is obscene. You wouldn't want your children to come across it," declared MacPhee. This justification addled the astute newspaperman. While he granted that Customs agents play an important role in searching for opium smugglers, "the collector has no duty to protect my children.... If he is going to pick up everything that is a menace to them, he is going to be confiscating night and day."

What caught the attention of the Customs men in connection with the *Howl* shipment was the name "Villiers." Not long before, they had seized copies of *Miscellaneous Man* for alleged obscenity; that magazine, published by William Margolis in Berkeley, was also printed by Villiers. The moral enforcers of the Tariff Act of 1930 were wise to the vulgar fare of the London-based printer. They went on a censorial hunt for anything that displayed the stamp "Villiers." It was up to the well-dressed MacPhee, who resembled the actor David Niven, to convince the public that *Howl* was such a threat to children that it must be quarantined. Lawrence Ferlinghetti, whose bundles of books were sequestered, was unconvinced: "I think MacPhee just saw the four-letter words in there, and wasn't capable of making any critical judgment on the literary or poetic value of the text."*

---

*It is interesting that the Customs officials seized *Howl and Other Poems* after Villiers had printed only asterisks alluding to such "four-letter words." Assuming that all of the mailed copies contained asterisks, it would then seem that Chester MacPhee found obscenity by implication. Such asterisks, however, did not appear in later American printings.

The City Lights Books publisher anticipated MacPhee's move when he had earlier contacted the American Civil Liberties Union to defend against any Customs actions. Happily, Ferlinghetti didn't need the ACLU's assistance for the first shipment of *Howl*, which passed through without incident. Now, however, he summoned them to lift the quarantine on the second shipment of his books; on April 3, the ACLU informed MacPhee that it would challenge the legality of the seizure. Even so, Lawrence did not limit himself to legal recourse. He saw to it that a stock of 2,500 photo-offset copies were printed in the U.S., thus depriving Customs officials of jurisdiction. And those books were quickly distributed for any and all to read. His shrewd move made a mockery of MacPhee's paternalistic logic—protecting American children from lurid lines of poetry.

The "obscene" author, of course, was in no place to assist his "obscene" publisher. Working in Tangier, Morocco, on Bill Burroughs' early draft of his ribald novel *Naked Lunch*, Ginsberg was both sympathetic and opportunistic. On the one hand, he wrote to Ferlinghetti, "I guess this puts you up shits creek financially. I didn't think it would really happen. . . . Sorry I'm not there." On the other hand, he figured, "I suppose the publicity will be good." He urged Lawrence to "prepare some sort of outraged and idiotic but dignified statement, quoting the Customs man," Eberhart's *New York Times* article, and William Carlos Williams's introduction to *Howl*. "Mimeograph it up," he urged, "and send it out as a sort of manifesto publishable by magazines and/or news release."

Lawrence first lent an ear to Allen's publicity advice and then wielded his pen. Because William Hogan, the *San Francisco Chronicle*'s book review editor, turned over his Sunday column, "Between the Lines," to the bookseller, Ferlinghetti could respond publicly to the government's actions. In his printed statement, he made three basic points: 1) The publicity argument: "The San Francisco Collector of Customs deserves a word of thanks for seizing *Howl and*

Other Poems and thereby rendering it famous. Perhaps we could have a medal made. It would have taken years for critics to accomplish what the good collector did in a day, merely by calling the book obscene." 2) The literary merits argument: "I consider 'Howl' to be the most significant single long poem to be published in this country since World War II, perhaps since Eliot's *Four Quartets*." 3) The dissent argument: If "Howl" is "a condemnation of our official culture, if it is an unseemly voice of dissent, perhaps this is really why officials object to it. In condemning it, however, they are condemning their own American world. For it is not the poet but what he observes which is revealed as obscene.... Considering the state of the world (not to mention the state of modern poetry) it was high time to howl."

With two slams from the *Chronicle*, Customs Collector MacPhee was put on the rhetorical run. But what really pulled the rug out from beneath him was notification that the U.S. Attorney's Office in San Francisco would take no legal action against *Howl*. With that, Customs had no alternative but to release the books, which it did on May 29. Ferlinghetti's two-pronged strategy, hitting hard on both the publicity and legal fronts, had worked beautifully. It was a victory for free speech: Allen's dissident bardic voice could now be heard. It was a victory for the free market: Lawrence's Pocket Poets books could now be sold.

Until, that is, William A. Hanrahan's "sting" operation. Unlike the critics who carped at MacPhee's warnings, the captain of the Juvenile Department of the San Francisco Police took them to heart. If the Customs officials were unable to "protect" San Francisco's children from Ginsberg's coarse verses, then he and his officers would come to their rescue. On May 21, 1957, Hanrahan sent two undercover agents to City Lights to buy a book of poems and a magazine. After paying Shigeyoshi ("Shig") Murao, the heavyset store manager who "looked like a Japanese sage but had the culture of a hip American," they left immediately with their contraband, *Howl and Other Poems* and *Miscellaneous Man*.

Within two weeks, the plainclothes officers came back to the scene of the crime and purchased yet another copy of *Howl*. Later on that same day—Monday, June 3, 1957—they returned to City Lights with two arrest warrants. Ferlinghetti and Murao were to be charged with the "willful and lewd" sale of "obscene and indecent" materials, and Lawrence with the publication, as well, in violation of Section 311.3 of the California Penal Code.

The task of making the poem-busts fell to officers Russell Woods and Thomas Pagee. They pulled up to the storefront, the one with the striped canopy that prominently advertised "BOOKS." Somewhat embarrassed, the two entered the small pie-shaped room, looking for their criminal suspects. They found only Shig and Kirby, Ferlinghetti's wife. When Kirby confronted them about the absurdity of it all, the response was routine: "It is all in the line of duty, ma'am." Though they looked like well-groomed college students and "were terribly nice," they were there on official business. A "John Doe" warrant was then handed to Shig. He took it in stride and even kidded that "Shigeyoshi Murao, a Japanese-American, was being arrested as a 'John Doe' white man." The officers smiled, but didn't laugh. Without being handcuffed, Murao was escorted out of the store and into the squad car. It was only three blocks to the Hall of Justice.

On arrival, the suspect was taken down to the basement, where he was fingerprinted. The Kafkaesque reality of being busted for selling poems hit home when the cops took his mug shots, front and side. Then, the stench of urine overwhelmed Murao as he approached his dim cell. When the door locked behind him, his eyes immediately fixed on the "piss-stained mattress on the floor." He was in the drunk tank. Someone had seen the need to post a penal code section on the cell wall; above it, scrawled as graffiti, was an obscene word—"COCKSUCKERS."

Murao suffered the stench as Ferlinghetti breathed in full lungs of fresh air in his Big Sur cabin,* the one near a canyon where gigantic "elbows of rock" rose up thousands of feet and then fell into the breaking waters of the Pacific. While there, he received word of the bust; he even got newspaper clippings and mailed one along with a letter to Allen in Tangier. On June 6, three days after Shig had been sprung by the ACLU on $500 bail, Lawrence left the enchanted redwood forest and turned himself in at the San Francisco Hall of Justice; "a picturesque return to the early Middle Ages," he described it.

The next day, Jack Kerouac, who was staying in Berkeley, wrote to Allen: some "local dumb Irish cops rushed up on their own initiative and bought HOWL in the store and arrested the nice Jap cat who was instantly bailed out by the Civil Liberties Union, but I went there & there were no more HOWLS on the shelf." Worse still, Kerouac feared that American intellectuals were "so gutless they might knuckle under the dumb fat Irish cops in time and it'll be like Germany, a police state. I'm really worried."

Allen was also anxious: "I guess this is more serious than the customs seizure since you can lose real money on this deal if they find you guilty," he wrote to Lawrence. And he had his suspicions, too: "Who or what is behind all this attention? It appears like Customs were burned up when they had to let go and someone must have called juvenile police from customs, and asked them to take up and carry the ball from there." One more thing: "Are local newspapers being sympathetic?"

Indeed, they were. Beyond the news stories, the *Chronicle* ran an editorial with a damning headline that read: MAKING A CLOWN OF SAN FRANCISCO. It published a column with the ominous headline: ORWELL'S 'BIG BROTHER' IS WATCHING OVER US. And it featured a

---

*It was at that cabin in August 1960 that Kerouac wrote most of what became his novel *Big Sur*, published in 1962.

cartoon that portrayed a bulldog-faced policeman pounding a notice on a bookstore door. The caption: "Hanrahan's Law All books must be fit for children to read—SFPD." And there was more of the same in other papers.

The editorial writers, columnists, and cartoonists lampooned what Captain Hanrahan had told reporters: "We have purchased" *Howl* and *Miscellaneous Man*. "They are not fit for children to read." To which came the editorial response: "Here is a new and startling doctrine and one which, if followed to the letter, would clear many of the world's classics from local bookstores, not excepting the Bible wherein is many a chapter and verse not recommended for perusal by tiny tots."

Gregory Corso was equally critical of the "Hanrahan's Law" mindset, but for different reasons: "How many children will read HOWL?" Some people are "afraid of what it might do to children—but children read nothing! Children know nothing—children are nothing!" Later, writing to Ferlinghetti from Paris, Corso was less flip. In a serious vein, he lamented the fate of those who print books by the Beats: "I think that you are perhaps the only great publisher in America and will have to suffer for it."*

---

*Around this time, Lawrence Ferlinghetti was preparing to publish the eighth book of his Pocket Poets Series—*Gasoline* by Gregory Corso.

PART IV

THE TRIAL &
TRIBULATION

*I'm afraid of what will happen in court—trial set for
August 6—maybe City Lights [will] lose, be out of
dough, & screw up the whole publishing deal.*
                                        —Allen Ginsberg

*The local prosecution cannot hope to win in the face of
the already made federal decision [not to prosecute].*
                                        —John G. Fuller

Previous page: Lawrence Ferlinghetti (left) and Shigeyoshi Murao (right) sit in the courtroom during their obscenity trial over selling Allen Ginsberg's Howl.

32.

ALLEN AND PETER frolicked in far-off Naples, Venice, Paris, and Amsterdam, strolling in museums and sitting in cafés while savoring the charms of European culture. Back in the U.S.A., Larry and Shig met with their ACLU lawyers and prepared for trial. Concerned as Allen was about the prosecution of *Howl and Other Poems*,* he was not the one within the punitive reach of the law.

Ferlinghetti, ever the radical poet, did not worry about his clash with Officialdom. He welcomed it. Even though he could be fined and jailed, he saw the golden lining in the storm clouds. Recall his sentiment: "It would have taken years for critics to accomplish what the good collector did in a day, merely by calling the book obscene." Notoriety had its benefits: a spike in sales and the prospect of long-term profits.

Indeed, before the trial was over, there would be several runs of *Howl* with more than ten thousand copies in print and an LP record

---

*By this time, the Beats had produced several other books. There was Kerouac's *The Town and the City*, Holmes's *Go*, Burroughs' *Junkie*, McClure's *Passage*, Corso's *The Vestal Lady on Brattle Street and Other Poems*, and Ferlinghetti's *Pictures of the Gone World*. But *Howl* was the lone book at the time that was the object of criminal prosecution. Eventually, that fate would also come to Bill Burroughs' *Naked Lunch*, but that time had yet to arrive. Since the editors of the scroll version of Kerouac's *On the Road* "desexed" several saucy scenes in the work, it never became a "cause" the way that the Ginsberg and Burroughs books did.

deal in the works. And *Life* magazine and others were profiling it all. Even if Ferlinghetti were convicted, the San Francisco poet and publisher seemed unflappable: "I thought, well, I could use some time in the clink to do some heavy reading."

Shigeyoshi Murao viewed the world through a different lens: "In jail I had no noble thoughts for fighting for freedom of the press....I had planned to live a quiet life of reading, listening to music, and playing chess the rest of my life. Yet here I was involved in a case for selling obscenity."

That charge weighed heavily on his mind and his cultural sense of self. As Ferlinghetti described Murao, he was a "Nisei whose family had been interned with thousands of other Japanese-Americans during the war" and "to be arrested for anything, even if innocent, was in the Japanese community of that time a family disgrace."

There was, however, far more at stake than the fate of two young men. For a conviction in this case surely would entice Captain Hanrahan and his officers to return to City Lights or other bookstores to scan the shelves for copies of other "obscene" types of avant-garde literature. The Juvenile Bureau chief suggested as much when he alluded to a literary cache that had caught his attention: "We will await the outcome of this case before we go ahead with other books." And a conviction in the *Howl* case would set a precedent for other jurisdictions to follow. If *Howl* could be banned in California, then it could be outlawed in Illinois, New York, Georgia, Massachusetts, or anywhere else in the nation.

Allen knew that, while the Beats had clashed with the law before, the *Howl* trial was the first time that their rebellious ideas and ideals were tested and tried by the state. It wasn't just *Howl*'s colorful words, such as "cock," "fucked," and "balled." It was also the poem's aggressive and activist message, those tirades against McCarthy-era politics and Norman Rockwell–era morality. That message was far more threatening to the conventions of the day than any barroom vernacular.

Exhibit A Pro-communist: "who distributed Supercommunist pamphlets in Union Square weeping and undressing while the sirens of Los Alamos wailed them down"

Exhibit B Pro-homosexual: "who blew and were blown by those human seraphim, the sailors, caresses of Atlantic and Caribbean love"

Exhibit C Pro-promiscuity: "who sweetened the snatches of a million girls trembling in the sunset, and were red eyed in the morning but prepared to sweeten the snatch of the sun rise, flashing buttocks under barns and naked in the lake"

Exhibit D Anti-capitalist: "Moloch whose mind is pure machinery! Moloch whose blood is running money! Moloch whose fingers are ten armies! Moloch whose breast is a cannibal dynamo! Moloch whose ear is a smoking tomb!"

Exhibit E Anti-American: "Go fuck yourself with your atom bomb," delivered in "America," one of the poems in the *Howl* collection. "I'm sick of your insane demands," Allen insisted in yet another declaration of anger and alienation in that poem.

Ginsberg railed against what America had become. This son of a communist mother and a socialist poet father loathed modern America's ethos, its logos, its "homophobos," and its mechanized mindset that produced uniformity at the expense of individuality. By that measure, Allen and his poems were un-American.

When the cultural lens widened, it became clear that the poem was political. Thus the battle the Beats now waged was not merely over some "dirty" words in literature, but over competing visions of the nation: the perspective of an Eisenhower-like America that many held dear versus that of a Whitman-like America that the Beats cherished. What was at stake was the right to *dissent*, the right to attack that "Moloch" America so determined to strangle the spirit of freethinking youths.

Defending *Howl*, then, meant defending alienated cultural outlaws who condemned modern America, the same outlaws who pointed to a new vision of America yearning to be born. With Allen on the sideline and Larry and Shig on the front line, the battle for America's soul was about to begin.

33.

TO LOOK AT HIM, you'd never know that Lawrence Speiser was an American Civil Liberties Union lawyer. He didn't fit the stereotype. He had middle America etched in the contours of his cheeks and fixed on his forehead.

At the time of the *Howl* trial, Speiser was thirty-four and had the face and frame of a football jock—clean-cut, clean-shaven, tall, and broad-chested. His all-American manner made him seem "square," the kind of guy the Beats lampooned. Few could guess that this World War II veteran would defend countercultural and radical types, even anarchists and communists. But defend them he did. Larry Speiser was part of a remarkable trio of pro bono lawyers who would represent the defendants (an anarchist publisher and his shop clerk) in *People v. Ferlinghetti* and *People v. Murao*.

As he prepared for the start of the trial in the Municipal Court of San Francisco, Speiser had his mind on another First Amendment case. This one did not involve poetry. It was a loyalty-oath case, in which he himself was the civil plaintiff/appellant and which he had recently lost in the California Supreme Court. Thus, at the very time Speiser was working on *Murao/Ferlinghetti*, he was also petitioning the U.S. Supreme Court to review the state's denial of a tax exemption because he refused to sign a loyalty oath.

Speiser had an impressive record as a civil liberties lawyer, especially for someone his age. True to that record, in the year following the *Howl* trial, he would win his own case in the Supreme Court. It was a 7–1 victory, with Justice William J. Brennan Jr. writing for the majority.*

As it turned out, that same Justice Brennan would play a pivotal, though indirect, role in the *Howl* case, too. That was due to his opinion in still other First Amendment cases, *Roth v. United States* and *Alberts v. California*, decided in June 1957, a few months before the *Murao/Ferlinghetti* trial began.

---

*According to Thomas Emerson, a noted First Amendment scholar, the Supreme Court's "*Speiser* decision broke new paths in its recognition of the importance of taking into account the dynamics of a system of freedom of expression."

34.

IT WAS A MERE thirty-two days after he was confirmed by the Senate, with Joe McCarthy railing against him, when William Brennan took his seat on the Supreme Court to hear oral arguments in case nos. 582 and 61, *Roth v. United States* and *Alberts v. California.* He was the junior player sitting alongside constitutional giants William O. Douglas, Hugo Black, John Harlan, Earl Warren, and Brennan's former Harvard Law School professor, Felix Frankfurter.

The Court chamber where the *Roth-Alberts* oral arguments took place was a monumental paean to the law's grandeur. The constitutional dialogue began under the majestic forty-four-foot ceiling supported by twenty-four columns of Italian marble.

Prior to oral arguments, the Justice Department had shipped materials under seal to the Court to demonstrate the kind of filth that would be legitimized if the justices reversed the convictions of Sam Roth and David Alberts for advertising and selling obscene books and magazines. Now Justices Tom Clark and William O. Douglas quietly distributed pornographic materials to their colleagues on the bench, out of the sight of those in the Court gallery, of course. In the very elevated quarters where decorum and propriety were the rule, some of the justices eyed "stroke" mags as they listened to the nuances of American procedural and constitutional law. If only Allen Ginsberg had known, it would have made for a saucy and satirical poem.

Justice Frankfurter was a pretentious jurist who wore his Harvard credentials on his lapel. He dominated the dialogue. The constitutionally conservative justice peppered the parties with procedural, evidentiary, and jurisdictional questions. With professorial fervor, he tried repeatedly to pin Roth's counsel down to exactly what his position was on the legal status of obscene materials. The more he asked, the worse it got. Exasperated, the justice said: "You can't just swim in the midst of the Pacific Ocean in these matters. You've got to get some footing on some... *terra firma*."

Throughout the oral arguments, the timid Brennan spoke only once and not for very long. He asked the deputy district attorney from California how he could identify an offending photograph or movie frame—namely, the point at which an erotic magazine or film crossed the line from the constitutionally protected to the legally obscene. The response was non-responsive, no defining point, just common knowledge: "Every man in the street knows what obscenity is."

When all was said and done, the highly technical oral arguments made it easy for the audience to drift off and stare at the sculpted marble panels surrounding the chamber. Moreover, no one reasonably could have predicted either the outcome of the case or the landmark status it would later attain.

It was Monday, June 24, 1957, when the Court handed down its rulings. Sam Roth's obscenity conviction was upheld by a 7–2 margin, as was that of David Alberts, though by a 6–3 vote. While the judgment of the Court and some of the language in Justice Brennan's majority opinion surely must have troubled the civil-rights attorney Lawrence Speiser, there were aspects of the opinion that promised a new measure of First Amendment freedom for his clients.

Indeed, Brennan's opinion read like a tribute to the Roman god Janus, the great gatekeeper with two faces gazing in opposite directions. It was an opinion that pleased conservatives and liberals alike, even as it troubled them.

There was the conservative face. This face of the opinion frightened libertarians and pleased those who would censor sexual expression. After all, Brennan declared: "[T]his Court has always assumed that obscenity is not protected by the freedoms of speech and press." And then this: "[I]mplicit in the history of the First Amendment is the rejection of obscenity as utterly without socially redeeming importance." Worse still, there was a big blow to those who used blue vernacular: "There are certain well-defined and narrowly limited classes of speech, the prevention and punishment of which have never been thought to raise any Constitutional problem. These include the lewd and obscene.... It has been well observed that such utterances are no essential part of the exposition of ideas, and are of such slight social value as a step to truth that any benefit that may be derived from them is clearly outweighed by the social interest in order and morality."

Obscenity was, by definition, worthless—no analysis or balancing necessary. For prosecutors, that meant that if they succeeded in branding a book, movie, play, or poem "obscene," that was typically the end of the matter: off to the local holding-tank with the moral offenders. Such a destiny might, then, await Ferlinghetti and Murao. Would their judge or jury conclude that *Howl and Other Poems* was "no essential part" of the exposition of important ideas?

Then there was the liberal face of the *Roth* opinion. On that side of the opinion, there was hope for those who defended sexual expression in literature and the arts. Brennan provided language that inspired that assessment: "[S]ex and obscenity are not synonymous." Obscene material, he continued, is "material having a tendency to excite lustful thoughts." And then Brennan delivered a big blow to those who sought to outlaw blue vernacular: "All ideas having even the slightest importance—unorthodox ideas, controversial ideas, even ideas hateful to the prevailing climate of opinion—have the full protection of the guaranties, unless excludable because they encroach upon the limited area of more important interests."

The upshot? Messages about sex were no longer categorically obscene. There was also a strong suggestion in the opinion that a finding of obscenity hinged on evidence that a work pushed libidinal buttons. Finally, when messages about sex commingled with social commentary, they ranked higher on the First Amendment scale.

Legally, the most important portion of the *Roth* opinion, the words that would find their way into numerous state and federal obscenity laws, was Justice Brennan's famous formula for determining obscenity:

[1] whether to the average person,

[2] applying contemporary community standards,

[3] the dominant theme of the material taken as a whole

[4] appeals to prurient interest.

Each of these four prongs had its peculiar relevance to the *Howl* case. For Ferlinghetti and Murao, the *Roth* test could prove promising in the hands of a judge sensitive to the nuances of the law and the literary value of *Howl's* unorthodox and controversial lines.

Murao/Ferlinghetti would be the first obscenity case in the nation to apply the new *Roth* test. How would the earliest progeny of *Roth* be fashioned? Would the *Howl* judge take his cue from William Brennan's application of the obscenity test? It was, recall, the young justice who had upheld the *Roth-Alberts* obscenity convictions. Or would the *Howl* judge turn instead to the more liberal side of the opinion for constitutional guidance?

Lawrence Speiser, the appellate law expert who resembled a defensive lineman, had to craft a constitutional argument that would spare Ferlinghetti and Murao the fate of Roth and Alberts. It was quite a formidable challenge, even for such a remarkable lawyer.

35.

THE TRIAL WAS SET for August 8, 1957. It was to be conducted at the Municipal Court for the City and County of San Francisco, located at 750 Kearny Street.* Judge Byron Arnold, a newly appointed Republican judge, was to preside. But things didn't play out that way. The case was delayed for eight days, and the matter reassigned to the Honorable Clayton W. Horn, with the case calendared for August 16.

Judge Horn was a Sunday school Bible teacher. He was a man who cared about the moral character of his world and those in it. God was in the letter of the law.

In the weeks before he presided over the *Howl* obscenity trial, Judge Horn had imposed his moral vision in an unusual manner, which placed him in the national limelight. He had sat in judgment on a case involving five women charged with shoplifting; finding they were guilty as charged, Judge Horn sentenced them to serve time at a movie theater.

The five convicted women were confined for 219 minutes in a local theater for a court-ordered movie viewing of *The Ten Commandments*. The cinematic sentence did not end with the ladies watching

---

*The courthouse was leveled long ago; a hotel is located at that address today.

Cecil B. DeMille's epic film starring Charlton Heston (Moses), Yul Brenner (Pharaoh Rameses), and Anne Baxter (Nefertiti). They had to put pen to paper and discuss, in essay form, the moral lessons to be drawn from the movie.

The judge's sentence drew harsh criticism from the editorial page of the *San Francisco Chronicle*: "Municipal Judge Clayton Horn's freewheeling excursion into movie-reviewing and *belles lettres* in weighing penalties for five petty shoplifters fills us with wonder and no little trepidation."

Worse still, that lesson in morality, the editors emphasized, required the five misdemeanants to sit through a film filled with "violence, lust, sex, and orgies." Alongside the editorial was a derisive cartoon of Horn clad as Moses in robe and sandals, holding a graven tablet that declared: "THOU SHALT NOT MISS 'THE TEN COMMANDMENTS'—Judge Clayton Horn."

The Bay Area jurist, who resembled the actor Gene Lockhart, would now sit in judgment over the much-publicized obscenity trial of Lawrence Ferlinghetti and Shigeyoshi Murao.

What were the chances that a judge who honored a vengeful God would rule in favor of the defendants? Would he castigate these purveyors of poetic protest because the works they published and sold were laced with lewd terms? Or would he, newly chastened by the media's charges of moral self-righteousness, approach the case with a nonjudgmental sensitivity to its significance for the American free-speech culture?

Whatever those chances were, the defense had to develop both a compelling trial strategy to convince Judge Horn of the legality of *Howl* and a compelling constitutional record in the event of an appeal. For those tasks, Ferlinghetti and Murao had a dream team of lawyers.

36.

LAWRENCE SPEISER, who had been staff counsel at the Northern California chapter of the ACLU, would take charge and select and prepare the witnesses for trial. If the defendants were to win this case, those witnesses were crucial to substantiate that *Howl* had serious literary value and did not primarily appeal to "prurient" interests.

Albert M. Bendich became the next member of the legal team. He was a bright but quiet twenty-eight-year-old lawyer, a recent graduate of the University of California's Boalt Hall Law School. Although a labor law practitioner, Bendich had desired for some time to work for the ACLU.

Having applied in the spring of 1957, he was hired by the civil-rights organization late in the summer and shortly before the *Howl* trial began to succeed Speiser as staff counsel. At the time that he came on board, Bendich met with Speiser over his impending workload. Speiser assigned Bendich immediately to *Howl*, his very first free-speech civil liberties case.

The formidable charge of researching the main statutory and constitutional arguments and writing the legal memoranda submitted to the court fell to this novice. In effect, Bendich was the one who had to reconcile the contrary strands of the *Roth* opinion with the facts of *Murao/Ferlinghetti*. And he had to do this against the backdrop of a body of pre-*Roth* law that was largely hostile to the use of vulgarity in literature.

Jacob Wilburn Ehrlich was the final member of the team. He took the lead both at the trial and in the limelight. Ehrlich—"Never Plead Guilty" or "the Master" as he was popularly known—was a San Francisco lawyer with a big ego and a bigger national reputation. In July 1948, for example, he defended condemned murderer Caryl Chessman, forestalling his execution in an appeal from death row, a case that drew international attention.*

Practicing since 1922 in San Francisco, "the Master" had won hundreds of murder cases. In one of them, he secured a jury acquittal in a mere four minutes. In another, it took the jury only thirteen minutes to find his client not guilty of murdering her boyfriend who died of three bullets to the back. He was also renowned as a divorce lawyer; he represented celebrities such as Errol Flynn, Billie Holiday, and Howard Hughes.

Ehrlich was a show horse, a man of both substance and flash. In his day, he published several widely used tracts on the law, including *Ehrlich's Blackstone*. And in the courtroom he was *the* man to be heard and seen.

Never modest in his style, he was an impressive oral advocate and an impeccable dresser. His trademark attire: expensive custom-tailored suits draped over well-polished cowboy boots. And then there were his legendary cuff links, some valued at more than $25,000. One of his favorite sayings spoke volumes on his sartorial tastes: "A man can always be underdressed, but never overdressed."

Little wonder then that he could command $1,000 per minute for a fifteen-minute court appearance for one of his well-heeled clients.

---

*The defendant had been condemned to death for non-capital offenses: robbery, kidnapping, and rape.

Even the less fortunate among them were not spared his astounding bills: "When I defend a man in a capital case," he often quipped, "my fee is EVERYTHING he owns. The way I have got it figured, if I win him his freedom it is worth it, and if I don't, he won't need it anyway." Ehrlich's sharp and showy career was perfect material for Hollywood: he eventually was fictionalized in *Sam Benedict*, a popular TV series, with Edmond O'Brien playing his character.

For all his experience in representing accused murderers and lovelorn spouses, Jake Ehrlich had never argued a First Amendment case. He did it—and this time, with no payment—for the glory and glitz that such a victory might promise.

Deputy District Attorney Ralph McIntosh was the prosecutor in the *Howl* trial. Once a linotype operator at a newspaper by day and a law student by night, he was now a man with years of prosecuting behind him. While nowhere as knowledgeable in constitutional law as Speiser and Bendich, and while hardly a courtroom match for the suave and seasoned Ehrlich, McIntosh had earned a local reputation for being tough on smut.

He had long set his prosecutorial sights on porn movie houses and bookstores, charging them for their dirty flicks and girly magazines. He even went after Howard Hughes's 1941 film, *The Outlaw*, the one in which Hughes, as an eccentric producer and Hollywood movie mogul, emphasized Jane Russell's voluptuous cleavage throughout the rough-and-tumble western. The film and its pulp-fiction-like poster—a racy pic of a reclining Jane, revealing her scantily-clad breasts while packing a pistol just above her hiked-up skirt—proved too much for the San Francisco prosecutor. He would not tolerate such filth in his fine city.

But going after "smutty" poetry was something new for the old prosecutor of porn. McIntosh had no sense of the poem; it was all gibberish to him. What he did understand, however, were all the dirty words, those disgusting references to "cock" and "cocksucker" and "asshole" and "fucked in the ass." Now that was obscene. That was something the California criminal law need not tolerate and the First Amendment should not protect.

Surely, the Supreme Court's new *Roth* standard for obscenity would not license such rubbish to be peddled in bookstores and elsewhere. And so, in the tradition of the notorious nineteenth-century moral crusader Anthony Comstock, Ralph McIntosh aimed to prosecute that which he really did not comprehend. He would do so simply because there were foul and corrupting words lurking between the black-and-white covers of *Howl and Other Poems*.

While McIntosh would confront formidable opponents in the team of Ehrlich, Speiser, and Bendich, he did have, to all appearances, a morally sympathetic judge and a new Supreme Court decision with some helpful language in it. More generally, the prosecutor could rely on a strong tradition hostile to the nonconformist ways of those who engaged in "sustained shrieks of frantic defiance," as M.L. Rosenthal of the *New York Times* tagged Ginsberg's poetry several months earlier.

To put it all another way, Ralph McIntosh had one big thing in his favor. He had the mighty "Moloch" on his side.

37.

IT WAS A DECLARATION of war reported on the front page of the *San Francisco Chronicle*. What was at stake was a generational struggle of ideologies and attitudes—the old versus the young; the established versus the rebellious; the traditional versus the unconventional; and the righteously proper versus the irreverently vulgar.

The Beat Generation's "nakedness of mind," as John Holmes put it in 1952, was being exposed for all to see in a San Francisco courtroom. In that venue, the Beats would proclaim through *Howl* their "*will* to believe," a will that manifested itself "even in the face of an inability to do so in conventional terms." The contest of wills and words had begun.

This battle, of course, had singular importance for Ferlinghetti and Murao. But from the broader perspective of Western history, it fell into a long line of conflicts over the government's power to control morals and manners, a tradition that stretched back at least to the elected censors of ancient Rome. In this sense, *Murao/Ferlinghetti* was the latest episode in a relentless campaign to purify what entered people's minds. In America, that crusade had attacked such noted works as Nathaniel Hawthorne's *The Scarlet*

Letter, Walt Whitman's *Leaves of Grass*, D.H. Lawrence's *Women in Love*, Radclyffe Hall's *The Well of Loneliness*, and James Joyce's *Ulysses*.

The larger implications of the *Howl* prosecution were certainly well understood by the San Francisco literary community. One day before the *Murao/Ferlinghetti* trial opened, Mayor George Christopher received a petition signed by twenty-one of the city's leading booksellers, urging him to "use all the power of your office" to stop police seizure of books. Decrying the "deplorable" arrests of Ferlinghetti and Murao, the petition declared: "This sort of censorship has no place in a democratic society" and "is harmful to San Francisco's reputation as a center of culture and enlightenment."

Although neither the first nor the last obscenity prosecution on American shores, the *Howl* trial nevertheless had a full measure of significance. Legal vindication of Ginsberg's poetry might confirm the cultural value of unorthodox literature more generally and might cast a wider protective net of liberty for the likes of Jack Kerouac, Bill Burroughs, John Clellon Holmes, and Ferlinghetti himself.

Accompanying the *San Francisco Chronicle's* headlines was a black-and-white courtroom picture of a new generation of young Americans sitting and standing there to witness history. It was all captured for posterity by press flash-bulb cameras allowed in the chamber.

The photographs reveal a high-ceilinged courtroom divided into two large sections of benches abutted by carved railing. Some 150 people sat there. Huge windows permitted the summer sunlight to pour in. Seated on a swivel chair to the left of the judge's bench, Lawrence Ferlinghetti wore an olive-green corduroy coat and tie. A pensive Shigeyoshi Murao, his right hand under his chin, sported a light blue summer suit, a white buttoned shirt, and a black knit tie. Jake Ehrlich was dressed with his typical sartorial splendor in a finely cut three-piece suit replete with a gold watch chain and a protruding multi-pointed handkerchief.

When the trial* finally got under way on Friday, August 16, the courtroom was jammed—standing room only. Henry Miller, the renowned author of *The Tropic of Cancer*, attended to show his support for Ferlinghetti and the First Amendment. Unknown admirers did the same, as they openly displayed copies of *Howl* that they had brought with them. By stark contrast, the prosecutor refused to contribute to the spectacle: he carried copies of *Howl* and *Miscellaneous Man* in a brown bag, as if to suggest that even the display of their all-too-innocent covers might be seen as injurious to the decorum of the court. Employing a different strategy, Jake Ehrlich kept his copy of *Howl* in plain view and even waved it boldly during the course of the hearings. As for Lawrence Ferlinghetti, he openly sold and publicly displayed numerous copies of *Howl* in his storefront window throughout the trial.

"Gentlemen, you may proceed." With those words from Judge Horn, the trial started.

The prosecution called its first witness, Russell Woods, the plainclothes officer who visited City Lights Bookshop on May 21 to pick up copies of *Howl* and *Miscellaneous Man* magazine. Ralph McIntosh's direct examination of the officer was surprisingly short and simple. Woods established that he had purchased and read *Howl*, and obtained an arrest warrant for the defendants. That was it. At this point, McIntosh offered a copy of Ginsberg's book into evidence and turned the witness over to the defense for cross-examination.

Jake Ehrlich did not reveal the defense's hand that day. "It will be of no value to commence cross-examination today or to put in a defense," Ehrlich explained, "unless and until Your Honor has read

---

*A largely complete transcript of the *People v. Ferlinghetti* trial is offered in *Howl of the Censor* (1961), edited by Jake W. Ehrlich. Unfortunately, the Ehrlich transcript omits, among other things, the closing arguments of Lawrence Speiser and Albert Bendich.

the book. Then we can call your attention to various parts." McIntosh offered no objection to a continuance. "You have the book before you," the prosecutor said to Judge Horn. "Naturally, you will have to read it to determine whether or not it is obscene or indecent." In complete accord, the judge postponed the trial for a week so that he could sample the forbidden fruit.

Since the defendants had waived a jury trial, the outcome lay with Clayton Horn. The trio of legal talents had made a calculated bet that their clients' fortune was better entrusted to a Bible-believing judge than to a potentially prim-and-proper San Francisco jury. That calculation, of course, was a risky one, and the defense now hoped that the judge would fully prepare himself to appreciate the grave meaning and great import of Ginsberg's poems.

38.

When success comes in America
it comes in a golden flood...
—Ann Charters

BY THE SUMMER of 1957, the scent of the literary life was everywhere in the air for the Beats. The *Evergreen Review*'s "San Francisco Scene" issue had recently come out. It focused on the "exciting phenomenon of a young group in the process of creating a new American culture." It brought together "for the first time" the "leading figures of the 'San Francisco Renaissance.'" The literary lineup included Lawrence Ferlinghetti, Allen Ginsberg, Jack Kerouac, Michael McClure, Henry Miller, Kenneth Rexroth, Gary Snyder, and Philip Whalen. (In far away Tangier, the final typing of Bill Burroughs' *Naked Lunch* was being completed.) Notably, the review reprinted Ginsberg's "Howl," and this at a time when the poem was under the glare of the San Francisco censors.

Meanwhile, *Time* magazine was eager to profile Allen and his prosecuted poem. To make matters sweeter still, the editors agreed to pay his round-trip travel from Venice to Rome plus two days' living expenses. A new trend was surely developing, something potentially big, and the editors wanted to catch the wave of the story.

Jack Kerouac was one of the Beats soon to ride the crest of that wave. In July he was back in Berkeley hanging with the gang (Cassady and Whalen) and dropping in on old haunts like The Place over on Grant Avenue. While drinking with the guys in that bohemian hangout, Kerouac could see news clippings about *Howl* tacked to the wall. If he didn't find his way to the courthouse, it was perhaps because he was too preoccupied with the long-awaited arrival of his second published novel.

Fiction had become reality, and Jack held that reality in his hands. The advance copies of *On the Road* had arrived from Viking and had been delivered to the Milvia Street cottage. A promotional wrapper encircled the shiny black dust jacket of each volume. The promotional blurb hailed the book as a "publishing event" destined to cause "violent conflicting reactions" among its readers. This, the ad hype continued, was the fictional account of a generation "roaming America in a wild, desperate search for identity and purpose." And then: "Jack Kerouac is the voice of this group and this is his novel."

Shortly afterward, he found himself in Mexico, before the official release of *On the Road*. Lodged in the Hotel Luis Moya, which he described as "an old 1910 whorehouse built of solid marble and tile," he busily worked on "About the Beat Generation," an essay for the *Saturday Review*. "The article is weird, I dunno if they'll even publish it—but I wish you could read it and comment on it for me right now," he wrote to his friend Phil Whalen. It was important to Jack that Phil evaluate it "before a thousand phonies start writing about the beat generation." As originator of the phrase, Kerouac wanted to "sneak in that it means religiousness, a kind of Second Religiousness... which *always* takes place in late civilization stage."

It was a fact: Jack Kerouac, age thirty-five, was not the man he was when he first began *On the Road*. Now he saw life through a more spiritual lens, a "beatific" one.

Sick with the Asiatic flu, Kerouac left Mexico on the heels of a deadly earthquake that demolished the huge apartment complex across the way from his hotel. He nonetheless escaped and returned to Orlando, where he stayed at his mother's home to recuperate. He had high fever and swollen testicles and was hardly able to walk about. As he suffered through his illness, he wondered whether his publicist at Viking had received his completed "About the Beat Generation."* And Jack wondered about traveling to New York to be interviewed by *Time*; he had received a letter from Allen and Peter, then in Venice, informing him that the editors wanted to interview him, too. Maybe they would fly him to New York? But one way or another, he had to get well and find a way to Manhattan, for soon his next novel would be launched, and his publisher had grand plans for its literary debut.

---

*The article, written for the *Saturday Review*, was never published there. It was, however, retitled as "Aftermath: The Philosophy of the Beat Generation" and published in *Esquire* in March 1958.

39.

WHEN THE TRIAL RESUMED on Thursday, August 22, the two P.M. hearing got off to a quirky start. The straight-laced prosecutor drew Judge Horn's attention to the bottom of *Howl*'s dedication page, which read: "All these books are published in Heaven."

"I don't quite understand that," Ralph McIntosh stated in all seriousness, "but let the record show, anyway, Your Honor, it's published by the City Lights Pocketbook Shop."

Had this evidence been offered with tongue-in-cheek, it might have suggested a playful understanding of Ginsberg's mindset. As it was, McIntosh's admission proved prophetic. It was the first of many examples of the linear mind clashing with the literary mind. Soon, it would become patently apparent that the elderly prosecutor was baffled by a great deal in *Howl*. Only time would tell whether his bewilderment would cripple the prosecution's obscenity case.

Rising from his chair, the confident and commanding Jake Ehrlich was now prepared to expose the legal strategy developed by the trio of attorneys for the defense. As was expected, he began by moving for a judgment that *Howl and Other Poems* was not obscene and that the defendants were not guilty of violating California Penal Code Section 311.3 for publishing and selling obscenity.

"I assume Your Honor has now read the book," Ehrlich asked. "The question then arises whether as a result of your reading you have been able to form a judgment as to whether this book is or is not obscene.... If Your Honor determines that the book is not obscene under the law, then, of course, that's the end of the issue."

Arguing for his motion, Ehrlich was careful to establish two key points of law critical to the defense. First, a prosecution for obscenity could not prevail on indecent words alone, taken out of context of the entire work. "I believe Your Honor will agree with me that individual words in and of themselves do not make obscene books," he urged. "Some people think that certain four-letter words in and of themselves destroy mankind from a moral standpoint. This, of course, is not the law." Ehrlich drove this point home by alluding to the notorious example of censorial overreaching against Whitman's celebrated work: "I presume that I could take the classic, *Leaves of Grass*, and by cutting it to pieces find a word here or there or an idea that some people may not like."

Second, the defense emphasized that California's obscenity law penalized only intentional acts—in other words, that the defendants' purpose in publishing and selling *Howl* must be to provide the public an obscene work. In this regard, Ehrlich claimed, the prosecution failed utterly to prove its case. "There is not one word in the record going to the intent of the defendant in the sale of this book," he argued. "Nor is there any evidence before this court that any representation was made concerning the contents of the book, nor is there any evidence before the court that ... the purpose of the sale was the selling of a salacious, lewd, or indecent book."

"The Master" had put the prosecutor on the ropes. Try as he might to disentangle himself, Ralph McIntosh's every effort seemed to enmesh him even more tightly. As he offered one counterargument after another, the frustrated prosecutor was rebuffed by the court at almost every turn:

Prosecutor's Argument: California's obscenity law prohibits obscene or indecent literature. Thus, a violation can be established by proof either of obscenity or indecency alone.

Court's Response: No—the words are essentially synonymous. "You are flying in the face of the First Amendment," Judge Horn asserted. "I can stop you right there as far as 'indecent' is concerned. This court...will follow the *Roth* decision as the basis of what may or may not be the subject of an...exception to the First Amendment, and these books are either obscene or not obscene." In Horn's mind, indecency was not a separate exception to the First Amendment. Thus, he concluded, "I am not going to quibble about the word 'indecent' or even consider that it is something lesser than obscene."

Prosecutor's Argument: When it comes to the defendant's purpose in selling obscenity, lewd intent may be proved by the character of the literature itself.

Court's Response: No—evidence that a book was sold, particularly where there is no suggestion of obscene character on its cover, is not sufficient alone to demonstrate lewd intent.

Prosecutor's Argument: An inference of lewd intent can be drawn from the fact that a publisher or seller must have knowledge of what he is doing.

Court's Response: No—at least as to Murao, the bookstore clerk. "Going back to the salesman," the judge posited, "there is nothing in the record showing that he has read these books or knew their contents or that there was any lewd intent on his part in selling them."

When the exchanges ended, even a cautious seer would have found the signs to be favorable for the defense. After all, Judge Horn had invoked the First Amendment as a shield against any prosecution under California criminal law for merely "indecent" words. Either *Howl*, taken as a whole, was obscene literature as defined by the *Roth* test, or it was protected expression.

Furthermore, Horn had managed to separate the prosecution's charges involving *Miscellaneous Man* from those involving *Howl*. Having done that, the case against the defendants for selling *Miscellaneous Man* could not stand. For one thing, the magazine had not been published by City Lights; for another, its innocuous cover gave no indication of its allegedly obscene character. Hence, McIntosh's failure to prove that the defendants had actual knowledge of its contents was fatal to the *Miscellaneous Man* charges.

Judge Horn also became increasingly cool toward the prosecution's entire case against Shigeyoshi Murao for criminal sale of an allegedly obscene work. Accordingly, he suggested that the charges against Ferlinghetti's clerk would soon be summarily dismissed. What remained to be seen was how the jurist would view the State's case against Ferlinghetti for the publication of *Howl*.

At this point, Judge Horn dealt a bad card to the defense. He denied its motion to dismiss the *Howl* case for insufficient evidence. So the trial was on. Now it fell to Ehrlich, Speiser, and Bendich either to submit the case to the court without a defense or to present testimony supporting the legality of *Howl*.

Judge Horn intended to keep tight reins on the trial proceedings. For example, he was quite precise as to the type of evidence that he would and would not entertain. He would accept opinion evidence from literary scholars, critics, or reviewers on the merits of *Howl*. In contrast, he would not hear testimony from psychiatrists or sociologists on the psychically damaging or socially corruptive potential of the work. On that score, Horn declared, "It is obvious that you are never going to get unanimous consent.... That's the reason why the freedom of the press should be so stringently protected, so that no one segment of the country can censor to the injury of the rest, what they can read, see, and hear." This was yet another blow to the prosecution. The judge was sounding more and more like an ACLU devotee.

The prosecutor objected strenuously that the hearing "could get out of hand" as both sides offered expert witnesses "telling Your Honor how you should decide." Judge Horn made it plain, however, who would be the Decider in his courtroom. He would not tolerate a panel of experts opining on *Howl*'s obscenity. For it was Judge Horn, and only Judge Horn, who would reach that conclusion as a matter of law. "I would not permit the direct question to be asked of such a witness, 'Do you consider this book obscene?' because that is something that the court has to determine," Horn confirmed.

After a brief conference with the attorneys in his chambers, the judge brought the hearing to a close. He set the date of Thursday, September 5, for presentation of expert testimony concerning *Howl*'s inherent value as a poetic creation.

—◦◦◦—

SIXTY-TWO HUNDRED miles away from all this legalese, Allen Ginsberg was still in Rome following his debacle of a *Time* magazine interview (which was never published).* He ventured to Naples to visit the "Secret Museum" (or "Secret Cabinet"), a part of the National Archaeological Museum there. Allen was eager to see the pornographic artifacts of ancient Pompeii, including erotic frescoes, shameless satyrs, and debauched Bacchuses. He even paid a call on the ruins of a bordello to examine the ribald Priapic depictions on the walls.

---

*According to one of Ginsberg's biographers, Barry Miles, the "interview itself was a depressing experience—the *Time* interviewer accused him of being insincere."

Finding a fisherman to ferry him to the Isle of Ischia, Allen hoped to drop in on W.H. Auden at his summer respite. Ginsberg found the famous Anglo-American poet and dramatist at an outdoor bar, seated with "a tableful of dull chatty literary old fairies," as Allen later characterized them. After consuming far too much wine, the youthful poet became contentious and boisterous when the aged poet admitted that he didn't relish rebellious poetry.

Insults began to fly.

Ginsberg called Auden a "bad poet." In turn, Auden denigrated *Howl* for its excessive self-pity. Auden criticized Ginsberg's beloved Walt Whitman for holding undemocratic views. Ginsberg then retorted that he was blind to the wisdom of Whitman.

As Allen told it, "I quoted the first line of Whitman, 'I celebrate myself,' etc., and Auden said, 'Oh, but my dear, that's so wrong, and so shameless, it's an utterly bad line.'" Allen left tanked, branding Auden and his company "a bunch of shits" as he walked off in a huff.

Writing to Ferlinghetti from Europe, Allen pestered him to publish Burroughs' sexually charged *Naked Lunch*, this even while *Howl's* publisher was in the throes of an obscenity trial! He also urged Ferlinghetti to reprint *Howl* without blanks in place of the "dirty" words. "[I]f we win the trial—is it possible to put in the whole words now??? If so that would be worth doing, as far as I'm concerned. I never liked the blanks and think they actually weaken the effect and make it shocking where it should be powerfully hip." Ginsberg added, "We put the blanks in to evade customs and protect Villiers—if we win have we green lite?"

Back in America, Jack Kerouac was anxious to leave Orlando, Florida, for New York City for the publishing debut of *On the Road*. He was so broke that he couldn't pay for the ticket to Manhattan. But there was his generous girlfriend, Joyce Johnson (then Glassman), and he prevailed on her to come to his financial rescue: "I'd sure like to be in N.Y. when ROAD comes out! Unless you'd like to ship me $30 and I could take a bus & come stay with you for a month—During the month I'll surely collect $ on *something*."

That was pure Kerouac. Jack had done much the same the first time he met Joyce earlier that year at the Howard Johnson's down on Eight Street in the Village. (It was a blind date that Allen had arranged.) They sat on bar stools, and chatted waiting for coffee.

"When the coffee arrived, Jack looked glum. He couldn't pay for it. He had no money, none at all," recalled Joyce. "He was waiting for a check from his publisher, he said angrily." Turning to her handsome stranger, clad in a "flannel lumberjack shirt," Joyce said, "Look, that's all right. I have money. Do you want me to buy you something to eat?"

Here she was, doing what his other lovers before her had done—paying for Jack. She sent him the dough for the New York trip, and Jack was back on the road, this time in a Greyhound bus instead of Neal Cassady's Hudson Hornet. He arrived in New York in the late afternoon of September 4. Then he hopped on the subway with his rucksack, exited at 68th Street, and walked to Joyce's new place.

Rebellious, carefree, and bright, the former Barnard College student was Jack's cup of tea. Joyce was also a writer busy on a novel, *Come and Join the Dance*. She had even worked for literary agents, including one who passed on three of Jack's novels (*On the Road* was one of them). Because this fair-haired girl felt at home in the bohemian quarters of Washington Square, she was especially appealing in Jack's eyes. He could barely wait to see her.

Meanwhile, as Joyce awaited Jack's return, "the phone started ringing with messages from Viking Press." It was Jack's publicist from Viking. He was anxious, very anxious. Joyce took the call, acting as Jack's secretary.

"Is Jack Kerouac there?" There was a clear sense of urgency in his tone.

"No," Joyce told him. He would be getting in later that day.

"Will you have him call as soon as he arrives? Will you tell him we have a lot of things lined up for him?"

His tone became more pressing with each new request. Among other things, he was eager to arrange a *Time* interview with Jack for the next day. This was extremely important.

"Will you make *sure* to tell him I called?" The man seemed on "the edge of being distraught." One more matter: "Who am I speaking to?"

Joyce spoke in her best college vernacular, thereby reassuring the man from Viking that she was not "one of those abandoned young women" about whom Jack had written in *On the Road*. She would convey the entire message, and Jack would call him immediately. And yes, she understood that this was extremely important.

But how would all this excitement play out with Jack, Joyce wondered? After all, he "had mixed feelings about *On the Road*. It had been written six years ago" when Jack was a very different man. His life had changed much since then. Moreover, Jack hated what the Viking editors had done to the spontaneity of the original work, which now had been edited to please a more mainstream taste. "Now, when it was too late, he regretted every revision they'd talked him into." Besides, his heart was now in two other works, *Doctor Sax* and *Visions of Cody*, but no publisher had any interest in those books, however important Jack Kerouac thought them to be.

When Jack finally got to Joyce's apartment, he was ready to be taken into Joyce's warm embrace. At last, he had arrived, decked out in a loud blue Hawaiian shirt. She looked into his gorgeous eyes with wild excitement, both about his love and his literary future. After they hugged, she told him the news soon enough, especially the news about the *Time* interview. Such an opportunity, Joyce appreciated, was the sort of break that Jack Kerouac needed to catapult him to fame and fortune.

40.

Its publication is a historic occasion...
—Gilbert Millstein
New York Times, September 5, 1957

IN THE WEE HOURS of the very day that the *Howl* trial would resume, Jack and Joyce took some rest after passionate entangling. It was "the black-out sleep that comes after making love," she recalled. But their sleep would be interrupted because there was to be a review of *On the Road* in tomorrow's *New York Times*. At least, that is what the Viking publicist had told them.

Jack was worried, Joyce was hopeful. "Maybe it'll be terrific. Who knows?" she said. He was doubtful; it would be hard for him to sleep, however tired he was.

Just before midnight, the two woke up, dressed, and rushed from her brownstone apartment to a newsstand at Broadway and 66th Street near the subway entrance. They watched with anticipation as the "old man at the stand" cut the brown cord that bundled that morning's papers. There, under a street lamp, they stood turning the pages until they found it on page 27—a column by Gilbert Millstein, entitled "Books of the Times." Jack's picture was next to it.

Joyce "felt dizzy reading Millstein's first paragraph—like going out on a Ferris wheel too quickly and dangling out over space, laughing and gasping at the same time." Jack was quiet at first. He read through the review, worried at the outset of each new paragraph.

"It's good, isn't it?"

Joyce was jubilant: "Yes, it's very, very good."

The review, as it would later be credited, "propelled both Kerouac and his beat-generation beatitudes from limbo to limelight." It was a new day.

Donnelly's Irish Bar was only a few blocks away, and the elated couple decided to celebrate over a beer. They spread the paper out on a table and went over the review line by line. And then they read it again, and yet again. They could hardly believe their eyes as they reexamined Jack's picture and reread Millstein's praise. "*On the Road* is the most beautifully executed, the clearest and the most important utterance yet made by the generation Kerouac himself named years ago as 'beat,' and whose principal avatar he is."

To Jack's amazement, the same man who in 1952 had rejected his essay on "The History of Bop" now ratcheted up the tribute to Kerouac's literary prowess. For Millstein, the book was more than a novel; it was a glorious declaration of generational independence. "Just as, more than any other novel of the Twenties, *The Sun Also Rises* came to be regarded as the testament of the "Lost Generation," so it seems certain that *On the Road* will come to be known as that of the 'Beat Generation.'"

And presciently, Millstein landed on what would become the book's most famous passage, a few lines taken from the first chapter: "The only people for me are the mad ones, the ones who are mad to live, mad to talk, mad to be saved, desirous of everything at the same time, the ones who never yawn or say a commonplace thing, but burn, burn, burn like fabulous yellow roman candles."

This fountain of acclaim was a source of unease for Jack. He "kept shaking his head. He didn't look happy, exactly, but strangely puzzled, as if he couldn't figure out why he wasn't happier than he was." The review "overwhelmed" and "frightened" him, Joyce recalled, "because he wasn't the kind of person who did very well being in the public eye." Joyce saw the bigger picture: "Thousands were waiting for a prophet to liberate them from the cautious middle-class lives they had been reared to inherit." And the Millstein review had proclaimed Jack Kerouac to be that prophet, a defiant prophet. "*On the Road*," she understood, "would bring them the voice of a supreme outlaw validated by his art, visions of a life at dizzying speed beyond all safety barriers, pure exhilarating energy."

With mixed emotions running high, the pair walked back to Joyce's apartment to get some needed sleep. "Jack lay down obscure for the last time in his life," she observed. "The ringing phone woke him the next morning and he was famous."

41.

*The trial, in its way, illustrated what
"Howl" was howling about.*
—Al Bendich

THE *MURAO/FERLINGHETTI* trial was a *cause célèbre* for the San Francisco literati. Grand literary poobahs appeared in Judge Horn's courtroom on Thursday, September 5, to testify in defense of *Howl*'s poetic merits.

Lawrence Speiser had lined up a formidable team of impressive witnesses. There were six college professors from different disciplines: among them, Herbert Blau, professor of humanities and language arts at San Francisco State College and director of the Actors' Workshop of the San Francisco Drama Guild; Leo Lowenthal, sociology and literature professor at the University of California, Berkeley, who had been a leading authority in the Frankfurt Institute before Hitler's rise; Mark Linenthal, professor of language arts and director of the Poetry Workshop at San Francisco State College; and Mark Schorer, chair of English graduate studies at UC Berkeley and a recognized novelist, short-story writer, and essayist.

In addition, a recognized newspaper book review editor, Luther Nichols of the *San Francisco Examiner*, would be called for the defense. And, to add the weight of international literary success, two celebrated authors were to testify for the defense: Walter Van Tilburg Clark, recognized primarily for his novel, *The Ox-Bow Incident*; and Kenneth Rexroth, the prolific poet, translator of poetry, and essayist who was simpatico with the Beat Generation.

Notwithstanding the imposing credentials of the defense's nine witnesses, notable was the absence of three witnesses: Allen Ginsberg, the man who wrote *Howl*; Lawrence Ferlinghetti, the man who published *Howl*; and Shigeyoshi Murao, the man who sold *Howl*. None of those voices was ever heard in the course of the trial that lasted for weeks. Judge Horn never heard Allen describe the relationship between life as he lived it and the poem as he wrote it. The jurist never heard Ferlinghetti explain why he decided to have the book printed abroad. Moreover, it was never clear whether Murao even read the poems or, if he did, what he made of them. Of course, one is left to wonder whether, if any or all of the three had taken the stand, the testimony would have helped or hindered the defense.

The defense's phalanx of outstanding literary authorities was assembled to serve one and the same important purpose. They were all to offer their expert opinions that *Howl*, in both its substance and its style, had serious literary merit, insofar as it dealt with significant social issues or offered an impassioned critique of contemporary American life or indicted the elements in modern society that corrupted, perverted, or destroyed "the best minds" of Ginsberg's generation. Of course, if *Howl* had such literary merit, then the defense attorneys could argue that the poetry was "a step to truth" and not "utterly without redeeming social importance." In short, it could not be obscene.

Each of the nine witnesses, in his own way, contributed to building the defense's case. For example, Mark Schorer was key to establishing that "*Howl*, like any work of literature, attempts and intends to make a significant comment on or interpretation of human experience as the author knows it."

Ever the pedagogue, Schorer clarified in his steady and serene drawl the aesthetic structure of the poem, as if he were instructing his English students. A Fulbright and Guggenheim Award–winning scholar, Schorer explained that Ginsberg created, in the first part of the poem, "the impression of a kind of nightmare world in which people representing 'the best minds of my generation'... are wandering like damned souls in hell." Part II turned to an "indictment" of "materialism, conformity, and mechanization leading to war," all "destructive of the best qualities in human nature." Finally, part III addressed a friend "who is mad and in a madhouse" and "is the specific representative of what the author regards as the general condition." Stylistically, the poem used "the language of ordinary speech, the language of vulgarity," terms "absolutely essential to the aesthetic purpose of the work."

Without ever giving a direct opinion on the obscenity of *Howl*, something that Judge Horn would not have permitted, Schorer's testimony was a masterpiece of indirection on that very issue. How could *Howl* be obscene when it had such literary merit in its very theme, organization, and vulgarity?

The other defense witnesses testified much to the same effect. Book critic Luther Nichols, the future West Coast editor for Doubleday, deftly characterized Ginsberg's life as a "vagabond one" that was "colored by exposure to jazz... to a liberal and bohemian education... to a certain amount of what we call bumming around." All that experience led to this "howl of pain." Similarly, Van Tilburg Clark, whose cowboy-frontier novels explored deep philosophical issues, found in "all of the poems" in *Howl* a "thoroughly honest poet, who is also a highly competent technician."

Clearly, the most laudatory judgment on *Howl* came from the poet Kenneth Rexroth. "Its merit is extraordinarily high," Rexroth stressed. "It is probably the most remarkable single poem published by a young man" since the Second World War.

When Al Bendich, who conducted the direct examination of Rexroth, asked him to describe the nature and theme of *Howl*, the poet of humanistic passion depicted Ginsberg's work as "the denunciation of evil...and a call to repent." It fit into a great biblical tradition: "This is prophetic literature: 'Woe! Woe! Woe! The City of Jerusalem!...[Y]ou must repent and do thus and so.'"

With these words, Rexroth's testimony moved Ginsberg from the status of a crude poet to that of a chastising prophet. Without doubt, this characterization must have caught the ear of the Bible-revering judge. And as for Ralph McIntosh, it must have been inconceivable for him to imagine biblical prophesies worded in the coarse vernacular of *Howl*.

As the defense witnesses aimed to demonstrate *Howl*'s serious literary merits, the prosecutor's cross-examination of them aimed to dethrone their lofty praise. In so doing, McIntosh hoped to convince Judge Horn that, indeed, Ginsberg's poetry was little more than its filth, its vulgarity, and its disgusting language—in short, obscene. McIntosh used two basic strategies to accomplish that.

First, there was the *What can this possibly mean?* strategy: demonstrate that the average person on the streets of San Francisco would likely have no idea of what *Howl* was all about. Then, in the words of Justice Brennan in *Roth*, Ginsberg's poetry might be viewed, under "contemporary community standards," as having little "social value as a step to truth." That was the point of McIntosh's cross-examination of Mark Schorer:

> *McIntosh:* You understand what "angelheaded hipsters burning for the ancient heavenly connection to the starry dynamo in the machinery of night" means?
> *Schorer:* Sir, you can't translate poetry into prose; that's why it's poetry...

McIntosh: In other words, you don't have to understand the words to—

Schorer: You don't understand the individual words taken out of their context....You can no more translate that back into logical prose English than you can say what a surrealistic painting means in words, because it's not prose...

McIntosh: Each word by itself certainly means something, doesn't it?

Schorer: No....I can't possibly translate, nor I am sure, can anyone in this room translate the opening part of this poem into rational prose.

McIntosh: That's just what I wanted to find out.

The prosecution employed a second strategy: *Were these words really relevant?* That is, demonstrate that Ginsberg's choice of "dirty" words was not really relevant to any socially valuable ideas. Then, applying the standards of *Roth*, Ginsberg's poetry (already shown to be incomprehensible "to the average person") might be viewed as little more than its lewd and sex-obsessed language, appealing primarily to the "prurient interests" of its readers. McIntosh's cross-examination of Luther Nichols emphasized this strategy:

McIntosh [reading "Footnote to Howl"]: "The world is holy! The soul is holy! The skin is holy! The nose is holy! The tongue and cock and hand and asshole holy!" Now, are those last words there, are they relevant to the literary value of Mr. Ginsberg's work?

Nichols:...He's showing that everything is holy within a sense, the sense that he is trying to convey here...

McIntosh [reading "America"]: "America when will we end the human war? Go fuck yourself with your atom bomb." Now, the word in there, that four-letter word, is that relevant to the literary merit of Mr. Ginsberg's work?

Nichols:...He doesn't want to temper it by saying it any less softly. He's angry, and when you are angry sometimes you do use words of this sort. I would say, yes, it's relevant; it's in keeping with the wrath he feels, with the language that he has used throughout most of these poems.

Interestingly, in deploying his cross-examination strategies, the prosecutor repeated again and again—indeed, no fewer than twenty-four times—the very four-letter and five-, six-, seven- and eight-letter words that he deemed "obscene" terms violating the California Penal Code. And all of this, of course, was done in open court.

Jake Ehrlich was prepared to bring the defense case to a close. Before resting, however, he offered into evidence copies of admiring reviews of *Howl*. Among them, a *New York Times Book Review* article by Richard Eberhart, published only three days earlier, described Ginsberg's poems as "profoundly Jewish in temper." Much like Rexroth, Eberhart depicted *Howl* as "biblical" in its catalogue of "evils of our time from physical deprivation to madness." There were other reviews, some positive and some mixed, published in magazines such as the *Nation* and literary journals.

Predictably, Ralph McIntosh objected to the admissibility of all the book reviews as being irrelevant. "The only possible reason that [Mr. Ehrlich] could offer those would be if there was some testimony by Mr. Ferlinghetti; if he were to take the stand and say that he relied upon those book reviews in selling this book." Then, the prosecutor explained, the reviews would be material to the publisher's intent in issuing *Howl*.

With some impatience, Judge Horn overruled this objection. Judicial consideration of literary reviews in obscenity cases had become an established practice in New York, Horn observed, and "California has so far adopted a more liberal attitude than the State

of New York." The book reviews were admitted, and the distinguished literary voices of Richard Eberhart, M.L. Rosenthal, and
others now chimed in with those of the nine defense witnesses.

From the very start, Ralph McIntosh had not relished the prospect of expert witness testimony in this obscenity prosecution. He
had argued vehemently at the end of the August 22 hearing that the
opinions of poets, professors, and pundits as to the literary merits of
Howl were entirely irrelevant. Hence, the prosecutor did not intend
to prolong what he viewed as a charade of poetic puffery. He brought
only two rebuttal witnesses to the trial for the sole purpose of dem-
onstrating that even the experts would disagree as to the redeeming
social value of Ginsberg's outlandish and tasteless creations.

The prosecution's witnesses paled, both as to credentials and
credibility, in comparison to the illuminati called by the defense.
David Kirk, an assistant professor of English at the University of
San Francisco, testified that *Howl* had "negligible" literary value
because it was "just a weak imitation of a form that was used eighty
to ninety years ago by Walt Whitman." On cross-examination,
however, Kirk proved no match for quick-witted Jake Ehrlich, as he
twisted the young Ph.D. candidate into knots of self-contradiction
and self-impeachment.

The comic relief of the *Howl* trial arrived with Gail Potter. Before
taking the stand for the prosecution, the middle-aged woman
had circulated small printed brochures to the courtroom spectators advertising her availability for private elocution lessons. On
the stand, the San Francisco speech teacher and freelance writer
declared with grandiose flare, "I have rewritten 'Faust'—took three
years to do that, but I did it; I rewrote 'Everyman.'"

When laughter exploded, Judge Horn interrupted: "Ladies and
gentlemen, we are not playing games; this is a trial that involves
serious issues. . . . Try to maintain decorum in the courtroom; otherwise, I will have to clear it."

Once order was restored, the prosecutor asked Ms. Potter for her opinion of *Howl and Other Poems*. "I think it has no literary merit," she put it decisively. "You feel like you are going through the gutter when you have to read that stuff." Shuddering with dramatic disgust, she concluded: "I didn't linger on it too long, I assure you." Defense attorney Ehrlich responded by declining any cross-examination.

"The People rest, Your Honor," McIntosh stated. It was now time for the prosecution to make its closing statement.

The deputy district attorney began by portraying the ordinary and unenlightened citizen of San Francisco as going to hell in a handbasket if exposed to such smut as *Howl*. "I made the comment in open court here that I read it; I don't understand it very well," he conceded. "In fact, looking it over, I think it is a lot of sensitive bullshit, using the language of Mr. Ginsberg. So, then, if the sale of a book is not being limited to just...experts on modern poetry, but falls into the hands of the general public, that is, the average reader, this court should take that into consideration in determining whether or not *Howl* is obscene."

Here was a contemporary Cassandra, crying out the fall of the beloved city. "I would like you to ask yourself, Your Honor," McIntosh bellowed, "would you like to see this sort of poetry printed in your local newspaper...to be read by your family...or would you like to have this poetry read to you over the air on the radio as a diet?" With emotional charge, the prosecutor concluded: "In other words, Your Honor, how far are we going to license the use of filthy, vulgar, obscene, and disgusting language? How far can we go?"

Jake Ehrlich's summation deflated the prosecution's dire warnings. Invoking James Joyce's *Ulysses* and Christopher Marlowe's "Ignoto," he elevated low-brow slang to high-brow status. "Fuck" was but a "plain, common Anglo-Saxon word...used in some beautiful poetry."

Reciting the whole of Marlowe's poem, he boldly proclaimed the final stanza:

I cannot buss thy fill, play with thy hair,
Swearing by Jove, "Thou art most debonnaire!"
Not I, by cock! But I shall tell thee roundly,
Hark in thine ear, zounds I can fuck thee soundly.

Throwing down the gauntlet, he asked: "Would we, if he were alive today, arrest Christopher Marlowe for writing his poem...?"

The defense lawyer then turned the tables on the prosecution: "You do not think common, lewd, or lascivious thoughts just because you have read something in a book, unless it is your mental purpose to do so." Directing himself to *Howl*, Ehrlich adroitly summed up the merits of the poems' substantive concepts and stylistic choices. When the poet howled, "'Go fuck yourself with your atom bomb,'" he asked, "what prurient interest is Ginsberg generating with that cry of pain? The man is at the end of the road. He is crying out in the wilderness. Nobody is listening." Moreover, the language of the poems harbored no lewd intent or salacious appeal: "It isn't for us to choose the words. When Ginsberg tells his story, he tells it as he sees it, uses the words as he knows them, and portrays in his language that which he sees."

Building momentum in pace and pitch, Ehrlich proclaimed: "The problem of what is legally permissible in the description of sexual acts and feelings in art and literature is of the greatest importance in a free society.... The battle of censorship will not be finally settled by Your Honor's decision, but you will either add to liberal educated thinking or, by your decision, add fuel to the fire of ignorance."

And then Ehrlich's climax: "Let there be light. Let there be honesty. Let there be no running from nonexistent destroyers of morals. Let there be honest understanding. In the end the four-letter words will not appear draped in glaring headlights, but will be submerged in the decentralization of small thinking in small minds."

Somber silence in the courtroom. No one spoke. No one moved. Moments passed. Finally, Judge Horn inquired, "Gentlemen, is the matter submitted?... October Third at two P.M. for decision."

The three-week trial had come to a close. Now the work of McIntosh, Ehrlich, Speiser, and Bendich was over, but the real work for Judge Clayton Horn had just begun. During the one-month recess before issuing his decision, he poured through James Joyce's *Ulysses* and the obscenity cases concerning it and carefully studied *Howl and Other Poems*.

42.

JACK KEROUAC couldn't purge the Millstein review from his brain. It was a cause for uninhibited celebration and for unnerving concern.* His publisher and friends wanted to memorialize his success by partying like there was no tomorrow, an activity that was not foreign to him. Still, Jack reacted to his success by medicating himself with alcohol to mitigate his neuroses, a malady that haunted him even in his dreams. To face up to his Beat celebrity persona, he was looped so often that he turned into a disaster waiting to happen at any party, press conference, TV or radio interview, or wherever he was in the public eye. What was once fun with Allen, Bill, Neal, and the gang had become frightening. His demons had begun to encircle him.

On the day after the Millstein review, Keith Jennison, one of his editors at Viking, dropped in at Joyce's apartment with a gift of a half case of champagne. First they toasted, and then Jack got toasted.

---

*"One of the great ironies of Kerouac's becoming famous for *On the Road*," notes Isaac Gewirtz, "was that by 1957 he had forsaken what might be called a 'road' lifestyle and had even begun to question the validity of 'hipsterism.' Instead, he found himself yearning for a more settled existence, which, in his idyllic vision, would still include late-night jazz-clubbing and getting drunk at parties and in bars." But at sunrise he staggered back to a normal existence with all of its traditional trappings. In a larger sense, there was more: "After reading carefully through Kerouac's diaries, journals, and fugitive autobiographical pieces," Gewirtz adds, "it is impossible to escape the oppressive reality of a psyche at war with itself."

As the three drank mimosas, the bell on the black telephone rang incessantly like a fire alarm on Benzedrine. *Ring! Ring! Ring!*—a friend calling to congratulate him. *Ring! Ring! Ring!*—a reporter asking for an interview. *Ring! Ring! Ring!*—a publicist inviting him to a PR bash. *Ring! Ring! Ring!*—sorry, wrong number.

Within no time, three bottles of champagne vanished. Stunned by Jack's compulsive consumption, Keith pulled Joyce aside. "Take care of this man," he advised.

As fate had it, somebody else wanted to raise a glass to Kerouac's rising star, the very man who had illuminated that star. It was his reviewer, Gilbert Millstein. Perhaps more than anyone else, Millstein had played a major role in thrusting Beat literature into the public limelight. Five years earlier, as the writer of book reviews and articles for the Sunday department of the *New York Times*, Millstein gave national notice to John Clellon Holmes's first novel, *Go*. And it was Millstein who, shortly thereafter, solicited Holmes to write his famous piece, "This Is the Beat Generation." It was that essay that first gave popular currency to the cultural catchphrase.

Now Millstein had done the same for Jack, and then some. Unquestionably, it was his *New York Times* review that gave *On the Road* its invincible status.

"I'm giving a party for Jack."

It was Millstein calling Holmes to request that he bring his friend Kerouac to commemorate the fame the reviewer had just heaped on him. Since the thirty-one-year-old newspaper man did not know Jack, he needed John's intervention. Holmes was happy to help.

"I went in alone." John mingled with Millstein and his friends, as more and more people arrived. "Hours went by, and people kept piling in." The party was in full swing, but "no Jack." More time passed, more people arrived. Still no Jack.

Through all of the music and chatter, a phone was heard ringing in the bedroom. It was Jack, calling from Joyce's apartment.

Incredibly, he would speak neither to Millstein nor his wife, only to John. John went into the room to take Jack's call.

"I can't come down. I'm hung over. I'm shivering. I've got the D.T.'s," Jack complained, "but I know you've come into town. Can you get out and come up and see me?"

"Sure," John replied.

Embarrassed and apologetic, John turned to Gilbert to explain the situation: "Look, Jack's in trouble. He's feeling bad. He's sick, and he can't make it, and I'm going to slip out because I'm in town really to see him, and I'm going to run up and see him."

"Gil understood completely," Holmes recalled. "So it was one of those ludicrous situations in which, here were thirty or forty people collected in this apartment to see this new, young Marlon Brando of literature, who had just called up to say he couldn't make it, he was in bed."

John rushed out of the party and ran uptown to Joyce's apartment on 67th Street between Columbus and Central Park West. When he got there, he discovered the crisis soon enough. All of the favorable fallout from Millstein's review—the endless demands for interviews and TV appearances—was torturing Jack. "He didn't know who he was, and he was just terrified. He was lying there in bed, holding his head." To make matters worse, the phone wouldn't stop ringing.

Kerouac's stress, Holmes observed, "so discombobulated him that for the rest of his life he never, never got his needle back on true north. Never."

43.

UNLIKE JACK KEROUAC, Clayton Horn was not getting smashed and carrying on in a frenzied and anxious state. His life was far more staid, more cerebral, or at least it had become that way with the advent of the *Howl* trial.

What the judge was doing was of far greater importance than the mundane day-to-day routine of the fender-bender fare he had in his courtroom. Now he was faced with momentous law— *constitutional law*. Now he had to study that law, especially the new obscenity standards mandated by the Supreme Court. And now he had to comprehend that law, apply it to the facts of the case and author a legal opinion, something rare for a municipal court judge.

As he read in his chambers or reclined on his sofa at home, Judge Horn studied both literature and law. When he was not perusing *Ulysses* or *Howl,* he paged through the official appellate reports of the federal and state courts and strove to make sense of complicated statutes. Fortunately, the studious jurist had a most helpful work to assist him, this one less literary, more legal; less poetic, more practical. It was a "Memorandum of Points and Authorities," composed by defense counsel Albert Bendich and submitted to the court for its consideration.

In clear and crisp prose, the document methodically laid out the constitutional and statutory arguments that formed the backbone of the defense's trial strategies. Not only did it outline the logical sequence of legal analysis, but it provided case authority supporting every key point. Moreover, excerpts from the testimony of expert witnesses illustrated that, indeed, the defendant's case had been proven at trial.

The memorandum was divided into three parts. Part I addressed the order in which the legal issues were to be considered by Judge Horn, as the First Amendment required it. Part II interpreted the standards for constitutionally unprotected obscenity that Justice Brennan provided in *Roth*. And, finally, part III examined the higher standards to be met under California law before a defendant could be convicted of obscenity.

Each link in this chain of reasoning was carefully conceived and crafted. And, at every point, the relevant law, whether the First Amendment or the California Penal Code, was given a reading that was both reasonable and strongly rights-protective. Of course, if the judge were convinced by that formidable chain, he would be led inescapably to a decision of "not guilty."

As Bendich understood the fundamental freedoms of speech and press, they prohibited the suppression of any literature by application of the obscenity test unless the trial court first determined that the work was utterly without socially redeeming value. Justice Brennan's majority opinion in *Roth*, Bendich explained, distinguished between "social speech" (that with redeeming value) and "non-social speech" (that without redeeming value), and it was only the latter that was to be tested under the "prurient interest" obscenity standard. "The *Roth* decision charges the trial court with the responsibility in every obscenity case," Bendich explained, "to see to it that this preference for freedom is not transmuted into a preference for prejudice."

This argument meant that Judge Horn needed to decide, first and foremost, whether *Howl and Other Poems* had any, even very slight, social value as a literary work. If it did, then a decision to acquit Ferlinghetti and Murao was to be made then and there, without any further consideration of the work's sexually stimulating potential.

Bendich marshaled piece after piece of powerful testimony from the defense's expert witnesses to persuade Horn that *Howl* must be viewed as having at least some literary merit. And the young ACLU attorney did not forget the jurist's penchant for Bible reading. Invoking the example of the Jewish prophet Hosea, he concluded: "Perhaps Ginsberg is a modern Hosea—only history will show whether, like Hosea, he will be considered a great social poet and critic. But it is obvious today that Ginsberg is saying much the same thing about our society as Hosea was saying about Israel."

And what was Ginsberg's connection to the prophet who chastised Israel for its infidelities? "Ginsberg, too, says that...we can save ourselves from destruction by our nightmare world...by focusing our attention upon the supreme values of love and reverence for everything human." That understood, the prosecution's case against *Howl* was a flimsy one—indeed, one not permitted by the First Amendment: "The prosecution has done no more than to question the meaning of the poem, admitting its ignorance in that regard, and has done no more than to cite out of context isolated words and phrases as questionable usage. The prosecution has not shown that this is a work which may be fairly described as hard core pornography or dirt for dirt's sake."

If the trial court were to determine, however, that *Howl*'s contents had essentially no redeeming value, then it would be required to move onto the *Roth* obscenity test. At that point, Bendich stressed, it was important to appreciate what the test was not about: "It does not consider whether material is shocking, degrading, vulgar, scatological or perverse where its tendency is to *disgust* the reader." In short, *Roth* had sliced off vulgarity from obscenity. What the test was about was "erotic allurement, sexual stimulation, aphrodisiac action." He put it plainly: "This comes very close to a requirement that the material be actually designed to 'sell sex' and, as such, to deal with no questions of social importance."

With this qualification, the obscenity test was designed to surgically remove from the community's discourse only that pornography that traded in acts rather than ideas. "A gesture calculated to excite lust, just as a picture or a story calculated to do the same, has no relevance to a question of how life should be lived by the community since it does not suggest social change or moral criticism," the memorandum stated. "[A] work which has as its probable effect no more than erotic arousal, or . . . stimulation to masturbation, does not argue social purpose."

Bendich contended that, under this constrained reading of *Roth*, *Howl* ought to survive the "prurient interest" test. "It is difficult in the extreme, if not impossible, to say logically that a work which has as its dominant theme the criticism of moral standards has also as its dominant theme the arousal of lustful desire. Here, at least, it would seem that the prosecution cannot have it both ways." He concluded: "The record is clear that all of the experts for the defense identified the main theme of *Howl* as social criticism. And the prosecution concedes that it does not understand the work, much less what its dominant theme is."

Much the same compelling logic guided Bendich's handling of the California obscenity statute and how it should be interpreted favorably to the defense. That is, the penal code required that both the obscenity of the work and the specific intent of the defendant be proved beyond a reasonable doubt and to a moral certainty.

But the facts could not establish that, Bendich argued. "No circumstantial evidence has been adduced by the prosecution . . . except that the defendant Ferlinghetti owns the City Lights Bookstore which is named as the publisher on the flyleaf of *Howl*." The memorandum continued: "There is no evidence...that Ferlinghetti sells erotica, that his bookstore caters to a prurient crowd. Indeed, so-called 'girlie' magazines will not be found there." Moreover, the bookstore was widely recognized for specializing in "literature for the intelligentsia."

Importantly, the civil-liberties lawyer observed, not even the feds had found Ginsberg's poetry to be criminal: "Although the Collector of Customs seized *Howl* on the charge that it was obscene, and referred the matter to the United States Attorney for institution of condemnation proceedings, the United States Attorney, after conferring with the United States Attorney General on the matter, notified the American Civil Liberties Union, which had provided counsel for the defendants throughout, that condemnation proceedings would not be instituted."

At this point, it was only left for Bendich to conclude: "It is thus apparent that defendants at all times acted on the conviction that the material in question was not obscene; there has never been anything furtive or clandestine about the way defendants handled the material in question."

Only fourteen pages long, the memorandum was a concise and convincing exercise of legal reasoning. Had Ginsberg and Ferlinghetti read the document, they likely would have found much of the subject matter ponderous, the writing technical, and the experience boring. But no other document, including *Howl* itself, might weigh as heavily on Judge Horn's mind as Bendich's memorandum of law. Perhaps even more than the trial testimony, that memorandum might best preserve their right to write as Beats.

Still, in all of this, there was a wild card. To what extent would the God-fearing jurist be persuaded by the defense?

44.

What they all have in common is the conviction that any
form of rebellion against American culture ... is admirable,
and they seem to regard homosexuality, jazz, dope-addiction,
and vagrancy as outstanding examples of such rebellion.
—Norman Podhoretz

THAT WAS THE JUDGMENT of the Beat Generation printed
on the pages of the "liberal" *New Republic* for September 16, 1957. By
a Columbia classmate of Allen's, no less. That critical take on *Howl*
and other Beat works was echoed by other mainstream critics:

James Dickey, *Sewanee Review*—*Howl* is an "exhibitionist welter
of unrelated associations, wish-fulfillment fantasies, and self-
righteous maudlinness."

John Ciardi, *Saturday Review*—the poem has "a kind of tireless
arrogance at least as refreshing as it is shallow."

John Hollander, *Partisan Review*—*Howl* is a "dreadful little
volume ... very short and very tiresome."*

---

*A few years later, Ginsberg responded to his critics: "Poetry has been attacked by an
ignorant and frightened bunch of bores who don't understand how it's made, & the
trouble with these creeps is they wouldn't know poetry if it came up and buggered them
in broad daylight."

While Allen took it on the chin in some high-brow literary venues, other poetry experts praised his work in Judge Horn's courtroom. It was that laudatory image of Ginsberg and the Beats that was magnified countless times in the popular culture, including a two-page spread of *Life* magazine.

The boldface title: BIG DAY FOR BARDS AT BAY: SAN FRANCISCO MUSE THRIVES IN FACE OF TRIAL OVER POEMS. The September 9, 1957, story gave a favorable assessment of the Beats: "As some of these photographs show, the poets are shouting their poems in night-clubs, at dance recitals, in art galleries, on radio and TV. Their work has gained respectful hearing from local and even national critics."

Four huge photographs depicted various Beat moments:

—Kenneth Rexroth, with head thrown back as if howling, recites poetry to the accompaniment of a jazz ensemble.

—Clad in a black dress and hat, a young amateur poet, Phyllis Diller, spoofs Dame Edith Sitwell, the English experimental poet.

—A "bohemian bard" performs his poetry, as a shirtless, muscular dancer in tights gives dramatic expression to his work.

—A hip Lawrence Ferlinghetti reads his "London," while a sassy black woman ("Mrs. Florence Allen") does a mock striptease with her brassiere in plain view.

The other two photographs were taken of the *Howl* trial:

—An impassioned Jake Ehrlich, leaning forward against a banister, addresses the court while brandishing an open copy of *Howl*.

—A brooding Ferlinghetti and contemplative Murao observe their fates on trial.

The photographic message of those juxtaposed images was clear: a rebellious movement was emerging in the culture and battling in the courtroom. It was cool—James Dean cool. Lawrence Ferlinghetti was right. Censorship was *Howl's* best publicity agent.

In stark contrast, Kerouac's publicity agent could take comfort in the fact that Gilbert Millstein's review immunized Jack's novel from the many scathing critiques that attacked it. Incredibly, the staying power of that review was so great as to deflect such critical comments as:

> R.W. Grandsden, *Encounter*—The novel is little more than a "series of Neanderthal grunts."

> Carlos Baker, *Saturday Review*—*On the Road* is a "dizzy travelogue" full of "verbal goofballs."

> Herbert Gold, the *Nation*—*On the Road* is "proof of illness," and Kerouac is the "perennial perverse bar mitzvah boy."

The countless reviews—"everyfuckingwhere," as Jack put it— drew ever more attention, even when highly critical. In the cultural rumble of it all, one thing was clear: Kerouac had become the "Great White Father" of the Beats. And the face of that father was soon to be seen by millions, as his image was broadcast on television.

Jack was invited to appear on John Wingate's popular WOR-TV talk show, *Nightbeat*. With tousled hair and frozen blue eyes, he looked "like a scared rabbit." As he shifted uncomfortably in his swivel chair, he "clammed up almost totally," feeling like "a kid dragged up before the cops." Wingate tried to extract some memorable sound bites from him about the rebellious Beat Generation that would interest his forty million viewers, but the stocky Kerouac went spiritual on him. He described the Beats as "basically a religious generation," and tersely declared, "I'm waiting for God to show his face."

It was exciting fare for the young Hunter S. Thompson and the crowd at the West End Bar, where Jack had once duked it out with two sailors.* Hundreds crammed into this "dim waystation of undergraduate debauchery" to catch Jack's first televised interview. They listened as he unleashed his stream of consciousness: "We love everything, Billy Graham, the Big Ten, rock and roll, Zen, apple pie, Eisenhower—we dig it all. We're in the vanguard of the new religion." Jack later felt foolish for having dragged the deity into the dialogue, but the West End kids received him approvingly. After all, he was revered as the "Bob Dylan of his day," recalled Thompson.

While *Howl* was enjoying modest success (some ten thousand copies were in print), the sales of *On the Road* zoomed like a rocket. It was on the best-seller list for five weeks; foreign rights were being sold; off-Broadway producers clamored for the chance to turn it into a play; and magazine editors sought Kerouac's pen. Warner Brothers was even willing to dish out $110,000 for the movie rights,[†] and Marlon Brando yearned to be the leading man, Dean Moriarty.

In effect, Ginsberg's *Howl* and *People v. Murao/Ferlinghetti* were the warm-up acts for *On the Road*. It was Kerouac who received the wild ovations from the popular culture. "Previously Jack had been grumbling to Allen that people kept introducing him as 'the guy

---

* "Ginsberg first met Neal Cassady and his wife Lu Anne at the West End," Bill Morgan noted, "just after their arrival in New York City in 1946." This was also the place where, in the summer of 1944, Jack drank with Lucien Carr not long before Lucien killed David Kammerer.

†Filmmaker Francis Ford Coppola has owned the film rights to *On the Road* since 1979. After several failed attempts to adapt the book to the screen, the project finally took shape in 2010 with Coppola as executive producer, Brazilian director Walter Salles, and screenwriter José Rivera. Released in 2012, the film stars Garrett Hedlund as Dean Moriarty (Neal Cassady), Sam Riley as Sal Paradise (Jack Kerouac), Kristen Stewart as Marylou (Lu Anne Henderson), Tom Sturridge as Carlo Marx (Allen Ginsberg), Viggo Mortensen as Old Bull Lee (William Burroughs) and Amy Adams as Jane (Joan Vollmer).

that Ginsberg's *Howl* is dedicated to,'" but now "he had fame of his own to contend with." On this very score, Allen wrote to Jack on September 28, 1957: "We saw *Times* Sept 5 review, I almost cried, so fine & true—well now you don't have to worry about existing only in my dedication & I will have to weep in your great shadow—what is happening in N.Y.—are you being pursued—is there a great mad wave of Fame crashing over your ears?"

"Everything's been happening here," Jack informed Allen. "Unbelievable number of events almost impossible to remember." In his letter of October 1, Kerouac wrote of his current life as "a big blurred Dostoyevskyan party with socialites where I was the Idiot." And then this bit of capitalized advice to his friend: "NOW LISTEN VIKING WANTS TO PUBLISH HOWL AND YOUR OTHERS AND ALSO GROVE. THEY RACING TO REACH YOU FIRST. TAKE YOUR CHOICE. I THINK HOWL NEEDS DISTRIBUTION. IT HAS NOT EVEN BEGUN TO BE READ."

Faithful to the publisher who had risked jail time and economic loss for him, Allen would not consider leaving the City Lights imprint. As he would later assure his friend Ferlinghetti, "I hear from Jack that both Viking and Grove interested in hardcover *Howl*, however that be wrong etc so don't worry as I said I won't go whoring in N.Y." That loyalty probably cost Ginsberg.

Worthy of Ginsberg's loyalty, Ferlinghetti wrote to his friend on Constitution Day (September 17, 1957): "Trial is not over yet—we're in court again this Thursday....Question of Fucked in the Ass not yet settled....Got to go. Later dad, Larry."

45.

APPROXIMATELY ONE MONTH after *People v. Ferlinghetti**
had been submitted for consideration, Judge Clayton Horn rendered
his decision. At two P.M. on Thursday, October 3, 1957, the judge
announced his judgment to a crowded audience that, according to
the *San Francisco Chronicle*, "offered the most fantastic collection
of beards, turtle-necked shirts and Italian hair-dos ever to grace the
grimy precincts of the Hall of Justice."

Remarkably, Horn issued his opinion in written form, a rare phenomenon for municipal judges. The typed opinion left little doubt
where this jurist stood on questions of free speech: "The authors of
the First Amendment knew that novel and unconventional ideas
might disturb the complacent, but they chose to encourage a freedom which they believed essential if a vigorous enlightenment was
ever to triumph over slothful ignorance.... The best method of censorship is by the people as self-guardians of public opinion and not
by government."

Horn's opinion was pure John Stuart Mill, pure Louis Brandeis,
pure Hugo Black, pure protection for dissident expression: "[L]ife

---

*When the opinion in the case was issued, the name changed to *People v. Ferlinghetti*
since the case against Murao had been dismissed.

is not encased in one formula whereby everyone acts the same or conforms to a particular pattern. No two persons think alike; we are all made from the same mold but in different patterns. Would there be any freedom of the press or speech if one must reduce his vocabulary to vapid and innocuous euphemism? An author should be real in treating his subject and be allowed to express his thoughts and ideas in his own words."

The Judge buttressed his rhetoric with legal analysis, carefully applying the rule of *Roth*. Obviously, the San Francisco jurist was impressed with Albert Bendich's Memorandum of Points and Authorities, as the structure and logic of his opinion closely tracked the defense attorney's rationales. Horn stressed: "[T]he majority opinion in *Roth* requires a trial court to ... decide in the first instance whether a work is utterly without social importance, *before* it permits the test of obscenity to be applied ... "

That crucial point was the first of twelve points Judge Horn listed for applying the law of *Roth* to the facts of *People v. Ferlinghetti*. "If the material has the slightest redeeming social importance it is not obscene," Horn wrote. Of course, this ruling alone could readily have ended the prosecution's case. Yet, the judge went on to elaborate eleven other criteria that needed to be considered before a work could be deemed obscene and a fit subject for censorship.

Among other things, the words contested must excite lascivious thoughts or arouse lustful desire to the point where they "present a clear and present danger of inciting antisocial or immoral action." Again tracking arguments made by Bendich, Judge Horn actually extended the protective reach of *Roth*, which nowhere demanded such a strict showing by the government. Moreover, added Horn, if the words used are "objectionable only because of coarse and vulgar language which is not erotic ... in character, [they are] not obscene."

Not surprisingly, then, the court ruled for the defense. *Howl and Other Poems* did, indeed, have "redeeming social importance," which meant that it was no longer criminal to sell Allen Ginsberg's lyrics in San Francisco.

It was poetic justice, a major victory for the cultural outsiders. Ginsberg, then vacationing in Paris, was vindicated (though he had yet to hear it); Ferlinghetti was liberated; and the cause of free speech was celebrated. The elated audience in the packed courtroom welcomed the ruling with applause and cheers.

The Bible-teaching judge had done it. He had demonstrated how *Roth* could be applied in ways faithful to full First Amendment freedoms. Admirably, this municipal officer, whose daily routine was traffic offenses and other petty infractions, had developed (with the able assistance of the defense lawyers) complex points in *Roth* that would take U.S. Supreme Court Justice Brennan more than a decade to work out in a multitude of First Amendment cases.

Judge Horn's opinion would have been a memorable one, sure to be widely cited by other courts, if only it had ever been officially published. It never was.

Lawrence Ferlinghetti had quipped about his prospect of jail time as a chance to catch up on his reading. Now, he was getting no such break for relaxing literary pursuits. After hearing Judge Horn's decision, the poet-publisher did not linger outside the courthouse to be interviewed by news reporters. He graciously took in the congratulatory wishes of friends and admirers and returned immediately to work. His very first task was to restack the front windows of City Lights Bookstore with even more copies of *Howl*.

46.

HOWL AGAIN MADE front-page news. The bold banner message in the *San Francisco Chronicle* proclaimed the victory of the Beats over the censors. The article highlighted the fact that Judge Horn's "most pointed comment was in French: '*Honi soit qui mal y pense*.' So the police and public might know, he translated: 'Evil to him who evil thinks.'" While Jake Ehrlich "crowed" excitedly over the judgment, Ralph McIntosh glumly brushed it aside: "It's just another case as far as the District Attorney's office is concerned."

Three days later, the *Chronicle* delivered its editorial reflections on Judge Horn's decision. Dubbing it a "Landmark of Law," the newspaper praised Horn's opinion as "sound and clear, foursquare with the Constitution and with the letter and spirit of various courts that have heretofore found the outcries of censorship lacking virtue." The editorial ended vividly with compliments to the jurist: "For a sharp and staggering blow to the chops of prurience and censorship, we congratulate Judge Clayton Horn." The journalistic tides had turned for the man who had been mocked only two months before as the "Ten Commandments" judge.

Allen Ginsberg first learned the good news about *Howl*'s vindication while in Amsterdam. On October 10, he received a letter from

314

Ferlinghetti containing clippings from the *Chronicle*. He was elated and relieved. But he was also eager to exploit the commercial possibilities that the trial story could create. Writing to Ferlinghetti the same day, he inquired, "Was decision news carried nationally anyway? Look up Harvey Breit on *Times*, he'll probably want to interview you."

With *Howl* no longer contraband, Ginsberg (the "PR genius of the Beat Generation") sought greater distribution of the work, and in some rather unlikely places: "If possible . . . would like to get the single poem 'Howl' reprinted more widely, perhaps in *Time, Life, Look, Cong. Record . . .*" Ever the solicitous son eager for his father's approval, he ended his letter to Ferlinghetti with a postscript: "Do me a favor, phone my papa Louis G., and tell him trial news—please. He'll be proud to hear, etc."

One news clipping that particularly pleased Allen was a *Life* magazine photograph of the *Howl* trial that he believed had captured Neal Cassady among the spectators. The embers of Ginsberg's affair with Cassady had cooled, but Allen's love and devotion for Neal never abated. Indeed, throughout 1957, Allen jotted short letters to Neal to share this or that tidbit about his travels with Peter and Gregory. The three wrote a joint letter from Paris to express their delight at having spied Neal at the trial hearing: "Saw your picture in *Life*, Neal, you were in the Court room looking in on how Allens Howl was progressing, just the side of your face with your hair back, yes it was you, Gregory just discovered it & told us we all said together Ha Neal was there seeing how things were going."

Once back in Paris, Ginsberg committed himself to finding a publisher for Bill Burroughs' recently completed draft of *Naked Lunch,* a "sensationalistic" novel that dealt graphically with the grotesque and bizarre world of drug addicts. Allen had carried it from Tangier to Paris in a knapsack months earlier and had dropped it off with Maurice Girodias, the editor of Olympia Press.

Allen believed that Olympia, the publisher of such works as *White Thighs* and *Sin for Breakfast*, would be perfect. After all, Girodias normally demanded an alluring title and sex scenes every few pages for the books he issued. With a title like *Naked Lunch* (suggested by Kerouac), and racy vernacular such as "asshole," "dick," and "fag" all in the very first paragraph, Burroughs' novel seemed a good fit for Olympia.

How unexpected and disappointing, then, when Girodias refused the work. Yes, it had its pornographic moments, but it was rather sickening and puzzling. What could one make, after all, of passages like "A beastly young hooligan has gouged out the eye of his confrere and fucked him in the brain. 'This brain atrophy already, and dry as grandmother's cunt'"?

Ginsberg would not give up being Burroughs' "agent," however. Through it all, Bill continued to write him with promises of more maddening manuscripts to place. And in letters to Ginsberg, Burroughs discussed his own self-analysis: "I feel myself closer and closer to resolution of my queerness which would involve a solution of that illness.... At least in my case, I have just experienced emergence of my non-queer persona as a separate personality." But that "solution" was still a ways off, as evidenced by the postscript of Bill's letter from Tangier: "Amsterdam sounds all right. Any boys?"

While Ginsberg reveled in greatness and Burroughs aspired to it, Kerouac found himself unable to deal with it. His health was suffering; the booze, the weed, the goofballs took their toll. The more his fans praised him and sought him out, the more withdrawn and anxious he became. He was, he told friends, experiencing "nervous breakdowns." When fame became his enemy, alcohol became his "liquid suit of armor," his "shield which not even Flash Gordon's super ray gun could penetrate." And it got continually worse, as "the Great God Public" crowned Jack "the King of the Beats."

Strange. Kerouac's celebrity turned his life into a Dostoyevskyan parody. In so many ways, he was like Prince Myshkin in *The Idiot*— a good man, an innocent and God-loving soul, who succumbed to blackouts and moments of insanity as he became hopelessly entangled in his society's affairs. Like Ginsberg in 1949 at the asylum, Kerouac in 1957 self-identified with Myshkin's crazed character. For Allen, that insight had come at the beginning of the road, but for Jack it pointed inevitably to the end of the road.*

In time, Myshkin's madness caught up with Jack. Meanwhile, "by 1957 Kerouac had burnt his way through several lifetimes."

---

*Dean Moriarty, the fictional archetype, was cast in a similar light. Ann Charters put it well: he "was the loner in *On the Road*, the hero left with nothing at the end of the road."

47.

*Howl is the confession of faith of the generation
that is going to be running the world
in 1965 and 1975—if it's still there to run.*
—Kenneth Rexroth

TIME MAGAZINE BILLED him the "Godfather of the Beats." He denied it: "An entomologist is not a bug." Yes, Kenneth Rexroth did study the Beats. But he was also a key part of their history. After all, he presided over the 6 Gallery readings and testified for the defense at the *Howl* trial, among other things. He was thus both a participant in the history of the Beat movement and a chronicler of it.

"Poetry has become an actual social force." And Allen Ginsberg is "certainly a poet of revolt if there ever was one." So Rexroth put it in a 1957 essay entitled "Disengagement: The Art of the Beat Generation." And what did he make of that generation?

"It is impossible to go on indefinitely saying: 'I am proud to be a delinquent,' without destroying all civilized values." His words.

"The end result must be the desperation of shipwreck—the despair, the orgies, ultimately the cannibalism of a lifeboat." More of his words.

"I believe that most of an entire generation will go to ruin... voluntarily, even enthusiastically." Yet more.

And then this: "What will happen afterwards I don't know, but for the next ten years or so we are going to have to cope with the youth we, my generation, put through the atom smasher."

And finally: "Social disengagement, artistic integrity, voluntary poverty—these are powerful virtues and may pull them through, but they are not the virtues we tried to inculcate; rather they are the exact opposite."

By the end of 1957, a new generation, a rebellious one, had been launched. And there in its midst was Jack Kerouac, perched high on a stool in Goody's Bar with a pack of smokes protruding from his shirt pocket. He sat there guzzling Schlitz. Forever the rambler, Kerouac repeated an old refrain that echoed back down the corridors of time to the early days with Allen and the boys.

"Man, I can't make it. I'm cutting out."

EPILOGUE LEGACY

In their discontent with American values...they had restored a sense of adventure to American culture. In their rejection of the boring, the conventional, and the academic, in their adoption of a venturesome lifestyle, they gave everyone the green light to plumb their own experience.

—Ted Morgan

Previous page: Allen Ginsberg photographed on a backpacking trip to the northern Cascades in Washington state by Gary Snyder in the summer of 1965.

SO HOW DID the stories of the great Beats end? How did their experiments with life and literature play out? Here are a few snapshots—fast-forward, much as they lived their lives.

NEAL CASSADY —

The racer, the jazzer, the chick-chaser extraordinaire, Neal Cassady was "catapulted from his status as an underground legend to a national cult figure" with the publication of *Howl* and *On the Road*. Still, for all his fame, he could not escape the bad moons that often hung over him.

In 1958, just as Kerouac's *Road* novel was immensely popular, Neal got on the wrong side of the law once again. Back in the days when selling pot was still a felony, he sold "three off-brand cigarettes" to an undercover agent at a San Francisco nightclub. When the legal dust settled, it landed him in San Quentin (prisoner No. A47667) where "his job was to sweep the floor of the textile mill." His cell door didn't open until June 1960 when he was paroled. He struggled to make it—accepting unemployment here, busting tires there—to feed his family.

But Neal Cassady was not a family man; he had his flirtatious eyes set on far too many women for that. Over time, the list had included Lu Anne (first wife), Carolyn (second wife), Diana Hansen (third wife), Natalie Jackson (girlfriend who committed suicide), Joan Anderson (girlfriend who attempted suicide), and numerous unnamed hookers.* There were, as well, all those other young women this "Cocksman of Adonis" had seduced. And, of course, there had been Allen Ginsberg, too. Then in early 1961 Neal set his sights on Anne Murphy, his latest girlfriend, who would remain so for the next eight years, though his infidelity continued almost unabated.

Things stayed bad. Just as Neal's parole ended in 1963, his dad died. "Well, my father died the same afternoon I left to see him," he wrote to Carolyn and the kids from Denver. Things got worse. Carolyn left him shortly afterward. The absences, the lying, the affairs—she once returned to their bedroom to find bloodstained bedsheets—brought their "fifteen-year marital roller-coaster ride to an end." As for his old pal Jack, Neal had stopped writing to him after he left San Quentin, disgusted with Kerouac for his excessive drinking.

Cassady was a beaten man, down on his luck. If his present were any sign of his future, he would be dead and forgotten. Still, Neal had not reached the end of his road. Soon enough, he would travel down a new one in the company of a fresh band of friends—after famed novelist Ken Kesey came into his life.

Neal first hooked up with Kesey around January 1963 at Ken's home in Palo Alto. Neal had read *One Flew over the Cuckoo's Nest* (1962), and decided he wanted to mix with its author. So, clad in T-shirt and chinos, he dropped in on Kesey and his wife, "bobbing up and down as if he were a boxer" and "jabbering, jabbering 'Yes, yes, yes, why hello Chief...'" In no time, said Kesey, "he just took over." Because Ken admired risk-takers and cultural outlaws, he particularly liked the real hero-outlaw of *On the Road*.

The union of Kesey and Cassady brought wonder back into Neal's existence. Kesey's kaleidoscopic sphere of drug-droppers,

---

*Cassady also fathered more than eight children, whose welfare he largely ignored. When, in 1965, his daughter Melany Jane saw him in San Francisco's Golden Gate Park, he did not recognize her.

free-lovers, and prankster-people swept Neal up readily as he moved from the Beat world to the hippie one. In that world, he was a cultural god to the young and spontaneous. "For Cassady, their worship meant easy access to their bountiful source of marijuana, Benzedrine, and LSD. Cassady's daily consumption of Benzedrine quickly grew into an addiction, causing his movements and speech to race far ahead of what most people's eyes and ears could reasonably follow."

This was a culture that Cassady embraced wholeheartedly. Neal throttled the Merry Pranksters' 1939 International Harvester school bus ("Furthur") through hitch-post towns along the map from Phoenix to New Orleans. "Sir Speed Limit" and his hippie friends spread their countercultural creed of love, happiness, and acid throughout America's redneck quarters. In town after town, and on long stretches of highway, music blared, cops stared, and film cameras captured the psychedelic frenzy of it all.

The Day-Glo pink, green, yellow, and red–painted bus traveled northbound away from Pensacola toward the Blue Ridge Mountains and then headed for New York. As Furthur cruised along the New Jersey Turnpike, "Captain Flag"—Kesey in pink sunglasses with his head draped turban style in an American flag—stood on its rear platform. While motorists zoomed by, he bellowed into the loudspeakers mounted on the bus: "Salute, dammit, salute!"

Outrageous as it was, Sir Speed Limit "wasn't destined to grow old," Lawrence Ferlinghetti once remarked. Indeed.

Death: February 4, 1968, at the age of forty-one, of unknown cause.

Different stories circulated about Neal's death, everything from a fatal mix of drugs and alcohol to overexposure during a long walk counting railroad ties. In any case, his body was discovered in Mexico alongside a railroad track, wearing nothing but a T-shirt and jeans. The death certificate declared: "generalized congestion."

He was cremated, and his ashes were given to his former wife, Carolyn.

Three years later, Lawrence Ferlinghetti published *The First Third*, the beginning of Cassady's autobiography. A decade afterward, an expanded version was released, which included fragments from Neal's writings and letters to Jack Kerouac and Ken Kesey. In 1990 Carolyn Cassady published her *Off the Road: My Years with Cassady, Kerouac, and Ginsberg*; and fourteen years later, Penguin Books issued Cassady's *Collected Letters, 1944–1967*, edited by Dave Moore and with an introduction by Carolyn Cassady.

JACK KEROUAC—

September 3, 1968: it was the night of the taping of William Buckley's nationally televised *Firing Line*. The tight fit of Jack Kerouac's buttoned, checker-patterned jacket constrained him a tad as he twisted in his chair, balancing a long and narrow cigar. He inhaled time and again as the nicotine pushed toward his brain. The TV cameras took aim at him; their red dots blinked and then faded into a blur. He clutched his coffee cup. It was filled with whiskey. But who knew?

As Kerouac sat in the studio, he felt the show within him playing out—the drag of the booze, the rush of the bennies, the mind games of the pot, and the kick of the nicotine's stimulation on his adrenal glands. His once photogenic image had transformed into a humiliating spectacle. His firm body had become flabby; boilermakers had dulled his sharp wit; and melancholy had overtaken his self-confidence so profoundly as to make normal social interaction nearly impossible. As the TV cameras targeted him, Jack's mind scattered in every which psychological direction. Meanwhile, he had to be cognitive—rational. He had to be quick—funny. He had to be awake—attentive. Could he do it? And could he summon up his old bravado and dare to speak truth to the Establishment's power?

Allen Ginsberg, sitting in the audience, hoped so. He himself had appeared on the conservative talk-show host's program in May of that same year and had flown the dissident's rhetorical flag with uninhibited flair. Now it was Jack's turn.

At the height of the counterculture—1968 was one of the most radical years in American history—Jack Kerouac was telling the world: "Listen, my politics haven't changed, and *I* haven't changed! I'm solidly behind Bill Buckley, if you want to know. Nothing I wrote in my books," he confessed in an earlier interview, "*nothing* could be seen as basically in disagreement with this." In fact, one of his aims for consenting to appear on the Buckley show was to spell out his "patriotic reasons" for holding onto his old romanticized vision of Chevrolet America.

The lead man to whom the revolutionary *Howl* had been dedicated now preached a tired political gospel as if he were an aging evangelist clinging onto his tattered faith-tent. It was a fact too enormous to hide: "*On the Road* looked to the future but its author was stuck in the past."

The azure of Bill Buckley's summer seersucker sport coat was nowhere as intense as the Yale blue of his young eyes. By stark contrast, Kerouac's eyes were vacant; that emptiness made him vulnerable. Buckley sensed his vulnerability and was raring to capitalize on it. The syndicated columnist and talk-show host loved to be devilishly satirical and even patronizing if he could weave condescension into his rhetorical web. Those talents were on full display the night he hosted the program with Jack Kerouac, Lewis Yablonsky (sociologist and author of *The Hippy Trip*), and Ed Sanders (a mild-mannered poet and member of the Fugs). With his trademark Ivy League smirk, Buckley began the evening's discussion.

Buckley: The topic tonight is the hippies, an understanding of whom we must, I guess, acquire or die painfully.

As Buckley spoke, Jack twisted in his chair, made foolish faces, and occasionally closed his eyes as if ready to doze off. The host continued.

> *Buckley*: We have before us a professional student of hippies and also someone who is said to have started the whole Beat Generation business. . . . Mr. Jack Kerouac . . . became famous when his book *On the Road* was published. It seemed to be preaching a life of disengagement, making a virtue out of restlessness. The irony is that when the book was belatedly published in 1958 [sic], seven years after it was written, Mr. Kerouac had fought his way out of the Beat Generation and is now thought of as orthodox, or at least a regular, practicing novelist whose thirteenth book, *Vanity of Duluoz*, is widely regarded as his best.

The falsity of Buckley's snide praise of *Vanity of Duluoz*—some reviewers savaged it—went unnoticed as the dialogue unfolded with Jack smoking, Jack drinking, Jack nodding, and Jack looking bored stiff as he sat in stoned silence. Meanwhile, the cultural war was hashed out as Yablonsky and Sanders engaged Buckley and defended the new morality. And then, as if from outer space, Jack hurled a verbal meteorite Allen's way.

> *Kerouac*: And I show my thumbs-down to Ginsberg over there in back. He's a nice fellow, yeah. We'll throw him to the lions.

Some took it to be a jab; but it was really no more than a drunken Jack Kerouac having a little fun. That he was only goofin' around was obvious in his lighthearted repartee with Bill Buckley. When Kerouac delivered a playful punch line, Buckley responded mischievously: "Give that man a drink." As the wild talk continued, however, Jack's intentions seemed more ambiguous.

Kerouac: The hippies are good kids, they're better than the Beats. The Beats, you see, Ginsberg and I, well... Ginsberg [is] boring. We're forty, we're all in our forties, and we started this and the kids took it up.

He became more intense, more critical.

Kerouac: But a lot of hoods, hoodlums, and communists, jumped on our backs, well my back, not his [gesturing to Allen in the audience]. Ferlinghetti jumped on my back and turned the idea that I had that the Beat Generation was a generation of Beatitude and pleasure in life and tenderness, but they called it in the papers the "Beat Mutiny," the "Beat Insurrection," words I never used, being a Catholic. I believe in order, tenderness, and piety.

Later, things turned even more personal and hostile.

Buckley: Will anybody be thinking about the hippies ten years from now? Other than in a sort of hula-skirt sense? As just something that happened?
Sanders: Well, no. By then, the Yippies will be in the Command Generation, and [everyone will be] "turned on" and articulate. [They will be] aware of Mr. Kerouac's and Mr. Ginsberg's great contribution to American society.
Kerouac: You hope. I'm not connected to Ginsberg, and don't you put my name next to his!
Sanders: Okay, Mr. Kerouac's contribution to American civilization. Those people will be in the "Command Generation" and will hopefully retain some of the humane.
Kerouac: Command Generation! *Heil Hitler!*

Jack Kerouac wanted no part of that future America. He disdained those who moved his beloved old nation in a new direction.

Since Allen was one of those people, he broke ranks with him, too, on national television for all to see and hear.

Don't you put my name next to his! Jack's message was clear: he and Allen were Beat brothers no more.

Hurtful as Kerouac was that televised night in September, Ginsberg let the wounding words be. As they stood outside the studio on the street corner, Allen touched Jack tenderly. With words as poignant as any he had recited that historic night at 6 Gallery, he spoke with deep sadness to the man he so loved: "Good-bye, drunken ghost."

Kerouac then turned away into the long dark of the night and sauntered off to the jazz clubs in the Village. "For old time's sake, Jack picked up a black hooker, but, as usual, nothing came of it."

Indeed, nothing, *nothing*...

Death: October 21, 1969, at the age of forty-seven, of a massive abdominal hemorrhage.

"It was the classic drunkard's death. The cirrhotic liver had rejected the blood that was supposed to flow through it. The backed-up blood broke through the weaker veins.... He drowned in his own blood." Kerouac was buried in the Sampas family burial plot at the Edson Catholic Cemetery in Lowell.

More than any of the Beats, Jack Kerouac was lionized by history. Numerous biographies were written of him, and in 2007 Viking Press published the original scroll version of *On the Road*. Six years earlier, the scroll sold at Christie's for $2.43 million, the highest price ever obtained at auction for a literary manuscript. Jim Irsay, the owner of the Indianapolis Colts, purchased the scroll and has allowed it to tour the nation for public viewing.

JOHN CLELLON HOLMES—

A writer, poet, and professor, John Holmes was widely regarded as a spokesman for the Beats. After all, he was the man who, in 1952, published the first article on the Beat Generation, popularizing the term that Kerouac coined in a semi-serious conversation with Holmes. Even so, John was more an observer than a participant: "Unlike the others in the group, who were emotionally and sexually involved with each other, Holmes was critical of what he considered his friends' destructive activities—drug addiction, alcoholism, and petty crime."

After his first novel, *Go*, Holmes authored thirteen more books, several of which were collections of essays and poems. He taught for eleven years at the University of Arkansas, where he established a creative writing program, and lectured at Yale and Brown Universities, among others. In 1988 he was the recipient of the Award in Literature from the American Academy and Institute of Arts and Letters.

Holmes's admiration for Jack Kerouac was resilient in ways that humbled him, as evidenced by the events of Friday, October 24, 1969. When the final moments of Jack Kerouac's burial ceremony neared, groups of people and photographers crowded toward the freshly dug grave. The coffin was poised over a raw hole. Meanwhile, nearby TV crews busily rushed around, setting up for interviews with Allen Ginsberg and Sterling Lord to take place as the casket was lowered into the ground.

"So, Mr. Ginsberg, I'll ask you to assess his career briefly, the camera's not rolling yet, but in a minute, and then you can make your statement and just stand a little further over to the left so that we can get it all in the picture." Allen waited stoically in his sandals.

Surreal, thought Holmes. "It seemed as meaningless as the commercials that interrupt the disasters on the TV news." As John tried to make sense of it all, a man from *Rolling Stone* tugged at his elbow, asking questions.

"Why did Jack drink? Was he, in your opinion, significant? What had he thought of rock?"

John was numb, "even to the irony."

When Allen walked over to the burial scene, a man in work clothes said to him: "Here, you should throw the dirt first." So he bent down, clenched a handful of soil and pebbles, and tossed it. Gregory Corso followed. And then John: "I took up the stones, too, and open-handed them down on Jack's head." As he did, memories flooded his mind.

Shortly thereafter, Sterling Lord, Jack's literary agent, got to thinking: who would write the biography of this "new Buddha of American prose"?

Sterling turned to John: "You know, John, you're really the one to do the *book*. You knew him from the inside, you were there when so much of it happened, but you stand away from it all now."

A twinge came over him as John stared at Sterling's stylish "blue shirt with the white collar and a dark necktie." Sterling's suggestion struck him as strange. Do a biography of the Great Jack Kerouac?

"No, really, you're the one to do it," Sterling continued.

John did not see it. The very idea of combining an authorized biography and a cool critical assessment of his friend "revolted" him. "It seemed," he believed, "a coffin no less adequate to contain the Jack I'd known than the one in which he lay."

And yet, John Holmes had a deep affection for Jack Kerouac. "If love is total involvement," he wrote in his journal, "deep emotional clairvoyance about the other's soul, fury & hunger all intermixed, [then] he was the only man I ever loved. He changed my life irrevocably." With the profound melancholy of a lifetime lover, he added: "He's gone. It's over. I don't know what to do."

"Word, words, words, words, words, words, words—"

John Holmes never acted on Lord's suggestion to author a full Kerouac biography. He did, however, write two books about Jack: one titled *Visitor: Jack Kerouac in Old Saybrook* (1981); the other, *Gone in October: Last Reflections of Jack Kerouac* (1985).

Death: March 30, 1988, at the age of sixty-two of cancer.

HERBERT HUNCKE—

Hobo, drug addict, criminal, hustler, con man, storyteller, and philosopher of the streets, Herbert Huncke was "the original hipster." Bill Burroughs heralded him as "a character, a rarity, a real picturesque antihero in the classical tradition." Both in the lives and literature of the Beats, Herbert became an icon: "He was the *Ur*-Beat: Kerouac's lonesome traveler, Burroughs' junkie, Ginsberg's angelheaded hipster." Yet, for all of his deviant celebrity, the "Duke of Deception" paid dearly; he spent many years in prison—in Sing Sing, in Dannemora, and in Rikers Island.

Unlike Kerouac's "beatific" Beat, this *miserable* of 42nd Street "always used 'beat' in its root sense, to signify the defeated, those not open to the insult of rehabilitation, those unable or unwilling to 'make it.'" He even celebrated that desperate meaning of life in his books: *Huncke's Journal* (1965), *The Evening Sun Turned Crimson* (1980), and *Guilty of Everything* (1990). To much the same effect, he penned a poem titled "The Needle" near the end of his life.

In his latter years, Herbert Huncke lived in a tiny room, No. 828 in the Chelsea Hotel, with rent paid by The Grateful Dead and others. He was on a methadone program to cope with his junk habit for some three decades. But then, one day in his final year, Herbert tested dirty at a methadone clinic: traces of cocaine, heroin, marijuana, and Valium showed up in his urine.

"Why do you do it?" his doctor asked.

"I've been doing it my whole life," Huncke answered. "Why can't you just let me be me?"

Death: August 8, 1996, at the age of eighty, of congestive heart failure.

One obituary bluntly depicted Huncke's fame: "Seldom has a life so lacking in any conventional virtues been so widely celebrated."

CARL SOLOMON—

Time largely ignored the antihero of "Howl." As in his days at the asylum, Solomon was a loner throughout the remainder of his life. There were, however, occasional exceptions, as in 1966 when City Lights Books published his *Mishaps, Perhaps* and in 1989 when another small house published his *Emergency Messages: An Autobiographical Miscellany*. This "marginal underground intellectual," as John Tytell tagged him, shared little of the buzz of the Beat Generation and the tumultuous years that followed it. By the early 1990s, he was slipping away. No one seemed to care, no one except Allen Ginsberg. He noticed Carl as his friend neared eternity.

It was around the time of the first World Trade Center bombing in 1993. Allen Ginsberg caught a D Train to the Bronx Veterans Hospital. There he beheld his skeletal friend whose old frail body was ridden with lesions. Fighting the demon of death, Carl sucked laboriously through an oxygen tube. With loving attention, the poet from Paterson bent over and gently removed Solomon's wide-framed glasses, and then cleaned them. Vision. Clarity. Carl looked up. Allen peered down, down into his beaten soul. When their eyes locked, Ginsberg leaned toward his dying friend and "asked Carl's forgiveness for having put him in the spotlight and making him a sensational cipher for universal suffering in *Howl*." Whatever Carl made of Allen's apology, Solomon remained "calmly surrealistic" as he faded. And then, in time...shhhhh. Silence.

Death: February 26, 1993, at the age of sixty-four, of lung cancer.

In the corridors of time, the great poet's mystical refrain continued to howl for old Carl Solomon:

> *I'm with you in Rockland*
> > *in my dreams you walk dripping from a sea-journey on the highway across America in tears to the door of my cottage in the Western night*

WILLIAM BURROUGHS—

Old Bull was "someone who strove to forge the unspeakable into an art form." By his own admission, his outlandish novel, *Naked Lunch* (1959), showcased "the most horrible things I can think of." He stressed: "Realize that—the most horrible dirty slimy awful niggardliest posture possible."

Burroughs' book was a raw account of a man's struggle with opiates—his hell, hallucinations, deviancy, and terrifying withdrawals. "What I am putting down on paper now is *literally* what is happening to me," he told Allen Ginsberg. "This is no land of the imagination.... And dangerous in a most literal sense." The work portrayed the human condition in rather sordid terms, a dystopia the very image of which made one's skin crawl.

In other words, William Burroughs didn't mind offending the public or tweaking bluenosed police and prosecutors. Indeed, this literary outlaw reveled in it.

His first significant run-in with official censors came with *Big Table*. A new and underground magazine designed to counter suppression of Beat literature, the inaugural issue featured excerpts of *Naked Lunch*, Kerouac's experimental poem "Old Angel Midnight," and three poems by Gregory Corso, among others. After the United States Postmaster impounded four hundred copies of the periodical, "In the Matter of *Big Table* Magazine" came before a postal hearing examiner in June 1959. The publication was deemed "obscene and filthy and thus non-mailable" due to Burroughs' and Kerouac's contributions. When a postal judicial officer affirmed the ruling, the ACLU took the matter to federal court. Judge Julius Hoffman reversed the order, finding the literature protected under the First Amendment.

But the bluenoses weren't finished with Burroughs yet. They came after *Naked Lunch* again—this time when the American edition of the book, which had been published earlier in Paris and sold

in England, France, Germany, and Italy, was released by Barney Rosset's Grove Press on November 20, 1962. The work sold quickly within
the United States; within a matter of weeks, eight thousand copies
of the strange book with a strange cover flew off bookstands and
shelves. The first Grove Press hardcover edition had a wraparound
band over the dust jacket. Its bold words read: RECOMMENDED FOR
SALE TO ADULTS ONLY. While that caught the attention of many
buyers, it also caught the eye of Boston's vice squad.

During the civil trial, which began in the Suffolk County Court
House on January 12, 1965, Massachusetts Assistant Attorney General William I. Cowin argued that the novel, standing alone, was
prima facie evidence of obscenity. Its many colorful words (such as
"fuck," "ass," "asshole," and "shit"), along with its offensive parade
of satirical scenes (such as a "talking asshole" and a father who treats
his son to a prostitute as a birthday present) were, in the state's
view, evidence enough of depraved and obscene material.

The task of defending *Naked Lunch's* twenty-five idiosyncratic chapters fell mainly to a young lawyer, Edward de Grazia,
who specialized in free-speech cases and who was on retainer
with Burroughs' American publisher. De Grazia collaborated with
Allen Ginsberg on legal strategy; not only did Allen agree to take
the stand as an expert witness for the defense, but he enlisted the
novelist Norman Mailer and the poet and arts critic John Ciardi as
additional witnesses. Burroughs was not personally involved, however, and did not attend the trial. Had Old Bull taken the stand,
his crude candor, open homosexuality, heroin addiction, and rap
sheet (not to mention the Vollmer killing) would surely have com-
pounded the defense's problems.

On March 23, 1965, Superior Court Judge Eugene Hudson issued
his ruling. He found *Naked Lunch* to be "obscene, indecent and
impure" and "taken as a whole is predominately prurient, hard-core
pornography, and utterly without redeeming social importance."

The howl of free-speech freedom was temporarily silenced. For the first time, a court of law had adjudged a Beat work to be obscene. This meant that other Beat books might also be banned in Boston and elsewhere.*

Edward de Grazia appealed, arguing his case before the Massachusetts high court on October 8, 1965. Nine months later, the state's Supreme Judicial Court rendered its ruling, with two justices dissenting. *Naked Lunch,* the majority concluded, did have some socially redeeming value. Its message and contents were therefore protected under the First Amendment.† Justice Paul Reardon sharply disagreed: "It is, in truth, literary sewage."

Far from fretting over the disgust of the dissent, Burroughs had little patience for the tepid liberalism of the majority. "I think that all censorship, any form of censorship, should be abolished," he emphasized with unnuanced resolve. As things played out, *Naked Lunch* was the last printed novel, without illustrations or photographs, to be deemed obscene by a court.

While the law challenged Bill Burroughs, pop culture embraced him. The emerging '60s counterculture delighted in his experimental writing techniques, such as folding together snippets of text in his "cut-up trilogy": *The Soft Machine* (1961), *The Ticket That Exploded* (1962), and *Nova Express* (1964). His subsequent novels, *Cities of the Red Night* (1981) and *Queer: A Novel* (1995), among others, received wide notice. In 2001 Grove Press published the restored text of the

---

*Only weeks after the Boston trial, a California criminal obscenity case against *Naked Lunch* was heard on January 28, 1965, in the Municipal Court of Los Angeles. Judge Allen G. Campbell determined that, although Burroughs' text was "revolting, nauseating, repugnant," it did not primarily appeal to prurient interest. "One person might say its predominant interest is to complete boredom," the judge opined. "And another one would say that no one in his right mind would have any interest in reading it."

†The Court's ruling did not, however, affect the possibility that those who sold *Naked Lunch* might still be prosecuted if they advertised the book "in a manner to exploit it for the sake of its possible prurient appeal."

original version of *Naked Lunch*. There have been two major biographies about him and numerous publications of his letters, interviews, and assorted writings.

Notably, Burroughs coined the phrase "heavy metal," influenced punk rock music, collaborated with the likes of Kurt Cobain and Tom Waits, appeared in a Nike TV commercial, and played a defrocked junkie priest alongside Matt Dillon in the 1989 movie *Drugstore Cowboy*.

Death: August 2, 1997, at the age of eighty-three, of a heart attack.

Bill Burroughs was the subject of a lengthy *New York Times* obituary (1,897 words). Few of those readers, no doubt, appreciated the irony that he had died in a hospital bed in Lawrence, Kansas. Perhaps only a handful of Beat devotees would recall Old Bull's shocking admonition: "God grant I never die in a fucking hospital! Let me die in some *louche* bistro, a knife in my liver, my skull split with a beer bottle, a pistol bullet through my spine, my head in spit and blood and beer, or half in the urinal so the last thing I know is the sharp ammonia odor of piss.... Anyplace, but not a hospital bed."

ALLEN GINSBERG—

Although there are various lenses through which to view the life of Allen Ginsberg, such as his great influences on the '60s and '70s counterculture and on more contemporary poets and artists, one lens that is particularly strong is his unwavering commitment to dissent. Through the remainder of his life, the bold poetic bard whose *Howl* made First Amendment history raised many a lance against government censorship of artistic and political expression. Regardless of the outcome, he never turned down an opportunity to engage in free-speech combat. On this front, as in *Howl*, he always sided with the outsider.

After the irreverent comedian Lenny Bruce was arrested in Manhattan in April 1964 for ribald word crimes committed in a Village coffeehouse, Allen circulated a petition in support of Bruce. Celebrities such as Bob Dylan, Norman Mailer, Susan Sontag, Elizabeth Taylor, Lionel Trilling, and Paul Newman signed on. Their typed press release began with the banner: ARTS, EDUCATIONAL LEADERS PROTEST USE OF NEW YORK OBSCENITY LAW IN HARASSMENT OF CONTROVERSIAL SATIRIST LENNY BRUCE. The body of the petition, the "manifesto," opened: "We the undersigned are agreed that the recent arrests of nightclub entertainer Lenny Bruce by the New York Police Department on charges of indecent performance constitute a violation of civil liberties as guaranteed by ... the United States Constitution." The *New York Times* and *Herald Tribune*, among others, ran with the story. Nonetheless, Allen's well-intentioned efforts* came to naught when Bruce was later convicted for obscenity. Similarly, Ginsberg's expert testimony on behalf of the defense in the Boston *Naked Lunch* trial did not deter the judge from finding Burroughs' bizarre book to be obscene, though it may well have contributed to the work's ultimate vindication by a higher court.

And then there was the time in August 1968 during the Democratic Convention in Chicago, where Allen, Abbie Hoffman, Jerry Rubin, and the Youth International Party (Yippies) sponsored a Festival of Life to protest the military draft and America's involvement in the Vietnam War. "We are here," Ginsberg declared at an earlier press conference in March, to manifest "a desire for the preservation of the planet," to end "a long period by the war gods and the older, menopausal leaders." Setting a mood for the new planetary peace consciousness, he reached over to open a small red leather box that contained his old harmonium. Playing the one-octave keyboard, he chanted a Hindu prayer, not stopping for ten minutes: *Hare Krishna, Hare Krishna, Krishnaaaaaaa, Rama Krishna, Hare*

---

*One such theatrical effort was Allen's mailing of his shorn locks and beard to the prosecutor in the Bruce case, Assistant District Attorney Richard Kuh.

Krishna, and on and on. Afterward, Judy Collins summoned young people to the Windy City in late August "for a testimonial for life."

By the time Allen got to Chicago, much had happened in the explosive months from April to August 1968 that stirred the passions of disaffected and angry youth. Dr. Martin Luther King was shot at Lorraine Motel in Memphis (April 4); not long after announcing his bid for the presidency, Robert F. Kennedy was assassinated at the Ambassador Hotel in Los Angeles (June 5); the Republican National Convention nominated Richard Nixon for president and Spiro Agnew for vice president, running on a "law and order" platform (August 23); and it appeared likely that the Democrats would nominate Senator Hubert Humphrey, a war supporter, to be their presidential candidate.

Signs of unyielding tension and impending conflict were everywhere to be found in Chicago's streets and parks. Tens of thousands of young people filled with rage came to the city, a resentment ready to be ignited by the Yippies, Black Panthers, Students for a Democratic Society, and "16,000 Chicago police officers, 4,000 state police, and 4,000 National Guard troops in full battle dress armed with machine guns, bazookas, and tanks." Although Ginsberg tried to obtain a permit for peaceful protests in the parks, he was unsuccessful; with fury building all around, however, any options for nonviolent action dwindled.

The spectacle of the festival drew hordes of print and electronic reporters. Allen was one of them, as were Bill Burroughs, Norman Mailer, Terry Southern (a noted novelist and screenwriter), and Jean Genet (the notorious French novelist, playwright, and poet). *Esquire* magazine hired them all to offer the countercultural take on what was about to happen. Bearing press credentials, beads, and love in his heart, Allen waded into an expansive sea of outraged youth, surrounded by blue-helmeted police wearing Plexiglas face-shields.

August 26, 12:20 A.M., Lincoln Park: Officers had ordered everyone to leave the park almost an hour and a half earlier, but the demand was ignored. Anticipating that the police might storm the park, protesters had erected makeshift barriers. Things escalated quickly, as the crowd of three thousand waved Vietcong, black anarchist, and peace flags, some of them howling "kill the pigs!" while police floodlights glared and bullhorns blared.

The amplified police message was clear: "This is a final warning. Please leave the park. The park is now closed. Anyone remaining in the park is in violation of the law. Everyone out of the park. This is a final notice."

The crowd's response was equally loud and clear: "Hell no, we won't go! Hell no, we won't go! Hell no, we won't go!"

Then, from nowhere, tear gas shells hissed through the night air as the police and National Guard, armed with shotguns, advanced into the crowd. Some protesters threw rocks, some hurled bottles, and others ran screaming as mottled brown-and-white clouds of gas forced the panicked demonstrators to retreat. But there, in the center of the chaos, were Allen Ginsberg and three hundred fellow Yippies standing their ground and chanting "Om, om." This was the only calmness witnessed that night.

The madness swelled a few nights later when the "Nightmare of Moloch," as Allen put it in "Howl," returned to Grant Park on the shores of Lake Michigan. After a day of tumultuous events, a mass rally was held there. In the glow of campfires burning in the summer night, young people openly smoked pot and passed hash pipes, while others sipped honey-flavored mixes spiked with acid. During the night's speech-making, Terry Southern downed tequila and took hits of "Panama Red." One reproach after another flew out from the stage: barbs were tossed at President Johnson, the war, and, of course, Chicago's contentious Mayor Richard J. Daley. Charged up by the denunciations, a few demonstrators headed for a flagpole and hauled down the American flag. A fight then broke out.

When Chicago's riot-ready police moved in, they were pelted with rocks and bricks. Screams of "Pig, pig, pig!" filled the post-midnight air. Some yelled, "Revolution now!" Others shouted, "The park belongs to the people!" Then a phalanx of Plexiglass-protected soldiers descended, wearing black leather gloves and wielding clubs, rifles, tear gas, and chemical mace. The fracas lasted about ten minutes, until some semblance of order returned. At that point, Allen Ginsberg stepped onto the park's band shell to deliver his message of peace over the loud speakers.

His voice cracked: "I lost my voice chanting in the park the last few nights." Clearing his throat, he continued: "The best strategy for you in cases of hysteria, overexcitement, or fear is still to chant 'Om' together. It helps to calm flutterings of butterflies in the belly. Join me as I try to lead you."

A *New York Times* news story recounted what happened next: "So as the policemen looked in astonishment out their Plexiglass face shields, the huge throng chanted the Hindu 'Om, om,' sending deep mystic reverberations off the glass office towers along Michigan Avenue." Calmness came over the crowd.

Jean Genet, Bill Burroughs, Norman Mailer, and comedian Dick Gregory spoke next. But as at 6 Gallery, the night belonged to Allen Ginsberg. With their peace work done, Ginsberg, Burroughs, and Genet left for New York, where they would write their stories for *Esquire* magazine ... and accidentally hook up with Jack Kerouac, who was in town to appear on William F. Buckley's *Firing Line*.

Well into his sixties, Allen Ginsberg continued to rant against censorship. Ironically, his later efforts were targeted, once again, at governmental suppression of his greatest works. More than thirty years after Judge Clayton Horn ruled that *Howl* could not be banned from San Francisco bookstores as an obscene work, the

Federal Communication Commission's regime of indecency regulations threatened to silence the public broadcasting of sexually explicit works, such as Ginsberg's poetry. At a meeting of the Federal Communications Bar Association, held on April 18, 1990, Allen delivered a powerful "Statement on Censorship." "In the last two decades," he explained, his "Howl," "Sunflower Sutra," "America," "Kaddish," and other poems had been "broadcast by university, public educational and listener supported stations." But now "FCC regulation could forbid broadcast of 'Howl.'" Any such "censorship of my poetry ... is a direct violation of our freedom of expression," he rebuked. "I am a citizen. I pay my taxes and I want the opinions, the political and social ideas and emotions of my art to be free from government censorship."

Four years later, Allen railed again—this time outside the U.S. Court of Appeals in Washington, D.C. Clad in a black suit (something he picked up at the Salvation Army), the poet addressed passersby who sipped from cups of Starbucks coffee. He read "Howl" aloud, "while lawyers representing him and others stood inside, arguing in markedly less colorful language" that the FCC's indecency regulations violated the First Amendment. Pacifica, a radio station in Berkeley, had stopped broadcasting "Howl" for fear of a stiff fine. "At a recent symposium," Ginsberg explained, an FCC commissioner "pulled out a copy of *Howl* and said, 'This is perfectly fine; all Mr. Ginsberg has to do is eliminate a couple of paragraphs.' That's their idea of freedom."*

---

*In a letter of April 4, 1995, to conservative congressman Randy "Duke" Cunningham (since convicted and sentenced for bribery, mail fraud, and tax evasion), Ginsberg again complained about censorship, this time related to funding for the National Endowment for the Arts. Alluding to FCC indecency regulations, he wrote: "The excuse is to guard the ears of minors from 'indecency,' but these same *Howl* and *Kaddish* poems of mine under ban are read in high school and college anthologies during the very hours the poems are banned off the radio." He added: "Now censorship is re-imposed on what is at present the main marketplace of ideas: radio, TV, and even now the information highway."

Death: April 5, 1997, at the age of seventy, of liver cancer.

Peter Orlovsky remained with Allen until the end.

Two years later. It was a novel picture of America. The famous 1966 photo* of Allen Ginsberg was featured on the cover of a Sotheby's catalogue. Its glossy black-and-white portrait blended the yin and yang of Allen's world. Here was the face of the counterculture mixed with its commercial opposite. A paper Uncle Sam top hat perched on his head, its stars and stripes shooting skyward out of his skull. The aura of it all was reminiscent of images of Walt Whitman taken a century earlier.

On October 7, 1999, the austere Manhattan auction house swarmed with the tailored set of the famous and wealthy along with an unkempt set of aging yuppies with receding hairlines, bulging bellies, and beaded necklaces. They were all eager to inspect and bid upon personal property from the estates of Allen Ginsberg, Jack Kerouac, William Burroughs, and other Beat figures.

As they bid and bought, many there that day remembered Allen's famous works, public awards, and his enormous impact on things literary, political, and cultural—everything from his role in free-speech struggles to his induction into the American Academy of Arts and Letters to his directorship of Naropa's Jack Kerouac School of Disembodied Poetics, and more.

Most had seen the *New York Times* front-page obituary. Remarkably, that 2,915-word story, replete with several photographs, was more than twice as long as the newspaper's obituaries for Elvis Presley (1,076 words), John Lennon (1,166 words), and even Allen's Beat brother, Jack Kerouac (1,273 words). In that same America where the "poet laureate of the Beat Generation" once howled against military power, students at the Virginia Military Institute now studied

---

*The photograph, taken on March 26, 1966, by Fred W. McDarrah was titled *Allen Ginsberg in Fifth Avenue Peace Demonstration to End the War in Vietnam*.

his rebellious poem as part of their curriculum; there is even a photograph of them doing so.

The Ginsberg canon is awe-striking. It includes three major biographies, some seventeen compilations of poetry and nineteen of prose, five photography books, nine collections of audio-recorded materials, two DVD documentaries, and a website entitled "The Allen Ginsberg Project."

LUCIEN CARR—

The "fallen angel" of the Beats, Lucien was the Columbia University muse who encouraged Allen Ginsberg to first read Rimbaud / who introduced Ginsberg to Jack Kerouac and Bill Burroughs and later all of them to Neal Cassady / who took David Kammerer's life in the dark of the night and thereby motivated Jack Kerouac and Bill Burroughs to collaborate on a novel titled *And the Hippos Were Boiled in Their Tanks* (first published 2008) / who disallowed Allen's dedication to him in *Howl* / and who inspired the besotted Kerouac to write of him repeatedly in *The Town and the City* (as Kenny Wood), *On the Road* (as Damion), *Visions of Cody* (as Julien Love), *The Subterraneans* (as Sam Vedder), *Desolation Angels* (as Julien Love), *Vanity of Duluoz* (as Claude de Maubrus), *Big Sur* (as Julian), and *Book of Dreams* (as Julien Love). All this, and yet Lucien never himself contributed to the Beat canon. While his crazy comrades hitchhiked and hauled across the country as merry vagabonds, Carr chose to "live apart from the disintegrating mayhem of the Beats."

There was, however, one occasion in September 1968 when Lucien hooked up with the old gang. This was, since 1953, the first time that the Beat circle had reconvened. It was a reunion made not in heaven, but on the elevated floors of the Hotel Delmonico on Park Avenue at 59th Street. Hours of drinking and reminiscing passed as the four middle-aged men (Burroughs, fifty-four; Carr, forty-three; Ginsberg, forty-two; and Kerouac, forty-six) savored those moments when their glorious past became present again—the tales, the laughter, the fraternity of it all.

But that was the exception. For the next thirty-seven years, Carr continued in his respectable career at United Press International. As UPI's assistant managing editor for national news, he "worked on every major story from the era of Eisenhower to the administration of the first George Bush." Admired, unflappable, and always professional, the enigmatic "Lou" stayed behind the scenes to the very end.

Death: January 28, 2005, at the age of seventy-nine, of bone cancer.

LAWRENCE FERLINGHETTI—

Poet, novelist, essayist, playwright, newspaper columnist, publisher, bookseller, painter, and activist, Lawrence Ferlinghetti has managed to keep all of these balls in the air without dropping a single one. And many of his achievements are record winners. His most famous book of poetry, *Coney Island of the Mind* (1958), has been translated into more than a dozen languages and has sold over a million copies, making it one of the best-selling poetry collections of all time. For more than a half-century, he has maintained the highly successful City Lights Bookstore in San Francisco, which was declared an official historic landmark in 2001, and has continued as editor and publisher of City Lights Books, which can boast of more than two hundred books in print. And the nearly ninety-five-year-old Renaissance man has accumulated a bevy of honors: among others, San Francisco named an alley after him, Via Ferlinghetti (1994), and awarded him the title of its first poet laureate (1998); he has received the Robert Frost Memorial Medal (2003) and membership in the American Academy of Arts and Letters (2003); the French Order of Arts and Letters named him Commandeur (2007); and the San Francisco Art Institute honored him with the Douglas MacAgy Distinguished Achievement Award (2012).

Over the years, his famous Pocket Poet Series has celebrated the likes of Robert Bly, Gregory Corso, Robert Duncan, Allen Ginsberg, Jack Kerouac, Philip Lamantia, Frank O'Hara, Kenneth Patchen, and Anne Waldman. As for himself, he has authored some fifteen collections of poetry, four books of prose (including two novels), and two volumes of plays; several audio recordings feature his poetry. Furthermore, there are four biographies of him.

The fighting spirit of the bearded activist is well captured in *Poetry as Insurgent Art* (2007). "Be subversive, constantly questioning reality and the status quo," he counseled. "Speak up. Act out. Silence is complicity," he warned. "Be the gadfly of the state and also its firefly," he urged. "Where are Whitman's wild children / where the great voices speaking out," he asked.

Lawrence's great voice spoke out, and forcefully, during a 2007 flap over airing "Howl" on broadcast radio. It began in late August of that year, when Ferlinghetti and others* petitioned New York Pacifica Radio station WBAI-FM to play Allen Ginsberg's twenty-four-minute 1959 recording of "Howl"—this in celebration of the fiftieth anniversary of the victory in the famous case. Though Janet Coleman, arts director at WBAI, favored the idea, and Pacifica's attorney, John Crigler, thought that airing the poem would make for "a great test case," fears of catastrophic FCC fines for alleged indecency ultimately prevailed. Program director Bernard White worried that the fine might be $325,000 for each of Ginsberg's dirty words, which could bankrupt the station. So WBAI opted for a safer alternative: running a program, "Howl against Censorship," on the Pacifica.org website, which is not subject to FCC regulation.

---

*In addition to the authors, who organized the petition effort, the following signed onto a letter emailed to Janet Coleman of Pacifica Radio: Al Bendich (*Howl* attorney), Christopher Finan (American Booksellers Foundation for Free Expression), Peter Hale & Bob Rosenthal (Ginsberg Trust), Eliot Katz (poet and activist), Bill Morgan (archivist and biographer), and Nancy J. Peters (City Lights).

The program included, among other things, Ginsberg's reading of "Howl" and a phone interview with Ferlinghetti.

"I look at the present situation," Lawrence began, "as a repeat in spades of what happened in the 1950s, which was also a repressive period. The current FCC policy . . . when applied to ['Howl'] amounts to government censorship of an important critique of modern civilization, especially of America and its consumerist society, whose breath is *money*, still." Responding to Coleman's question about what Ginsberg would have said today, he sighed: "Ah, well, I'm sure he'd have plenty to say about it. I often lament that he isn't around to say it."* Ferlinghetti asked if he could end by reciting his poem, "Pity the Nation":

> *Pity the nation whose people are sheep,*
> *and whose shepherds mislead them.*
> *Pity the nation whose leaders are liars, whose sages are*
> *   silenced.*

The old poet closed with lines that echoed down the halls of time, back to the words of Walt Whitman:

> *Pity the nation—oh, pity the people who allow their rights to*
> *   erode*
> *and their freedoms to be washed away.*
> *My country, tears of thee, sweet land of liberty.*

THE END

---

*In a *New York Times* editorial, titled "A Muse Unplugged," the editors wrote: "If Ginsberg were still alive with us, he would undoubtedly pen a mocking line or two about his poem being banned from the airwaves 50 years after it was ruled not to be obscene." The piece closed by quoting Ginsberg: "'Whoever controls the media, the images, controls the culture.'"

Acknowledgments

NO WRITER UNDERTAKES a literary journey without discovering the trails of those who have traveled there before. Our experience in writing this book is no different. While the bibliography and notes reveal our tracks, certain people and works deserve special mention. We are happy to recognize our debt to them, even if some of them may take exception to our "outsider" status, our occasional irreverence, and our unwillingness to blindly join them in worshipping at the altar of their literary gods. They have their canons, which they expect others to honor even if it means disregarding the very spirit that made their sacred men great. To them, our only defense: we wrote the story as we found it...the good, the bad, and everything in between.

A manuscript draft of *Mania* circulated as early as 2004. Some of those who saw it objected to its candor and preferred to offer a more sanitized version of our story. In the end, however, the real uncensored story is the one that documents both the glorious highs and the ruinous lows of its subjects. It is the latter story that we elected to bring to light in the several years since our typed words were first distributed to various Beat scholars and others.

So, on to the credits. Beyond the archival tombs in New York, California, and elsewhere, there is a long list of people whose help—either directly by personal contact or indirectly by their writings—merits acknowledgment.

We begin with the keeper of the canon: Ann Charters, the *grande dame* and ardent defender of all things Beat. Her books, biographies, and assorted writings have long defined Beat culture.

Barry Miles deserves serious recognition for his many and insightful works on the Beats. Those books proved vital to our project.

Michael Schumacher's *Dharma Lion* is a heroic work of scholarship that is essential to anyone writing in the field. Like many others, we were the beneficiaries of Bill Morgan's exhaustive (and ongoing) archival efforts dedicated to preserving the genius of Allen Ginsberg. His own biography of Ginsberg, the Ginsberg journals he coedited with Juanita Lieberman-Plimpton, and the Ginsberg letters he edited were also helpful to us.

In the Kerouac corner, some names deserve special mention. Gerald Nicosia's *Memory Babe* is a sober and sensible biography of Kerouac—quite a feat in that arena. It was a book we had regularly by our side. More recently, Gerald has written (with Anne Marie Santos) a valuable new edition to Beat literature, namely, *One and Only: The Untold Story of On the Road*. His abiding love and respect for Jack Kerouac is evidenced by his commitment to bringing to print *Jan Kerouac: A Life in Memory*. Ellis Amburn's *Subterranean Kerouac* is at once passionate and candid in its portrayal of Jack. There is also the more recently published *On the Road: The Original Scroll*, edited by Howard Cunnell. That book, with its original text and insightful commentaries, proved crucial to us. Most recently there is Joyce (Glassman) Johnson's voluminous and perceptive biography, *The Voice Is All: The Lonely Victory of Jack Kerouac*. John Leland's *Why Kerouac Matters* is simply a work to behold, both in the remarkable way it captures Kerouac's essence and in the astute way it gives new and vital meaning to *On the Road*. We hope that Douglas Brinkley will continue to write in this area, since his work has already illuminated the vast Kerouac universe. Isaac Gewirtz's publication, *Beatific Soul: Jack Kerouac on the Road*, is, to be sure, a treasure trove of reliable and insightful information. One more thing: much Kerouac research traces back to Ann Charters' early biography of Kerouac.

Anyone interested in William Burroughs must consult the exhaustive biography by Ted Morgan. In much the same vein, there is the dedicated work of James Grauerholz, the author of a forthcoming biography of Burroughs. His unpublished scholarly essay on the Joan Vollmer shooting is definitive, and his more recently published afterword to *And the Hippos Were Boiled in Their Tanks* is vital to any understanding of the killing of David Kammerer. Not to be ignored is Oliver Harris's superb collection of Burroughs' letters and Sylvère Lotringer's equally valuable collection of Burroughs interviews. All of these works, and others, contributed to our portrayals of "Old Bull."

The life of Herbert Huncke is set out in his revealing autobiography, *Guilty of Everything*, and in Benjamin Schafer's *The Herbert Huncke Reader*. Most recently, Hilary Holladay has published a hefty biography entitled *American Hipster: A Life of Herbert Huncke*.

Bill Morgan and Nancy Peters (of City Lights fame) assisted us mightily with their *Howl on Trial*. There is also Lawrence Ferlinghetti's significant essay "Horn on 'Howl.'" And we are grateful to him, as well, for granting us an interview.

We have also profited considerably from the comments and writings of Matt Theado, whose impressive work and insights have greatly guided us. Thanks also to Dave Moore, who has a vast knowledge and very keen corrective eye, and who was always very supportive; to Brad Parker for his careful comments; and to Paul Maher whose writings on Kerouac (including his remarkable book of Kerouac interviews) helped us at many a turn. They are great guys, and we owe them more than a few Coronas.

No study of the Beats could be complete without some meaningful reference to *The Beats: Literary Bohemians in Postwar America*, a marvelous two-volume encyclopedia edited by Ann Charters. There is also her compilation of the Kerouac letters and Dave Moore's important collection of Neal Cassady's letters. John Tytell's interviews with Herbert Huncke and Carl Solomon were indispensable.

Some of the dead are entitled to special thanks, as well. The most important of them all is John Clellon Holmes. He was one of the founders and great chroniclers of the Beat Generation. His novel *Go* and his later works on Kerouac and the Beats were vital to us. Ann and Samuel Charters have written a book about Holmes, titled *Brother Souls: John Clellon Holmes, Jack Kerouac, and the Beat Generation*. Likewise, we are indebted to the work of Jake Ehrlich, whose *Howl of the Censor* prevented the truths of a great trial from being lost to the dustbin of history.

We first met Al Bendich, whose legal skills saved *Howl*, years ago when we were writing *The Trials of Lenny Bruce*. He also helped us find our way with the *Howl* trial. Al is a prize to his profession and to those who value civil liberties. We are happy to join in the chorus of well wishers who sing his praises.

Brenda Knight's superb *Women of the Beat Generation* helped us to focus on what is too often overlooked, namely, the role of women in the Beat lives of the main characters profiled in *Mania*. By that measure, we benefited from the many valuable insights offered by Joyce Johnson in *Minor Characters* and Carolyn Cassady in her remarkable book, *Off the Road*, which showed us another side of the Cassady world; moreover, there are Carolyn Cassady's candid, seasoned, and sage words in Christopher Felver's *Beat*. There is also Joan Haverty Kerouac's *Nobody's Wife*, a book that opened many biographical doors to us, and Edie Parker-Kerouac's *You'll Be Okay: My Life With Jack Kerouac*, which offered us yet another invaluable lens by which to see the Kerouac story.

Among the Beat commentators we have read, a few stand out: Bruce Cook, Ann Douglas, Herbert Gold, Jane Kramer, and Seymour Krim.

We gladly recognize our debts to the wonderful librarians at the Stanford Archives (Ginsberg), the New York Public Library (Kerouac), and the Library of Congress. We love librarians.

More could be said about the works of the likes of David Amram, Carolyn Anspacher, James Campbell, Diane Di Prima, Barry Gifford and Lawrence Lee, Mikal Gilmore, Dennis McNally, Gilbert Millstein, David Pearlman, Jonah Raskin, Bob Rosenthal, David Sandison and Graham Vikers, Anne Waldman, and Regina Weinreich, among others. But enough: we will let the curtain draw there.

Let us not forget those who gave us vision—those whose lenses showed us the many pictorial sides of our heroes and heroines: Grahan Caveney, Christopher Felver, Allen Ginsberg, Mellon Tytell, Steve Turner's offerings in *Jack Kerouac: Angelheaded Hipster,* and the Whitney Museum of Art collection as reproduced in *Beat Culture and the New America: 1950–1965.* Chris Felver's book, *Beat,* is a wonderful and wondrous work. Likewise the books by Steven Watson, Matt Theado, and Isaac Gewirtz contained many priceless pictures of people, places, and any variety of printed materials.

Alex Lubertozzi has been a trooper since the early days when he was our editor for *The Trials of Lenny Bruce.* He is one of the rare few in his business (both as an editor and publisher) who still values the *art* of writing, even in these dismal days when bookstores seem to be going the way of phone booths. Moreover, Alex believed in us when others were diplomatically dismissive or outright cowardly about publishing a "Beat book."

Special thanks to James L. Swanson, our *ex officio* agent, who tried in ever so many ways to make this book happen and who also provided some truly remarkable editing suggestions. James, a most accomplished writer himself, has been a faithful supporter who kept the spirit of this project alive. Thanks for your faith in us, James.

The folks at Seattle University School of Law were supportive in countless ways. We are immensely grateful for the generous research and travel budget provided by former Dean Kellye Testy and Vice Dean Annette Clark, and current Dean Mark Niles and Associate Dean Rick Bird. We owe thanks for the unstinting administrative assistance given by Nancy Ammons; for the excellent library assistance given by Susan Kezele, Kelly Kunsch, and Bob Menanteaux; and for the superb research work done by Jason Eric Bernstein and Stacey Scriven Bernstein to reinsert authoritative citations in the *People v. Ferlinghetti* opinion found in the appendix. We much appreciate, as well, the mighty efforts of our colleagues, Professors Richard Delgado and Jean Stefancic, who kindly read and edited our manuscript and helped promote our work in the most generous of ways. Our mighty thanks, as well, to Jay Gairson, who has been along for the ride for several years now, first as a student assistant and then as an attorney knowledgeable in the law of intellectual property. We owe him a great debt in steering our project in ways both affordable and equitable. Thank you, Jay, for helping us in ensuring that all the legal hatches were nailed down.

A special debt of gratitude is owed to Dave Moore, Peter Hale, Matthew Theado, and Kevin Naud, who read our manuscript and offered their editorial suggestions while affirming our enterprise.

Ron Collins: This work would have remained shipwrecked on the shores of bad luck if it were not for my co-author in life and letters, David Skover. At one point, we actually returned the advance paid to us, and walked away from a publishing contract—this to publish the book *our way*. I doubt that many co-authors would have remained in the game in such circumstances, but David did. And that is the story, or part of it, of David's life. It is the story of struggle in the face of strife, of determination in the face of disappointment, and of relentless hope in the midst of the worst of times.

He is the soldier who returns again and again to the battlefield to fight another day, and to carry on his shoulder his wounded friends. Most of the time, as in my case, he succeeds, though he has suffered his own painful tragedy. And yet, he returns to rise again like the great Phoenix. Rise, rise, rise!

Like the works before and after it, this book would have also been impossible but for the love and support provided to me by my soulmate, Susan Cohen. It is true: behind every husband of even moderate success, there is a great wife. Even though she is a sun in her own universe, for a quarter-century she has ventured into mine to shed much needed light. Always calm, even-keeled, and sober-minded, she provides a vital counterweight to my sometimes eccentric ways. To Susan: thanks for being the wonderful soul you are and have always been. As for Dyl, he needs no extra thanks (see my dedication).

Bunny Kolodner was in on this book, too, lending her own sage support from the beginning and during all of the maniacal times. A tip of the hat to Bunny.

Linda Hopkins did her share, too—always counseling me to hang on: "Your time will come," she likes to say. Until whenever that day is, I thank her for investing in my life in ways far too numerous and private to put to print.

David Skover: In this as in so many other ventures, I must thank Sean Patrick O'Reilly (1959–2009), who was with me at the beginning of *Mania* but did not live to celebrate its publication. With your untimely death, Sean, you left me as your legacy, and I strive to draw wisdom and strength from your incomparable sweetness, light, optimism, and love of life. So many times I find myself asking "What would Sean think? What would Sean say? What would Sean do?"—and the answers sustain me in all that is good in my small universe. The example of your unconditional devotion enabled me to prevent the walls of my heart from closing inward, and now encourages me to stretch those walls even wider in order to accommodate nascent love. I am eternally grateful for what you gave me over our seventeen and one-half years together and for what you give me still.

And to Ron, my partner of the pen: As only you know best, this work has proven more maniacal than we could ever have imagined it to be. But in the madness, you did not fail me. Professionally, you shared my buoyant hopes and shouldered with me the burdens of dashed expectations. Personally, you reveled in the glory of sunny days and consoled me when rain clouds let loose. Like our Beat friends, we have been together on the road for many an adventure over many a year. We may not know how long that journey will be or when and how it will end, but it has clearly been one of the most exciting, productive, and memorable of my life. I thank you from the bottom of my heart for being my travel companion. And now, here's to our newest venture: Let no *Dissent* be heard to the idea that the best may be yet to come!

Appendix: People v. Ferlinghetti (1957)*

IN THE MUNICIPAL COURT OF THE CITY AND COUNTY
OF SAN FRANCISCO, STATE OF CALIFORNIA

HONORABLE CLAYTON W. HORN, JUDGE

PEOPLE OF THE STATE OF CALIFORNIA
Plaintiff

vs.

LAWRENCE FERLINGHETTI, NO. B27585
Defendant

Thomas C. Lynch, District Attorney
Ralph McIntosh, Deputy District Attorney
for the People

J.W. Ehrlich
Lawrence Speiser
Albert Bendich
for the Defendants

---

*Copyright © 2013 by Ronald K.L. Collins & David M. Skover. Originally, the case name read *People of the State of California, Plaintiff vs. Shigeyoshi Murao, No. B27083 and Lawrence Ferlinghetti, No. B27585, Defendants.* The case against Murao was dismissed before Judge Horn issued his opinion in the matter of *People vs. Ferlinghetti.* None of the surviving and incomplete versions of *People vs. Ferlinghetti* contained authoritative citations within the body of the opinion. After much research and analysis, the authors inserted citations and quotations in all of the appropriate places. Hence, this is the sole definitive version of the opinion in print.

HORN, CLAYTON W., J. The defendant is charged with a violation of Section 311.3 of the Penal Code of the State of California. Defendant pleads Not Guilty. The complaint alleged that the defendant did wilfully and lewdly print, publish and sell obscene and indecent writings, papers and books, to wit: "Howl and Other Poems."

It is to be noted that the statute requires proof of criminal intent, namely, that the defendants did wilfully and lewdly commit the acts specified. It should also be noted that no reference to minors is made in the statute.

It must be borne in mind that the prosecution has the burden of proving beyond a reasonable doubt and to a moral certainty two things: first, that the book is obscene and, second, that the defendants wilfully and lewdly committed the crime alleged. It is elementary that where a statute makes a specific intent an element of an offense, such intent must be proved. *People v. Wepplo*, 78 Cal. App. 2d Supp. 959, 965, 178 P.2d 853, 857 (1974). The proof may be circumstantial; but if so, the circumstances must be such as reasonably to justify an inference of the intent. *Id.* at 857–58.

The prosecution has advanced the theory that the word "indecent" means something less than obscene.

In their broadest meaning the words indecent and obscene might signify offensive to refinement, propriety and good taste. A penal statute requiring conformity to some current standard of propriety defined only by statutory words would make the standard in each case, ex post facto.

Unless the words used take the form of dirt for dirt's sake and can be traced to criminal behavior, either actual or demonstrably imminent, they are not in violation of the statute. Indecent as used in the Penal Code is synonymous with obscene, and there is no merit in the contention of the prosecution that the word indecent means something less than obscene.

The evidence shows that "Howl" was published by the defendant and therefore it remains to be seen whether said book is obscene and if so, whether this defendant wilfully and lewdly published it. The prosecution contends that having published the book defendant had knowledge of the character of its contents and that from such knowledge a lewd intent might be inferred.

The mere fact of knowledge alone would not be sufficient. The surrounding circumstances would be important and must be such as reasonably to justify an inference of the intent. To illustrate, some might think a book obscene, others a work of art, with sincere difference of opinion. The bookseller would not be required to elect at his peril. Unless the prosecution proved that he acted lewdly in selling it, the burden would not be met.

Written reviews of "Howl" were admitted in evidence on behalf of the defendants, over the objection of the District Attorney. One was from the *New York Times Book Review*, dated September 2, 1956; one from the *San Francisco Chronicle*, dated May 19, 1957, which included a statement by Ferlinghetti; one from the *Nation* dated February 23, 1957. All of the reviews praised "Howl."

The practice of referring to reviews in cases of this nature has become well established. Opinions of professional critics publicly disseminated in the ordinary course of their employment are proper aids to the court in weighing the author's sincerity of purpose and the literary worth of his effort. These are factors which, while not determining whether a book is obscene, are to be considered in deciding that question.

Over the objection of the prosecution the defense produced nine expert witnesses, some of them with outstanding qualifications in the literary field. All of the defense experts agreed that "Howl" had literary merit, that it represented a sincere effort by the author to present a social picture, and that the language used was relevant to the theme. As Professor Mark Schorer put it: "'Howl,' like any work of literature, attempts and intends to make a significant comment on, or interpretation of, human experience as the author knows it."

The prosecution produced two experts in rebuttal, whose qualifications were slightly less than those of the defense. One testified that "Howl" had some clarity of thought but was an imitation of Walt Whitman, and had no literary merit; the other and by far the most voluble, that it had no value at all. The court did not allow any of the experts to express an opinion on the question of obscenity because this was the very issue to be decided by the court.

Experts are used every day in court on other subjects and no reason presents itself justifying their exclusion from this type of case when their experience and knowledge can be of assistance. The court also read many of the books previously held obscene or not for the purpose of comparison.

In determining whether a book is obscene it must be construed as a whole. *Wepplo*, 78 Cal. App. 2d Supp. at 961, 178 P.2d at 855. The courts are agreed that in making this determination, the book must be construed as a whole and that regard shall be had for its place in the arts.

The freedoms of speech and press are inherent in a nation of free people. These freedoms must be protected if we are to remain free, both individually and as a nation. The protection for this freedom is found in the First and Fourteenth Amendments to the United States Constitution, and in the Constitution of California, Art. I, sec. 9 which provides in part:

> Every citizen may freely speak, write, and publish his sentiments on all subjects, being responsible for the abuse of that right; and no law shall be passed to restrain or abridge the liberty of speech or of the press...

The Fourteenth Amendment to the Federal Constitution prohibits any State from encroaching upon freedom of speech and freedom of the press to the same extent that the First Amendment prevents the Federal Congress from doing so. *Commonwealth v. Gordon*, 66 Pa. D. & C. 101, 138–39 (1949).

These guarantees occupy a preferred position under our law to such an extent that the courts, when considering whether legislation infringes upon them, neutralize the presumption usually indulged in favor of constitutionality. *Id.* at 139.

Thomas Jefferson in his bill for establishing religious freedom wrote that "to suffer the Civil Magistrate to intrude his powers into the field of opinion, and to restrain the profession or propagation of principles on supposition of their ill tendency, is a dangerous fallacy which at once destroys all religious liberty... it is time enough for the rightful purposes of civil government for its officers to interfere when principles break out into overt acts against peace and good order." *Id.* at 139–40 (quoting Thomas Jefferson, "A Bill for Establishing Religious Freedom," 12 June 1779).

The now familiar "clear and present danger" rule represents a compromise between the ideas of Jefferson and those of the judges, who had in the meantime departed from the forthright views of the great statesman. Under the rule the publisher of a writing may be punished if the publication in question creates a clear and present danger that there will result from it some substantive evil which the legislature has a right to proscribe and punish. *Id.* at 140.

Mr. Justice Brandeis maintained that free speech may not be curbed where the community has the chance to answer back. He said: "those who won our independence by revolution were not cowards. They did not fear political change. They did not exalt order at the *cost* of liberty. To courageous, self-reliant men, with confidence in the power of free and fearless reasoning applied through the processes of popular government, no danger flowing from speech can be deemed clear and present, unless the incidence of the evil apprehended is so imminent that it may befall before there is opportunity for full discussion. If there be time to expose through discussion the falsehood and fallacies, to avert the evil by the processes of education, the remedy to be applied is more speech, not enforced silence. Only an emergency can justify repression. Such must be the rule if authority is to be reconciled with freedom. Such, in my opinion, is the command of the Constitution. It is therefore always open to Americans to challenge a law abridging free speech and assembly by showing that there was no emergency justifying it." *Whitney v. California*, 274 U.S. 357, 377, 47 S.Ct. 641, 648–49 (1927) (Brandeis, J., concurring).

"Moreover, even imminent danger cannot justify resort to prohibition of these functions essential to effective democracy, unless the evil apprehended is relatively serious. Prohibition of free speech and assembly is a measure so stringent that it would be inappropriate as the means for averting a relatively trivial harm to society—the fact that speech is likely to result in some violence or in destruction of property is not enough to justify its suppression. There must be the probability of serious injury to the State. Among free men, the deterrents ordinarily to be applied to prevent crime are education and punishment for violations of the law, not abridgment of the rights of free speech and assembly." *Gordon*, 66 Pa. D. & C. at 140–42.

The authors of the First Amendment knew that novel and unconventional ideas might disturb the complacent, but they chose to encourage a freedom which they believed essential if vigorous enlightenment was ever to triumph over slothful Ignorance. *Id.* at 143 (quoting *Martin v. Struthers*, 319 U.S. 141, 143 [1943]).

I agree with the words of Macaulay who finds it "difficult to believe that in a world so full of temptations as this, any gentleman, whose life would have been virtuous if he had not read Aristophanes and Juvenal, will be made vicious by reading them." *Id.* at 155.

I do not believe that "Howl" is without redeeming social importance. The first part of "Howl" presents a picture of a nightmare world; the second part is an indictment of those elements in modern society destructive of the best qualities of human nature; such elements are predominantly identified as materialism, conformity, and mechanization leading toward war. The third part presents a picture of an individual who is a specific representation of what the author conceives as a general condition.

"Footnote to Howl" seems to be a declamation that everything in the world is holy, including parts of the body by name. It ends in a plea for holy living.

The poems, "Supermarket," "Sunflower Sutra," "In the Baggage Room at Greyhound," "An Asphodel," "Song" and "Wild Orphan" require no discussion relative to obscenity. In "Transcription of Organ Music" the "I" in four lines remembers his first sex relation at age 23 but only the bare ultimate fact and that he enjoyed it. Even out of context it is written in language that is not obscene, and included in the whole it becomes a part of the individual's experience "real or imagined," but lyric rather than hortatory and violent, like "Howl."

The theme of "Howl" presents "unorthodox and controversial ideas." Coarse and vulgar language is used in treatment and sex acts are mentioned, but unless the book is entirely lacking in "social importance" it cannot be held obscene. This point does not seem to have been specifically presented or decided in any of the cases leading up to *Roth v. United States*, 354 U.S. 476 (1957).

No hard and fast rule can be fixed for the determination of what is obscene, because such determination depends on the locale, the time, the mind of the community and the prevailing mores. Even the word itself has had a chameleon-like history through the past, and as Mr. Justice [Holmes] said: "A word is not a crystal, transparent and unchanged. It is the skin of living thought and may vary greatly in color and content according to the circumstances and the time in which it is used." *Towne v. Eisner*, 245 U.S. 418, 425 (1918). The writing, however, must have a substantial tendency to deprave or corrupt its readers by inciting lascivious thoughts or arousing lustful desires. *Commonwealth v. Isenstadt*, 318 Mass. 543, 550, 62 N.E.2d 840, 844 (1945).

The effect of the publication on the ordinary reader is what counts. The Statute does not intend that we shall "reduce our treatment of sex to the standard of a child's library in the supposed interest of a salacious few." *United States v. Roth*, 237 F.2d at 812 (1956). This test, however, should not be left to stand alone, for there is another element of equal importance—the tenor of the times and the change in social acceptance of what is inherently decent.

The modern rule is that obscenity is measured by the erotic allurement upon the average modern reader; that the erotic allurement of a book is measured by whether it is sexually impure—i.e., pornographic, "dirt for dirt's sake," a calculated incitement to sexual desire—or whether it reveals an effort to reflect life, including its dirt, with reasonable accuracy and balance; and that mere coarseness or vulgarity is not obscenity. *Gordon*, 66 Pa. D. & C. at 136.

Sexual impurity in literature (pornography, as some of the cases call it) is any writing whose dominant purpose and effect is erotic allurement; a calculated and effective incitement to sexual desire. It is the effect that counts, more than the purpose, and no indictment can stand unless it can be shown. *Id.* at 151.

In the *Roth* case no question of obscenity was involved or considered by the court. The sole question was whether obscenity as such was protected by the constitution and the court held it was not. *Roth v. United States*, 354 U.S. at 481 (1957). In the appeals involved the material was obviously pornographic, it was advertised and sold as such. The United States Supreme Court refers to the various rules on obscenity by stating that: "sex and obscenity are not synonymous. Obscene material is material which deals with sex in a manner appealing to prurient interest. The portrayal of sex, e.g., in art, literature and scientific works is not itself sufficient reason to deny material the constitutional protection of freedom of speech and press." *Id.* at 486–87.

The following instruction, given in the *Alberts* case, is approved in *Roth*: "The test is not whether it would arouse sexual desires or sexual impure thoughts in those comprising a particular segment of the community, the young, the immature or the highly prudish, or would leave another segment, the scientific or highly educated or the so-called worldly-wise and sophisticated indifferent and unmoved. The test in each case is the effect of the book, picture or publication considered as a whole, not upon any particular class, but upon all those whom it is likely to reach. In other words, you determine its impact upon the average person in the community. The books, pictures and circulars must be judged, as a whole, in their entire context, and you are not to consider detached or separate portions in reaching a conclusion. You judge the circulars, pictures and publications which have been put in evidence by present-day standards of the community. You may ask yourself does it offend the common conscience of the community by present-day standards. In this case, ladies and gentlemen of the jury, you and you alone are the exclusive judges of what the common conscience of the community is, and in determining that conscience you are to consider the community as a whole, young and old, educated and uneducated, the religious and the irreligious, men, women and children." *Id.* at 490.

Mr. Chief Justice Warren, concurring in the result in the *Roth* case, stated: "I agree with the result reached by the court in these cases, but the line dividing the salacious or pornographic from literature or science is not straight and unwavering, the personal element in these cases is seen most strongly in the requirement of scienter. Under the California law, the prohibited activity must be done 'wilfully and lewdly.'" *Id.* at 494.

There are a number of words used in "Howl" that are presently considered coarse and vulgar in some circles of the community; in other circles such words are in everyday use. It would be unrealistic to deny these facts. The author of "Howl" has used those words because he believed that his portrayal required them as being in character. The People state that it is not necessary to use such words and that others would be more palatable to good taste. The answer is that life is not encased in one formula whereby everyone acts the same or conforms to a particular pattern. No two persons think alike; we were all made from the same mold but in different patterns. Would there be any freedom of press or speech if one must reduce his vocabulary to vapid innocuous euphemism? An author should be real in treating his subject and be allowed to express his thoughts and ideas in his own words.

In *People v. Viking Press*, the court said: "The Courts have strictly limited the applicability of the statute to works of pornography and they have consistently declined to apply it to books of genuine literary value. If the statute were construed more broadly than in the manner just indicated, its effect would be to prevent altogether the realistic portrayal in literature of a large and important field of life.... The Court may not require the author to put refined language into the mouths of primitive people," 174 Misc. 813, 814–816, 264 N.Y.S. 534 (1933), and in *People v. Vanguard Press*, the court observed: "The speech of the characters must be considered in relation to its setting and the theme of the story. It seems clear that use of foul language will not of itself bring a novel or play within the condemnation of the statute." 192 Misc. 127, 129, 84 N.Y.S.2d 427 (1947). "As I have indicated above, all but one of these books are profoundly tragic, and that one has its normal quota of frustration and despair. No one could envy or wish to emulate the characters that move so desolately through these pages. Far from inciting to lewd or lecherous desires, which are sensorially pleasurable, these books leave one either with a sense of horror or of pity for the degradation of mankind. The effect upon the normal reader, *l'homme moyen sensuel* (there is no such deft precision in English), would be anything but what the vice hunters fear it might be. We are so fearful for other people's morals; they so seldom have the courage of our own convictions." *Gordon*, 66 Pa. C. & D. at 109.

In *Commonwealth v. Gordon*: "the test for obscenity most frequently laid down seems to be whether the writing would tend to deprave the morals of those into whose hands the publication might fall by suggesting lewd thoughts and exciting sensual desires." *Id.* at 113. "The statute is therefore directed only at sexual impurity and not at blasphemy or coarse and vulgar behavior of any other kind. The word in common use for the purpose of such statute is 'obscenity.'" *Id.* The "familiar four-letter words that are so often associated with sexual impurity are, almost without exception, of honest Anglo-Saxon ancestry, and were not invented for purely scatological effect. The one, for example, that is used to denote the sexual act is an old agricultural word meaning "to plant" and was at one time a wholly respectable member of the English vocabulary. The distinction between a word of decent etymological history and one of smut alone is important; it shows that fashions in language change as expectably as do the concepts of what language connotes. It is the old business of semantics again, the difference between word and concept. But there is another distinction. The decisions that I cite have sliced off vulgarity from obscenity. This has had the effect of making a clear division between the words of the bathroom and those of the bedroom; the former can no longer be regarded as obscene, since they have no erotic allurement, and the latter may be so regarded, depending on the circumstances of their use. This reduces the number of potentially offensive words sharply." *Id.* at 114.

"The law does not undertake to punish bad English, vulgarity, or bad taste, and no matter how objectionable one may consider the book on those grounds, there is no right to convict on account of them." *Id.* at 122 (citing *Commonwealth v. Dowling*, 14 Pa. C. C. 607 [1894]). The dramatization of the song "Frankie and Johnnie" caused much furor, but the court there held that "the language of the play is coarse, vulgar and profane; the plot cheap and tawdry. As a dramatic composition it serves to degrade the stage where vice is thought by some to lose 'half its evil by losing all its grossness.'" *Id.* at 134. "That it is indecent from every consideration of propriety is entirely clear, but the court is not a censor of plays and does not attempt to regulate manners. One may call a spade a spade without offending decency, although modesty may be shocked thereby. The question is not whether the scene is laid in a low dive where refined people are not found or whether the language is that of the bar room rather than the parlor. The question is whether the tendency of the play is to excite lustful and lecherous desire." *Id.* (internal citations omitted).

"To determine whether a book falls within the condemnation of the statute, an evaluation must be made of the extent to which the book as a whole would have a demoralizing effect on its readers, specifically respecting sexual behavior. Various factors must be borne in mind when applying the judicially accepted standards used in measuring that effect. Among others, these factors include the theme of the book, the degree of sincerity of purpose evidenced in it, its literary worth, the channels used in its distribution, contemporary attitudes toward the literary treatment of sexual behavior and the types of readers reasonably to be expected to secure it for perusal." *People v. Creative Age Press*, 192 Misc. 188, 190–191, 79 N.Y.S. 198 (1948).

Material is not obscene unless it arouses lustful thoughts of sex and tends to corrupt and deprave *l'homme moyen sensuel* by inciting him to anti-social activity or tending to create a clear and present danger that he will be so incited as the result of exposure thereto.

If the material is disgusting, revolting or filthy, to use just a few adjectives, the antithesis of pleasurable sexual desires is born, and it cannot be obscene.

In *United States v. Roth*, a footnote to the concurring opinion of Judge Frank is of interest: "The very argument advanced to sustain the statute's validity, so far as it condemns the obscene, goes to show the invalidity of the statute so far as it condemns 'filth,' if 'filth' means that which renders sexual desires 'disgusting.' For if the argument be sound that the legislature may constitutionally provide punishment for the obscene because, antisocially, it arouses sexual desires by making sex attractive, then it follows that whatever makes sex disgusting is socially beneficial." *United States v. Roth*, 237 F.2d at 801.

"To date there exist, I think, no thoroughgoing studies by competent persons which justify the conclusion that normal adults reading or seeing of the 'obscene' probably induces anti-social conduct. Such competent studies as have been made do conclude that so complex and numerous are the causes of sexual vice that it is impossible to assert with any assurance that 'obscenity' represents a ponderable causal factor in sexually deviant behavior. Although the whole subject of obscenity censorship hinges upon the unproved assumption that 'obscene' literature is a significant factor in causing sexual deviation from the community standard, no report can be found of a single effort at genuine research to test this assumption by singling out as a factor for study the effect of sex literature upon sexual behavior. What little competent research has been done, points definitely in a direction precisely opposite to that assumption." *Id.* at 812.

While the publishing of "smut" or "hard core pornography" is without any social importance and obscene by present-day standards, and should be punished for the good of the community, since there is no straight and unwavering line to act as a guide, censorship by Government should be held in tight rein. To act otherwise would destroy our freedoms of free speech and press. Even religion can be censored by the medium of taxation. The best method of censorship is by the people as self-guardians of public opinion and not by government. So we come back, once more, to Jefferson's advice that the only completely democratic way to control publications which arouse mere thoughts or feelings is through non-governmental censorship by public opinion.

From the foregoing certain rules can be set up, but as has been noted, they are not inflexible and are subject to changing conditions, and above all each case must be judged individually.

1. If the material has the slightest redeeming social importance it is not obscene because it is protected by the First and Fourteenth Amendments of the United States Constitution, and the California Constitution.
2. If it does not have the slightest redeeming social importance it may be obscene.
3. The test of obscenity in California is that the material must have a tendency to deprave or corrupt readers by exciting lascivious thoughts or arousing lustful desire to the point that it presents a clear and present danger of inciting to anti-social or immoral action.
4. The book or material must be judged as a whole by its effect on the *average adult* in the community.
5. If the material is objectionable only because of coarse and vulgar language which is not erotic or aphrodisiac in character it is not obscene.
6. Scienter must be proved.
7. Book reviews may be received in evidence if properly authenticated.
8. Evidence of expert witnesses in the literary field is proper.
9. Comparison of the material with other similar material previously adjudicated is proper.
10. The people owe a duty to themselves and to each other to preserve and protect their constitutional freedoms from any encroachment by government unless it appears that the allowable limits of such protection have been breached, and then to take only such action as will heal the breach.
11. I agree with Mr. Justice Douglas: I have the same confidence in the ability of our people to reject noxious literature as I have in their capacity to sort out the true from the false in theology, economics, politics, or any other field.
12. In considering material claimed to be obscene it is well to remember the motto: *"Honi soit qui mal y pense."* (Evil to him who evil thinks.)

Therefore, I conclude the book "Howl and Other Poems" does have some redeeming social importance, and I find the book is not obscene.

The defendant is found not guilty.

Notes

Prologue

Epigraph quote: Kerouac (4) at 262.

In writing this section we have benefited from, among others, the insightful comments of Brad Parker.

Re: the Kammerer killing and related events: The most extended historical account from the period of the Kammerer killing and the events leading up to and following it is offered in Kerouac's autobiographical novel *Vanity of Duluoz* (1958) in Kerouac (4) at 211–43. Kerouac devoted an entire "book" with twenty-one parts and thirty-two-some pages to the topic. That account is regularly quoted or relied upon by all who write of the Kammerer episode. Kerouac's wife at the time, Stella Sampas Kerouac, said this of that work and its treatment of the Kammerer killing: It "imparts events 'truthfully,' filling in some of the gaps in the earlier, more fictional treatment. He had promised Lucien Carr he never would write about the murder of David Kammerer, but included it in *Vanity of Duluoz with only the most minimal disguising of facts.*" Quoted in Gillford & Lee at 306 (emphasis added).

Kerouac's editor at the time, Ellis Amburn, noted the following in his biography of Kerouac: "As Kerouac's biographer, I have attempted to cross-check everything in his novels, using not only his letters, but also interviews and numerous other primary and secondary sources.... Even prior to negotiations for *Vanity of Duluoz*, Kerouac assured me that his fiction was entirely factual, and that he hoped future biographers, if there were any, would regard his *oeuvre* as his truthful autobiography." Amburn at 6. As Amburn also noted, Kerouac discussed with him the idea of "including Lucien's story in *Vanity of Duluoz.*" Amburn at 81.

Other writings—such as Kerouac's journals and letters, along with those of his contemporaries, and newspaper accounts of the time—corroborate much of that account. Drawing on the totality of the aforementioned, and assisted by the able commentary of several respected Kerouac scholars, we offer the composite set out in the text. While this or that detail may be subject to debate, the overall portrait taken as a whole is as close to the truth mark as we could make it based on the numerous materials now available to us.

Our narrative is also generally consistent with the overall accounts set out in various factual forms in the leading works on the matter. See, e.g., Burroughs & Kerouac at 185–214 (Grauerholz afterword); Aaron Latham, "The Columbia Murder that Gave Birth to the Beats," *New York Magazine*, 19 April 1976, p. 41 (the most detailed account as of this date, though not sourced); Amburn at 87–89; Charters (1) at 42–54; Clark at 59–65; Gifford & Lee at 35–69; Maher (1) at 122–26; McNally at 62–74; Miles (1) at 33–41; Miles (4) at 38–43; Morgan (1) at 37–49, 77–80; T. Morgan at 104–11; Nicosia at 127–30; and Schumacher at 41–45. Notwithstanding, whenever Kerouac's *Vanity of Duluoz* account differed from factual accounts (such as those in newspapers from the time), we deferred to the factual accounts in our rendition of the events portrayed concerning the Kammerer killing and related matters. Such factual accounts include, but are not limited to, the following: Frank S. Adams, "Columbia Student Kills Friend and Sinks Body in Hudson River," *New York Times*, 17 August 1944, p. 1; "Student is Silent on Slaying Friend," *New York Times*, 18 August 1944, p. 14; "Student is Indicted in 2D-Degree Murder," *New York Times*, 25 August 1944, p. 15; "Student Slayer Sent to the Reformatory," *New York Times*, 7 October 1944, p. 15; "Young Slayer Goes to Elmira," *New York Times*, 10 October 1944, p. 38; "Simon Carr," *New York Times* Magazine, 5 November 1995, p. 39; "Lucien Carr," *The Telegraph*, 1 January 2, 2005; Ed Gold, "Trying to Get a Bead on the 'Beats' Mysterious Muse," *The Villager*, March 30–April 5, 2005; Wilborn Hampton, "Lucien Carr, a Founder and a Muse of the Beat Generation, Dies at 79," *New York Times*, 30 January 2005, p. 35. One final point: a noted Kerouac commentator, John Leland, has taken exception to the practice of relying on Kerouac's "novels as factual accounts." Leland at 203. Nonetheless, Leland himself occasionally engages in that very practice. See, e.g., Leland at 77 (relying on *Visions of Gerard*), 78 (relying on *Vanity of Duluoz*).

4   Background information on Carr: Amburn at 80–84, 88, 91, 92, 313–14; Burroughs & Kerouac at 185–214 (Grauerholz afterword); Schumacher at 26–29, 33–34, 38–40, 41–47, 49, 50, 54; Campbell at 11–13, 18, 22–24, 27–32, 34, 51; Aaron Latham, "The Columbia Murder that Gave Birth to the Beats," *New York Magazine*, 19 April 1976, p. 41; Patricia Cremins, "Lucien Carr: Last Original Member of the Beats," *The Independent* (London), 2 February 2005, p. 32; "Obituary of Lucien Carr," *The Daily*

Telegraph (London), 1 February 2005, p. 23; "Lucien Carr," *The Hollywood Reporter*, 2 February 2005; Wilborn Hampton, "Lucien Carr, a Founder and a Muse of the Beat Generation, Dies at 79," *New York Times*, 30 January 2005, p. 35.

4 Lucien and Allen: Ginsberg (6) at 301.

4 "the most angelic" and "romantically glorious": Amburn at 81.

5 "drug-induced visions": Amburn at 84 (quoting Amburn).

5 Kerouac's fatal attachment: Amburn at 81, 83; see also Kerouac (4) at 213; Campbell at 18. Joyce Johnson (née Glassman), one of Kerouac's girlfriends, claimed: "In my own experience with Jack, he never gave me reason to think he was sexually attracted to men." Nonetheless, she conceded: "To me it has always seemed a futile pursuit to try to affix labels of sexual identity to Jack." Johnson (3) at 186.

5 "prettier than any woman": Amburn at 83; see also Kerouac (4) at 211.

5 buck-toothed grin: Kerouac (4) at 220.

5 Burroughs and Carr: Miles (4) at 25, 29, 34–35.

6 "I'm sure I ruined": Amburn at 81.

6 Burroughs and Kammerer in St. Louis: Miles (4) at 27.

6 Supervisor in various junior-high school activities: Miles (4) at 38. According to James Grauerholz: "Kammerer had been Lucien Carr's youth-group leader when Lucien was in junior high..." Burroughs (4) at 10. Michael Schumacher described him as a "former St. Louis physical education instructor and college English teacher who had known Carr as a boy..." Schumacher at 28. Gerald Nicosia maintains that, when he was 14 years old, Carr met Kammerer, who was his "physical education instructor." Nicosia at 117. Bill Morgan identifies Kammerer as Carr's "Boy Scout troop leader" in St. Louis, and claims that Kammerer had a Masters degree and "went on to teach English and physical education for the school where he met Lucien." Morgan (1) at 38.

6 Description of Kammerer: Amburn at 81; Morgan (1) at 38; Campbell at 12–13; Aaron Latham, "The Columbia Murder that Gave Birth to the Beats," *New York Magazine*, 19 April 1976, p. 41; Frank S. Adams, "Columbia Student Kills Friend and Sinks Body in Hudson River," *New York Times*, 17 August 1944, p. 1; "Student in Indicted in 2D-Degree Murder," *New York Times*, 25 August 1944, p. 15. See also Burroughs & Kerouac at 185–214 (Grauerholz afterword).

6 menial jobs: Morgan (1) at 38.

6 Lionel Trilling: Ed Gold, "Trying to Get a Bead on the 'Beats' Mysterious

Muse," *The Villager*, March 30–April 5, 2005.

7 Mother Kammerer: Amburn at 86.

7 Cat story: Schumacher at 42.

7 "Gotta get away," "We'll write poetry": Kerouac (4) at 214.

7 "Where's Lucien?": Kerouac (4) at 220–21.

8 "an indecent proposal" and Riverside Park: Amburn at 87; Frank S. Adams, "Columbia Student Kills Friend and Sinks Body in Hudson River," *New York Times*, 17 August 1944, p. 1.

9 Burroughs-Carr exchange: T. Morgan at 104.

11 *Four Feathers*: Kerouac (4) at 224–25; McNally at 70.

11 Marion Carr was flabbergasted: Morgan (1) at 51.

11 amazing story: Frank S. Adams, "Columbia Student Kills Friend and Sinks Body in Hudson River," *New York Times*, 17 August 1944, p. 1.

12 City morgue: Kerouac (4) at 232–34; Campbell at 33.

12 "Heterosexuality all the way": Kerouac (4) at 230.

12 "Lissen, my father is": Kerouac (4) at 239; accord Clark at 64–65; Knight at 78; and Aaron Latham, "The Columbia Murder that Gave Birth to the Beats," *New York Magazine*, 19 April 1976, p. 41, 53. Barry Miles and James Campbell tell the wedding story slightly differently by suggesting that marriage was the idea of Edie Parker's parents, this as a condition for them posting his bail. But neither offers any support for that portrayal of things. Miles (4) at 42 and Campbell at 33, 289. Paul Maher, by contrast, maintains that Eddie made Jack agree to marry her as a condition for paying his bail. Maher (1) at 124, 125, 500 (n. 42, citing *What happened to Kerouac?*, a 2001 movie with an interview with Edie Parker). Ann Charters suggests that the marriage idea was a mutual one. Charters (1) at 48.

12 Footnote re Edie Parker's account: Kerouac-Parker at 157–58.

13 Marriage: Kerouac-Parker at 193–97.

13 "low, evil decadence": Kerouac (4) at 259.

13 "Dark bridge waters" and Baudelaire quote: Kerouac (4) at 217; Campbell at 11.

13 Kerouac and Burroughs' mystery thriller & Burroughs quote: Miles (4) at 42–43; see also Burroughs (4) at 13 (Grauerholz commentary). Says Grauerholz: After years and years, the text "turned up at the offices of Kerouac's agent, Sterling Lord, in the early 1970s. The jejune text cannot be published as a serious novel, but 'Hippos'—and the earlier draft—will undoubtedly be published, with biographical commentary, someday."

Indeed, the book has recently been published with commentary. See Burroughs & Kerouac at 185–214 (Grauerholz afterword).

14 "Kammerer, Kammerer": Morgan (1) at 53.

14 *West End Sunday*: Ginsberg (6) at 55–61 (draft of novel); Miles (1) at 51–52; Morgan (1) at 55–56; Schumacher at 49–50.

14 "The homosexual and the insane person": Ginsberg & Ginsberg at 6, 7 (letter of Louis Ginsberg to Allen Ginsberg, Fall 1944)

14 "And now this curtain" and "The libertine circle": Ginsberg (6) at 63.

PART I: The Chase
Epigraph: Tytell at 10, 11.

Chapter 1
19 "It was a nice day": Ginsberg (2) at 58, reproduced in Ginsberg (6) at 307.

19 "Sunny and warm...rain": *New York Times*, 22 April 1949, p. 1.

19 Description of 1401 York Avenue: Charters (1) at 94–95; Miles (1) at 106; Tytell at 91.

20 "Conversational bits": Huncke (1) at 106.

20–24 Description of car chase, accident, and characters: Ginsberg (2) vol. 1 at 59–64; Ginsberg (6) at 308–12; Holmes (2) at 280; Kramer at 126–27; Miles (1) at 115; Morgan (1) at 79, 108–14; Raskin at 88; Schumacher at 111–13; "'Cinderella's Shoe' Traps 4 in Thefts," *Daily Mirror*, 23 April 1949, p. 5; Aaron Latham, "The Lives They Lived: Allen Ginsberg; Birth of a Beatnik," *New York Times*, 4 January 1998; "One-Way Street Violation Traps Four as Robbers," *New York Herald Tribune*, 23 April 1949, p. 11; "Wrong-Way Turn Clears Up Robbery," *New York Times*, 23 April 1949; T. Morgan at 164.

Chapter 2
Epigraph quote: Huncke & Schafer (3) at ix.

25 Biographical background: Clark at 71; "Obituary: Herbert Huncke," *The Independent* (*London*), 16 August 1996, p. 11; Huncke (2) at 5; Morgan (1) at 25; Morgan (2) at 65–66; Raskin at 82–83; Robert McG. Thomas Jr., "Herbert Huncke, the Hipster Who Defined 'Beat,' Dies at 81," *New York Times*, 9 August 1996, sec. B, p. 7.

25 Kerouac "the evil bar": Kerouac (4) at 260.

26 Allen's sublet apartment episode: Campbell at 89; Raskin at 83; Schumacher at 107–8.

26 Huncke's appearance: Campbell at 40; Ginsberg (6) at 244; Miles (1) at 62.

27 "They were all so very, very intellectual": Huncke (3) at 155.

27 William S. Burroughs description: Amburn at 81; James Grauerholz, "The Name Is Burroughs," in Burroughs (4) at 7 (marriage); Campbell at 6 ("he was 'definitely' fruit"); Jennie Skerl, "William S. Burroughs," in Charters (5), vol. 1 at 45 (marriage), 48 (occupations).

27 William S. Burroughs meets Huncke: Campbell at 6, 42–43; Ginsberg (6) at 293; Robert M. Thomas Jr., "Herbert Huncke, the Hipster Who Defined 'Beat,' Dies at 81," *New York Times*, 9 August 1996, sec. B, p. 7.

28 A "sort of grifter's realism": Clark at 62–63.

28 Letter to Jack Kerouac of September 20, 1947: Cassady (1) at 57.

Chapter 3

30 Kinsey: Amburn at 96; Huncke (3) at 251–54; "Herbert Huncke, the Hipster Who Defined 'Beat,' Dies at 81," *New York Times*, 9 August 1996, sec. B, p. 7.

Chapter 4

32 "actual damned soul": Miles (1) at 107–8.

33 "letter on Rikers Island": Ginsberg (6) at 262–63. Elsewhere in his journal, Ginsberg states that he sent his letter to Huncke to "the Bronx County Jail." See Ginsberg (6) at 281.

33 Huncke's return to Ginsberg's apartment: Ginsberg (6) at 262–63; Allen Ginsberg, "Herbert Huncke: The Hipster's Hipster," *New York Times*, 29 December 1996, sec. A, p. 1; Huncke (1) at 97–98; Kramer at 123–25; Miles (1) at 107–8; Schumacher at 106–7; Tytell at 91; Watson at 110.

34 Huncke's recovery: Ginsberg (6) at 269–70; Huncke (1) at 105; Kramer at 123–25; Miles (1) at 107, 111; Morgan (1) at 111; Schumacher at 108; Tytell at 92.

35 Footnote re Allen's detailed journal descriptions of Huncke: Ginsberg (6) at 242–44, 262–63, 267–75, 280–85.

Chapter 5

36 *Beggar's Opera*: Ginsberg (6) at 282; Huncke (1) at 105; Kramer at 123–25; Miles (1) at 107, 111; Morgan (1) at 111; Schumacher at 108; Tytell at 92.

37 "My feelings at the time were mixed": Miles (1) at 111–12; Schumacher at 110.

37 Manifesto: Morgan (1) at 112–13.

37 Huncke's use of Ginsberg's clothes: Ginsberg (6) at 282.

37 Burroughs' letters: Miles (1) at 112–13; Morgan (1) at 37–42, 50–52; Schumacher at 107–9; Tytell at 92–93.

38 Footnote re growing marijuana on Texas farm: Ginsberg (6) at 188.

Chapter 6

39 Carr's two-year sentence and "he carved": Aaron Latham, "The Columbia Murder that Gave Birth to the Beats," *New York Magazine*, 19 April 1976, p. 41, 53.

40 "Large autobiographical work of fiction": Morgan (1) at 112.

40 February 24, 1947 journal entry re "real hip sex": Ginsberg (6) at 176.

40 July 24, 1947 journal entry re "glass room-cage-bathroom": Ginsberg (6) at 258.

40 July 29, 1947 journal entry re two uniformed cops: Ginsberg (6) at 191.

40 Drug-related journal entries: Ginsberg (6) at 240 (journal entry of 13 December 1947), 189 (journal entry of May–June, 1947), 167 (journal entry of 8 January 1947), 168 (journal entry of 13 January 1947), 294–95, 302 ("The Fall"), 190–91 (journal entry of 29 July 1947).

Chapter 7

42 Allen's efforts to assist publication of Jack's novel: Charters (1) at 107; Morgan (1) at 111.

42 Footnote re Kerouac's birth name: Amburn at 9; Charters (1) at 22–23; Maher (3) at 29; Nicosia at 23–24.

43 March 29, 1949 letter to Ed White: Kerouac (1) at 185.

43 Allen's antics at parties: Charters (1) at 95.

43 Bill Cannastra: Holmes (2) at 270–71; Amburn at 151–52; Morgan (2) at 52–53; Theado (1) at 410 (comments by Holmes).

43 Tennessee Williams and W.H. Auden: Amburn at 151–52.

43 Footnote re Kammerer's stabbing and *The Town*: Charters (1) at 65–66.

43 Kerouac and God: Douglas Brinkley, "The Kerouac Papers," *The Atlantic Monthly*, November 1998, p. 52 (Kerouac poem); Kerouac (2) at 17 (July 1947 entry).

44 John Clellon Holmes: Gifford & Lee at 72, 74.

44 April 20, 1949 caper and the felonious gang at the party: Clark at 84; McNally at 116–17; Gifford & Lee at 59–60; Huncke at 105–6.

44 Footnote re Little Jack & Kerouac: Ginsberg (6) at 303.

45 Allen's conversation with Kerouac: Ginsberg (6) at 304; Miles (1) at 113–14.

46 Huncke's post-party activities: Gifford & Lee at 59–60.

46 Plan of action: Aaron Latham, "The Lives They Lived: Allen Ginsberg; Birth of a Beatnik," *New York Times*, 4 January 1998; Kramer at 125–26; Miles (1) at 114; Raskin at 88.

Chapter 8

47 Bickford's: Campbell at 52; Bill Morgan (3) at 22–23.

47 Vicki, Allen, and Huncke at the apartment before the bust: Ginsberg (6) at 311; Huncke (1) at 106; Huncke (3) at 309.

47 Description of York Avenue apartment: Ginsberg (6) at 311; Holmes (2) at 16; Miles (1) at 106; Morgan (1) at 106.

48–51 Arrest at the apartment and charges: Ginsberg (2) vol. 2 at 1–3 (statements recast as questions); Ginsberg (6) at 311–12; Holmes (2) at 290; Kramer at 127; "One-Way Street Violation Traps Four as Robbers," *New York Herald Tribune*, 23 April 1949, p. 11; Raskin at 88–89; Schumacher at 111–12; Watson at 111; "Wrong Way Turn Clears Up Robbery," *New York Times*, 23 April 1949; "Columbia Grad, Girl, Seized in Theft Ring," *Brooklyn Eagle*, 22 April 1949.

Chapter 9

52 Allen's interrogation: Ginsberg (6) at 312–13; Kramer at 124–25; "One-Way Street Violation Traps Four as Robbers," *New York Herald Tribune*, 23 April 1949, p. 11; Raskin at 40, 55; Schumacher at 108–10; "Wrong Way Turn Clears Up Robbery," *New York Times*, 23 April 1949. In "The Fall," Ginsberg's notebook confession typewritten for his lawyer Ilo Orleans, Allen apparently transposed his numbers when referring to the precinct station to which he and his criminal cohorts had been brought by the police. He first writes: "We were all taken to the 68th Street precinct." Subsequently he states that the police "took me back to the 86th Street station." See Ginsberg (6) at 312–13. We have reconciled this supposed error.

53 Footnote re Henry Pieretti: Morgan (1) at 113.

56 The Upanishads: Holmes (2) at 290.

56 Charges, arraignment, bail: Huncke (1) at 107; Miles (1) at 115; Schumacher at 112; "Wrong Way Turn Clears Up Robbery," *New York Times*, 23 April 1949; "Columbia Grad, Girl, Seized in Theft Ring," *Brooklyn Eagle*, 22 April 1949.

Chapter 10

Epigraph quote: Diana Trilling, "The Other Night at Columbia: A Report from the Academy," reprinted in Hyde at 56 (originally published in the *Partisan Review*, Spring 1959).

57   News articles on car chase & robbery: "Wrong Way Turn Clears Up Robbery," *New York Times*, 23 April 1949; "One-Way Street Violation Traps Four as Robbers," *New York Herald Tribune*, 23 April 1949, p. 11; "'Cinderella's Shoe' Traps 4 in Thefts," *Daily Mirror*, 23 April 1949, p. 5; Holmes (2) at 291 (patrol wagon); "Columbia Grad, Girl, Seized in Theft Ring," *Brooklyn Eagle*, 22 April 1949.

58   "almost literal truth": Holmes (2) at xvii.

59   News articles on Lucien Carr: Frank S. Adams, "Columbia Student Kills Friend and Sinks Body in Hudson River," *New York Times*, 17 August 1944, p. 1; "Student is Silent on Slaying Friend," *New York Times*, 18 August 1944, p. 14; "Student Slayer Sent to the Reformatory," *New York Times*, 7 October 1944, p. 15.

59   Footnote re Ginsberg suspension: Morgan (1) at 62–64. See also Miles (1) at 56–58; Schumacher at 53–55, 67.

60   Reactions of friends & professors: Ginsberg (6) at 276 (letter of Allen Ginsberg to Lionel Trilling, April 1949); Kramer at 128; Aaron Latham, "The Lives They Lived: Allen Ginsberg; Birth of a Beatnik," *New York Times*, 4 January 1998; McNally at 118; Raskin at 45–46; Schumacher at 109.

60   Van Doren, Trilling & Wechsler: Kramer at 128–29; McNally at 115; Morgan (1) at 5–6; Schumacher at 112–13; Lewin Tamar, "Herbert Wechsler, Legal Giant, Is Dead at 90," *New York Times*, 28 April 2000. Re Ginsberg's late-night calls to Trilling, see Diana Trilling, "The Other Night at Columbia: A Report from the Academy," reprinted in Hyde at 56 (originally published in the *Partisan Review*, Spring 1959).

62   Ilo Orleans & "The Fall": Albert Camus, *La Chute* (Paris: Gallimard, 1956), rpt. *The Fall*, trans. by Justin O'Brien (London: Hamish Hamilton, 1957); Allen Ginsberg (2); "Ilo Orleans, a Poet and Lawyer, Was 65," *New York Times*, 27 September 1962, p. 37; Ruskin at 89–90.

62   Footnote re Huncke in Bellevue prison ward: Ginsberg (6) at 284.

62–63 Corman & Hogan: Ronald K.L. Collins & David M. Skover, *The Trials of Lenny Bruce: The Rise and Fall of an American Icon* (Naperville, IL: Sourcebooks, 2002) at 201; Schumacher at 113; Tytell at 94.

63   Hearing on psychological disability & Cott: Campbell at 91; Miles (1) at

94–96; Raskin at 90.

64 Fagin, Burroughs & Kerouac: Kerouac (2) at 186; Campbell at 91.

65 "he avoided jail": Burroughs (1) at 70, n. 10 (note by Oliver Harris). See also T. Morgan at 164 ("Vicki's magistrate father got her a suspended sentence. Little Jack's family arranged for him to be sent to Pilgrim State Hospital for observation even though he had a record of eighteen previous arrests, and was released later in the custody of his mother.")

65 Ginsberg's writings before commitment: Campbell at 85; Schumacher at 113.

66 "psychological portrait": Ginsberg (6) at 259 (January 24, 1949 journal entry).

66 Footnote re Billie Holiday: Ginsberg (6) at 290.

66 Mississippi: Morgan (1) at 111.

66 Cooper Union College, *New York Times* & Associated Press: Ginsberg (6) at 260, 257, 292–93; Holmes (2) at 298–99 (re A.P.)

PART II: The Asylum
Epigraph quote: Holmes (2), at 10.

Chapter 11

69 Townsend Harris & High School: See generally Lebow; "Townsend Harris: America's First Consul to Japan," at www.cgj.org/150th/ html/ nyepiE2a.htm; Association of the Bar of the City of New York, *Report of the Commission on the Future of CUNY: Part I Remediation and Access: To Educate the "Children of the Whole People,"* 1999.

70 Carl Solomon's early background: Tom Collins, "Carl Solomon," in Charters (5), vol. 2, at 501–502; Miles (1) at 116; T. Morgan at 165; Schumacher at 116; Theado (1) at 51.

71 "jumped ship in France": Miles (1) at 116–17.

71 Street scene: Tom Collins, "Carl Solomon," in Charters (5), vol. 2, at 503; Miles (1) at 116–17; T. Morgan at 165; John Tytell, "The Comedian as Common Denominator," in Solomon (2) at xii, xv. In his interview with John Tytell, Carl Solomon noted, contrary to what some commentators maintain, that the young man whom he saw in the street was not Artaud, who was then a middle-aged man in an asylum. See Theado (1) at 51–52 (quoting Solomon in Tytell interview).

71 "a lunatic is a man": T. Morgan at 165 (quoting Antonin Artaud, *Van Gogh, The Man Suicided by Society*).

72 Footnote re Ronnie Gold: Dudley Clendinen & Adam Nagourney, *Out for Good: The Struggle to Build a Gay Rights Movement in America* (New York: Simon & Schuster, 1999), p. 190–97, 210–14, 299–300.

72 Dadaist demonstration scene: Tom Collins, "Carl Solomon," in Charters (5), vol. 2, at 503; Miles (1) at 117; Theado (1) at 51–52 (quoting Solomon in Tytell interview).

72 Le crime gratuite scene: Miles (1) at 117; T. Morgan at 165; Schumacher at 116; John Tytell, "The Comedian as Common Denominator," in Solomon (2) at xii.

72 "The only legitimate acts of free will": Tom Collins, "Carl Solomon," in Charters (5), vol. 2, at 503–504.

73 "The tendency toward crime among the young men": Solomon (2) at 9.

73 "I picked up a peanut butter sandwich": Solomon (2) at 67.

73 "Things seemed so sick": Theado (1) at 52 (quoting Solomon in Tytell interview).

73 Columbia Presbyterian Psychiatric Institute: Eric Levy, "The New York State Psychiatric Institute: Revolutionizing the Study of Mental Illness," *P&S*, 23: Fall 2003, p. 1–2.

73 Insulin shock therapy: T. Morgan at 166; Solomon (2) at 105–8.

75 Myshkin/Kirilov: Miles (1) at 116; Schumacher at 113–14.

75 "psychological penetration": "Fyodor Dostoyevsky" in Encyclopedia Britannica (DVD, 2004).

75 "There is a boy here": Ginsberg (6) at 324 (letter of Allen Ginsberg to Jack Kerouac, 13 July 1949); T. Morgan at 166 (quoting Solomon).

75 "I take my madhouses seriously": Ginsberg (16) at 51 (letter of Allen Ginsberg to Jack Kerouac, 14 July 1949). We note that Ginsberg (6) dates the excerpts from this letter as July 13th, whereas Ginsberg (16) dates the full letter as July 14th. For citation purposes, we chose to remain faithful to the editors' conflicting designations.

75 "Be careful while convincing the docs": Miles (1) at 120 (letter of Jack Kerouac to Allen Ginsberg, 5 July 1949).

75 "Be smart, now": Kerouac (1) at 209 (letter of Jack Kerouac to Allen Ginsberg, 26 July 1949).

76 Footnote re Kerouac's stint in Navy's psychiatric ward: Gewirtz at 57–58.

76 "I wouldn't let them croakers": Burroughs (1) at 51 (letter of William Burroughs to Jack Kerouac, 24 June 1949).

76 "The Problem": Columbia Presbyterian Psychiatric Institute Clinical Summary, on file at the Allen Ginsberg Trust, New York, NY (Ginsberg's

entire medical report from the CPPI is on file here).

76 Daily schedule: Miles (1) at 121–22.

76 Psychotherapy sessions: Miles (1) at 121.

76 "ghouls of mediocrity": John Tytell, "The Comedian as Common Denominator," in Solomon (2) at xiii (quoting letter of Allen Ginsberg to Jack Kerouac).

77 "I am torn": Ginsberg (6) at 321–22 (journal entry of 29 June 1949).

77 "As I look out the Washington Bridge": Ginsberg (6) at 322 (journal entry of 4 July 1949); Miles (1) at 120.

77 "I was just writing prose": Schumacher at 120 (quoting Allen Ginsberg interview).

77 Solomon and Ginsberg introducing each other to literature: Tom Collins, "Carl Solomon," in Charters (5), vol. 2, at 504; Miles (1) at 122; Schumacher at 116.

78 Debate on Wordsworth and "dopey daffodil": Miles (1) at 122; Schumacher at 116; John Tytell, "The Comedian as Common Denominator," in Solomon (2) at xiii.

78 Piano scene: Miles (1) at 121.

78 Letter to T.S. Eliot: Solomon (2) at 178–81.

79 "I am beginning to hate my mother": Miles (1) at 120 (quoting letter of Allen Ginsberg to Jack Kerouac).

Chapter 12

80 Camp Nitgedayget: Miles (1) at 12–13; Morgan (1) at 18; Schumacher at 9. Morgan's spelling of the camp, which we believe to be accurate, differs from that of Miles and Schumacher, who apparently rely on Allen's spelling ("Camp Nicht-Gedeigat") in Part II of *Kaddish*.

81 Naomi's background and marriage: Miles (1) at 4–7; Schumacher at 4–6.

81 Marital fights: Morgan (1) at 12; Schumacher at 9.

81 Bloomingdale Sanatorium: Miles (1) at 7–9; Morgan (1) at 13; Schumacher at 8–9.

81 Naomi's symptoms: Miles (1) at 15–16; Morgan (1) at 12–13; Schumacher at 10.

82 Greystone: Miles (1) at 15–16; Schumacher at 11–12.

82 "It stank, sour smell of wards": Miles (1) at 16.

83 Naomi's suicide attempt: Ginsberg (6) at 5–6; Ginsberg & Ginsberg at 283–84 (quoting from Louis Ginsberg's "My Son the Poet"); Miles (1) at 21; Morgan (1) at 22; Schumacher at 13. While Louis Ginsberg's account

has Naomi opening the door, all other accounts (including Allen's contemporaneous one) describe Louis as breaking the glass door.

83 "What traumas": Ginsberg & Ginsberg at 284 (quoting from Louis Ginsberg's "My Son the Poet").

83 Footnote re *Everlasting Minute*: Morgan (1) at 22.

84 Naomi and Allen's dialogue re 1941 psychotic episode: Miles (1) at 27–31; Schumacher at 17–21.

85 "rambling on": Schumacher at 19.

85 Rest home scene: Miles (1) at 29–30; Schumacher at 20.

86 Things becoming apparent: Miles (1) at 31, 93–94; Schumacher at 21, 53, 88–89.

86 Lobotomy: Miles (1) at 94; Morgan (1) at 98; Schumacher at 88.

86 "Allen, don't die": Ginsberg (6) at 239 (journal entry of 25 November 1947).

Chapter 13

87 Prognosis for cure: Miles (1) at 122–23; Schumacher at 118–19.

88 "He is partly homosexual": Miles (1) at 123.

88 Form of insanity and menace to society: Ginsberg & Ginsberg at 6 (quoting letter of Louis Ginsberg to Allen Ginsberg, Fall 1944)

88 "a certificate stating": Morgan (1) at 122.

88 "A turning point has been reached": Miles (1) at 123 and Morgan (1) at 124 (both sources quoting letter of Allen Ginsberg to Jack Kerouac, 27 February 1950). We note that, in a different work, Bill Morgan dates this letter as 24 February 1950. Ginsberg (16) at 56.

88 "I wish that I could meet": Ginsberg (16) at 56, Morgan (1) at 124, and Schumacher at 119 (quoting letter of Allen Ginsberg to Jack Kerouac, 24 January 1950).

88 Allen meets Helen Parker: Morgan (1) at 121.

88 "There *is* something new": Miles (1) at 127 and Morgan (1) at 124 (both sources quoting letter of Allen Ginsberg to Jack Kerouac, 8 June 1950).

89 "I'm a man": Ginsberg (16) at 58–60, McNally at 130 (quoting letter of Allen Ginsberg to Jack Kerouac, 8 July 1950).

89 "I am more than a little dubious": Burroughs (1) at 68–69 (letter of William Burroughs to Allen Ginsberg, 1 May 1950).

89 "Laying one woman or a thousand:" Burroughs (1) at 88–90 (letter of William Burroughs to Allen Ginsberg, May 1951).

89 Allen's newspaper career: Miles (1) at 125, 129; Morgan (1) at 123–24;

Schumacher at 119–20. Unlike Miles and Schumacher, Morgan maintains that Allen "found a job as an office boy with the *New Jersey Labor Herald*."

89 New home in Paterson: Miles (1) at 123.

90 Ribbon factory: Maher (1) at 219; Miles (1) at 129.

90 "pick up all the broken threads": Miles (1) at 129.

90 "I would daydream": Miles (1) at 129.

90 *Book of Doldrums* & Giroux quote: Morgan (1) at 122–23.

90 William Carlos Williams: see generally Paul Mariani, *William Carlos Williams: A New World Naked* (New York: McGraw-Hill, 1981).

90 "I would like to make my presence known": Paul Mariani, *William Carlos Williams: A New World Naked* (New York: McGraw-Hill, 1981) at 604 (quoting letter of Allen Ginsberg to William Carlos Williams, 30 March 1950).

91 "rhythmical construction": Miles (1) at 125 (quoting Williams).

91 "I refuse to use Benny": Ginsberg & Cassady at 68 (letter of Allen Ginsberg to Neal Cassady, Summer 1950).

91 Solomon's New Year's Eve party: Tom Collins, "Carl Solomon," in Charters (5), vol. 2, at 505; Solomon (2) at xiii; Tytell at 96.

92 San Remo: Morgan (2) at 88–89; Watson at 119–21.

92 "the strongest espresso": Ronald Sukenick, *Down and In: Life in the Underground* (New York: Macmillan, 1987), p. 19 (quoting Gloria Sukenick).

92 "amid the discussion": Watson at 120–21.

93 "For all his apparent attempts": Schumacher at 125.

Chapter 14

Epigraph quote: Plummer at 33.

94 San Remo: Ginsberg (6) at 336–37 (journal entry of 11 October 1950).

94 Cannastra's appearance: J.H. Kerouac at 19.

94 Cannastra's antics: Amburn at 152 (stripping and streaking); J.H. Kerouac at 22, 30–31 (alcoholic consumption), 47–48 (voyeurism); McNally at 130 (ledges); Nicosia at 215 (peepholes), 216 (palm tree & stripping and streaking), at 330 ("guzzled liquor so fast"), at 331 ("like the swoosh," quoting Howard Moss); Plummer at 33 (Bach fugues); Schumacher at 130 (broken glass, ledges, lying in street).

95 Allen's envy and wondering: Ginsberg (6) at 337 (journal entry of 11 October 1950).

95 Tennessee Williams: Lyle Leverich, *Tom: The Unknown Tennessee Williams* (New York: Crown, 1995), p. 541–42.

96 Trendsetting Parties at Loft: Amburn at 151–52; J.H. Kerouac at 20, 35, 80–82; Nicosia at 217, 330–31 (quoting John Snow).

96 Legal life & jobs: J.H. Haverty at 19–24; Tim Hunt, "Interview with John Clellon Holmes," *Quarterly West* (Winter 1978), reprinted in Theado (1) at 410; Nicosia at 214–15, 331; Schumacher at 130.

97 "Wop" incident: Ginsberg (6) at 337–38 (journal entry of 11 October 1950).

97 "Up your ass with Mobilgas": Kerouac (1) at 240 (letter of Jack Kerouac to Neal Cassady, 3 December 1950).

97 "Buy me a drink": Tim Hunt, "Interview with John Clellon Holmes," *Quarterly West* (Winter 1978), reprinted in Theado (1) at 410.

97 "Bill was of more value": J.H. Kerouac at 50.

97 "Why don't you fuck somebody?": Ginsberg (6) at 339 (journal entry of 11 October 1950).

97 Cannastra's stutter: Lyle Leverich, *Tom: The Unknown Tennessee Williams* (New York: Crown, 1995), p. 542. See also Holmes (2) at 73. In order to portray more accurately Cannastra's speech pattern, we have embellished a bit on the text as recounted by Ginsberg.

98 Cannastra & Williams: Amburn at 157; Donald Spoto, *The Kindness of Strangers: The Life of Tennessee Williams* (Boston: Little, Brown and Co., 1985), p. 185–86; Tennessee Williams, *Memoirs* (New York: New Directions, 2006), p. 105–6.

98 Joan Haverty: J.H. Kerouac at 47–49; Nicosia at 331; Schumacher at 131.

98 "When women are protected": J.H. Kerouac at 21–22.

98 "He's a writer, and *mensch*": J.H. Kerouac at 49–50.

99 Cannastra & Ginsberg conversation: Ginsberg (6) at 338–39 (journal entry of 11 October 1950); Ginsberg (16) at 61 (letter of Allen Ginsberg to Helen Parker, 12 October 1950).

99 Cannastra's death: Amburn at 156–57; Ginsberg & Cassady at 70–71 (letter of Allen Ginsberg to Neal Cassady, 31 October 1950); Ginsberg (16) at 61 (letter of Allen Ginsberg to Helen Parker, 12 October 1950); Miles (1) at 130; Nicosia at 332; Schumacher at 129–30; Watson at 135. See also Holmes (2) at 302.

100 Haverty's reaction to death: J.H. Haverty at 55–57.

100 Footnote re Ginsberg's question: Ginsberg & Cassady at 71 (letter of Allen Ginsberg to Neal Cassady, 31 October 1950); Nicosia at 214 (mother's attempted suicide).

101 Ginsberg's reaction to death: Ginsberg (16) at 62 (letter of Allen Ginsberg to Helen Parker, 12 October 1950); Ginsberg & Cassady at 71–72 (letter of Allen Ginsberg to Neal Cassady, 31 October 1950).

101 Auden's reported reaction to death: Leverich at 542.

Chapter 15

Epigraph: J.H. Kerouac at 128. To be accurate, at the time that this statement was published, her full name was Joan Haverty Kerouac. For dramatic purposes, we chose to use her maiden name.

103 Kerouac meets Haverty: Amburn at 158; J.H. Kerouac at 52 (Lashinsky), 69–72, 77; Kerouac (1) at 315, 318 (lofts). See also "Jack Kerouac's Typescript Scroll of *On the Road*," Christie's New York, 22 May 2001, p. 18; Kerouac (11) at 304; Maher (1) at 220–21; Nicosia at 333–34; Matt Theado, "Revisions of Kerouac: The Long, Strange Trip of the *On the Road* Typescripts," p. 4 (unpublished article on file with authors).

104 Kerouac proposes to Haverty: J.H. Kerouac at 93–96; Nicosia at 333–34.

105 Reasons for marriage: J.H. Haverty at 89–90, 128–29; Nicosia at 333–34.

105 Footnote re Jack and children: Gifford & Lee at 237 (quoting Joyce Johnson).

106 Wedding: Amburn at 159; J.H. Kerouac at 130–32; Maher (1) at 221–22; McNally at 331; Nicosia at 333.

106 Reception & wedding night: Amburn at 159; Ginsberg (16) at 62–64 (letter of Allen Ginsberg to Neal Cassady, 18 November 1950); J.H. Kerouac at 132–34; "Jack Kerouac's Typescript Scroll of *On the Road*," Christie's New York, 22 May 2001, p. 18; Nicosia at 333–34; Schumacher at 131–32.

107 Day after wedding: J.H. Kerouac at 137–38; "Jack Kerouac's Typescript Scroll of *On the Road*.," Christie's New York, 22 May 2001, p. 18.

Chapter 16

Epigraph: Kerouac (17) at 167.

108 "I first met Neal": Kerouac (16) at 109 (quotation from the original scroll version of *On the Road*); compare Kerouac (11) at 1. Note that the original scroll, as recently reproduced, contained errors, such as the one in the first sentence of the work (i.e., "met met"). And the line "after my father died" was changed in the final version to read "after my wife and I split up."

109 Typewriter: Kerouac (1) at 294 (letter of Jack Kerouac to Neal Cassady, January 10, 1951). In his correspondence with Neal, Jack mentions that

he was using "this antique L.C. Smith typewriter" to write the letter, and that he planned to take the typewriter to California with him the following month. (The trip never happened.) Since the scroll version of *On the Road* was begun three months later, it is likely that this was the typewriter he used for that purpose. We are grateful to Dave Moore for alerting us to this.

109 Typing scene: "Jack Kerouac's Typescript Scroll of *On the Road*," Christie's New York, 22 May 2001, p. 25; Kerouac (1) at 318 (letter of Jack Kerouac to Neal Cassady, 10 June 1951); Nicosia at 343; Matt Theado, "Revisions of Kerouac: The Long, Strange Trip of the *On the Road* Typescripts" at 6–8, 10, 12 (unpublished article on file with authors).

109 Journals & notebooks: Douglas Brinkley, "In the Kerouac Archive," *Atlantic Monthly*, November 1998, p. 53; Ann Charters, "Introduction," in Kerouac (11) at xx; Howard Cunnell, "Fast This Time: Jack Kerouac and the Writing of *On the Road*," in Kerouac (16) at 24; "Jack Kerouac's Typescript Scroll of *On the Road*," Christie's New York, 22 May 2001, p. 19; Kerouac (1) at 46; Matt Theado, "Revisions of Kerouac: The Long, Strange Trip of the *On the Road* Typescripts" at 12, 14 (unpublished article on file with authors). Although he believes that Kerouac used his notebooks, journals, and plot-lines when typing the scroll version of *On the Road*, Professor Matt Theado informed us that some recent evidence suggests that Jack may have referred to them only in the process of revising and retyping the book.

110 "produced thousands" & "NIGHT NOTE": Gewirtz at 61–62, 86.

110 Joan & Jack conversation: J.H. Haverty at 201–2.

110 "Memory Babe": "Jack Kerouac's Typescript Scroll of *On the Road*," Christie's New York, 22 May 2001, p. 18; Nicosia at 39.

110 Footnote re five attempts: See Hunt at xxxvii, 77–78, 83–142; Tim Hunt, *Off the Road: The Literary Maturation of Jack Kerouac* (Ithaca, NY: Cornell University Press, 1975), p. 11; Dave Moore, "*On the Road*—The Scroll Revealed," *The Kerouac Connection*, No. 10, April 1986, 3, at 4.

110 "I have another novel in mind": Kealing at 5 (quoting Kerouac notebook entry of 24 July 1948).

111 Scroll paper: Howard Cunnell, "Fast This Time: Jack Kerouac and the Writing of *On the Road*," in Kerouac (16) at 24; J.H. Kerouac at 141; Kerouac (1) at 316; Dave Moore, "On the Road—The Scroll Revealed," *The Kerouac Connection*, April 1986, p. 3; Matt Theado, "Revisions of Kerouac: The Long, Strange Trip of the *On the Road* Typescripts" at 4

(unpublished article on file with authors).

111 "With the coming of Neal": Kerouac (16) at 109 (quotation from the original scroll version of *On the Road*); compare Kerouac (11) at 1.

111 "just flung it down": Gifford & Lee at 156–57 (quoting John Clellon Holmes).

111 "drawing a breath": Penny Vlagopoulos, "Rewriting America: Kerouac's Nation of 'Underground Monsters,'" in Kerouac (16) at 65 (quoting Jack Kerouac).

111 "IT'S NOT THE WORDS": Leland at 131–32 (quoting Kerouac journal entry).

112 "They danced down the street": Kerouac (16) at 113 (quotation from the original scroll version of *On the Road*); compare Kerouac (11) at 5–6.

112 "burn, burn, burn like fabulous yellow roman candles": Kerouac (11) at 6.

112 "When one writes": Cassady (1) at 69–70 (letter of Neal Cassady to Jack Kerouac, 7 January 1948).

112 "My first impression of Neal": Kerouac (16) at 110 (quotation from the original scroll version of *On the Road*); compare Kerouac (11) at 2.

113 Neal Cassady's background & attributes: Amburn at 107, 111; John Clellon Holmes, "The Gandy Dancer," in Holmes (3) at 202; Kerouac (9) at 47–49, 338–39; T. Morgan at 138–39; Nicosia at 146; Schumacher at 61, 70–73.

113 "a walking, breathing hard-on": Leland at 92.

113 "To him, sex was": Kerouac (16) at 110 (quotation from the original scroll version of *On the Road*); compare Kerouac (11) at 2.

114 "Sounds, sights, personalities": J.H. Kerouac at 176–77.

114 "In the bar I told Neal": Kerouac (16) at 111 (quotation from the original scroll version of *On the Road*); compare Kerouac (11) at 3.

115 "siren singing freedom": McNally at 89.

115 "Allen was queer in those days": Kerouac (16) at 113 (quotation from the original scroll version of *On the Road*); compare Kerouac (11) at 5.

116 Ginsberg & Cassady sexual relations: Amburn at 111; Nicosia at 173; Schumacher at 74–76.

116 "Having spent a wild weekend": Ginsberg (6) at 169 (journal entry of 21 January 1947).

116 "Try him laying me again": Ginsberg (6) at 176.

116 "I *really don't* know": Ginsberg & Cassady at 11 (letter of Neal Cassady to Allen Ginsberg, 30 March 1947).

116 "dirty, double crossing": Ginsberg & Cassady at 17 (Ginsberg quoted in letter of Neal Cassady to Allen Ginsberg, 10 April 1947).

116 "I can't promise a darn thing": Ginsberg & Cassady at 17 (letter of Neal Cassady to Allen Ginsberg, 10 April 1947).

117 Triple-dipping schedule: Leland at 87; McNally at 94; Schumacher at 81–82.

117 New Waverly: Amburn at 120–21; Ginsberg (6) at 224 (journal entry of 1 September 1947), 358 (journal entry of 30 March 1952); Miles (4) at 52; T. Morgan at 144–45; Schumacher at 83–84.

117 "Fastestmanalive": Schumacher at 72.

117 End of first day of writing: Kerouac (1) at 315 (letter of Jack Kerouac to Neal Cassady, 22 May 1951) (12,000 words); Ann Charters, "Introduction" in Kerouac (11) at xix (sweating); Nicosia at 343 (sweating).

Chapter 17

118 Footnote re abortion: Nicosia & Santos at 80.

118 "He had lived happily": Kerouac (16) at 213 (quotation from the original scroll version of *On the Road*); compare Kerouac (11) at 110.

119 Scene & dialogue: C. Cassady at 73–77.

121 Footnote re 191 words in the scroll version referencing episode: Kerouac (16) at 213 (quotation from the original scroll version of *On the Road*); compare Kerouac (11) at 110. Re "The truth of the matter": Kerouac (16) at 224 (quotation from the original scroll version of *On the Road*); compare Kerouac (11) at 122.

121 "fraternity of undesirables": Leland at 128.

121 Footnote quotation re Kerouac's "female characters": Leland at 94.

Chapter 18

Epigraph quote: Burroughs (1) at 37–38 (letter of William Burroughs to Allen Ginsberg, 30 January 1949)

122 Original title: Leland at 4, 161.

123 "He was roaring": Kerouac (16) at 214 (quotation from the original scroll version of *On the Road*); compare Kerouac (11) at 111.

123 Al and Helen Hinckle: T. Morgan at 153–54; Plummer at 50–51; Sandison & Vickers at 165, 169; Schumacher at 102.

123 Lu Anne Henderson: T. Morgan at 154; Sandison & Vickers at 169, 172; Schumacher at 103; see generally Nicosia & Santos.

124 "Neal, Louanne, and Al Hinkle roared east": Kerouac (16) at 215 (quotation from the original scroll version of *On the Road*); compare Kerouac (11) at 112.

124 Great Plains snowstorm: Amburn at 131; T. Morgan at 154; Schumacher at 103–4.

125 "The only way we could make it": Nicosia & Santos at 86.

125 "mudsplattered '49 Hudson": Kerouac (16) at 212 (quotation from the original scroll version of *On the Road*); compare Kerouac (11) at 107.

126 Christmas: Amburn at 131; Plummer at 51; Sandison & Vickers at 169–70; Schumacher at 104.

127 "We packed my sister's boxes": Kerouac (16) at 218 (quotation from the original scroll version of *On the Road*); compare Kerouac (11) at 116.

127 Cassady travel plan: Amburn at 131; Sandison & Vickers at 169–70; compare Kerouac (16) at 216, 219–24 and Kerouac (11) at 113–14, 118–22.

128 "Everything since the Greeks": Kerouac (16) at 221 (quotation from the original scroll version of *On the Road*); compare Kerouac (11) at 120.

128 "This is what *it's* about, man": Amburn at 131.

128 "So now Neal had come": Kerouac (16) at 219 (quotation from the original scroll version of *On the Road*); compare Kerouac (11) at 117.

Chapter 19

Note: John Leland's *Why Kerouac Matters* influenced this chapter. We gladly acknowledge our debt to Mr. Leland and his superb commentary.

129 "Bill had a sentimental": Kerouac (16) at 246 (quotation from the original scroll version of *On the Road*); compare Kerouac (11) at 144.

130 Goethe quote: Leland at 51 (quoting Goethe's *Faust*).

130 Footnote reference to Sal Paradise: Leland at 19, 187.

130 "We bent down": Kerouac (16) at 196–97 (quotation from the original scroll version of *On the Road*); compare Kerouac (11) at 96.

131 "The one thing": Kerouac (16) at 225 (quotation from the original scroll version of *On the Road*); compare Kerouac (11) at 124.

131 "Neal stood outside the windows": Kerouac (16) at 407 (quotation from the original scroll version of *On the Road*); compare Kerouac (11) at 306.

132 "That's a lousy way": J.H. Kerouac at 187.

132 "So in America" & next passage: Kerouac (16) at 408 (quotation from the original scroll version of *On the Road*); compare Kerouac (11) at 307.

132 Footnote re "God is Pooh Bear": Kerouac (11) at 307.

133 "Still we travel": Leland at 200. He then adds: "At some point we read *On the Road*, which turns this elemental recognition into a lively story, with girls, visions, everything."

133 Single-spaced paragraph: Charters, "Introduction," in Kerouac (11) at xix.

133 Footnote re "beat": Kerouac (11) at 195; Gewirtz at 11, 23.

133 Facts re scroll: "Jack Kerouac's Typescript Scroll *On the Road*," Christie's New York, 22 May 2001, p. 15, 22. Although Isaac Gewirtz, the New York Public Library curator, has characterized the scroll as having 12 foot long strips, Professor Matt Theado informed us that Jim Canary, the Indiana University librarian who took personal care of the scroll, claims that the strips of paper are of varying lengths.

Chapter 20
Epigraph quote: Kerouac (1) at 315–16 (letter of Jack Kerouac to Neal Cassady, 22 May 1951).

135 Robert Giroux profile: Amburn at 137, 138–40.

135 Giroux phone conversation with Kerouac: *On the Road to Desolation* (David Stewart, dir.) (BBC/NVC Arts Co-production, 1997) (Giroux interview).

136 "complete departure from *Town and City*": Kerouac (1) at 315 (letter of Jack Kerouac to Neal Cassady, 22 May 1951).

137 Office conversation: Derived and reasonably adapted from Amburn at 166; Howard Cunnell, "Fast This Time: Jack Kerouac and the Writing of *On the Road*," in Kerouac (16) at 32; Donald Hall, "Robert Giroux: Looking for Masterpieces," *New York Times Book Review*, 6 January 1980, p. 22; *On the Road to Desolation* (David Stewart, dir.) (BBC/NVC Arts Co-production, 1997) (Giroux interview); Nicosia at 349.

138 "typing and revising": Kerouac (1) at 317 (letter of Jack Kerouac to Neal Cassady, 22 May 1951).

138 Crayon edits: Ann Charters, *A Bibliography of Works by Jack Kerouac* (New York: Phoenix Book Shop, 1967), p. 5. We are indebted, yet again, to Dave Moore for his assistance in fine-tuning our work on these points.

139 Demise of Kerouac marriage: J.H. Kerouac at 202–6; Maher (1) at 235–36.

139 Footnote re Potchky: "Jack Kerouac's Typescript Scroll of *On the Road*," Christie's New York, 22 May 2001, p. 25–26; Matt Theado, "Revisions of Kerouac: The Long, Strange Trip of the *On the Road* Typescripts, at 19 (unpublished article on file with authors).

139 Footnote re paternity denial: Amburn at 167; Charters (1) at 217–18; Maher (1) at 235–36; McNally at 136, 152, 191; Nicosia at 631.

139 "I'm completely fucked": Kerouac (1) at 320 (letter of Jack Kerouac to Neal Cassady, 24 June 1951).

140 Rae Everitt: Howard Cunnell, "Fast This Time: Jack Kerouac and the

Writing of *On the Road*," in Kerouac (16) at 33; Nicosia at 349; Matt Theado, "Revisions of Kerouac: The Long, Strange Trip of the *On the Road* Typescripts, at 23–25 (unpublished article on file with authors).

140 Carl Solomon & Ace Book Contract: Amburn at 170; Tom Collins, "Carl Solomon," in Charters (5), vol. 2, at 505; Howard Cunnell, "Fast This Time: Jack Kerouac and the Writing of *On the Road*," in Kerouac (16) at 34–36; Leland at 69; Nicosia at 357, 368, 371, 415; Matt Theado, "Revisions of Kerouac: The Long, Strange Trip of the *On the Road* Typescripts, at 23–25 (unpublished article on file with authors).

141 "Prose sketching": Kerouac (1) at 335 (letter of Jack Kerouac to John Clellon Holmes, 12 March 1952), 356 (letter of Jack Kerouac to Allen Ginsberg, 18 May 1952); McNally at 139–40; Schumacher at 146.

141 "The wainscot effect of dark": Kerouac (9) at 6.

142 Footnote re *Hippos*: Tom Collins, "Carl Solomon," in Charters (5), vol. 2, at 505. See Burroughs & Ginsberg.

142 Ace Books rejection: Howard Cunnell, "Fast This Time: Jack Kerouac and the Writing of *On the Road*," in Kerouac (16) at 34–36; Nicosia at 415.

143 Footnote: "a holy mess": Ginsberg (16) at 81–82.

142 "I don't see how it will ever be published": Kerouac (1) at 372–74 (letter of Allen Ginsberg to Jack Kerouac, 11 June 1952).

143 Footnote re "a holy mess": Ginsberg & Cassady at 130 (letter of Allen Ginsberg to Jack Kerouac, 3 July 1952).

143 "We've had a reading": Howard Cunnell, "Fast This Time: Jack Kerouac and the Writing of *On the Road*," in Kerouac (16) at 36 (quoting letter of Carl Solomon to Jack Kerouac, 30 July 1952).

143 "I believe 'On the Road'": Kerouac (1) at 376–77 (letter of Jack Kerouac to Carl Solomon, A. A. Wyn, and Miss James, 5 August 1952). A photo of the original draft of that letter, which has notable differences, is contained in Theado (1) at 154. At the end of his letter, Kerouac wrote: "Please let me know what you intend to do as quickly as possible." Not long after, Ace Books rejected the book. Nicosia at 415. Per Jack's prediction, much of the "spontaneous prose" draft of *On the Road* was eventually published, under the title *Visions of Cody* in 1972, three years after his death.

143 "This is to notify you": Kerouac (1) at 377–80 (letter of Jack Kerouac to Allen Ginsberg, 8 October 1952).

144 "I feel like an Indian": Kerouac (1) at 381–82 (letter of Jack Kerouac to John Clellon Holmes, 12 October 1952). Kerouac's rapid change of

sentiment toward Holmes, only four days after Jack had impugned John in his letter to Allen, was entirely consistent with the off-again, on-again character of Kerouac's friendships; after bitter tirades against them, he would soon sweeten up and rebuild the fences he had knocked down. On this point, see Schumacher at 149 and Ann Charters, "Introduction," in Kerouac (11) at xviii.

145 Carl Solomon's relapse: Amburn at 177; McNally at 161–62.

145 Jack's world collapsing around him: Derived from Leland at 187 (1952 letter of Jack Kerouac to John Clellon Holmes).

145 Publisher rejections: Listed in Theado (1) at 145.

145 *Go* and *Junk*: Maher (3) at 271; Theado (1) at 5.

Chapter 21

Epigraph quote: Burroughs (1) at 79.

146 "He is exceedingly interested in guns": Miles (4) at 51 (quoting letter of Herbert Huncke to Allen Ginsberg, March 1947).

146 "I always carry a gun": Burroughs (1) at 39 (letter of William S. Burroughs to Allen Ginsberg, 30 January 1949).

146 Shoulder-holster: C. Cassady (1) at 112 (quoting Helen Hinkle).

146 "I've got enough guns": Burroughs (1) at 27 (letter of William S. Burroughs to Jack Kerouac and Allen Ginsberg, 30 November 1948).

146 Gun types: Burroughs (8) at 415, 416, 555, 566, 571, 605, 606, 637; Miles (4) at 37–38 (bug-spray gun).

147 "Shooting is my principal pastime": Burroughs (1) at 27 (letter of William S. Burroughs to Jack Kerouac and Allen Ginsberg, 30 November 1948).

147 Duck-hunting: T. Morgan at 35.

147 Sophomore year at Harvard: Schumacher at 31; T. Morgan at 59.

147 Unregistered gun and narcotics bust: Burroughs (1) at 47 (letter of William S. Burroughs to Allen Ginsberg, 16 April 1949); Miles (4) at 53–54; T. Morgan at 167–68.

147 "Maybe I will feel a little better": Burroughs (1) at 258 (letter of William S. Burroughs to Allen Ginsberg, 21 January 1955).

147 "All my life I've never considered suicide": Burroughs (8) at 644 (quote from 1987 interview).

147 Painting by gun: Burroughs (8) at 657, 679, 701, 703.

147 Footnote re Van Gogh: Miles (4) at 34–35; T. Morgan at 73–76; Schumacher at 33; Burroughs (2) at xxxvii–xxxviii (Burroughs' prologue to *Junky*).

148 Texas shooting: McNally at 99; Miles (4) at 51; T. Morgan at 134–37; Schumacher at 84; Burroughs (1) at 13 (letter of William S. Burroughs to Allen Ginsberg, 11 March 1947).

148 Louisiana shooting: Nicosia at 257–58.

148 Mexico City shooting: T. Morgan at 184–85.

148 .380 Star pistol: R. Johnson at 148, 153–54; Miles (4) at 57; T. Morgan at 194.

148 Footnote re Robert Addison: James Grauerholz, *The Death of Joan Vollmer: What Really Happened?* (unpublished essay prepared for the Fifth Congress of the Americas at Universidad de Las Americas / Puebla, October 18, 2001; final manuscript dated January 7, 2002) (hereinafter Grauerholz, *The Death of Joan Vollmer*), at 32, 47.

149 Knife-sharpening scene: Miles (4) at 57.

149 Healy's apartment: Grauerholz, *The Death of Joan Vollmer*, at 26, 33, 39; R. Johnson at 148, 152–54; T. Morgan at 194–95. We gladly acknowledge our immense debto to Mr. Grauerholz, whose unpublished paper was vital to the writing of this chapter.

150 Joan Vollmer description: Amburn at 78–79, 94–95; Knight at 49–55; Maher (3) at 135–37; Miles (4) at 44; T. Morgan at 92–93, 115.

150 Footnote re Hal Chase: Nicosia at 135–36; Miles (4) at 44; T. Morgan at 94, 97, 115.

150 Footnote re Joan's daughter: Amburn at 78–79, 94–95; T. Morgan at 93–94.

150 Burroughs' literary taste: Miles (4) at 36; McNally at 74; Schumacher at 40.

150 "'Tis too starved a subject": Miles (4) at 40–41; T. Morgan at 89.

150–51 "Jack and I decided": Miles (4) at 44 (quoting Allen Ginsberg).

151 "Women are a perfect curse": Burroughs (5) at 116.

151 "You're supposed to be a faggot": Amburn at 97; T. Morgan at 123.

151 Benzedrine: Amburn at 98–99, 104; Miles (4) at 48–50; T. Morgan at 115, 125, 131–32; Nicosia at 135–36, 153–54; Schumacher at 60–61, 65–66.

151 "I got way off the beam": Grauerholz, *The Death of Joan Vollmer*, at 6 (letter of Joan Vollmer to Edie Kerouac, 29 December 1946).

151 Bellevue Hospital: Amburn at 104; Miles (4) at 50–51; T. Morgan at 131–33; Schumacher at 66.

152 Footnote re William Burroughs III: Grauerholz, *The Death of Joan Vollmer*, at 6–7.

152 Appearance of Vollmer & Burroughs: T. Morgan at 178, 179.

152 Phony drug prescriptions: Amburn at 104; Grauerholz, *The Death of Joan Vollmer*, at 5; Miles (4) at 43–44, 48; T. Morgan at 125; Schumacher at 66.

152 Drunk driving and public indecency: Grauerholz, *The Death of Joan Vollmer*, at 10; Miles (4) at 53–54; T. Morgan at 170–71.

152 Footnote re intercourse in car and parenting style: Grauerholz, *The Death of Joan Vollmer*, at 10, 11.

152 Heroin possession: Grauerholz, *The Death of Joan Vollmer*, at 12–13; Miles (4) at 53–54; T. Morgan at 170–71.

152 MCC enrollment: Grauerholz, *The Death of Joan Vollmer*, at 16–17; Miles (4) at 54–55; T. Morgan at 168, 170–73.

152 "My case in New Orleans": Burroughs (1) at 56 (letter of William S. Burroughs to Jack Kerouac, 2 November 1949).

153 "I always say": Burroughs (1) at 63 (letter of William S. Burroughs to Jack Kerouac, 22 January 1950).

153 Vollmer's appearance in Mexico City: Miles (1) at 134; T. Morgan at 191, 193.

153 Burroughs slaps Joan: Grauerholz, *The Death of Joan Vollmer*, at 19; T. Morgan at 176.

153 Boy bars: Grauerholz, *The Death of Joan Vollmer*, at 17; Miles (4) at 55 (letter of William S. Burroughs to Allen Ginsberg, 18 March 1949); T. Morgan at 173–74.

153 Lewis Marker and Ecuador *yagé*: Grauerholz, *The Death of Joan Vollmer*, at 23–24, 26–27; Miles (4) at 56–57; T. Morgan at 188–91; Schumacher at 136.

153 Filing for divorce: Grauerholz, *The Death of Joan Vollmer*, at 21; T. Morgan at 177.

153 "How fast can this heap go?": Grauerholz, *The Death of Joan Vollmer*, at 27; Schumacher at 136–37.

153 "Go on! Go on!": Grauerholz, *The Death of Joan Vollmer*, at 27–28; Miles (1) at 135; T. Morgan at 192.

154 "I'm not going to make it": T. Morgan at 193.

154 Healy living-room scene: Grauerholz, *The Death of Joan Vollmer*, at 2, 30, 33, 39; T. Morgan at 194–96.

154 "we'll starve to death": Grauerholz, *The Death of Joan Vollmer*, at 34 (quoting June Woods Overgaard's account of Vollmer's statement)

154 "William Tell act": T—Morgan at 194.

154 "Put that glass": Grauerholz, *The Death of Joan Vollmer*, at 33.

154 Texas orchard shootings: R. Johnson at 155 (quoting Ted Marak's statements in Matt McClung, *Border Beats* (unreleased documentary film, 2002–2003)).

155 "I can't watch this": Grauerholz, *The Death of Joan Vollmer*, at 33.

155 Shooting scene: Grauerholz, *The Death of Joan Vollmer*, at 33–34, 39, 50; R. Johnson at 148, 154–55; T. Morgan at 194–96.

155 Post-shooting events: Grauerholz, *The Death of Joan Vollmer*, at 37–41; R. Johnson at 148–51; Schumacher at 137.

156 Footnote re *El Nacional*: Grauerholz, *The Death of Joan Vollmer*, at 40.

156 "The point is": Grauerholz, *The Death of Joan Vollmer*, at 41 (quoting *La Prensa* report of Jurado's statement).

157 "Quiso Demonstrar": Newspaper photograph in Grauerholz, *The Death of Joan Vollmer*, at 45.

157 September 8 hearing: Grauerholz, *The Death of Joan Vollmer*, at 46–48; T. Morgan at 201.

157 "The pistol slipped": Grauerholz, *The Death of Joan Vollmer*, at 46. Although the statements in the text derive from a prepared script that Burroughs recited to news reporters on September 7th, his testimony at the September 8th hearing essentially reiterated those claims, among others.

158 Footnote re 1965 interview and 1955 letter: Burroughs (8) at 76 (interview with Conrad Knickerbocker in *Paris Review*); Burroughs (1) at 263–64 (letter of William S. Burroughs to Allen Ginsberg, 7 February 1955).

158 "Black Palace of Lecumberri": Grauerholz, *The Death of Joan Vollmer*, at 45–46; T. Morgan at 202.

158 *Formal prisión*, bail, *amparo*, *imprudencia criminal*: Grauerholz, *The Death of Joan Vollmer*, at 48–52, 54–56; T. Morgan at 201; Schumacher at 137–38. In contrast to Grauerholz, on whom we have largely relied for the legal proceedings, the Morgan and Schumacher accounts report that Burroughs pled guilty to *imprudencia criminal* and was released on bail until his sentencing one year later.

158 Vollmer's burial: Grauerholz, *The Death of Joan Vollmer*, at 53; T. Morgan at 203.

159 Kerouac books, Ginsberg poems, and Burroughs introduction: Amburn at 168–69, Burroughs (10) at xxii.

159 Julie and Billy: Grauerholz, *The Death of Joan Vollmer*, at 53; Miles (4) at 57–58.

159 Burroughs and Jurado flee Mexico: Amburn at 181; Grauerholz, *The Death of Joan Vollmer*, at 56.

Chapter 22

Epigraph quote: Kerouac (1) at 346 (letter of Jack Kerouac to Allen Ginsberg, March or April 1952).

160 Thomas Hobbes: See generally Laurence Berns, "Thomas Hobbes," in Leo Strauss & Joseph Cropsey, *History of Political Philosophy* (Chicago: University of Chicago Press, 3ʳᵈ ed.), p. 399–402.

160 John Clellon Holmes' background: Richard Kirk Ardinger, "John Clellon Holmes," in Charters (5), vol. 1, at 249–50; Schumacher at 93.

160 *The Beat Generation*: Holmes (2) at xviii; Nicosia at 342.

160 Footnote re title of novel: Ann Charters, "Introduction," in Kerouac (11) at xviii; Holmes (2) at xxi; Nicosia at 342.

161 "almost literal truth": Holmes (2) at xvii.

161 Spanish Harlem party: Richard Kirk Ardinger, "John Clellon Holmes," in Charters (5), vol. 1, at 250; Holmes (2) at xii; Schumacher at 93.

161 "excitable, infectious, direct": Holmes (1) at 51.

161 "drugs, madness, visions": Holmes (2) at xx.

161 Kerouac's nights at Holmes's apartment: Amburn at 124; Nicosia at 224.

161 "should write immense novels": Kerouac (1) at 199–200 (letter of Jack Kerouac to John Clellon Holmes, 24 June 1949).

162 Footnote re Holmes-Kerouac contrast: John Clellon Holmes, "The Great Rememberer," in Maher (2) at 116 (quoting from Holmes, *Gone in October: Last Reflections on Jack Kerouac*).

162 "John was reserved": Seymour Krim, "Afterword," in Holmes (2) at 314.

162 "sweet and generous": McNally at 107 (quoting Ginsberg).

162 "exhaustive work-journals": Holmes (2) at xviii.

163 "tourist in the underworld": Holmes (2) at xiii (quoting James Atlas).

163 "goddamn fool": Holmes (2) at 303.

163 "more interested in self-preservation": Holmes (2) at xiii.

163 "suddenly knew" and "outraged, violated": Holmes (2) at 310.

163 "he held her closer": Holmes (2) at 311.

164 Scribner's publication: Richard Kirk Ardinger, "John Clellon Holmes," in Charters (5), vol. 1, at 251; Holmes (2) at xx.

164 "With considerable reluctance": Holmes (2) at xx–xxi.

164 Renaming of novel: Holmes (2) at xxi.

164 *Go* cover: See http://mysite.orange.co.uk/holmes-books/GO_Scribners _1952.jpg.

164 Reviews of *Go*: Frederic Morton, "Three A.M. Revels," *The New York Herald Tribune Books*, 12 October 1952, p. 33; "Be-Bop and Blues," *The Saturday Review*, 11 October 1952, p. 36–37; Gilbert Millstein, "The 'Kick' that Failed," *The New York Times Book Review*, 9 November 1952, p. 50.

165 Bantam paperback sale: Richard Kirk Ardinger, "John Clellon Holmes,"

in Charters (5), vol. 1, at 251; Holmes (2) at xxi.

165 Footnote re Ace Book edition: Holmes (2) at xxi.

165 "John Holmes' Novel is No good": Ginsberg & Cassady at 122 (letter of Allen Ginsberg to Neal Cassady and Jack Kerouac, 15 February 1952).

165 "John Holmes, who as everybody knows": Kerouac (1) at 378–79 (letter of Jack Kerouac to Allen Ginsberg, 8 October 1952).

165 *New York Times Magazine* article: Clellon Holmes, "This Is the Beat Generation," *New York Times Magazine*, 16 November 1952, p. 10.

166 "latecomer" and "pryer-intoer": Kerouac (1) at 345 (letter of Jack Kerouac to Allen Ginsberg, March or April 1952).

166 Footnote re "History of Bop": Nicosia at 429. In a July 27, 2007 email from Gerald Nicosia, he surmised that Kerouac had sent his essay to Millstein after reading the Holmes essay.

166 "It was Jack Kerouac": Clellon Holmes, "This Is the Beat Generation," *New York Times Magazine*, 16 November 1952, p. 10.

166 Millstein invitation: Nicosia at 423; Schumacher at 150.

166 Excerpts from *New York Times Magazine* article: Clellon Holmes, "This Is the Beat Generation," *New York Times Magazine*, 16 November 1952, p. 10, 19, 20, 22.

167 "Your *Beat Generation* article liked by everyone": Kerouac (1) at 388 (letter of Jack Kerouac to John Clellon Holmes, 9 December 1952).

167 "sleek beasts and middleclass subterraneans": Nicosia at 429 (quoting letter of Jack Kerouac to John Clellon Holmes, 9 December 1952).

168 Burroughs in male whorehouse: Tytell (1) at 46.

168 Cassady humping paramours: Gerald Nicosia, "Neal Cassady," in Charters (5), vol. 2, at 110.

168 Kerouac begging Carolyn Cassady: C. Cassady (1) at 196–204; Kerouac (1) at 386–87 (letter of Jack Kerouac to Neal and Carolyn Cassady, 9 December 1952).

Chapter 23

Epigraph quote: Bill Burroughs quoted in Gewirtz at 19.

169 Contract for *Junk*: Oliver Harris, "Introduction" in Burroughs (2) at xii–xiii, xxvii; Miles (4) at 61; T. Morgan at 205.

169 "You really are a sweetheart": Burroughs (1) at 111 (letter of William S. Burroughs to Allen Ginsberg, 5 April 1952).

169 Description of *Junk*: Oliver Harris, "Introduction," in Burroughs (2) at x; Miles (4) at 56; Schumacher at 134.

170 "real horror of junk": Burroughs (1) at 83 (letter of William S. Burroughs to Allen Ginsberg, 5 May 1951).

170 "When I wrote the original MS": Miles (4) at 56.

170 Portrait of Huncke and omission of Vollmer: Oliver Harris, "Introduction," in Burroughs (2) at xv.

170 "forced to the appalling conclusion": Burroughs (10) at xxii; Miles (4) at 58; T. Morgan at 199.

170–71 Publication issues: Oliver Harris, "Introduction" in Burroughs (2) at xii–xiii.

171 Footnote re *Junky*: Oliver Harris, "Introduction" in Burroughs (2) at xiii.

171 *Narcotics Agent*: Miles (1) at 149; T. Morgan at 206.

171 Pseudonym: Oliver Harris, "Introduction" in Burroughs (2) at xii; Miles (4) at 61.

171 A.A. Wyn's stalling and *Queer*: Oliver Harris, "Introduction" in Burroughs (2) at xxvii; Miles (4) at 61.

171 "Get form without deforming the language": Miles (1) at 125 (quoting William Carlos Williams).

171 Allen writing "actual talk rhythms": Raskin at 102–3.

171 Notebook-derived poems: Schumacher at 139–40.

171 "a bunch of short crappy scraps": Schumacher at 140 (quoting letter of Allen Ginsberg to Jack Kerouac and Neal Cassady, ca. February 1952).

172 "How many such poems do you own?": Schumacher at 140 (quoting letter of William Carlos Williams to Allen Ginsberg, 27 February 1952).

172 "Now you realize you old bonepoles": Schumacher at 140 (quoting letter of Allen Ginsberg to Jack Kerouac and Neal Cassady, ca. February 1952).

172 "Blow, baby, blow!": Schumacher at 140 (quoting letter of Jack Kerouac to Allen Ginsberg, 15 March 1952).

172 *Empty Mirror* submission and rejection: Schumacher at 148–49 (quoting letter of Random House editor Shirley Neitlich to Allen Ginsberg, 8 September 1952).

172 "This young Jewish boy": William Carlos Williams, "Introduction" to *Empty Mirror*, in Lewis Hyde, ed., *Under Discussion: On the Poetry of Allen Ginsberg* (Ann Arbor, MI: University of Michigan Press, 1984), at 17–18.

173 Literary journal rejections: Miles (1) at 145.

173 Publication of *Junkie*: Oliver Harris, "Introduction" in Burroughs (2) at xxvi.

173 *New York Times* ad for *Junkie*: *New York Times Book Review*, 18 April 1953, p. 22.

174　Footnote re Kerouac's refusal to promote: Kerouac (1) at 397 (letter of Jack Kerouac to Allen Ginsberg and Phyllis Jackson, 21 February 1953). See also Ginsberg (16) at 84–86 (letter of Allen Ginsberg to Jack Kerouac, 24 February 1953).

174　Phyllis Jackson: Amburn at 186–87; Nicosia at 419, 427–428.

174　Malcolm Cowley: Howard Cunnell, "Fast This Time: Jack Kerouac and the Writing of *On the Road*," in Kerouac (16) at 39.

175　$50,000 prediction: Nicosia at 427.

175　Experimental works & Buddhism: Amburn at 196–97, 199, 200; Charters (1) at 217–20; George Dardess, "Jack Kerouac" in Charters (5), vol. 1, at 295–96; Nicosia at 445–451, 456–459. In a May 1954 letter to Allen Ginsberg, Kerouac enthusiastically elaborated upon his discovery of Buddhism. See Kerouac (1) at 409–417 (letter of Jack Kerouac to Allen Ginsberg, early May 1954).

175　"How's your fellow": Amburn at 187.

175　"muttering": Theado (1) at 159 (quoting letter of Phyllis Jackson to Malcolm Cowley, 12 May 1953).

176　*Yagé Letters*: McNally at 175–76; Miles (1) at 151–52.

176　"schlupping": McNally at 176; Miles (1) at 152–53.

176　"junkie-organic-protoplasmic schlup": Kramer at 138 (quoting Allen Ginsberg).

176　Gregory Corso: McNally at 174; Miles (1) at 131–33; Nicosia at 358; Schumacher at 140–41.

177　Kerouac meets Sterling Lord: Sterling Lord, "The Kerouac Saga: Extended Version," *Publishers Weekly*, 23 August 2007, at http://www.publishersweekly.com/index.asp?layout=articlePrint&articleID=CA6471371. Although Lord recalls that he met Kerouac in 1951 and implies that he began working as his agent shortly thereafter, other sources establish that it was around May 1954, through the recommendation of Robert Giroux, that Jack first met Sterling and engaged him as an agent. See Amburn at 203; Charters (1) at 217; Clark at 134; Maher (3) at 281; McNally at 187. Given that Phyllis Jackson represented Jack in 1953 when he first met Malcolm Cowley, we consider the 1954 date to be the more reliable.

177　Sterling Lord and "Beat Generation": Amburn at 203; McNally at 187; "Jack Kerouac's Typescript Scroll of *On the Road*," Christie's New York, 22 May 2001, p. 26–27. Several sources named Stanley Colbert, Sterling Lord's partner, as Jack's agent. See Gifford & Lee at 189; Nicosia at 453.

An exchange of letters between Sterling Lord and the Alfred A. Knopf publishing house in 1954 confirms that Lord was clearly acting as an agent for Jack, at least in this regard. See Matt Theado, "Revisions of Kerouac: The Long, Strange Trip of the *On the Road* Typescripts" (unpublished article on file), at 26–27. It is, of course, entirely possible that Lord and Colbert were working together on placing *On the Road*.

177 "sent out again and again": Cook at 76 (quoting Sterling Lord).

178 Excerpts in literary quarterlies: Amburn at 188, 202; Ann Charters, "Introduction," in Kerouac (11) at xxvi–xxvii; Matt Theado, "Revisions of Kerouac: The Long, Strange Trip of the *On the Road* Typescripts" (unpublished article on file), at 27–28. Recently, Sterling Lord set forth his recollections: "After almost four years of trying to sell Jack's manuscript—now called *On the Road*—to a U.S. publisher, I sold a piece of his to the *Paris Review*. A few months later, I sold one piece and then another of the manuscript to *New World Writing*." Sterling Lord, "The Kerouac Saga: Extended Version," *Publishers Weekly*, 23 August 2007, at http://www.publishersweekly.com/index.asp?layout=articlePrint& articleID=CA6471371.

178 Jean-Louis pseudonym: Howard Cunnell, "Fast This Time: Jack Kerouac and the Writing of *On the Road*," in Kerouac (16) at 41–42; Maher (1) at 291.

178 Kerouac's visit with the Cassadys: Amburn at 197 (2)00; Maher (1) at 281–82; McNally at 181; Nicosia at 457–460.

178 Ginsberg's travels: Miles (1) at 153–63; Morgan (1) at 161–74; Schumacher at 158–74.

Chapter 24

Epigraph quote: Miles (1) at 169 (quoting Allen Ginsberg).

180 Joys of American middle-class life: Miles (1) at 168, 170.

180 "When I get married": Ginsberg (16) at 64 (letter of Allen Ginsberg to Neal Cassady, 18 November 1950).

181 "What a doll": Miles (1) at 167 (quoting letter of Allen Ginsberg to Jack Kerouac, 7 September 1954).

181 "finer than *any* girl": Schumacher at 183 (quoting letter of Allen Ginsberg to Jack Kerouac, 7 September 1954).

181 "living in splendor": Ginsberg (16) at 110 (letter of Allen Ginsberg to Jack Kerouac, 9 November 1954).

181 Romantic relationship with Sheila Williams: Miles (1) at 167–69. She

remarried in the summer of 1955, and became Sheila Williams Boucher. See Morgan (1) at 202.

181 "really fell in love": Miles (1) at 169 (quoting Allen Ginsberg)

181 Secret past: Schumacher at 183.

181 Footnote re Carolyn Cassady: Ginsberg (16) at 101 (letter of Allen Ginsberg to Jack Kerouac, 5 September 1954).

181 "ex-singer, big buddy of Brubeck": Miles (1) at 167 (quoting letter of Allen Ginsberg to Jack Kerouac, 7 September 1954).

181 "The queers of Remo": Kerouac (1) at 434 (letter of Jack Kerouac to Allen Ginsberg, 23 August 1954).

181 "I did not think": Burroughs (1) at 205–7 (letter of William S. Burroughs to Jack Kerouac, 22 April 1954).

181 "Now Allen is talking": Burroughs (1) at 233 (letter of William S. Burroughs to Jack Kerouac, 3 September 1954).

182 "frantic and possessive": Miles (1) at 169–70 (quoting letter of Allen Ginsberg to Jack Kerouac, September 1954).

182 "I think I'm responsible": Miles (1) at 171 (quoting Allen Ginsberg).

182 Kenneth Rexroth: Brown Miller & Ann Charters, "Kenneth Rexroth," in Charters (5), vol. 2, at 456–458; Miles (1) at 168–69; Schumacher at 184.

182 "Depression now": Ginsberg (13) at 61 (journal entry of 12 October 1954); see also Ginsberg (13) at 65 (journal entry of 9 November 1954).

183 "girlish psychological self-dramatization": Schumacher at 186 (quoting Allen Ginsberg).

183 Collapse of Ginsberg-Williams relationship: Miles (1) at 173–74; Morgan (1) at 183–85; Schumacher at 186–87.

183 Peter Orlovsky's appearance and background: Miles (1) at 179; Morgan (1) at 187–88; Schumacher at 188–89; Watson at 178.

183 Peter Orlovsky's portraits: "Head of the Poet Peter Orlovsky" in Ginsberg (7) at 6; "Nude with Onions" in Morgan (1) at 187.

184 Meeting Robert LaVigne: Miles (1) at 174; Morgan (1) at 187; Schumacher at 187.

184 Footnote re Robert LaVigne: Sheila Farr, "The Beats Go On in LaVigne's Portraits," *Seattle Times*, 8 March 2002, sec. H, p. 40.

184 Natalie Jackson: C. Cassady (1) at 253; Miles (1) at 174; Morgan (1) at 192; Sandison & Vickers at 232; Schumacher at 190.

185 Footnote re photograph of Natalie Jackson & Neal Cassady: Pivano at 77. A second photograph of the two lovers is reproduced in Pivano at 82.

185 "needed a sweet companion": Miles (1) at 174 (quoting Robert LaVigne).

185 "Ooh, don't mock me": Morgan (1) at 189 (quoting Allen Gisnberg).

185 "What are you asking *me* for?" and "Oh God, not again!": Miles (1) at 174 (quoting Allen Ginsberg).

185 First night with Peter: Miles (1) at 175; Schumacher at 190. Bill Morgan presents one of Allen's accounts of this night, in which he "screwed Peter in the ass, after which Peter began to cry." Noting conflicts with other accounts, Morgan carefully concludes that "it is impossible" from Ginsberg's journals or recollections "to clearly date when he first consummated his love for Peter." Morgan (1) at 189–90.

186 Final visit to Naomi: Schumacher at 190.

186 Complexity of love lives increased: Ginsberg (13) at 73 (journal entry of 1 January 1955); Morgan (1) at 193–95; Morgan (3) at 142–43; Schumacher at 192.

186 "I sit up looking": Ginsberg (13) at 74–75 (journal entry of 2 January 1955).

187 Doctor Philip Hicks: Miles (1) at 177; Morgan (1) at 185, 196; Schumacher at 186, 192–93.

187 Foster's Cafeteria: Morgan (3) at 119; Watson at 179.

188 Exchange of Vows: Allen and Peter's promises were crafted from descriptions of the vows in Miles (1) at 177–78 (quoting Allen Ginsberg); Morgan (1) at 196–97; Schumacher at 193–94 (quoting Allen Ginsberg).

188 Footnote re Towne-Oller: Miles (1) at 182.

188 "Peter, I feel as if I'm in heaven": Miles (1) at 178 (quoting Allen Ginsberg). In mid-August of 1955, Allen wrote to Jack Kerouac: "I enclose first draft scribble notes of a poem I was writing, nearer in your style than anything." Ginsberg (16) at 117.

PART III: The Poem & Prosecution
Epigraph quote: Raskin at xi.

Chapter 25
Epigraph quote: Allen Ginsberg, "Notes Written on Finally Recording *Howl*," in Ginsberg (4) at 229.

191 "I am no closer": Schumacher at 200 (quoting Allen Ginsberg's journal entry of 10 June 1955).

191 "Money problems of reality": Schumacher at 199 (quoting Allen Ginsberg).

191 Spousal problems: Miles (1) at 180; Schumacher at 199.

191 Footnote re Ms. Philips: Morgan (1) at 201.

191 Girlfriend problems: Miles (1) at 181–82 (quoting Sheila Williams).

192 Vollmer dream: Ginsberg (13) at 136; Watson at 180. See also Ginsberg's poem titled "Dream Record: June 8, 1955" in Allen Ginsberg (15) at 125.

192 Writer's block: Schumacher at 197, 705 note 197.

192 "Rules for Spontaneous Writing": Morgan (3) at 25. When published, the "Rules" were given the formal title of "Essentials of Spontaneous Prose" in Charters (3) at 484–85.

192 "trouble deaf heaven": Schumacher at 199 (letter of Allen Ginsberg to Jack Kerouac, 5 June 1955).

192 Appearance of 1010 Montgomery Street room: Ginsberg (13) at 147 (photograph of 1010 Montgomery Street bedroom/study taken in August of 1955); Miles (1) at 180; Morgan (3) at 25.

192 Peter in New York: Morgan (1) at 202–3.

192 "I saw the best minds": Ginsberg (1) at 13.

193 Footnote re journal entry: Ginsberg (13) at 159.

193 "*come* from within, out": "Essentials of Spontaneous Prose" in Charters (3) at 485.

193–95 Strophes from first typewritten draft: Ginsberg (1) at 12, 14, 16, 20.

195 Typing into darkness: Raskin at 163.

195 "bardic breath": Allen Ginsberg, "Notes Written on Finally Recording *Howl*," in Ginsberg (4) at 229.

196 Seven pages: Ginsberg (1) at 12–25.

196 Footnote re Kerouac and Burroughs: Miles (1) at 186; Schumacher at 202.

196 "gesture of wild solidarity": Allen Ginsberg, "Reintroduction to Carl Solomon," in Ginsberg (1) at 111.

196 "Carl Solomon!": Ginsberg (1) at 89; Miles (1) at 187; Schumacher at 202–3.

197 "Your HOWL FOR CARL SOLOMON": Kerouac (1) at 508 (letter of Jack Kerouac to Allen Ginsberg, 19 August 1955).

197 "I realize how right you are": Morgan & Peters at 33 (letter of Allen Ginsberg to Jack Kerouac, 25 August 1955). See also Miles (1) at 188; Schumacher at 203–4.

197 "MEXICO CITY BLUES": Kerouac (1) at 510 (letter of Jack Kerouac to Sterling Lord, 19 August 1955).

197 "saw him as another": Lawrence Ferlinghetti, "Introduction: 'Howl' at the Frontiers," in Morgan & Peters at xii.

197–98 Ferlinghetti & Ginsberg relationship: Cherkovski at 97; Schumacher at 204, 224; Silesky at 62.

198 "the most significant single long poem": "Between the Lines," *San Francisco Chronicle*, 19 May 1957, in Morgan & Peters at 107 (publishing statement of Lawrence Ferlinghetti in defense of *Howl*).

198 "City Lights Bookstore here": Miles (1) at 190 (quoting Allen Ginsberg).

198 Lafcadio Orlovsky: Morgan (1) at 204; Schumacher at 204–5.

198 1624 Milvia Street: Ginsberg (13) at 160 (journal entry of 1 September 1955); Raskin at 141; Schumacher at 205.

198 "35 per mo.": Ginsberg (16) at 119–20, Morgan & Peters at 31 (letter of Allen Ginsberg to Eugene Brooks, 16 August 1955). See also Ginsberg (16) at 123 (letter of Allen Ginsberg to John Allen Ryan, mid-September 1955).

Chapter 26

199 Kerouac & crucifixion: Douglas Brinkley, "In the Kerouac Archive," *Atlantic Monthly*, November 1998, at 52.

199 Columbia college days: Maher (3) at 78.

199 Kerouac on Bach: See Jack Kerouac, "On the Origins of a Generation," in Kerouac (19) at 56.

199 Listening to *St. Matthew Passion*: Miles (1) at 191; Schumacher at 213.

199 Kerouac images: Amburn at 220–21; McNally at 201–2; Nicosia at 490–491; C. Cassady (1) at 262–67 ("We never really slept, so afraid were we to miss a minute of being together; we only dozed now and then, clinging to each other's warmth and our hopeless dreams. A little before dawn [Jack] too his sleeping bag and went outside so the children wouldn't find him in my bed."). Amburn's and Nicosia's accounts do not mention any visit to Neal and Carolyn Cassady in advance of arriving in San Francisco.

200 Michael McClure conversation re 6 Gallery: Amburn at 224; Miles (1) at 190–91; Schumacher at 211–12; Silesky at 63.

200 Kerouac declines to read: Miles (1) at 192; Morgan (1) at 297; Schumacher at 213.

200 Gary Snyder: Miles (1) at 190–91; Raskin at 1–2; Schumacher at 212–13; Silesky at 63–64.

200 Philip Whalen: Miles (1) at 191–92; Schumacher at 214; Silesky at 64.

200 Kerouac's description of Snyder: Kerouac (6) at 7. For consistent characterizations, see also Amburn at 223; Allen Ginsberg, "The Six Gallery Reading," in Ginsberg (4) at 241.

200 Kerouac's description of Whalen: Kerouac (6) at 7. For consistent characterizations, see also Amburn at 223–24; Allen Ginsberg, "The Six

Gallery Reading," in Ginsberg (4) at 240.

201 Kerouac's description of Rexroth: Kerouac (6) at 7, 11. For consistent characterization, see Nicosia at 492.

201 *Pure Land Sutra* scenario: Nicosia at 491.

201 Philip Lamantia: Nicosia at 366. See also Miles (1) at 192; Raskin at 2; Silesky at 52, 64.

201 Kerouac's description of Lamantia: Kerouac (6) at 7.

201 Postcard: Liner Notes to CD Collection, *Howls, Raps & Roars: Recordings from the San Francisco Poetry Renaissance* (Berkeley, CA: Fantasy Studios, 1993), at 13; Theado at 63.

202 Epigraph quote: Mikal Gilmore, "Allen Ginsberg: 1926–1997," in George-Warren at 235.

202–8 Six Gallery event: Our narrative sketches derive from Amburn at 225–28; Frank Bidart, "A Cross in the Void," in Shinder at 246–54; Cherkovski at 99; Charters (1) at 240–41; Laszlo Géfin, "Ellipsis: The Ideograms of Ginsberg," in Hyde at 272–87; Allen Ginsberg, "Reading at the Six Gallery, October 7, 1955," in Ginsberg (1) at 165–66; Kerouac (1) at 524 (letter of Jack Kerouac to John Clellon Holmes, 12 October 1955); Kerouac (6) at 9–11; Michael McClure, *Scratching the Beat Surface*, reprinted in Ginsberg (1) at 168; McNally at 203–4; Miles (1) at 192–94; Morgan (1) at 208–9; Morgan (3) at 109–10; Nicosia at 492–493; "Peter Orlovsky & Allen Ginsberg Interview, 1975," reprinted in Ginsberg (1) at 167; Raskin at 17–18; Michael Rumaker, "Allen Ginsberg's 'Howl'," in Hyde at 36–40; Sandison & Vickers at 241–42; Schumacher at 214–17; Silesky at 64–65; Theado at 61–64. See generally Hyde at 1–84, 221–370, 401–454; Shinder at 19–58, 143–214, 260–72.

202 Footnote re 6 Gallery: Miles (1) at 192; Morgan (3) at 109–10; Schumacher at 214; Silesky at 60–61.

204 Footnote re performance of Part I: Barry Miles, "A Note on the Manuscript," in Ginsberg (1) at xiii.

208 Sam Wo's: Miles (1) at 194; Schumacher at 216; Silesky at 65.

208 "We had gone beyond a point of no return": Michael McClure, *Scratching the Beat Surface*, reprinted in Ginsberg (1) at 168.

208 Ferlinghetti telegram: Cherkovski at 99; Lawrence Ferlinghetti, "Introduction: 'Howl' at the Frontiers," in Morgan & Peters at xii; Miles (1) at 194; Raskin at 19–20; Schumacher at 216; Silesky at 54, 65–66.

208–9 Footnote re Ferlinghetti telegram: Morgan (1) at 209; Letter of Allen Ginsberg to Fernanda Pivano, 30 July 1964 (Treviso, Italy: Fernanda and

Riccardo Pivano Library); email of Bill Morgan to authors, 31 July 2007 (establishing 30 July 1964 letter as basis for statement in his text); email of Michael Schumacher to authors, 26 July 2007 (re interviews with Allen Ginsberg and Lawrence Ferlinghetti); Justin Kaplan, "Introduction" in Walt Whitman, *Leaves of Grass* (New York: Bantam Dell, 2004) at xxi (letter of Ralph Waldo Emerson to Walt Whitman, 21 July 1855).

Chapter 27

210 Moloch: See generally Day; *Leviticus* 18:21 in Bruce M. Metzger & Ronald E. Murphy, eds., *The New Oxford Annotated Bible* (New York: Oxford University Press, 1991).

210 Moloch viewings: Allen Ginsberg, "Notes Written on Finally Recording *Howl*," in Ginsberg (4) at 230; Ginsberg (13) at 61, 63 (journal entry of 18 October 1954); Morgan & Peters at 31; Schumacher at 205–6.

211 "We wandered on Peyote all downtown": Morgan & Peters at 34 (quoting letter of Allen Ginsberg to Jack Kerouac, 25 August 1955).

211 Writing of part II: Miles (1) at 189–90, 194–95; Schumacher at 206–7, 217; Raskin at 138–39, 141–42, 168–72.

211 "No 'spontaneous' poem was more thoroughly rewritten": Raskin at 168.

211 seventeen subsequent typewritten drafts: Ginsberg (1) at 56–87.

211–12 part II excerpts: Ginsberg (1) at 6–7.

212 "Moloch who reaches up at night": Ginsberg (1) at 56 (quoting Gary Snyder).

212 Writing of part III: Allen Ginsberg, "Notes Written on Finally Recording *Howl*," in Ginsberg (4) at 230; Miles (1) at 195–96; Raskin at 139–40.

213 Footnote re Solomon: Ginsberg (3) at 489 ("sympathetic attentiveness"); Raskin at 156–57 (derived from Ellen Pearlman, "Biography, Mythology and Interpretation," *Vajradhatu Sun*, April—May 1990, p. 17, quoting Allen Ginsberg). See also Morgan (1) at 318 (noting Solomon's anger with Ginsberg re use of his name).

213–14 part III excerpts: Ginsberg (1) at 7–8.

214 "a little rose-covered cottage": Kerouac (6) at 11–12.

214 Writing of part IV (later called "Footnote to Howl"): Allen Ginsberg, "Notes Written on Finally Recording *Howl*," in Ginsberg (4) at 230–31; Miles (1) at 196; Schumacher at 217–18; *Isaiah* 6:7 in Bruce M. Metzger & Ronald E. Murphy, eds., *The New Oxford Annotated Bible* (New York: Oxford University Press, 1991).

214–15 Excerpts of part IV ("Footnote to Howl"): Ginsberg (1) at 8.

215 "Look what I have done with the long line": letter from Ginsberg to Williams, 9 December 1955, Ginsberg (1) at 150.

215 "a weak spot toward the end": letter from Williams to Ginsberg, 17 March 1956, Ginsberg (1) at 151.

216 "It's a hot geyser of emotion": letter from Louis Ginsberg to Allen Ginsberg, 29 February 1956, Ginsberg (1) at 150.

Chapter 28

Epigraph quote: C. Cassady (1) at 271 (variation on Biblical maxim).

217 Edgar Cayce: C. Cassady (1) at 231–33, 237–38, 257. See also Amburn at 197–98; Miles (1) at 164; Schumacher at 174–75. See generally "Who Was Edgar Cayce?" at www.edgarcayce.org/ edgar-cayce2.html and the Edgar Cayce's Association for Research and Enlightenment at http:// www.edgarcayce.org/.

217 "Cayce had said": C. Cassady (1) at 257.

218 "it could be that I": C. Cassady (1) at 233.

218 Love notes: C. Cassady (1) at 258–60; Cassady (1) at 391–92.

218 Divorce and separation: C. Cassady (1) at 259–61.

219 Elsie Sechrist: C. Cassady (1) at 259.

219 Scoville's phone call: C. Cassady (1) at 270; Sandison & Vickers at 242; Schumacher at 226.

219 "It took every ounce of grit" & Christian maxims: C. Cassady (1) at 271.

220 Carolyn's bedside note: C. Cassady (1) at 270–71; Cassady (1) at 393–94.

220 "Scientific" gambling system and losses: C. Cassady (1) at 269, 271; Sandison & Vickers at 242.

221 December 1, 1955, news article: C. Cassady (1) at 273.

221–22 Death of Natalie Jackson: C. Cassady (1) at 273–74. See also Kerouac (6) at 82–85; Miles (1) at 198; Sandison & Vickers at 243; Schumacher at 226.

223 Ginsberg poem to Natalie Jackson: Miles (1) at 198.

Chapter 29

224 City Lights Books: Cherkovski at 80–82; Miles (1) at 180–81; Morgan (3) at 1 ("head, heart, and undersoul"), 2–4, 6–7; Schumacher at 221; Silesky at 56–57.

224 Lawrence Ferlinghetti: Cherkovski at 45–46, 49–60, 67, 77–79, 82; Miles (1) at 181 ("left-leaning, libertarian, anarchistic political philosophy"); Julia Older, "Poetry's Eternal Graffiti: Late-Night Conversations with Lawrence

Ferlinghetti," *Poets & Writers*, March–April, 2007, p. 38, 40; Schumacher at 221, 223; Silesky at 1–2, 25–29, 34–35, 42–45, 47, 57–58, 66, 92.

225 "It seemed like the logical thing to do": Silesky at 57.

225 "I was the last of the Bohemian generation": Julia Older, "Poetry's Eternal Graffiti: Late-Night Conversations with Lawrence Ferlinghetti," *Poets & Writers*, March–April, 2007, p. 40. See also Silesky at 82–83.

226 "would be busted": Lawrence Ferlinghetti, "Introduction: 'Howl' at the Frontiers," in Morgan & Peters at xiii.

226 "We were just a little" & ACLU: Lawrence Ferlinghetti interview with authors, San Francisco: City Lights Bookstore, 27 July 2001; Schumacher at 252.

226 "Civil Liberties Union here": Ginsberg (1) at 151 (quoting letter of Allen Ginsberg to Louis Ginsberg, March 1956); Schumacher at 288.

226 Revisions & selections of poems: Miles (1) at 201; Silesky at 66–67.

226 "call it simply *Howl*": Lawrence Ferlinghetti, "Introduction: 'Howl' at the Frontiers," in Morgan & Peters at xii.

227 Footnote re Ferlinghetti statement on omission of one-page section: Andrew P. Madden, "Interview with Lawrence Ferlinghetti, 1998," in Plimpton at 44 (interview originally published in *The Paris Review*).

227 "Footnote to Howl": Cherkovski at 99–100; Silesky at 66.

227 Williams's introduction: William Carlos Williams, "Introduction," in Ginsberg (8) at 7–8. See also Cherkovski at 100; Miles (1) at 201–2; Silesky at 67.

227 "Song of Myself": Whitman at 43.

227–28 Dedication: Ginsberg (8) at 3. See also Miles (1) at 204, 207; Schumacher at 238–39.

228 Footnote re Lucien Carr: Ginsberg (1) at 159 (letter of Lucien Carr to Allen Ginsberg, 21 September 1956); Morgan & Peters at 52–53 (letter of Allen Ginsberg to Lawrence Ferlinghetti, 15 January 1957).

228 Ditto copies: Felver (4) at 5; Miles (1) at 201; Schumacher at 238; Silesky at 69.

228 "beautiful gentleness": Schumacher at 238 (quoting letter of John Clellon Holmes to Allen Ginsberg, 26 September 1956).

228 "Thought your *Howl*": Ginsberg (1) at 150 (letter of Lucien Carr to Allen Ginsberg, 13 February 1956).

228 Berkeley reading: Amburn at 226; Miles (1) at 199–200; Schumacher at 228; Silesky at 68. A recent discovery of a reel-to-reel tape recording of Allen Ginsberg reciting *Howl* establishes that the first recorded performance

of the first part of the poem occurred on Valentine's Day in 1956 in a student hostel at Reed College in Portland, Oregon, three months before the Berkeley reading. Nevertheless, the March 1956 recording made in Berkeley is the earliest known recording of the entire poem. John Suiter, "When the Beats Came Back," *Reed Magazine*, Winter 2008, p. 20–25; Peter Edidin, "The Sound of 'Howl,'" *New York Times*, 16 February 2008, sec. B, p. 10.

229 "You have no idea": Morgan & Peters at 38 (letter of Allen Ginsberg to Louis Ginsberg, late March 1956).

229 Eberhart letter: Ginsberg (16) at 130–39, Charters (2) at 208–21 (letter of Allen Ginsberg to Richard Eberhart, 18 May 1956).

229 "I'm afraid I have to tell you": Ginsberg (1) at 156 (letter of Lionel Trilling to Allen Ginsberg, 29 May 1956).

230 Telegram re Naomi's death: Miles (1) at 202–3; Schumacher at 232. Compare Morgan (1) at 216 (telegram from Louis Ginsberg received when Allen on *Pendleton*).

230 Plans to move Naomi: Miles (1) at 202; Schumacher at 232.

230 "Everything changes toward death": Miles (1) at 203–4.

230 Footnote re letter from Naomi: Ginsberg (1) at 156 (letter of Naomi Ginsberg to Allen Ginsberg, 11 June 1956).

231 Villiers: Cherkovski at 100–101; Lawrence Ferlinghetti interview with authors, San Francisco: City Lights Bookstore, 27 July 2001; Lawrence Ferlinghetti, "Introduction: 'Howl' at the Frontiers," in Morgan & Peters at xii–xiii; Schumacher at 252; Silesky at 68–69.

231 galley corrections: Miles (1) at 204, 206; Schumacher at 233–34, 237–38.

231 "This being my first book": Morgan & Peters at 43–44 (letter of Allen Ginsberg to Lawrence Ferlinghetti, 3 July 1956).

231–32 "Everything worked out fine": Ginsberg (1) at 158 (letter of Allen Ginsberg to Lawrence Ferlinghetti, 9 August 1956).

232 complimentary copies: Schumacher at 238; Silesky at 69.

232 Ezra Pound: Miles (1) at 202; Schumacher at 239.

232 "If he's yours why don't yu": Ginsberg (1) at 157 (letter of Ezra Pound to William Carlos Williams, June 1956).

232 Richard Eberhart's piece: Richard Eberhart, "West Coast Rhythms," *New York Times Book Review*, 2 September 1956, p. 4.

233 *Life* and *Mademoiselle*: Schumacher at 240.

233 "Beginning to get long admiring letters": Ginsberg (1) at 159 (letter of Allen Ginsberg to Jack Kerouac, Fall 1956).

Chapter 30

Epigraph quote: Kerouac (1) at 561–62 (letter of Jack Kerouac to Sterling Lord, 24 February 1956).

234 "was not a work of fiction": Amburn at 221 (quoting Malcolm Cowley).

234 "theory of writing": Kerouac (1) at 516 (letter of Jack Kerouac to Malcolm Cowley, 11 September 1955).

235 "I saw the little midget": Kerouac (16) at 160.

235 "Justin W. Brierly": Kerouac (16) at 140–41.

235 "Allen was queer": Kerouac (16) at 113.

235 Keith Jennison: Ann Charters, "Introduction," in Kerouac (11) at xxvi–xxvii; Milton Crane, "A Young Man at Point," *Chicago Daily Tribune*, 8 August 1954, sec. G, p. 4 ("a young man at the crossroads," reviewing *The Green Place*); Joseph Henry Jackson, "Bookman's Notebook," *Los Angeles Times*, 19 July 1954, sec. A, p. 5 (review of *The Green Place* referring to *Half-Open Road*); Matt Theado, "Revisions of Kerouac: The Long, Strange Trip of the *On the Road* Typescripts," at 27–28 (unpublished article on file with authors).

236 Rocky Mount, NC: Amburn at 214; Kerouac (1) at 493 (letter of Jack Kerouac to Malcolm Cowley, 4 July 1955).

236 Footnote re Sterling Lord & other manuscripts: Maher (3) at 300.

236 Evelyn Levine memorandum: Maher (3) at 309; Nicosia at 476.

237 "Any changes you want to make okay with me" & title: Kerouac (1) at 518–19 (letter of Jack Kerouac to Malcolm Cowley, 20 September 1955).

237 Publishing problems—financial, geographical, legal: Amburn at 243, 247; Howard Cunnell, "Fast This Time: Jack Kerouac and the Writing of *On the Road*," in Kerouac (16) at 28–31, 44–45; Gifford & Lee at 206; Maher (3) at 300–303; Matt Theado, "Revisions of Kerouac: The Long, Strange Trip of the *On the Road* Typescripts," at 32 (unpublished article on file with authors).

237 "constantly falling between the cracks at Viking": Amburn at 247.

237 Structural changes & libel releases: Gifford & Lee at 206; Matt Theado, "Revisions of Kerouac: The Long, Strange Trip of the *On the Road* Typescripts," at 32 (unpublished article on file with authors).

238 "for the benefit of American literature": Howard Cunnell, "Fast This Time: Jack Kerouac and the Writing of *On the Road*," in Kerouac (16) at 45.

238 "pure shining original": Amburn at 259–60 (quoting Jack Kerouac); Arthur & Kit Knight, *The Beat Journey* (California, PA: Tuvoti, 1978), p. 50 (letter of Jack Kerouac to John Clellon Holmes, 23 June 1957).

238 "Well, Jack did something": Gifford & Lee at 206 (quoting Malcolm Cowley).

238 Extraneous adventures: Howard Cunnell, "Fast This Time: Jack Kerouac and the Writing of *On the Road*," in Kerouac (16) at 28.

238 "more of a continuous narrative": Amburn at 259 (quoting Malcolm Cowley).

238 February 24, 1956 letter: Kerouac (1) at 561 (letter of Jack Kerouac to Sterling Lord).

238 May 9, 1956 letter: Kerouac (1) at 575 (letter of Jack Kerouac to Malcolm Cowley).

238 September 17, 1956 letter: Kerouac (1) at 587 (letter of Jack Kerouac to Sterling Lord).

238–39 October 7, 1956 letter: Kerouac (1) at 588–589 (letter of Jack Kerouac to Sterling Lord).

239 December 26, 1956 letter: Kerouac (1) at 592 (letter of Jack Kerouac to John Clellon Holmes).

239 Trip to New York & arrival at Viking: Howard Cunnell, "Fast This Time: Jack Kerouac and the Writing of *On the Road*," in Kerouac (16) at 46–47; Matt Theado, "Revisions of Kerouac: The Long, Strange Trip of the *On the Road* Typescripts," at 34 (unpublished article on file with authors).

239 Chugging "prodigious amounts": Kerouac (5) at 6.

240 Viking's copy department & lawyer approval: Amburn at 259–60; Howard Cunnell, "Fast This Time: Jack Kerouac and the Writing of *On the Road*," in Kerouac (16) at 30–31; Matt Theado, "Revisions of Kerouac: The Long, Strange Trip of the *On the Road* Typescripts," at 29 (unpublished article on file with authors). Having compared the first pages of the Viking bound book with the original scroll version, Kerouac scholar Dave Moore surmised that "the published version of Kerouac's *On the Road* closely follows the original scroll typescript." Whatever the differences in style and punctuation between the two, Moore concluded: "The book as we have it today preserves the freshness and vitality of Kerouac's original high-speed outpouring of 35 years ago." Dave Moore, "On the Road—The Scroll Revealed," *The Kerouac Connection*, April 1986, p. 5.

240 Cowley & Jennison acceptance report: Theado (1) at 169–70 (reproduction of the manuscript acceptance report). See also Amburn at 260; Howard Cunnell, "Fast This Time: Jack Kerouac and the Writing of *On the Road*," in Kerouac (16) at 46.

241 "Sterl, I'm real worried": Kerouac (5) at 53–54 (letter of Jack Kerouac to Sterling Lord, 26 June 1957).

241 A dozen more books: Leland at 17; see also Maher (3) at 491.

242 "I wouldn't be surprised if Viking Press got chickenshit": Kerouac (5) at 52 (letter of Jack Kerouac to Gary Snyder, 24 June 1957).

Chapter 31

243 "[H]ow absurd of that man": Morgan & Peters at 59 (letter of Gregory Corso to Allen Ginsberg, 6 May 1957).

243 "Morning Report": Abe Melinkoff, "Morning Report: Iron Curtain on The Embarcadero," *San Francisco Chronicle*, 28 March 1957.

244 Villiers & *Miscellaneous Man*: Lawrence Ferlinghetti, "Horn on 'HOWL'," *Evergreen Review*, vol. 2 (1957), p. 145.

244 "I think MacPhee": Lawrence Ferlinghetti Interview with Authors, San Francisco: City Lights Bookstore, 27 July 2001.

245 ACLU: Lawrence Ferlinghetti, "Horn on 'HOWL'," *Evergreen Review*, vol. 2 (1957), at 146; Miles (1) at 224–25; Schumacher (1) at 252.

245 Photo-offset copies: Lawrence Ferlinghetti, "Horn on 'HOWL'," *Evergreen Review*, vol. 2 (1957), p. 146; Miles (1) at 224–25; Morgan & Peters at 58–59 (letter of Allen Ginsberg to Don Allen, 18 April 1957); Schumacher (1) at 252.

245 "I guess this puts you up shits creek": Ginsberg (16) at 149–50, Morgan & Peters at 56–58 (letter of Allen Ginsberg to Lawrence Ferlinghetti, 3 April 1957).

245–46 Ferlinghetti's statement in William Hogan's column: William Hogan, "Between the Lines," *San Francisco Chronicle*, 19 May 1957, p. 34.

246 U.S. Attorney & Customs release: Cherkovski at 102; Lawrence Ferlinghetti, "Horn on 'HOWL'," *Evergreen Review*, vol. 2 (1957), p. 147; Miles (1) at 224–25.

246 "Sting" operation: Cherkovski at 102; Morgan & Peters at 61; Schumacher at 254; Silesky at 70.

246 "looked like a Japanese sage": Morgan (3) at 50.

247 June 3 arrest & charges: Cherkovski at 103; Miles (1) at 224; Schumacher at 254; Silesky at 70–71.

247 "it is all in the line of duty, ma'am" & "terribly nice": Silesky at 70 (quoting Kirby Ferlinghetti's recollections of officers).

247 "Shigeyoshi Murao, a Japanese-American": Shigeyoshi Murao, "Footnotes to My Arrest for Selling *Howl*," in Ginsberg (1) at 170.

247 Fingerprinting, mug shots: Shigeyoshi Murao, "Footnotes to My Arrest for Selling *Howl*," in Ginsberg (1) at 170; Miles (1) at 224; Schumacher at 254.

247 "piss-stained mattress" & "cocksuckers": Shigeyoshi Murao, "Footnotes to My Arrest for Selling *Howl*," in Ginsberg (1) at 170.

248 "elbows of rock": Kerouac (14) at 14–15.

248 ACLU bail: Shigeyoshi Murao, "Footnotes to My Arrest for Selling *Howl*," in Ginsberg (1) at 171; Miles (1) at 224; Schumacher at 254.

248 Ferlinghetti turns himself in: "Bookshop Owner Surrenders," *San Francisco Chronicle*, 7 June 1957, p. 2.

248 "picturesque return": Lawrence Ferlinghetti, "Horn on 'HOWL,'" *Evergreen Review*, vol. 2 (1957), p. 147.

248 Ferlinghetti receives word of bust while in Big Sur: Ginsberg (16) at 154–58, Morgan & Peters at 62 (letter of Allen Ginsberg to Lawrence Ferlinghetti, 10 June 1957). We base this assertion on the following line in Ginsberg's letter: "Received your June 4 letter today, with clipping."

248 "local dumb Irish cops": Kerouac (5) at 46 (letter of Jack Kerouac to Allen Ginsberg, 7 June 1957).

248 "I guess this is more serious": Morgan & Peters at 62, 63–64 (letter of Allen Ginsberg to Lawrence Ferlinghetti, 10 June 1957).

248–49 *Chronicle* pieces: "Making a Clown of San Francisco," *San Francisco Chronicle*, 6 June 1957, reprinted in Morgan & Peters at 111–12; William Hogan, "Bookman's Notebook: Orwell's 'Big Brother' Is Watching over Us," *San Francisco Chronicle*, 6 June 1957, reprinted in Morgan & Peters at 113–14; "Hanrahan's Law," *San Francisco Chronicle* 1957, reprinted in Morgan & Peters at 110.

249 "We have purchased" & "They are not fit for children": "Making a Clown of San Francisco," *San Francisco Chronicle*, 6 June 1957, reprinted in Morgan & Peters at 111 (quoting Captain William Hanrahan).

249 "Here is a new and startling doctrine": "Making a Clown of San Francisco," *San Francisco Chronicle*, 6 June 1957, reprinted in Morgan & Peters at 111.

249 "How many children will read HOWL?": Morgan & Peters at 59 (letter of Gregory Corso to Allen Ginsberg, 6 May 1957). Although Corso opined on censorship efforts of Customs Collector MacPhee, his commentary was equally applicable to those of Captain Hanrahan.

249 "I think that you are perhaps the only great publisher": Morgan & Peters at 66 (letter of Gregory Corso to Lawrence Ferlinghetti, late July 1957).

PART IV: The Trial & Tribulation
Epigraph quotes: Allen Ginsberg, letter to Louis Ginsberg, 26 July 1957, reproduced in Morgan & Peters at 66; Fuller, "Trade Winds," 5 October 1957, reproduced in Morgan & Peters at 117–18.

Chapter 32

253 Footnote re *On the Road* references: see Leland at 89.

253 Ferlinghetti's reactions to his arrest: Ginsberg (1) at 71 (letter of Allen Ginsberg to Lawrence Ferlinghetti, 23 September 1957), 78 (letter of Allen Ginsberg to Lawrence Ferlinghetti, 10 October 1957), 107 (quoting Ferlinghetti's *San Francisco Chronicle* article of 19 May 1957); Morgan & Peters at xiii.

254 Murao's reactions to his arrest: Ginsberg (1) at 170; Morgan & Peters at xiii.

254 Hanrahan's declaration: David Perlman, "How Captain Hanrahan Made 'Howl' a Best-Seller," *The Reporter*, 12 December 1957, p. 37.

255 "America": Ginsberg (8) at 39.

Chapter 33

257 Legal cases: *Speiser v. Randall, 48 Cal. 2d 903, 311 P.2d 546 (Cal. 1958)*; *Speiser v. Randall*, 357 U.S. 513 (1958); *Roth v. United States*, 354 U.S. 476 (1957); *Alberts v. California*, 354 U.S. 476 (1957).

258 Footnote on Emerson: Emerson at 195.

Chapter 34

259 Supreme Court setting for *Roth-Alberts*: Eisler at 142.

260 Oral exchanges with Justices Frankfurter and Brennan: Friedman at 15, 54.

262 Opinion excerpts: *Roth v. United States*, 354 U.S. 476, 484–485, 487–489 (1957)

Chapter 35

264 Original schedule for trial: Morgan & Peters at 3.

264 *Ten Commandments* sentence: "Court Rules on Biblical Essays (1) Wins, 1 Loses," *San Francisco Chronicle*, 7 August 7 1957, p. 1.

265 Press reactions to *Ten Commandments* sentence: Editorial, "Creative Writing in Horn's Court," *San Francisco Chronicle*, 8 August 1957, at 20.

Chapter 36

266 Albert Bendich: Al Bendich Interview; Morgan & Peters at 213–20.

267 Jake Ehrlich: Silesky at 71; "Jake Ehrlich, Criminal Lawyer Who Won Murder Cases, Dies," *New York Times*, 25 December 1971, p. 20; "Jake Ehrlich Sr. Quotes" at http:// www.neverpleadguilty.com.

268 Ralph McIntosh: de Grazia at 335; Morgan & Peters at 203, 215–16; Fiona Paton, "Banned Beats," http://lib.newpaltz.edu/events/bannedbooks.html.

269 "sustained shrieks of frantic defiance": M.L. Rosenthal, "Poet of the New Violence," *The Nation*, 23 February 1957, at 162.

Chapter 37

270 Headlines: Carolyn Anspacher, "Battle of the Books is On: 'Howl' Trial Starts—Big Crowd," *San Francisco Chronicle*, 17 August 1957, p. 1.

270 "nakedness of mind": John Clellon Holmes, "This Is the Beat Generation," *New York Times Magazine*, 16 November 1952, p. 10.

270–71 censored works: Sova at 209–12 (*Scarlet Letter*), 166–67 (*Leaves of Grass*), 237–39 (*Well of Loneliness*); de Grazia at 7–13 (*Ulysses*).

271 Petition: "Bookmen Ask Mayor to Ban Cop Censors," *San Francisco Chronicle*, 16 August 1957, p. 1.

271–72 Description of Ferlinghetti, Murao, Ehrlich, and of the booklets on display at the trial hearing: Carolyn Anspacher, "Battle of the Books is On: 'Howl' Trial Starts—Big Crowd," *San Francisco Chronicle*, 17 August 1957, p. 1; Ginsberg (1) at 171.

272–73 Proceedings at the August 16 hearing: Ehrlich (1) at 3–5.

Chapter 38

Epigraph quote: Charters (1) at 287.

274 *Evergreen Review*: *Evergreen Review*, vol. 1, no. 2, 1957; cover and table of contents reprinted in Theado (1) at 73; Amburn at 272.

274 *Time* interview: Schumacher at 267; Miles (1) at 227.

275 Kerouac in Berkeley: Amburn at 270; Charters (1) at 286; Watson at 189.

275 Advance copies of *On the Road*: Amburn at 270; Maher (1) at 349.

275 "About The Beat Generation": Kerouac (5) at 65–69 (letters to Phil Whalen, mid-August 1957, and to Joyce Glassman, 18 August 1957); Amburn at 272.

276 Jack in Orlando: Maher (1) at 353; Kerouac (5) at 71–72 (letter of Jack Kerouac to Joyce Glassman, 23 August 1957).

276 Footnote on "About the Beat Generation": Kerouac (3) at 552.

Chapter 39

277 Arguments at the August 22 hearing: Ehrlich (1) at 6–23.

277–81 Description of the August 22 hearing: Carolyn Anspacher, "'Obscene' Book Trial: Dismissal for 'Howl' Clerk Indicated," *San Francisco Chronicle*, August 23, 1957, p. 4.

281 Footnote on *Time* interview: Miles (1) at 227.

281–82 Allen Ginsberg in Naples & Ischia: Miles (1) at 227–28; Morgan (1) at 251–52; Schumacher at 267–68.

282 Allen Ginsberg correspondence with Ferlinghetti: Morgan (1) at 252; Morgan & Peters at 69.

282 Kerouac's return to New York: Amburn at 273–74; Kerouac (5) at 69; McNally at 112.

283 Joyce (Glassman) Johnson meeting Kerouac: J. Johnson at 127.

283 Joyce Johnson's background: Knight at 167–68.

283–84 Viking publicist and Jack's return: J. Johnson at 180–83. Minor changes were made in the tense of the passages quoted to accommodate the narrative. The tense that we have used may well be truer to the original.

Chapter 40

Epigraph quote: Gilbert Millstein, "Books of the Times," *New York Times*, 5 September 1957, at 27.

285 Jack, Joyce, and the Millstein review: J. Johnson at 180–86. See also Amburn at 274–76; Gifford & Lee at 238; Kerouac (5) at 72–73; Knight at 167–68. The newspaper excerpts derive from Gilbert Millstein, "Books of the Times," *New York Times*, 5 September 1957, p. 27.

286 "from limbo to limelight": Jay Sharbutt, "An Old-school Editor Keeps NBC up to Date," *Los Angeles Times*, January 3, 1986.

286 "The History of Bop": Nicosia at 428.

Chapter 41

Epigraph quote: Al Bendich, "Award to Lawrence Ferlinghetti," 12 December 1999, reprinted in Charters (2) at 17.

288 Defense witnesses: "Clark, Walter van Tilberg," in *Encyclopedia Britannica*, at www.britannica.com/eb/article-9024214; "Lowenthal, Leo (1900–1993)," in "Glossary of People," *Encyclopedia of Marxism*, at www.marxists.org/glossary/people/l/o.htm#lowenthal-leo; "Rexroth, Kenneth," in *Encyclopedia Britannica*, at www.britannica.com/eb/article-9063377; "Schorer, Mark 1908–1977, in "Notable Wisconsin

Authors," *Wisconsin Library Association*, at www.wla.lib.wi.us/lac/notable/index.htm; Ehrlich (1) at 23–69.

290 Direct testimony of defense witnesses: Ehrlich (1) at 26–27 (Schorer), 39 (Nichols), 54 (Van Tilburg Clark),

291–93 Cross-examination testimony of defense witnesses: Ehrlich (1) at 30–31 (Schorer), 49–52 (Nichols).

293 Book reviews of *HOWL*: Richard Eberhart, "West Coast Rhythms," *New York Times Book Review*, 2 September 1956; M.L. Rosenthal, "Poet of the New Violence," *The Nation*, 23 February 1957, p. 162.

293–94 Admissibility of book reviews: Ehrlich (1) at 72–75.

294 David Kirk testimony: Ehrlich (1) at 76–91.

294 Gail Potter testimony: Ehrlich (1) at 91–94; David Perlman, "How Captain Hanrahan Made 'Howl' a Best-Seller," *The Report*, 12 December 1957, p. 37, 39.

295–97 Summations: Ehrlich (1) at 94–113.

Chapter 42

298 Footnote re "One of the great ironies": Gewirtz at 27, 29, 31.

298 Background information: Amburn at 277–79; Charters (1) at 299; Maher (1) at 355; McNally at 242–43.

299 "Take care of that man": Amburn at 277.

299 Millstein influence: Gilbert Millstein, "The 'Kick' that Failed," *New York Times*, 9 November 1952, p. 50 (review of *Go*); John Clellon Holmes, "This Is the Beat Generation," in Charters (2) at 222; Eric Pace, "Gilbert Millstein, 83, Reviewer Who Gave Early Boost to Kerouac," *New York Times*, 11 May 1999, sec. B, p. 10.

299 Millstein party: Amburn at 280–81; Gifford & Lee at 238–40; Maher (1) at 355.

300 "so discombobulated": Gifford & Lee at 241.

Chapter 43

301–5 Memorandum: *People v. Ferlinghetti* and *People v. Murao*, Memorandum of Points and Authorities, Municipal Court of the City and County of San Francisco, Nos. B-27585 & B-27083 (filed September 1957).

Chapter 44

Epigraph quote: Norman Podhoretz, "A Howl of Protest in San Francisco," *New Republic*, 16 September 1957, p. 26.

306 Negative reviews of *HOWL*: James Dickey, "From Babel to Byzantium," *Sewanee Review*, vol. 65, July–September 1957, p. 510; John Ciardi, "Writers As Readers of Poetry," *Saturday Review*, 23 November 1957, p. 33; John Hollander, "Poetry Chronicle," *Partisan Review*, vol. 24, Spring 1957, p. 298; McNally (1) at 241, 375.

306 Footnote quotation: Allen Ginsberg, "Notes Written on Finally Recording 'Howl,'" reprinted in Parkinson at 30.

307 *Life* magazine: "Big Day for Bards at Bay: San Francisco Muse Thrives in Face of Trial over Poems," *Life*, 9 September 1957, p. 105.

308 Negative reviews of *On the Road*: Carlos Baker, "Itching Feet," *Saturday Review*, 7 September 1957, p. 19; R.W. Grandsden, "Adolescence and Maturity," *Encounter*, August 1958, p. 84; Herbert Gold, "Hip, Cool, and Frantic," *Nation*, 16 November 1957, p. 349.

308 "Great White Father": Jack Kerouac, "After Me, the Deluge," *Chicago Tribune*, 28 September 1969, p. 120 (quoting the editor of the newspaper who introduced Kerouac's op-ed).

308 *Nightbeat*: Amburn at 278–79; Kerouac (5) at 73; Maher (2) at 356; McNally at 243; Morgan (2) at 14; Watson at 254.

309 Hunter S. Thompson: Thompson at 510.

309 Footnote on West End Bar: Morgan (2) at 14.

309 *HOWL*'s commercial success: Morgan & Peters at 78 (letter of Allen Ginsberg to Lawrence Ferlinghetti, 10 October 1957).

309 *On the Road*'s commercial success: Watson at 253–54.

309 Footnote on the filming of *On the Road*: "Kerouac's 'On the Road': 55 Years Later, with Lots of Sex and Some Poetry," *Forbes.com*, 23 May 2012; "The Beats Hit the Road Again on Screen," *NYTimes.com*, 23 May 2012.

309–10 "Jack had been grumbling": Miles (2) at 36.

310 Ginsberg letter to Kerouac (28 September 1957): Kerouac (5) at 73; Miles (2) at 36; Schumacher at 268.

310 Kerouac letter to Ginsberg (1 October 1957): Kerouac (5) at 76–77.

310 Ginsberg letter to Ferlinghetti (10 October 1957): Morgan & Peters at 78.

310 Ferlinghetti letter to Ginsberg (17 September 1957): Morgan & Peters at 70–71.

Chapter 45

311 "offered the most fantastic collection": David Perlman, "'Howl' Not Obscene, Judge Rules," *San Francisco Chronicle*, 4 October 1957, p. 1.

312 Description of opinion: Ginsberg (1) at 173–74; Morgan & Peters at 197–99.

313 Ferlinghetti after decision: Silesky at 78; David Perlman, "'Howl' Not Obscene, Judge Rules," *San Francisco Chronicle*, 4 October 1957, p. 1.

Chapter 46

314 *Chronicle* report and editorial: David Perlman, "'Howl' Not Obscene, Judge Rules," *San Francisco Chronicle*, 4 October 1957, p. 1; "'Howl' Decision Landmark of Law," *San Francisco Chronicle*, 7 October 1957, p. 18.

315 "PR genius": Kerouac (6) at xvi (quoting Ann Douglas).

315 Ginsberg reactions: Morgan & Peters at 78 (letter of Lawrence Ferlinghetti to Allen Ginsberg, 10 October 1957); Ginsberg & Cassady at 189 (letter of Allen Ginsberg to Neal Cassady, 3 December 1957).

315 Burroughs: Burroughs (1) at 369–70; Burroughs (3) at 37; Campbell at 227–28; Silesky at 78; Schumacher at 271.

316 "nervous breakdowns": Maher (1) at 358.

316 "liquid suit of armor" & "Great God Public:" McNally at 242–43.

317 Charters footnote: Charters (1) at 290 (referring to Neal Cassady, the inspiration for Dean Moriarty).

317 "By 1957 Kerouac": Kerouac (6) at ix (quoting Ann Douglas).

Chapter 47

Epigraph quote: Hyde at 32 (quoting Rexroth from 1957 *Evergreen Review* piece titled "San Francisco Letter").

318 "Godfather": "Rexroth, Kenneth," in *Encyclopedia Britannica*, at www.britannica.com/eb/article-9063377.

318 Rexroth reflections: Kenneth Rexroth, "Disengagement: The Art of the Beat Generation," 1957, reprinted in Charter (2) at 507, 508.

319 Kerouac in Goody's Bar: Jeremy Talmer, "Back to the Village," reprinted in Maher (2) at 44.

Epilogue: Legacy

Epigraph quote: T. Morgan at 310.

323–26 Neal Cassady: "catapulted": Gerald Nicosia, "Neal Cassady," in Charters (5), vol. 1, at 112 / Neal Cassady's background: See generally C. Cassady (1); Plummer; and Sandison & Vikers / "his job was to sweep": Morgan (3) at 217; Gerald Nicosia, "Neal Cassady," in Charters (5), vol. 1, at 111–13 / "Three off-brand cigarettes": Gerald Nicosia, "Neal Cassady," in Charters (5) vol. 1, at 112. As Nicosia recounts it, Neal took "money from a known narcotics agent with the promise to procure him marijuana; and when the deed failed to get him arrested, he gave 'three off-brand cigarettes' to another undercover policeman, who had previously arrested a friend of Cassady's on a narcotics charge. The first grand jury Cassady came before refused to indict him. Released in April, he was arrested the next day on slightly altered charges, which resulted in a felony conviction." / Neal's women: C. Cassady (1) at 116–18, 253–54, 258–59, 273–74, 377–78; Cassady (1) at 424; Gerald Nicosia, "Neal Cassady," in Charters (5) vol. 1, at 97–112 / Daughter Melany Jane: Gerald Nicosia, "Neal Cassady," in Charters (5), vol. 1, at 113 / "Well, my father died:'": Cassady (1) at 426 (letter of Neal Cassady to Carolyn Cassady, 21 July 1963) / bloodstained sheets: Sandison & Vikers at 279. See also Plummer at 120 / "fifteen-year marital": Sandison & Vikers at 278 / disgust with Kerouac: Charters (1) at 363 / "bobbing up": Plummer at 119 / "For Cassady, their worship": Gerald Nicosia, "Neal Cassady," in Charters (5) vol. 1, at 113 / "Salute, dammit, salute!": Perry & Babbs at 51 (quoting Ken Kesey) / Ferlinghetti re Cassady's death: Quoted in *The Source* (written, directed, and produced by Chuck Workman) (New York: Fox Lorber, 2000) (VHS) / "generalized congestion": Plummer at 157–58; see also "Neal Cassady: Debunking the Myths," website at http://www.nealcassadyestate.com/ neal.html / *The First Third*: See generally Cassady (2) / *Off the Road*: see C. Cassady (1). In 1996, Carolyn Cassady published *Heart Beat: My Life with Jack and Neal*: see C. Cassady (2) / *Collected Letters*: see Cassady (1).

326–30 Jack Kerouac: description of Buckley show: Amburn at 366–67; McNally at 338; *What Happened to Kerouac?* (New York: Shout!, 1986) (DVD) / Ginsberg on Buckley TV show: Ginsberg (3) at 76–102 (taped 7 May 1968, aired 24 September 1968) / "Listen, my politics": Cook at 88 (quoting Jack Kerouac) / "patriotic reasons": Kerouac (5) at 517 (letter of Jack Kerouac to Sterling Lord, 24 August 1968) / text of Buckley's *Firing Line* (3 September 1968), reproduced in Maher (2) at 328–55 / "many reviewers were savage": see, e.g., Thomas Lask, "Books of the Times: Road to Nowhere," *New York Times*, 17 February 1968, p. 27 / "Goodbye, drunken ghost": McNally at 338, 389 (quoting Allen Ginsberg) / "For old time's sake": Nicosia at 691 / Kerouac's death: Clark at 216 / Nicosia at 697 / Joseph Lelyveld, "Jack Kerouac, Novelist, Dead; Father of the Beat Generation," *New York Times*, 22 October 1969; "Jack Kerouac Dead at 47," *United Press International*, 21 October 1969. That evening, Walter

Cronkite announced the news to the nation: "Jack Kerouac, the novelist who wrote *On the Road*, reached the end of it today. The 47-year-old spokesman for the Beat Generation died of a massive hemorrhage in a St. Petersburg, Florida hospital." Quoted in *The Source* (written, directed and produced by Chuck Workman) (New York: Fox Lorber, 2000) (VHS) / "classic drunkard's death": T. Morgan at 450 / Edson cemetery: Maher (2) at 424–469 (drawing on John Clellon Holmes, *Gone in October*) / sale of scroll: "Jack Kerouac's Typescript Scroll of *On the Road*," *Christie's New York*, 22 May 2001 (Christie's catalogue); Regina Weinrich, "Road Trips," *Washington Post Book World*, 2 September 2007, p. 8.

330–32 John Clellon Holmes: "unlike the others in the group": Charters (3) at 153–54 / Edson Cemetery scenes: Maher (2) at 424–469 (drawing on John Clellon Holmes, *Gone in October*); Kerouac-Parker at 29–35 / "So, Mr. Ginsberg" & accompanying Holmes quote: Maher (2) at 461 (drawing on John Clellon Holmes, *Gone in October*) / *Rolling Stone* questions: Maher (2) at 461 (drawing on John Clellon Holmes, *Gone in October*) / Sterling Lord and John Holmes: Maher (2) at 448–449, 457 / "If love is total": Holmes (3) at 155–56 (journal entry of 21 October 1969) / Background and Death of Holmes: John T. McQuiston, "John Clellon Holmes, 62, Novelist and Poet of the Beat Generation," *New York Times*, 31 March 31 1988, sec. B, p. 11.

333 Herbert Huncke: "original hipster": Charters (2) at 238 / "*Ur*-Beat": Huncke (3) at xv (introduction by Raymond Foye) / "He was a character": Huncke (3) at ix (foreword by William S. Burroughs) / "Duke of Deception": Huncke (3) at xvi (introduction by Raymond Foye) / years in prison: Huncke (3) at xxiii (biographical sketch by Jerome Poynton) / "always used 'beat'": Charters (2) at 238 (quoting Ann Douglas) / Chelsea Hotel: Huncke (3) at xvii (introduction by Raymond Foye) / methadone clinic & dialogue with doctors: Huncke (3) at xxv (biographical sketch by Jerome Poynton) / obituaries: "Beat Generation's Herbert Huncke," *Chicago Tribune* 11 August 1996, sec. C, p. 4; James Campbell, "Herbert Huncke," *The Independent* (London), 16 August 1996, p. 11; Stephen Schwartz, "Herbert Huncke," *San Francisco Chronicle*, 9 August 1996, sec. A, p. 19; Robert McG. Thomas, "Herbert Huncke, the Hipster Who Defined 'Beat,' Dies at 81," *New York Times*, 9 August 1996, sec. B, p. 7; Elizabeth Young, "Herbert Huncke, First of the Beats on a Long Rough Road," *The Guardian* (London), 10 August 1996, p. 32.

334 Carl Solomon: "marginal underground intellectuals": Solomon (2) at xvi (Tytell introduction) / "asked Carl's forgiveness for having put him" & "calmly surrealistic": Tytell (2) at 176. There is a haunting photo, taken by Mellon, of Solomon in a hospital bed. See also Miles (1) at 551 / Morgan (1) at 624 (placing Solomon's death in February of 1993) / Date of Solomon's death: RecordsArea.com / "I am with you": Ginsberg (8) at 26.

335–38 William Burroughs: William Burroughs: "someone who strove to forge": Charters (2) at 63 (quoting Vince Passaro) / "the most horrible things": Charters (3) at 103 (quoting Bill Burroughs) / "What I am putting down": Burroughs (1) at 420 (letter of William Burroughs to Allen Ginsberg, July 1959) / description of *Naked Lunch:* See Jennie Skerl, "William S. Burroughs," in Charters (5) at 53–55 / *BIG TABLE* postal controversy: Barry-Goodman at 24–101. See also *In the Matter of the Complaint that BIG TABLE Magazine is nonmailable under 18 U.S. Code 1461* (Post Office Department, Docket No. 1/150) (12 August 1959); Ira Lurvey, "Beatniks Fight for Banned Verse," *Daily Defender,* 28 January 1959, sec. A, p. 4; "Shavians Meet the Beatniks," *Shaw Society Newsletter,* vol. 2, no. 1, February 1959; "U.S. Gives Up Postal Fight on Magazine," *Chicago Daily Tribune,* 12 August 1960, p. 7 / *BIG TABLE* federal court hearing: *Big Table v. Schroeder,* 186 F. Supp. 254 (N.D., IL, 1960) (defendant Schroeder was the Chicago postmaster); Barry-Goodman at 87–101; "U.S. Gives Up Postal Fight on Magazine," *Chicago Daily Tribune,* 12 August 1960, p. 7 / American edition of *Naked Lunch*: T. Morgan at 327 / cover wrap-around text: see Theado (1) at 297 / 25 idiosyncratic "chapters": See Burroughs (12) (table of contents). Technically, there are no chapters in the book, which is partitioned instead by italicized lower-case headings. Compare Campbell at 279 ("the book's twenty-two chapters") / Suffolk County trial: The trial and related obscenity accounts are drawn largely from Barry Goodman at 1–110, 142–230, 235–49; Burroughs (3) at ix–xlvii; Burroughs (4) at 115–20 (Grauerholz); Burroughs (11) at 233–48 (Miles & Grauerholz); de Grazia 481–495; and T. Morgan at 313, 342–59. The *Naked Lunch* proceedings originally began as a criminal proceeding against Theodore Mavrikos, who owned a bookstore in the "combat zone" and sold *Naked Lunch*. He was arrested for obscenity when he sold a copy of the book, which he kept under the counter, to an undercover vice-squad detective. Mavrikos's criminal trial was delayed pending the *in rem* civil proceeding held before Judge Eugene Hudson. See Barry-Goodman at 172–76. As Michael Barry-Goodman recounts: "On May 1,

1964, de Grazia formally requested on behalf of Grove Press that the Attorney General bring action against Burroughs' book. On September 30, 1964, the Attorney General's office filed a petition with the Superior Court, stating that there was reason to believe that *Naked Lunch* was obscene.... A show-cause hearing took place [before Superior Court Judge Francis Good] on October 13, and a date for a court trial in January 1965 was set." Barry-Goodman at 175 (notes omitted). As Ted Morgan recounts it, de Grazia "arranged with the Massachusetts attorney general's office that instead of proceeding with a criminal trial against a single bookseller, the book itself should be put on [civil] trial for obscenity.... [de Grazia] waived a jury trial." T. Morgan at 343 / Judge Hudson: "Judge Eugene Hudson," *New York Times*, 22 April 1972, p. 36 (obituary) / Edward de Grazia: T. Morgan at 343. Barney Rosset, Grove Press's publisher, had previously hired de Grazia on retainer to represent his press in connection with several other books, including one by Jean Genet (*Our Lady of the Flowers*). Telephone interview with Edward de Grazia, 22 August 2007. See also de Grazia at 247, 251, 367–69, 481 / Judge Hudson's ruling: "Findings of Material Facts and Order for Decree," Massachusetts Superior Court, 23 March 1965, quoted in part in Barry-Goodman at 235 / State high court opinion: *Attorney General v. Naked Lunch*, 351 Mass. 298 (MA 1965); Barry-Goodman at 236–46 / Footnote re Los Angeles criminal obscenity trial: Barry-Goodman at 232–33 (quoting trial transcript from *California v. Galanti/Frank*, Los Angeles Municipal Court, Division 2A, 28 January 1965) / "I think that all censorship": Burroughs (5) at 70 / Last literary work to be banned: Barry-Goodman at 249; de Grazia at 495. In August of 2005, federal obscenity charges were brought against Karen Fletcher, the author and webmistress of "Red Rose," a commercial website containing "explicit stories about adults have sex with children." U.S. District Court Judge Conti denied motions to dismiss the charges in August of 2007, making the Fletcher prosecution the first federal obscenity case in decades to be tried solely for written words, albeit not in a printed novel but in short stories on the Internet. See Neil A. Lewis, "A Prosecution Tests the Definition of Obscenity," *New York Times*, 28 September 2007; Jason Cato, "Trial Set for Washington County Woman," *Pittsburgh Tribune Review*, 31 August 2007 / "cut-up" trilogy: Burroughs (4) at 179–244; Miles (4) at 115–33; Jennie Skerl, "William S. Burroughs," in Charters (5) at 56–60; Theado (1) at 309–14 / biographies: see Miles (4) and T. Morgan / publications of letters and assorted writings: see Burroughs (1), Burroughs (4), Burroughs (5), Burroughs (8), Burroughs (9), Burroughs (11), and Burroughs & Ginsberg; see generally Oliver Harris, "William Seward Burroughs," in Hemmer at 31–37 / restored text of *Naked Lunch*: see Burroughs (12) / Burroughs' influence on pop culture: William S. Burroughs, *The Soft Machine* (New York: Grove, 1966) ("heavy metal"); Bockris (2) at 181–82 (His influence notwithstanding, Burroughs did say "I am not a punk and I don't know why anybody would consider me the Godfather of punk." The grunge rocker Kurt Cobain provided guitar backup for Burroughs' 1993 CD, "'The Priest' They Called Him."); Connie Lauerman, "The Broad Reach of the Beats; Generations Later, the Literary Rebels Still Have a Cause," *Chicago Tribune*, 24 October 1999, sec. C, p. 5 (Nike ads); Theado (1) at 8 (*Drugstore Cowboy*) / Richard Severo, "William S. Burroughs Dies at 83; Member of the Beat Generation Wrote 'Naked Lunch,'" *New York Times*, 4 August 1997, sec. B, p. 5 / "God grant I never die": Burroughs (4) at 119 (Grauerholz quoting Burroughs).

338–45 Allen Ginsberg: Lenny Bruce: Collins & Skover at 222–24 / Footnote re letter to Kuh: Ginsberg (16) at 296 (letter of Allen Ginsberg to Richard Kuh, 16 June 1964) / "We are here": Miles (1) at 410 (quoting Allen Ginsberg) / Yippie press conference: Nicholas von Hoffman, "Yippies Unveil 'Politics of Ecstasy,'" *Washington Post*, 20 March 1968, sec. A, p. 3; Miles (1) at 410 (mistakenly citing March 7, 1968 as date of press conference); Schumacher at 503–504 (mistakenly citing date of press conference as March 17, 1968 / "16,000 Chicago police officers": Miles (1) at 444 / Chicago demonstrations: Kurlansky at 272–83; Miles (1) at 412–413; Morgan (1) at 452–456; T. Morgan at 444–446; Sylvan Fox, "300 Police Use Tear Gas to Breach Young Militants Barricade in Chicago Park," *New York Times*, 27 August 27 1968, p. 29; D.J. Bruckner, "Chicago Police Use Tear Gas to Rout Thousands," *Los Angeles Times*, 28 August 1968, p. 1; J. Anthony Lukas, "Police Battle Demonstrators in Streets," *New York Times*, 29 August 1968, p. 1; "Ginsberg Enters Hall After Startling Police," *New York Times*, 29 August 1968, p. 23 / Ginsberg statements: Quoted in J. Anthony Lukas, "Police Battle Demonstrators in Streets," *New York Times*, 29 August 1968, p. 1, 23 / "Statement on Censorship": Federal Communications Bar Association, "What's Indecent? Who Decides?" program materials, 18 April 1990 (on file with authors); Ginsberg (4) at 177–80 / reading *Howl* in front of U.S. Court of Appeals: Laura Lippman, "Ginsberg 'Howls' Again as Lawyers Battle FCC Rule," *Baltimore Sun*,

20 October 1994, sec. D, p. 1 / Footnote re National Endowment of the Arts funding: Ginsberg (16) at 440–442 (letter of Allen Ginsberg to Randy "Duke" Cunningham, 4 April 1995); John M. Broder, "Lawmaker Quits after He Pleads Guilty to Bribes," *New York Times*, 29 November 2005; Sotheby catalogue & auction events: See Sotheby's—Ginsberg (cover portrait & listing of lots); Michael Ellison, "The Beat Goes On at Ginsberg Auction," *The Guardian* (London), 8 October 1999, p. 19; "Ginsberg's Belongings Auctioned Off at Sotheby's," *The Globe and Mail* (Canada), 8 October 1999, sec. A, p. 19; Kathryn Shattuck, "Sotheby's to Auction Ginsbergiana," *New York Times*, 7 October 1999, sec. E, p. 3; "They'll 'Howl' over Ginsberg Sales," *New York Post*, 5 October 1999, p. 9; David Usborne, "Sotheby's Sells Off Allen Ginsberg Estate, *Hamilton Spectator* (Ontario, Canada), 8 October 1999, sec. F, p. 11 / Ginsberg Obituary: Wilborn Hampton, "Allen Ginsberg, Master Poet of Beat Generation, Dies at 70," *New York Times*, 6 April 1997, sec. A, p. 1. Hilborn would later write Lucien Carr's obituary. See below / Lennon Obituary: Les Lesbetter, "John Lennon of Beatles Is Killed; Suspect Held in Shooting at Dakota," *New York Times*, 9 December 1980, sec. A, p. 1 / Presley Obituary: Molly Ivins, "Elvis Presley Dies; Rock Singer Was 42," *New York Times*, 17 August 1977, p. 1. Of course, the deaths of Lennon and Presley were unexpected, unlike Allen's. Moreover, the number of stories about Lennon and Presley in the immediate aftermath of their deaths and thereafter far exceeded those about Ginsberg. Still, it is noteworthy that the Ginsberg story received the coverage and placement that it did. / Kerouac Obituary: Joseph Lelyveld, "Jack Kerouac, Novelist, Dead; Father of the Beat Generation," *New York Times*, 22 October 1969 / Ginsberg's achievements & influences: Morgan (1) at 491–492; Molly Hall, "In the Spirit of Kerouac: School Is Born from the Beat Generation," *Chicago Tribune*, 4 August 1994, sec. C, p. 8 / "the poet laureate": Wilborn Hampton, "Allen Ginsberg, Master Poet of Beat Generation, Dies at 70," *New York Times*, 6 April 1997, sec. A, p. 1 / cadets read *Howl* at the Virginia Military Institute: *The Rolling Stone Book of the Beats* (Holly George-Warren, ed.) (New York: Hyperion, 1999), p. 60–61 / Ginsberg canon: see Bibliography in this book.

345–46 Lucien Carr: "fallen angel," "disintegrating mayhem" and "every major story": Eric Homberger, "Lucien Carr: Fallen Angel of the Beat Poets, Later an Unflappable News Editor with United Press," *The Guardian* (U.K.), 9 February 2005 / Beat reunion: McNally at 336 / Hotel

Delmonico: Amburn at 365; Clark at 21–3l; Cook at 180–81; McNally at 336; T. Morgan at 446–447; Nicosia at 690; Charles V. Bagli, "Trump Buys Hotel Delmonico for $115 Million," *New York Times*, 30 November 2001, sec. D, p. 1 / death of bone cancer: Wilborn Hampton, "Lucien Carr, a Founder and a Muse of the Beat Generation, Dies at 79," *New York Times*, 30 January 2005.

346–48   Lawrence Ferlinghetti: copies and translations *Coney Island of the Mind*: see www.citylights.com / City Lights bookstore, City Lights Books, and honors: William Lawlor, "Ferlinghetti, Lawrence," in Hemmer at 98–101 / Pocket Poet Series: *City Lights Pocket Poets Anthology* (Lawrence Ferlinghetti, ed.) (San Francisco: City Lights Books, 1995) / Ferlinghetti's publications: see Bibliography in this book / *Poetry as Insurgent Art*: Ferlinghetti (4) at 8, 31, 73 / WBAI flap: Joe Garofoli, "'Howl' Too Hot to Hear," *San Francisco Chronicle*, 3 October 2007; Lydia Hailman King, "'Howl' Obscenity Prosecution Still Echoes 50 Years Later," First Amendment Center, article posted on 3 October 2007, at www.firstamendmentcenter.org; Patricia Cohen, "'Howl' in an Era That Fears Censorship," *New York Times*, 4 October 2007, sec. B, p. 3; footnote re NYT editorial: "A Muse Unplugged," *New York Times*, 8 October 2007, sec. A, p. 22 / Pacific interview & Ferlinghetti reading: "Howl Against Censorship," *Pacifica.org*, 3 October 2007 at www.pacifica.org/program-guide/op,segment-page/ segment_id,469/.

Bibliography

Books

Amburn, Ellis. *Subterranean Kerouac: The Hidden Life of Jack Kerouac.* New York: St. Martin's Griffin, 1999.

Ash, Mel. *Beat Spirit: The Way of the Beat Writers as a Living Experience.* New York: Jeremy P. Tarcher/Putnam, 1997.

Averbusch, Bernard, and John Wesley Knoble. *Never Plead Guilty.* Farrar Straus & Cudahy, 1955.

Barry-Goodman, Michael. *Contemporary Literary Censorship: The Case History of Burroughs' Naked Lunch.* Metuchen, NJ: The Scarecrow Press, Inc., 1981.

Bierowski, Thomas R. *Kerouac in Ecstasy: Shamanic Expression in the Writings.* Jefferson, NC: McFarland, 2011.

Bockris, Victor (1). *With William Burroughs: A Report from the Bunker.* New York: Seaver, 1981.

———— (2). *Beat Punks.* Cambridge, MA: Da Capo Press, 2000.

Brinkley, Douglas. *The Majic Bus: An American Odyssey.* Foreword by Brian Lamb. New York: Thunder's Mouth Press, 2003.

Burroughs, William S. (1) *The Letters of William S. Burroughs, 1945–1959.* Edited by Oliver Harris. New York: Viking, 1993.

———— (2). *Junky.* New York: Penguin, 1977. Rpt. *Junky: The Definitive Text of 'Junk.'* Edited with an introduction by Oliver Harris. New York: Penguin, 2003.

———— (3). *Naked Lunch.* New York: Grove Press, 1959 (1990 ed.)

———— (4). *Word Virus: The William S. Burroughs Reader.* James Grauerholz & Ira Silverberg, editors. New York: Grove Press, 1998.

———— (5). *The Job: Interviews with William S. Burroughs.* Daniel Odier, editor. New York: Penguin, 1989.

———— (6). *Exterminator!* New York: Penguin, 1986.

———— (7). *My Education: A Book of Dreams.* New York: Penguin, 1996.

———— (8). *Burroughs Live: The Collected Interviews of William S. Burroughs, 1960–1997.* Edited by Sylvère Lotringer. Los Angeles: Semiotext(E), 2001.

——— (9). *Last Words*. Edited and Introduction by James Grauerholz. Fort Lauderdale, FL: Flamingo Press, 2001.

——— (10). *Queer: A Novel*. New York: Penguin, 1995.

——— (11). *Interzone*. Edited by James Grauerholz. New York: Viking, 1989.

——— (12). *Naked Lunch: The Restored Text*. Edited by James Grauerholz & Barry Miles. New York: Grove Press, 2001.

——— (13). *Rub Out the Words LP: The Letters of William S. Burroughs 1959–1974*. Edited by James Grauerholz. New York: Harperluxe, 2012.

Burroughs, William S., and Allen Ginsberg. *The Yagé Letters Redux*. Edited with an introduction by Oliver Harris. San Francisco: City Lights Books, 2006.

Burroughs, William S., and Jack Kerouac. *And the Hippos Were Boiled in Their Tanks*. With an afterword by James W. Grauerholz. New York: Grove Press, 2009.

Burroughs, William S. Jr. *Cursed from Birth: The Short, Unhappy Life of William S. Burroughs, Jr.* Edited by David Ohle. New York: Soft Skull Press, 2006.

Campbell, James. *This Is the Beat Generation: New York, San Francisco, Paris*. London: Secker & Warburg, 1999. Rpt. Berkeley: University of California Press, 2001.

Cassady, Neal (1). *Collected Letters, 1944–1967*. New York: Penguin, 2005.

——— (2). *The First Third*. San Francisco: City Lights, 1971. Revised ed. *The First Third: A Partial Autobiography and Other Writings*. San Francisco: City Lights, 1981. Rpt. San Francisco: City Lights, 2003.

——— (3). *Grace Beats Karma: Letters from Prison: 1958–1960*. New York: Blast Books, 1993.

Cassady, Carolyn (1). *Off the Road: My Years with Cassady, Kerouac, and Ginsberg*. New York: William Morrow, 1990.

——— (2). *Heart Beat: My Life with Jack and Neal*. Berkeley: Creative Arts Press, 1976.

Caveney, Graham. *Screaming with Joy: The Life of Allen Ginsberg*. New York: Broadway Books, 1999.

Charters, Ann (1). *Kerouac: A Biography*. San Francisco: Straight Arrow Books, 1973. Rpt. New York: St. Martin's Press, 1974.

——— (2), ed. *Beat Down to Your Soul: What Was the Beat Generation?* New York: Penguin, 2001.

——— (3), ed. *The Portable Beat Reader*. New York: Penguin, 1992.

——— (4). "Introduction." In *On the Road*, by Jack Kerouac. New York: Penguin, 1991.

———— (5), ed. *The Beats: Literary Bohemians in Postwar America*. Detroit: Gale Research Company, 1983, 2 vols.

Cherkovski, Neeli. *Ferlinghetti: A Biography*. New York: Doubleday, 1979.

Ciuraru, Carmela. *Beat Poets*. New York: Alfred A. Knopf, 2002.

Clark, Tom. *Jack Kerouac: A Biography*. San Diego: Harcourt Brace Jovanvich, 1984. Rpt. New York: Paragon House, 1990.

Collins, Ronald K.L., and David M. Skover. *The Trials of Lenny Bruce: The Fall and Rise of an American Icon*. Naperville, IL: Sourcebooks, 2002.

Cook, Bruce. *The Beat Generation*. New York: Scribner, 1971. Rpt. Westport, CT: Greenwood Press, 1983.

Corso, Gregory (1). *Elegaic Feelings American*. New York: New Directions, 1970.

———— (2). *Gasoline, The Vestal Lady of Brattle and Other Poems*. San Francisco: City Lights Books, 1981.

Cowley, Malcolm. *Conversations with Malcolm Cowley*. Jackson, MS: University Press of Mississippi, 1986.

Davidson, Michael. *The San Francisco Renaissance: Poetics and Community at Mid-century*. New York: Cambridge University Press, 1989.

Day, John. *Molech: A God of Human Sacrifice in the Old Testament*. New York: Cambridge University Press, 1989.

de Grazia, Edward. *Girls Lean Back Everywhere: The Law of Obscenity and the Assault on Genius*. New York: Random House, 1992.

Di Prima, Diane (1). *Memoirs of a Beatnik*. New York: Olympia, 1969. Rpt. New York: Penguin Books, 1998.

———— (2). *Recollections of My Life as a Woman: A Memoir*. New York: Viking, 2001.

Dittman, Michael J. *Jack Kerouac: A Biography*. Westport, CN: Greenwood Press, 2004.

Dylan, Bob. *Chronicles, Volume One*. New York: Simon & Schuster, 2004.

Ehrlich, J.W. (1). *Howl of the Censor: The Four-Letter Word on Trial*. San Carlos, CA: Nourse Publishing, 1961.

———— (2). *A Life in My Hands: An Autobiography*. New York: G.P. Putnam's Sons, 1965.

———— (3). *The Holy Bible and the Law*. New York: Oceana Publications, 1962.

———— (4). *A Reasonable Doubt*. Cleveland: World Publishing Co., 1964.

———— (5), ed. *Ehrlich's Blackstone*. New York: Capricorn, 1959.

Eisler, Kim. *A Justice for All*. New York: Simon & Schuster, 1993.

Emerson, Thomas I. *The System of Freedom of Expression*. New York: Random House, 1970.

Evans, Mike. *Beats: Kerouac to Kesey, an Illustrated Journey through the Beat Generation*. Philadelphia: Running Press, 2007.

Feldman, Gene, ed. *The Beat Generation and the Angry Young Men*. New York: Dell, 1960.

Felver, Christopher (1). *Ferlinghetti Portrait*. Salt Lake City, UT: Gibbs-Smith, 1998.

———— (2). *Beat*. San Francisco: Last Gasp Books, 2007.

———— (3). *The Late Great Allen Ginsberg: A Photo Biography*. New York: Thunder's Mouth Press, 2002.

———— (4). *Beat: Photographs/Commentary*. San Francisco: Last Gasp, 2007.

Ferlinghetti, Lawrence (1). *The Canticle of Jack Kerouac*. Boise, Idaho: Limberlost Press, 1993.

———— (2), ed. *City Lights Pocket Anthology*. San Francisco: City Lights Books, 1995.

———— (3). *A Coney Island of the Mind*. New York: New Directions Books, 1958.

———— (4). *Poetry as Insurgent Art*. New York: New Directions, 2007.

———— (5). *These are My Rivers: New and Selected Poems: 1955–1993*. New York: New Directions Books, 1994.

Ferlinghetti, Lawrence, and Nancy J. Peters. *Literary San Francisco: A Pictorial History from Its Beginnings to the Present Day*. San Francisco: City Lights Books and Harper & Row, 1980.

French, Warren. *Jack Kerouac*. New York: Macmillan, 1986.

Friedman, Leon, ed. *Obscenity: The Complete Oral Arguments before the Supreme Court in the Major Obscenity Cases*. New York: Chelsea House Publishers, 1970.

George-Warren, Holly, ed. *The Rolling Stone Book of the Beats*. New York: Hyperion, 1999.

Gewirtz, Isaac. *Beatific Souls: Jack Kerouac's On the Road, 1957–2007*. London: Scala Publishers, 2007.

Gifford, Barry. *Kerouac's Town*. Santa Barbara, CA: Capra Press, 1973.

Gifford, Barry, and Lawrence Lee. *Jack's Book: An Oral Biography of Jack Kerouac*. New York: St. Martin's Press, 1978.

Ginsberg, Allen (1). *Howl: Original Draft Facsimile, Transcript & Variant Versions, Fully Annotated by Author, with Contemporary Correspondence, Account of First Public Reading, Legal Skirmishes, Precursor Texts & Bibliography*. Edited by Barry Miles. New York: Harper & Row, 1985. Rpt. New York: HarperPerennial, 1995, 2006. *Howl* was originally published in

1956 by City Lights Book, San Francisco, CA; see Ginsberg, *HOWL and Other Poems.*

———— (2). *The Fall.* Unpublished memorandum held at Department of Special Collections, Stanford University Libraries, "Allen Ginsberg" Journals, Box 3.

———— (3). *Spontaneous Mind: Selected Interviews, 1958–1996.* Edited by David Carter. Preface by Václav Havel and Introduction by Edmund White. New York: HarperCollins, 2001. Rpt. New York: Perennial, 2002.

———— (4). *Deliberate Prose: Selected Essays, 1952–1995.* Edited by Bill Morgan. Foreword by Edward Sanders. New York: HarperCollins, 2000. Rpt. New York: Perennial, 2001.

———— (5). *Journals: Early Fifties, Early Sixties.* Edited by Gordon Ball. New York: Grove Press, 1977.

———— (6). *The Book of Martyrdom and Artifice: First Journals and Poems, 1937–1952.* Cambridge, MA: Da Capo Press, 2006.

———— (7). *Photographs.* Altadena, CA: Twelvetrees Press, 1990.

———— (8). *HOWL and Other Poems.* San Francisco: City Lights Books, 1956.

———— (9). *Kaddish and Other Poems, 1958–1960.* San Francisco: City Lights Books, 1961.

———— (10). *The Fall of America: Poems of These States, 1965–1971.* San Francisco: City Lights Books, 1972.

———— (11). *Psychiatric Record, New York Psychiatric Institute, June 2, 1949– February 27, 1950.* On file at Allen Ginsberg Archives, New York, New York.

———— (12). *Poems for the Nation: A Collection of Contemporary Political Poems.* Edited by Allen Ginsberg with Andy Clausen and Eliot Katz. Introduction by Eliot Katz and Bob Rosenthal. New York: Seven Stories Press, 2000.

———— (13). *Journals: Mid-Fifties.* Edited by Gordon Ball. New York: HarperCollins, 1995.

———— (14). *Snapshot Poetics: A Photographic Memoir of the Beat Era.* San Francisco: Chronicle Books, 1993.

———— (15). *Collected Poems: 1947–1957.* New York: HarperCollins, 2006.

———— (16). *The Letters of Allen Ginsberg.* Edited by Bill Morgan. Cambridge, MA: Da Capo Press, 2008.

Ginsberg, Allen, and Neal Cassady. *As Ever: The Collected Correspondence of Allen Ginsberg and Neal Cassady.* Edited by Barry Gifford. Berkeley: Creative Arts, 1977.

Ginsberg, Allen, and Louis Ginsberg. *Family Business : Two Lives in Letters and Poetry*. Edited by Michael Schumacher. London: Bloomsbury Publishing, 2001.

Ginsberg, Allen, and Gary Snyder. *The Selected Letters of Allen Ginsberg and Gary Snyder, 1956–1991*. Edited by Bill Morgan. Berkeley, CA: Counterpoint, 2008.

Grace, Nancy. *Jack Kerouac and the Literary Imagination*. New York: Palgrave Macmillan, 2007.

Gray, Michael. *The Bob Dylan Encyclopedia*. New York: Continuum, 2006.

Hajdu, David. *Positively Fourth Street: The Lives and Times of Joan Baez, Bob Dylan, Mimi Baez Farina, and Richard Farina*. New York: Farrar, Straus and Giroux, 2001.

Hamalian, Linda. *A Life of Kenneth Rexroth*. New York: W.W. Norton & Co., 1991.

Harris, Oliver. *William Burroughs and the Secret of Fascination*. Carbondale, IL: Southern Illinois University, 2006.

Hayes, Kevin J., ed. *Conversations with Jack Kerouac*. Jackson, MS: University of Mississippi Press, 2005.

Hedin, Benjamin, ed. *Studio A: The Bob Dylan Reader*. New York: W.W. Norton, 2004.

Hemmer, Kurt. *Encyclopedia of Beat Literature*. New York: Facts on File, 2006.

Heylin, Clinton. *Bob Dylan: Behind the Shades Revisited*. New York: HarperCollins, 2001.

Hipkiss, Robert A. *Jack Kerouac: Prophet of the New Romanticism*. Lawrence KS: Regents Press, 1976.

Holladay, Hilary. *American Hipster: A Life of Herbert Huncke, The Times Square Hustler Who Inspired the Beat Movement*. New York: Magnus Books, 2012.

Holladay, Hilary, and Robert Holton, eds. *What's Your Road, Man? Critical Essays on Jack Kerouac's On the Road*. Carbondale, IL: Southern Illinois University Press, 2008.

Holmes, John Clellon (1). *Nothing More to Declare*. New York: E.P. Dutton, 1967.

——— (2). *Go: A Novel*. New York: Thunder's Mouth Press, 1952. Rpt. New York: Thunder's Mouth Press, 1997.

——— (3). *Representative Men: The Biographical Essays*. Fayetteville: University of Arkansas Press, 1988.

—— (4). *Passionate Opinions: The Cultural Essays*. Fayetteville: University of Arkansas Press, 1988.

—— (5). *Displaced Person: The Travel Essays*. Fayetteville: University of Arkansas Press, 1987.

Hrebeniak, Michael. *Action Writing: Jack Kerouac's Wild Form*. Carbondale, IL: Southern Illinois University Press, 2008.

Huncke, Herbert (1). *Guilty of Everything*. Foreword by William S. Burroughs. New York: Paragon House, 1990.

—— (2). *Huncke's Journal*. New York: Poets Press, 1965.

—— (3). *The Evening Sun Turned Crimson*. New York: Cherry Valley, 1980.

Huncke, Herbert, and Benjamin G. Schafer, eds. *The Herbert Huncke Reader*. New York: William Morrow, 1997.

Hunt, Tim. *Kerouac's Crooked Road: The Development of a Fiction*. Foreword by Ann Charters. Berkeley, CA: University of California Press, 1981. Rpt. Berkeley, CA: University of California Press, 1996.

Hyde, Lewis, ed. *On the Poetry of Allen Ginsberg*. Ann Arbor, MI: The University of Michigan Press, 1984.

Jennison, Keith. *The Best of Times: Keith Jennison on Becoming a Book Publisher*. Tucson, AZ: Marshall Jones Co., 1995.

Johnson, Rob. *The Lost Years of William S. Burroughs: Beats in South Texas*. Austin, TX: Texas A&M University Press, 2006.

Johnson, Joyce (1). *Minor Characters*. Boston: Houghton Mifflin, 1983.

—— (2). *Door Wide Open*. New York: Viking, 2000.

—— (3). *The Voice Is All: The Lonely Victory of Jack Kerouac*. New York: Viking, 2012.

Kealing, Bob. *Kerouac in Florida: Where the Road Ends*. Orlando, FL: Arbiter Press, 2004.

Kerouac, Jack (1). *Selected Letters, 1940–1956*. Edited by Ann Charters. New York: Viking, 1995.

—— (2). *Windblown World: The Journals of Jack Kerouac, 1947–1954*. Edited and with an introduction by Douglas Brinkley. New York: Viking, 2004.

—— (3). *The Portable Jack Kerouac*. Edited by Ann Charters. New York: Penguin, 1995.

—— (4). *Vanity of Duluoz*. New York: Coward-McCann, 1968. Rpt. New York: Penguin, 1994.

—— (5). *Selected Letters, 1957–1969*. Edited by Ann Charters. New York: Viking, 1999.

—— (6). *The Dharma Bums*. Introduction by Ann Douglas. New York:

Viking Press, 1958. Rpt. New York: Penguin Books, 2006.

—— (7). *Desolation Angels*. Introduction by Seymour Krim. New York: Coward-McCann, 1965.

—— (8). *The Town and the City*. New York: Harcourt, 1950. Rpt. Fort Washington, PA: Harvest Books, 1970.

—— (9). *Visions of Cody*. New York: McGraw-Hill, 1972. Rpt. New York: Penguin, 1993.

—— (10). *Desolation Angels*. Introduction by Joyce Johnson. New York: Riverhead Books, 1995.

—— (11). *On the Road*. Introduction by Ann Charters. New York: Penguin Books, 2003.

—— (12). *Old Angel Midnight*. Edited by Donald Allen with prefaces by Ann Charters & Michael McClure. San Francisco: Grey Fox Press, 2001.

—— (13). *Book of Haikus*. Edited with an introduction by Regina Weinreich. New York: Penguin Poets, 2003.

—— (14). *Big Sur*. Foreword by Aram Saroyan. New York: Penguin Books, 1992.

—— (15). *On the Road: 50th Anniversary Edition*. New York: Viking, 2007.

—— (16). *On the Road: The Original Scroll*. Edited by Howard Cunnell with introductions by Howard Cunnell, Penny Vlagopoulos, George Mouratidis and Joshua Kupetz. New York: Viking, 2007.

—— (17). *Road Novels 1957–1960*. Edited by Douglas Brinkley. New York: Library of America, 2007.

—— (18). *Mexico City Blues*. New York: Grove Press, 1990.

—— (19). *Good Blonde & Others*. Edited by Donald Allen with preface by Robert Creeley. San Francisco: Grey Fox Press, 1993.

—— (20). Jack Kerouac. *Collected Poems*. Edited by Marilene Phipps-Kettlewell. New York: The Library of America, 2012.

Kerouac, Jack, and Joyce Johnson. *Door Wide Open: Jack Kerouac & Joyce Johnson*. New York: Penguin Books, 2000.

Kerouac-Parker, Edie. *You'll Be Okay: My Life with Jack Kerouac*. Edited by Timothy Moran and Bill Morgan. San Francisco: City Lights Books, 2007.

Kerouac, Joan Haverty. *Nobody's Wife: The Smart Aleck and the King of Beats*. Introduction by Jan Kerouac. Foreword by Ann Charters. Berkeley, CA: Creative Art Books, 1995.

Kesey, Ken. *The Further Inquiry*. New York: Viking, 1990.

Knight, Brenda, ed. *Women of the Beat Generation*. Berkeley, CA: Conari Press, 1996.

Kramer, Jane. *Allen Ginsberg in America*. New York: Random House, 1969. Rpt. with a new introduction by the author. New York: Fromm International, 1997.

Kraus, Michelle P. *Allen Ginsberg: Ann Annotated Bibliography, 1969–1977*. Metuchen, NJ: Scarecrow Press, 1980.

Krim, Seymour. *The Beats*. Greenwich, CT: Fawcett Publications, 1960.

Kurlansky, Mark. *1968: The Year That Rocked the World*. New York: Ballantine Books, 2004.

Lawlor, William. *The Beat Generation: A Bibliographical Teaching Guide*. Lanham, MD: The Scarecrow Press, 1998.

Leary, Timothy. *Flashbacks*. New York: G. P. Putnam's Sons, 1983.

Lebow, Eileen F. *The Bright Boys: A History of Townsend Harris High School*. Westport, CT: Greenwood Press, 2000.

Leland, John. *Why the Beats Matter: The Lessons of* On the Road (*They're not what you think*). New York: Viking Press, 2007.

Leverich, Lyle. *Tom: The Unknown Tennessee Williams*. New York: Crown Publishers, Inc., 1995.

Lipton, Lawrence. *The Holy Barbarians*. New York: Julian Messner, 1959.

Lyndenberg, Robin, and Jennie Skerl. *William S. Burroughs at the Front: Critical Reception, 1959–1989*. Carbondale: Southern Illinois University Press, 1991.

Maher, Paul Jr. (1). *Kerouac: The Definitive Biography*. Foreword by David Amran. Lanham, MD: Taylor Trade Publishing, 2004.

—— (2), ed. *Empty Phantoms: Interviews and Encounters with Jack Kerouac*. New York: Thunder's Mouth Press, 2005.

—— (3). *Kerouac: His Life and Work: Revised and Updated*. Foreword by David Amran. Lanham, MD: Taylor Trade Publishing, 2007.

—— (4). *Jack Kerouac's American Journey: The Real-Life Odyssey of* On the Road. Berkeley, CA: Thunder's Mouth Press, 2007.

Mahoney, Dennis, Richard L. Marin, and Ron Whitehead, eds. *A Burroughs Compendium: Calling the Toads*. New London, CN: Hozomeen Press, 1998.

Mariani, Paul. *William Carlos Williams: A New World Naked*. New York: McGraw-Hill, 1981.

Marqusse, Mike. *Chimes of Freedom: The Politics of Bob Dylan's Art*. New York: The New Press, 2003.

Maynard, Joe, and Barry Miles. *William S. Burroughs: A Bibliography, 1953–1973*. Charlottesville: University Press of Virginia Bibliographical Society, 1978.

McCarthy, Mary. *A Bolt from the Blue and Other Essays*. New York: New York Review of Books, 2002.

McClure, Michael (1). *Passage*. Big Sur, CA: Jonathan Williams, 1956.

——— (2). *Huge Dreams: San Francisco and Beat Poems*. New York: Penguin Books, 1999.

——— (3). *Scratching the Beat Surface: Essays on New Vision from Blake to Kerouac*. New York: Penguin Books, 1994.

——— (4). *Rebel Lions*. New York: New Directions, 1991.

McDarrah, Fred W. *Kerouac & Friends: A Beat Generation Album*. New York: William Morrow & Co., 1985.

McDarrah, Fred W., and Gloria S. McDarrah. *Beat Generation: Glory Days in Greenwich Village*. New York: Schirmer Books, 1996.

McNally, Dennis. *Desolate Angel: Jack Kerouac, the Beat Generation, and America*. New York: Random House, 1979. Rpt. New York: McGraw-Hill, 1980.

Meltzer, David, ed. *San Francisco Beat: Talking with the Poets*. San Francisco: City Lights Books, 2001.

Merrill, Thomas F. *Allen Ginsberg*. New York: Twayne Publishers, 1969.

Miles, Barry (1). *Ginsberg: A Biography*. New York: Simon & Schuster, 1989. Rpt. revised edition. London: Virgin Books, 2001.

——— (2). *The Beat Hotel: Ginsberg, Burroughs, and Corso in Paris, 1957–1963*. New York: Grove Press, 2000.

——— (3), ed. *The Beat Collection*. London: Virgin Books, 2005.

——— (4). *William Burroughs, El Hombre Invisible: A Portrait*. New York: Hyperion, 1993.

Milewski, Robert J. *Jack Kerouac: An Annotated Bibliography of Secondary Sources*. Metuchen, NJ: The Scarecrow Press, 1991.

Morgan, Bill (1). *I Celebrate Myself: The Somewhat Private Life of Allen Ginsberg*. New York: Viking Press, 2006.

——— (2). *The Beat Generation in New York: A Walking Tour of Jack Kerouac's City*. San Francisco: City Lights Books, 1997.

——— (3). *The Beat Generation in San Francisco: A Walking Tour of Jack Kerouac's City*. San Francisco: City Lights Books, 2003.

——— (4). *The Response to Allen Ginsberg, 1926–1994: A Bibliography of Secondary Sources*. Westport, CT: Greenwood Press, 1996.

——— (5). *Beat Atlas: A State by State Guide to the Beat Generation in America*. San Francisco: City Lights Books, 2011.

——— (6). *The Typewriter Is Holy: The Complete, Uncensored History of the*

Beat Generation. Counterpoint, 2011.

Morgan, Bill, and Nancy Peters, eds. *Howl on Trial: The Battle for Free Expression.* San Francisco: City Lights Books, 2006.

Morgan, Ted. *Literary Outlaw: The Life & Times of William S. Burroughs.* New York: Henry Holt, 1998.

Mottram, Eric. *William Burroughs: The Algebra of Need.* London: Marion Boyars, 1977.

Nicosia, Gerald. *Memory Babe: A Critical Biography of Jack Kerouac.* New York: Grove Press, 1983.

Nicosia, Gerald, and Anne Marie Santos. *One and Only: The Untold Story of On the Road.* Berkley, CA: Viva Editions, 2011.

Nieme, Robert. *The Ultimate, Illustrated Beats Chronology.* New York: Soft Skull Press, 2011.

Noble, John Wesley, and Bernard Averbuch. *Never Plead Guilty: The Story of Jake Ehrlich.* New York: Farrar, Straus & Cudahy, 1955.

Olson, Kirby. *Gregory Corso: Doubting Thomas.* Carbondale: Southern Illinois University Press, 2002.

Orlovsky, Peter. *Clean Asshole Poems and Smiling Vegetable Songs.* San Francisco: City Lights Books, 1978.

Osborne, Charles. *W.H. Auden: The Life of a Poet.* New York: M. Evans & Co., 1995.

Parker, Brad. *Jack Kerouac: An Introduction Printed for the Twentieth Anniversary of Kerouac's Death.* Lowell, MA: Lowell Corporation for the Humanities, 1989.

Parkinson, Thomas, ed. *A Casebook on the Beat.* New York: Thomas Y. Crowell, 1961.

Patchen, Kenneth. *Poems of Humor and Protest.* San Francisco: City Lights Books, 1955.

Paul, James C.N., and Murray L. Schwartz. *Federal Censorship: Obscenity in the Mail.* New York: The Free Press, 1961.

Perry, Paul, and Ken Babbs. *On the Bus: The Complete Guide to the Legendary Trip of Ken Kesey and the Merry Pranksters and the Birth of the Counterculture.* Edited by Michael Schwartz & Neil Ortenberg. New York: Thunder's Mouth Press, 1991.

Phillips, Lisa. *Beat Culture and the New America: 1950–1965.* New York: Whitney Museum of American Art in association with Flammarion, 1995.

Pivano, Fernanda. *Beat & Pieces: A Complete Story of the Beat Generation.* Photographs by Allen Ginsberg. Milan, Italy: Photology, 2005.

Pivano, Fernanda, and Massimo Vitali. *Kerouac in Milan, 1966: Photographs by Massimo Vitali*. St. Paul, MN: Five Ties Publishing, 2007.

Plimpton, George, ed. *Beat Writers at Work: The Paris Review*. New York: The Modern Library, 1999.

Plummer, William. *The Holy Goof: A Biography of Neal Cassady*. New York: Prentice Hall, 1981. Rpt. New York: Thunder's Mouth Press, 2004.

Raskin, Jonah. *American Scream: Allen Ginsberg's* Howl *and the Making of the Beat Generation*. Berkeley: University of California Press, 2004.

Reich, Charles. *The Greening of America*. New York: Random House, 1970.

Reynolds, David S. *Walt Whitman's America: A Cultural Biography*. New York: Knopf, 1995.

Sanders, Ed (1). *The Poetry and Life of Allen Ginsberg*. New York: Scribner, 2002.

——— (2). *The Tales of Beatnik Glory*. New York: Carol Publishing, 1990.

Sandison, David, and Graham Vikers. *Neal Cassady: The Fast Life of a Beat Hero*. Chicago: Chicago Review Press, 2006.

Schlesinger, Arthur M. *Robert Kennedy and His Times*. New York: Ballantine Books, 1978.

Schumacher, Michael. *Dharma Lion: A Critical Biography of Allen Ginsberg*. New York: St. Martin's Press, 1992.

Shinder, Jason, ed. *The Poem That Changed America: "Howl" Fifty Years Later*. New York: Farrar, Straus and Giroux, 2006.

Silesky, Barry. *Ferlinghetti: The Artist in His Time*. New York: Warner Books, 1990.

Skerl, Jennie. *William S. Burroughs*. Boston: Twayne Publishers, 1985.

Skerl, Jennie, and Robin Lydenberg, eds. *William S. Burroughs at the Front, Critical Reception, 1959–1989*. Carbondale, IL: Southern Illinois University Press, 1991.

Skir, Leo. *Elise Cowen: A Brief Memoir of the Fifties*. Evergreen Review, 1967.

Snyder, Gary. *The Gary Snyder Reader*. New York: Counterpoint, 2000.

Solomon, Carl (1). *Mishaps, Perhaps*. Edited by Mary Beach. San Francisco, CA: City Lights Books, 1966.

——— (2). *Emergency Messages: An Autobiographical Miscellany*. Edited and with a foreword by John Tytell. New York: Paragon House, 1989.

Sotheby's. *Allen Ginsberg and Friends, including property from the Estates of Allen Ginsberg, Jack Kerouac and William S. Burroughs*. October 7 1999. New York Auction Catalogue. Introductory Note by Peter Hale, foreword by Bill Morgan.

Saroyan, Aram. *Genesis Angles: The Saga of Lew Welch and the Beat Generation.* New York: William Morrow & Co., 1979.

Sounes, Howard. *Down the Highway: The Life of Bob Dylan.* New York: Grove Press, 2001.

Sova, Dawn B. *Banned Books: Literature Suppressed on Social Grounds.* New York: Facts On File, 1988.

Spitz, Bob. *Dylan: A Biography.* New York: W.W. Norton, 1989.

Stephenson, Gregory. *The Daybreak Boys: Essays on the Literature of the Beat Generation.* Foreword by Carolyn Cassady. Carbondale, IL: Southern Illinois University, 1990.

Stevens, Michale. *The Road to Interzone: Reading William S. Burroughs Reading.* Archer City, TX: Suicide Press, 2009.

Swartz, Omar. *The View From On the Road: The Rhetorical Vision of Jack Kerouac.* Carbondale, IL: Southern Illinois Press, 1999.

Theado, Matt, ed. (1). *The Beats: A Literary Reference.* New York: Carroll & Graf, 2001.

———— (2). *Understanding Jack Kerouac.* Columbia: University of South Carolina Press, 2000.

Thompson, Hunter S. *The Proud Highway: The Fear and Loathing Letters; Volume 1: Saga of a Desperate Southern Gentleman 1955–1967.* Douglas Brinkley, editor. New York: Ballentine Books, 1998.

Tonkinson, Carole, ed. *Big Sky Mind: Buddhism and the Beat Generation.* New York: Riverhead Books, 1995.

Trigilio, Tony. *Allen Ginsberg's Buddhist Poetics.* Carbondale, IL: Southern Illinois University Press, 2007.

Turner, Steve. *Jack Kerouac: Angelheaded Hipster.* New York: Viking, 1996.

Tytell, John (1). *Naked Angels: Kerouac, Ginsberg, Burroughs.* New York: Grove Press, 1976. Rpt. Chicago: Ivan R. Dee, 1991.

———— (2). *Paradise Outlaws: Remembering the Beats.* New York: William Morrow & Company, 1999.

Waldman, Anne, ed. *The Beat Book: Writings from the Beat Generation.* Foreword by Allen Ginsberg. Boston: Shambhala Publications, 2007.

Warner, Simon. *Text, Drugs, And Rock 'n' Roll: The Beats And Rock, from Kerouac to Cobain.* New York: Continuum International Publishing Group, 2007.

Watson, Steve. *The Birth of the Beat Generation: Visionaries, Rebels, and Hipsters, 1944–1960.* Afterword by Robert Creeley. New York: Pantheon Books, 1998.

Weinreich, Regina. *Kerouac's Spontaneous Poetics: A Study of the Fiction.* Berkeley, CA: Thunder's Mouth Press, 2002.

Welch, Lew (1). *I Remain: The Letters of Lew Welch and the Correspondence of His Friends.* Donald Allen, ed. San Francisco: Grey Fox, 1980.

———— (2). *Leo: An Unfinished Novel.* San Francisco: Grey Fox, 1977.

———— (3). *Ring of Bone: Collected Poems, 1950–1971.* San Francisco: Grey Fox, 1979.

Whitman, Walt. *Leaves of Grass.* Introduction by Justin Kaplan. New York: Bantam Classics, 2004.

Williamson, Nigel. *The Rough Guide of Bob Dylan.* London: Strand, London, 2004.

Wolfe, Tom. *The Electric Kool-Aid Acid Test.* New York: Farrar Straus & Giroux, 1968.

Worth, Richard. *Jack Kerouac: The Road Is Life.* Berkeley Heights, NJ: Enslow Publishers, 2006.

Zott, Lynn M. *The Beat Generation: A Critical Companion.* 3 vols., foreword by Anne Waldman. Detroit: Thompson/Gale, 2003.

Library Collections

Burroughs—Papers: Ohio State University.

Cassady—Papers: University of Texas, Austin.

Cowley—Papers: Newberry Library.

Ferlinghetti—Papers: University of California, Berkeley; University of Connecticut, Columbia University; Southern Methodist University; Washington University (St. Louis).

Ginsberg—Papers: Stanford University and University of North Carolina.

Holmes—Papers: Kent State University.

Huncke—Papers: Columbia University.

Kerouac—Papers: University of Massachusetts (Lowell) and New York Public Library.

T. Morgan—Papers: Arizona State University.

Orlovsky—Papers: University of Texas, Austin.

Legal Opinions and Related Documents

Alberts v. California, 354 U.S. 476 (1957).

Memoirs v. Massachusetts, 383 U.S. 413 (1966).

Roth v. United States, 354 U.S. 476 (1957).

Speiser v. Randall, 357 U.S. 513 (1958).

Torcaso v. Watkins, 367 U.S. 488 (1961).

Big Table v. Schroeder, 186 F. Supp. 254 (N.D. IL, 1960).

In the Matter of the Complaint that BIG TABLE Magazine is nonmailable under 18 U.S. Code 1461 (Post Office Department, Docket No. 1/150) (12 August 1959).

Attorney General v. A Book Named Naked Lunch, 351 Mass. 298 (1959).

Attorney General v. A Book Named Tropic of Cancer, 345 Mass. 11 (1958).

People v. Ferlinghetti, unpublished opinion, October 3, 1957. Printed in Ehrlich (1) (without citations).

Speiser v. Randall, 48 Cal. 2d 903, 311 P.2d 546 (Cal. 1958).

Attorney General Edward W. Brooke v. A Book Named Naked Lunch, Massachusetts Superior Court, docket # 83001, January 12–13, 1965 (trial transcript).

Scholarly Articles, Monographs, Dissertations, Reports, and Proceedings

Benas, Betram B. "The Holy Bible and the Law by J.W. Ehrlich." 26 *Modern Law Review* 6 (November, 1963), p. 731–733.

Caplan, Gerald M. "A Reasonable Doubt by Jacob W. Ehrlich." 73 *Yale Law Journal* 8 (July 1964), p. 1508–1512.

Charters, Ann. "The Beats, Literary Bohemians in Postwar America." In *Dictionary of Literary Biography*, vol. 16. Detroit: Gale, 1983.

Grauerholz, James. *The Death of Joan Vollmer: What Really Happened?* Unpublished essay prepared for the Fifth Congress of the Americas at Universidad de Las Americas / Puebla, October 18, 20001 (final manuscript dated January 7, 2002).

Hunt, Tim. *Off the Road: The Literary Maturation of Jack Kerouac.* Cornell University, PhD Thesis, 1975.

International Writers' Conference. Edinburgh International Festival, 20–24 August 1962.

Report of the Special Committee of the Student Government Organization in re: The Chicago Review, University of Chicago, 1959.

Sigler, S.A. "Customs Censorship." 15 *Cleveland Law Review* (January 1966), p. 63.

Select Magazine, Newspaper, & Internet Articles

"3 Named for Appeals Court." *Washington Post*, March 24, 1979, sect. C, p. 5

"300 Police Use Tear Gas to Breach Young Militant's Barricade in Chicago." *New York Times*, 27 August 1968, p. 29.

"A Howl of Protest in San Francisco." *New Republic*, 16 September 1957, p. 26.

"A Muse Unplugged." *New York Times*, 8 October 2007, sec. A, p. 22.

Adams, Frank S. "Columbia Student Kills Friend and Sinks Body in Hudson River." *New York Times*, 17 August 1944, p. 1.

Anspacher, Carolyn. "'Battle of Books is on: 'Howl' Trial Starts Big Crowd." *San Francisco Chronicle*, 17 August 1957, p. 1.

———. "'Obscene' Book Trial: Dismissal for 'Howl' Clerk Indicated." *San Francisco Chronicle*, 23 August 1957, p. 4.

Aaron, David. Book Review. *Commonweal*, 5 May 1967 (reviewing Holmes' *Nothing More to Declare*).

Aronowitz, Alfred G. "The Beat Generation." *New York Post*. 1 March 1959–21 March 1959 (12-part series).

———. "Pop Scene." *New York Post*. 15 August 1972, p. 36 (review of *Kaddish*).

———. "The Yen for Zen." *Escapade Magazine*. October, 1960, p. 50.

Baker, Carlos. "Itching Feet." *Saturday Review*, 7 September 1957, p. 19

Barber, David. "The Legend of 'Howl'." *Boston Globe*, 30 April 2006, sec. E, p. 2.

"Bay City Teacher Fired in Red Case." *Los Angeles Times*, 10 December 1953, p. 22.

Bess, Donovan. "Poetic Justice: Court Rules on Biblical Essays—1 Wins, 1 Loses." *San Francisco Chronicle*, 7 August 1957, p. 1.

"Big Day for Bards at Bay: San Francisco Muse Thrives in Face of Trial over Poems." *Life*, 9 September 1957, p. 105.

Blumenthal, Michael. "Allen Ginsberg: Millionaire?" 29 October 1994, at http://www.nytimes. com/books/01/04/08/specials/ginsberg-millionaire. html.

"Bookmen Ask Mayor to Ban Cop Censors." *San Francisco Chronicle*, 16 August 1957, p. 1.

Brame, Gloria G. "An Interview with Poet Allen Ginsberg." *Eclectic Literary Forum*, Summer, 1996.

Brinkley, Douglas. "In the Kerouac Archive." *Atlantic Monthly*, November 1998, p. 49–76.

Bruckner, D. J. R. "Chicago Police Use Tear Gas to Rout Thousands." *Los Angeles Times*, 28 August 1968, p. 1.

Burroughs, William. S. "Censorship." *Transatlantic Review*, 11: Winter 1962, p. 5.

———. "Final Words." *New Yorker*. 18 August 1997, p. 109.

———. "Kerouac." *High Times*. March, 1979, p. 52.

"Buyers Howl for Ginsberg Poetry and Other Stuff He Loved." *Star-Ledger* (Newark, NJ), 8 October 1999, p. 35.

Carvajal, Doreen. "A New Generation Chases the Spirit of the Beats." *New York Times*, 11 December 1997.

Ciardi, John. "The Book Burners and Sweet Sixteen." *Saturday Review*, 27 July 1959, p. 22.

———. "Writers as Readers of Poetry." *Saturday Review*, 23 November 1957, p. 33.

Clarke, Roger. "Missing the Beat." *Evening Standard* (London), 6 October 1999, p. 31.

Clarke, Terence. "'Howl,' Your Morals, and the FCC." *Blogcritics Culture*, 6 October 2007, at http://blogcritics.org/archives/2007/10/06/111547.php.

"Coast Loyalty Test for Tax Aid is Upset." *New York Times*, 11 February 1955, p. 24

Coe, Robert. "Kerouac Roles Only Half-Beat." *Washington Post*, 15 September 1960, sec. B, p. 14.

Cohen, Noam S. "Lawrence Speiser, 68, a Civil Liberties Lawyer," *New York Times*, September 12, 1991, p. 38

Collier, Peter. "Lawrence Ferlinghetti: Doing His Own Thing." *New York Times Book Review*, 21 July 1968, p. 4.

"Columbia Grad, Girl, Seized in Theft Ring." *Brooklyn Eagle*, 22 April 1949.

Coolidge, Clark. "Jack." *Village Voice Literary Supplement*, April 1995, p. 1.

"Cops Don't Allow No Renaissance Here." *San Francisco News*, 4 August 1957, p. 17.

"Court Rules on Biblical Essays—1 Wins, 1 Loses." *San Francisco Chronicle*, 7 August 1957, p. 1.

"Creative Writing in Horn's Court." *San Francisco Chronicle*, 8 August 1957, p. 20.

Dickey, James. "From Babel to Byzantium." *Sewanee Review*, 65: July–September 1957, p. 510.

Douglas, Ann. "On the Road Again." *New York Times Book Review*, 9 April 9, 1995, p. 1.

Dreisinger, Baz. "'Howl,' Ginsberg's Time Bomb, Still Setting Off New Explosions." *New York Observer*, 10 April 2006.

Eberhart, Richard. "West Coast Rhythms." *New York Times Book Review*, 2 September 1956.

Eckman, Frederick. "Neither Tame nor Fleecy." *Poetry*, September 1957, p. 387.

Ellison, Michael. "The Beat Goes on at Ginsberg Auction." *Guardian* (London), 8 October 1999, p. 19.

"End of the Road." *Time*, 31 October 1969, p. 10.

"FCC Sends Kansas City Station Letter on Indecency." *Television Digest Communications Daily*, 13 January 1988, p. 1.

Ferlinghetti, Lawrence. "Horn on 'Howl'." *Evergreen Review* 2: 1957, p. 145.

Fink, John. "Who Is Jack Kerouac?" *Chicago Tribune*, 28 September 1968, p. 13.

Fletcher, Martin. "Smut or Art? Barred Magazine, P.O. Tangle at Hearing." *New York Post*, 24 June 1959, p. 6.

Fuller, John G. "Trade Winds." *Saturday Review of Literature*, 5 October 1957.

Gallix, Andrew. "Cutting-Edge Literary News from Around the Global Village." 3 *A.M. Magazine*, May 2001, at www.3ammagazine.com/ buzzwords/may 2001_buzzwords.html.

Joe Garofoli, "'Howl' Too Hot to Hear: 50 Years after Poem Ruled Not Obscene, Radio Fears to Air It." *San Francisco Chronicle*, 3 October 2007.

Gates, David. "Breaking up with the Beats." *Salon.com*, 12 April 1999, at www. salon.com/ books/feature/1999/04/12/beats/.

Ginsberg, Allen. "Herbert Huncke: The Hipster's Hipster." *New York Times*, 29 December 1996.

———. "Review of *The Dharma Bums*." *Village Voice*, 12 November 1958, p. 3

"Ginsberg Enters Hall After Startling Police." *New York Times*, 29 August 1968, p. 23.

"Ginsberg's Belongings Auctioned Off at Sotheby's: Poet's Lover, Nephews, Nieces Likely to Get Money." *Globe and Mail* (Toronto, Canada), 8 October 1999, sec. A, p. 19.

Girodias, Maurice. "Confessions of a Booklegger's Son." *Censorship* 3:1965, p. 10.

Gold, Ed. "Trying to Get a Bead on the 'Beats' Mysterious Muse." *Villager*, March 30—April 5, 2005.

Gold, Herbert. "Hip, Cool, and Frantic." *Nation*, 16 November 1957, p. 349.

———. "Instead of Love, the Fix." *New York Times Book Review*, 25 November 1962, p. 4.

———. "Squaring off the Corners." *Saturday Review*, 22 September 1962, p. 29.

———. "The Beat Mystique." *Playboy*, February 1958, p. 20.

Grandsden, R.W. "Adolescence and Maturity." *Encounter*, August 1958, p. 84.

Gross, John. "Disorganization Man." *New Statesman*, 8 February 1963, p. 202.

Gussow, Adam. "Bohemia Revisted: Malcolm Cowley, Jack Kerouac, and *On the Road.*" *Georgia Review*, 38: Summer 1984, p. 298.

Hall, Donald. "Robert Giroux: Looking for Masterpieces." *New York Times Book Review*, 6 January 1980, p. 22.

Hall, Molly. "In the Spirit of Kerouac; School Is Born from the Beat Generation." *Chicago Tribune*, 4 August 1994, p. 8.

Hampton, Wilborn. "Lucien Carr, a Founder and a Muse of the Beat Generation, Dies at 79." *New York Times*, 30 January 2005, p. 35.

———. "Allen Ginsberg, Master Poet of Beat Generation, Dies at 70." *New York Times*, 6 April 1997.

Henry III, William A. "In New York, *Howl* Becomes a Hoot." *New York Times*, 7 December 1981, p. 8.

Hishmeh, Richard E. "Marketing Genius: The Friendship of Allen Ginsberg and Bob Dylan." *Journal of American Culture*, 29: December 2006, p. 395.

Hogan, William. "Between the Lines." *San Francisco Chronicle*, 19 May 1957, p. 34.

Hollander, John. "Poetry Chronicle." *Partisan Review*, 24: Spring 1957, p. 298.

Holmes, John Clellon. "This Is the Beat Generation," *New York Times Magazine*, 16 November 1952, p. 10.

———. "The Philosophy of the Beat Generation." *Esquire*, February 1958, p. 35.

"'Howl' Decision Landmark of Law." *San Francisco Chronicle*, 7 October 1957, p. 18.

Hunt, Tim. "Interview with John Clellon Holmes." *Quarterly West*, Winter 1978, p. 50–58.

Keller, Mitch. "When 'On the Road' Was 'On the Subway.'" *New York Times*, 14 September 2007.

Kerouac, Jack. "After Me, the Deluge." *Chicago Tribune*, 28 September 1969, p. 120.

Kirsch, Robert R. "The Beats Are Back, Man." *Los Angeles Times*, 29 April 1960, sec. B, p. 3.

Knickerbocker, Conrad. "William Burroughs: An Interview." *Paris Review*, 35: 1965, p. 13.

"Ilo Orleans, A Poet and Lawyer, Was 65." *New York Times*, 27 September 1962, p. 37.

"Irwin Allen Ginsberg." The Knitting Circle: Poetry, at www.knittingcircle. org.uk/ allenginsberg. html.

"Jack Kerouac's Typescript Scroll of *On the Road.*" Christie's New York, 22 May 2001.

"Jake Ehrlich, Criminal Lawyer Who Won Murder Cases, Dies." *New York Times*, 25 December 1971, p. 20.

Johnson, Joyce. "Reality Sandwiches." *American Book Review*, 18: August–September 1997, p. 13.

"Kammerer's Parents Prominent." *New York Times*, 17 August 1944, p. 13.

Kirsch, Robert. "Insight into Mexican Culture." *Los Angeles Times*, 3 April 1959, sec. B, p. 5.

King, Lydia Hailman. "'Howl' Obscenity Prosecution Still Echoes 50 Years Later." First Amendment Center, at http://www.firstamendmentcenter. org/news.aspx?id=19132.

Lask, Thomas. "Books of the Times: Road to Nowhere." *New York Times*, 17 February 1968, p. 27.

Latham, Aaron. "The Lives They Lived: Allen Ginsberg; Birth of a Beatnik." *New York Times*, 4 January 1998.

———. "The Columbia Murder that Gave Birth to the Beats." *New York Magazine*, 19 April 1976, p. 41.

Lauderman, Connie. "The Broad Reach of the Beats: Generations Later, the Literary Rebels Still Have a Cause." *Chicago Tribune*, 24 October 1999, sec. C, p. 5.

Leonard, William. "In Chicago, We're Mostly Unbeat." *Chicago Daily Tribune*, 9 November 1958, sec. G, p. 8

Lewin, Tamar. "Herbert Wechsler, Legal Giant, Is Dead at 90." *New York Times*, 28 April 2000.

Lingerman, Richard R. "Charting the Course." *New York Times Book Review*, 9 April 1967, p. 42–43.

Lippman, Laura. "Ginsberg 'Howls' Again as Lawyers Battle FCC Ruling." *Baltimore Sun*, 20 October 1994.

"Lucien Carr." *The Telegraph*, 2 January 2005.

Lukas, J. Anthony. "Allen Ginsberg Meets a Judge and Is Clearly Misunderstood." *New York Times*, 12 December 1969.

———. "Police Battle Demonstrators in Streets." *New York Times*, 29 August 1968, p. 1.

Lurvey, Ira. "Beatniks Fight for Banned Verse." *Daily Defender*, 28 January 1959, sec. A, p. 4.

Lyon, Herb. "Tower Ticker." *Chicago Daily Tribune*, 30 January 1959, sec. A, p. 2.

Mabley, Jack. "Filthy Writing on the Midway." *Chicago Daily News*, 25 October 1959, p. 1.

Mailer, Norman. "The Faith of Graffiti." *Esquire*, May 1974, p. 77.

"Making a Clown of San Francisco." *San Francisco Chronicle*, 6 June 1957, p. 22.

Malcolm, Donald. "The Heroin of Our Times." *The New Yorker*, 2 February 1963, p. 114.

Marcus, Griel. "Classic Beat." *New York Times Book Review*, 9 April 2006, p. 24.

Margolick, David. "An Unlikely Home for Ginsberg's Archive." *New York Times*, 20 September 1994, sect. C, p. 15.

McCarthy, Mary. "Burroughs' *Naked Lunch*." *Encounter*, April 1963, p. 92.

McGowen, Richard. "Smut Dealers: How Far Can They Go?" *New York Daily News*, 20 March 1959, p. 36.

McLuhan, Marshall. "Notes on Burroughs." *Nation*. 28 December 1964, p. 517.

McCoy, Mike. "Ellis Amburn: Editing the Final Words." *Moody Street Irregulars*, 9: Winter/Spring 1981, p. 10.

McDougal, Dennis. "FCC Firm on Decency Code; 'Howl' Muffled." *Los Angeles Times*, 8 January 1988, pt. 6, p. 1.

———. "Obscenity Issue Still Unresolved." *Los Angeles Times*, 4 January 1988, pt. 6, p. 1.

McQuiston, John T. "John Clellon Holmes, 62, Novelist and Poet of the Beat Generation." *New York Times*, 31 March 1988, sec. B, p. 11.

Louis Menand. "Drive, He Wrote." *The New Yorker*, 1 October 2007, p. 88.

Millstein, Gilbert. "Books of the Times." *New York Times,* 5 September 1957, p. 27.

———. "The 'Kick' that Failed." *New York Times*, 9 November 1952, p. 50.

———. "In Each a Self-Portrait." *New York Times Book Review*, 17 January 1960, p. 7.

Moon, Eric. "Review of *Naked Lunch*." *Literary Journal*, 1 December 1962, p. 4454.

Moore, Dave. "*On the Road*—The Scroll Revealed." *Kerouac Connection*, April 1986, p. 3–8.

——— . "Jack Kerouac Book Covers," at http://mysite.orange.co.uk/jkbooks /index.html (extensive collection, foreign covers included).

"New Test for Obscenity." *Nation*, 9 November 1957, p. 314.

Oates, Joyce Carol. "Down the Road." *New Yorker*, 27 March 1995, p. 96.

Older, Julia. "Poetry's Eternal Graffiti: Late-Night Conversations with Lawrence Ferlinghetti." *Poet's & Writers*, March–April, 2007, p. 38–46

O'Neill, Paul. "The Only Rebellion Around." *Life,* 47: 30 November 1959, p. 115.

Onishi, Norimitsu. "Free Spirits Flock to Park to Hear Ginsberg Poetry." *New York Times,* 29 September 1997.

Pace, Eric. "Gilbert Millstein, 83, Reviewer Who Gave Early Boost to Kerouac." *New York Times,* 11 May 1999, sect. B, p. 10.

Paton, Fiona. "Banned Beats." September 28, 2006, at http://lib.newpaltz.edu/events/ bannedbooks.html.

Patterson, Robert. "'Jake'—One of Famed Line of Men Who Symbolized SF." *San Francisco Examiner,* 24 December 1971.

Perlman, David. "'Howl' Not Obscene, Judge Rules." *San Francisco Chronicle,* 4 October 1957, p. 1.

———. "How Captain Hanrahan Made 'Howl' a Best-Seller." *Reporter,* 12 December, 1957, p. 37–39.

Perry, Tony. "The Beats are Cool—and Hot." *Los Angeles Times,* 2 August 1994, sec. A, p. 1.

Podell, Albert N. "Censorship on the Campus: The Case of the *Chicago Review.*" *San Francisco Review* 1: 2 (1959), p. 73.

Podhoretz, Norman. "A Howl of Protest in San Francisco." *New Republic,* 16 September 1957, p. 26.

———. "The Know-Nothing Bohemians." *Parisian Review,* Spring 1958, p. 305.

"Post Office Morals." *The Nation,* 30 May 1959, p. 486.

Raskin, Jonah. "Still Howling after 50 Years." *Columbia Spectator,* 21 April 2006.

"References in *On the Road.*" *Wikipedia* (with travelogue & character key), at http:// en.wikipedia.org/wiki/ References_in_On_the_Road.

Rexroth, Kenneth (1). "San Francisco's Mature Bohemians." *Nation,* 23 February 1957, p. 159.

——— (2). "It's an Anywhere Road for Anybody Anyhow." *San Francisco Chronicle,* 1 September 1957, p. 18.

——— (3). "The Voice of the Beat Generation Has Some Square Delusions." *San Francisco Chronicle* (This World Magazine), 16 February 1958, p. 23.

——— (4). "Discordant and Cool." *New York Times Book Review.* 29 November 1959, p.14.

——— (5). "San Francisco Letter." *Evergreen Review.* Summer, 1957.

Rodriquez, Suzanne. "And the Beat Goes On…" *Oregonian,* 23 April 2006.

Rosenbloom, Ron. "Interview with Bob Dylan." *Playboy,* March 1978.

Rosenthal, M.L. "Poet of the New Violence." *Nation*, 23 February 1957, p. 162.

Rothschild, Matthew. "Allen Ginsberg: 'I'm Banned from the Main Marketplace of Ideas in My Own Country.'" *Progressive*, August 1994.

Rumaker, Michael. "Allen Ginsberg's *Howl*." *Black Mountain Review* 7: Fall 1957.

Russell, Jenna. "Kerouac's 'Road' Will Be Unrolled: Original Scroll Set for Publication." *The Boston Globe*, 27 July 2006, at http://www.boston.com/news/local/articles/2006/ 07/27/ kerouacs_road_will_be_unrolled/.

Sante, Luc. "On the Road Again." *New York Times Book Review*, 19 August 2007, p. 1.

Scheuer, Philip K. "Sensitive Film Tale Views Gropings of Beatniks." *Los Angeles Times*, 31 July 1960, sec. F, p. 1.

"Shavians Meet the Beatniks." 2 *Shaw Society Newsletter* 1 (February, 1959).

Shattuck, Kathryn. "For Burroughs at 82, A Legion of Fans under the Influence." *New York Times*, 26 November 1996, sec. C, p. 11.

———. "Kerouac's 'Road' Scroll is Going to Auction." *New York Times*, 22 March 2001, sec. E, p. 1.

———. "Sotheby's to Auction Ginsbergiana." *New York Times*, 7 October 1999, sec. E, p. 3.

Shannon, Don. "High Court Strikes Out State Tax Loyalty Oath; 7–1 Decision Upholds Religious Groups and Veterans in Their Refusal to Comply." *Los Angeles Times*, 1 July 1958, p. 1.

"Simon Carr." *New York Times* Magazine, 5 November 1995, p. 39.

Skenazy, Lenore. "Catchy Beats a Hit with New Group of Rebels." *Advertising Age*, 22 February 1988, p. 45.

Skerl, Jennie. "Ginsberg on Burroughs: An Interview." *Modern Language Studies*, 16: Summer 1986, p. 271.

Smith, Dinitia. "Chanting in Homage to Allen Ginsberg." *New York Times*, 16 May 1998.

———. "How Allen Ginsberg Thinks His Thoughts." *New York Times*, 8 October 1996.

———. "Scholars and Survivors Tatter Kerouac's Self-Portrait: Pursuing the Beat from Courtrooms to Chat Rooms." *New York Times*, 9 July 1998, sec. E, p. 1.

Smith, J.Y. "Lawrence Speiser Dies: Championed Civil Rights." *Washington Post*, 31 August 1991.

Suiter, John. "When the Beats Came Back." *Reed Magazine*, Winter 2008, p. 20.

Stinson, Charles. "*The Subterraneans'* Pretentious Charade." *Los Angeles Times*, 2 September 1960, p. 27.

"Student Is Indicted in 2d-Degree Murder." *New York Times*, 25 August 1944, p. 15.

"Student Is Silent on Slaying Friend." *New York Times*, 18 August 1944, p. 14.

"Student Slayer Sent to the Reformatory." *New York Times*, 7 October 1944, p. 15.

"Ten San Francisco Poets." *Chicago Review*, Spring 1958.

"The Neal Cassady Issue." *Spit in the Ocean* 6: 1981.

"They'll 'Howl' over Ginsberg Sale." *New York Post*, 5 October 1999, p. 9.

Thomas Jr., Robert M. "Herbert Huncke, the Hipster Who Defined 'Beat,' Dies at 81." *New York Times*, 9 August 1996, sec. B, p. 7.

"Thou Shalt Not Miss." *San Francisco Chronicle*, 8 August 1957, p. 20 (political cartoon).

Trott, William C. "Poet Howls about Censorship." United Press International, 7 January 1988.

Ulin, David L. "Song of Himself." *Los Angeles Times*, 9 April 2006, p. 2.

Usborne, David. "Sotheby's Sells Off Allen Ginsberg Estate." *Hamilton Spectator* (Ontario, Canada), 8 October 1999, sec. F, p. 11.

"'Use all the power of your office.' Bookmen Ask Mayor to Cop Censors." *San Francisco Chronicle.* 16 August 1957.

"U.S. Court to Rule on State Loyalty Oath." *Los Angeles Times*, 26 November 1957, p. 14.

"U.S. Gives Up Postal Fight on Magazine." *Chicago Daily Tribune*, 12 August 1960, p. 7.

Wain, John. "The Great Burroughs Affair." *New Republic*, 1 December 1962, p. 21.

Weiland, Matt. "You Don't Know Jack." *New York Times Book Review*, 19 August 2007, p. 13.

Weiler, A.H. "Screen: *Subterraneans*—Kerouac's World of the Beatniks on View." *New York Times* movie review, 7 July 1960, p. 26 (accessed August 20, 2012, from: http://movies.nytimes.com/movie/112144/The-Subterraneans/overview).

Weinrich, Regina. "Road Trips." *Washington Post Book World*, 2 September 2007, p. 8.

Well, Martin. "Jake Ehrlich, Criminal Lawyer, Dies." *Washington Post*, 25 December 1971.

Will, George W. "Along Via Ferlinghetti, the Beat Goes On." *Washington*

Post, 14 June 2002, sect. A, p. 31.

"William Tell Shot Denied: Husband Insists Slaying of Wife Was Accident." *Los Angeles Times*, 8 September 1951, p. 5.

Williamson, Eric Miles. "He Saw the Best Minds of His Generation." *Washington Post Book World*, 16 April 2006, p. 4.

Wordsworth, William. "Ode: Limitations of Immorality from recollections of Early Childhood." In M.H. Abrams, ed. *Norton Anthology of English Literature*. New York: W.W. Norton, 2003, p. 210.

"Wrong-Way Auto Tips Off Police to Narcotics-Ruled Burglary Gang." *New York World-Tribune*, 23 April 1949.

"Wrong-Way Turn Clears Up Robbery." *New York Times*, 3 April 1949.

Yarrow, Andrew L. "Allen Ginsberg's 'Howl' in a New Controversy." *New York Times*, 6 January 1988, sec. C, p. 22.

"Young Slayer Goes to Elmira." *New York Times*, 10 October 1944, p. 38.

Interviews

Al Bendich Interview. Berkeley, CA: Fantasy Studios. 27 August 2001.

Lawrence Ferlinghetti Interview. San Francisco: City Lights Bookstore. 27 July 2001.

Records, CDs, Films, and DVD Documentaries

Allen Ginsberg Audio Collection, The. Caedmon, HarperCollins, 2006.

Aronson, Jerry. *The Life and Times of Allen Ginsberg*. New York: New York Video, 2006.

Beat Generation, The. Santa Monica, CA: Rhino Records, 1992 (CD).

Best of William Burroughs from Giorno Poetry Systems, The. New York: Mercury, 1998 (4 CD box).

Burroughs, William. *Call Me Burroughs*. Santa Monica, CA: Rhino /World beat, 1995.

Burroughs, William & Kurt Cobain. *The 'Priest' They Called Him*. Portland. OR: Tim Kerr Records, 1993.

Don't Look Back. D.A. Pennebaker, producer. Ashes and Sand, 1967 (now in DVD).

Dylan, Bob. *Bringing It All Back Home*. New York: Columbia Records, 1965.

Frank, Robert & Alfred Leslie. *Pull My Daisy*. New York: G-String Enterprises, 1959.

Ginsberg, Allen. *Holy Soul Jelly Roll: Poems and Songs, 1949–1993*. Los Angeles: Rhino, 1994.

Howls, Raps & Roars: Recordings from the San Francisco Poetry Renaissance. Berkeley, CA: Fantasy Studios, 1993 (CD).

Kerouac, Jack. *The Jack Kerouac Collection.* Santa Monica, CA: Rhino/World Beat, 1993.

Kill Your Darlings. Directed by John Krokidas and produced by Benaroya Pictures, 2013.

Life and Times of Allen Ginsberg, The: A Film by Jerry Aronson. New York: New Yorker Video, 2007 (DVD).

On the Road. Directed by Walter Salles and executive produced by Francis Ford Coppola, 2012.

On the Road with Jack Kerouac: King of the Beats. Active Home Video, 1990 (VHS).

Source, The. Written, directed, and produced by Chuck Workman. New York: Fox Lorber, 2000 (VHS).

What Happened to Kerouac? New York: Shout! 1986 (DVD).

Index

Photo Credits

Photographs appearing at the beginning of the prologue and parts I, II, and III are copyright © Allen Ginsberg LLC, and are used with permission of the Wylie Agency LLC.

Photographs appearing at the beginning of part IV and the epilogue are courtesy of Corbis Images.

About the Authors

RON COLLINS and **DAVID SKOVER** are friends.

Ron lives in the East, David in the West.

They have been writing together for almost three decades. Their work is a joint effort, with David manning the keys and Ron pacing.

This is their third book together, *The Death of Discourse* (1996, 2nd ed. 2005) being the first and *The Trials of Lenny Bruce* (2002, enhanced ebook ed. 2012) following it. (In 2003 they successfully petitioned the governor of New York to posthumously pardon Lenny Bruce.) *Mania* is the latest installment in their continued work on popular culture and free speech. Their next book, *On Dissent*, will be published by Cambridge University Press in 2013.

Ron, who grew up in Southern California, is the Harold S. Shefelman Scholar at the University of Washington Law School. David, who grew up in Wisconsin, is the Fredric C. Tausend Professor of Constitutional Law at Seattle University.

Both are law graduates. Ron went to law school at Loyola in Los Angeles, David at Yale in New Haven.

Both clerked for appellate judges—Ron for Justice Hans A. Linde of the Oregon Supreme Court (and later as a judicial fellow in the United States Supreme Court), and David for Judge Jon O. Newman of the United States Court of Appeals for the Second Circuit.

In a prior life, David sang in professional operatic and musical theater productions. He admires the music of Stephen Sondheim. He often performs in theaters and at cabarets in Seattle.

Ron likes to probe Plato, Camus, Wittgenstein, and Simone Weil. He admires the thought of Louis Brandeis and is intrigued by the life and writings of Oliver Wendell Holmes Jr. By a different measure, he is charmed by the fiction of Patricia Highsmith and T.C. Boyle and has begun to craft his own brand of fiction.

Both have written numerous scholarly articles (often together) in journals such as the *Harvard* and *Stanford Law Reviews* and in the *Supreme Court Review.*

Ron has penned some 150 or so newspaper op-ed pieces, coauthored *We Must Not be Afraid to Be Free* (2011) (with Sam Chaltain) and edited *The Fundamental Holmes* (2010), *The Death of Contract* (1995), and *Constitutional Government in America* (1981). In 2010 Ron was selected as a Norman Mailer fellow in fiction writing. His next book is *Nuanced Absolutism: Floyd Abrams and the First Amendment* (2013). David coauthored (with Pierre Schlag) *Tactics of Legal Reasoning* (1986).

A Note on the Type

The text of this book was set in Garvis, a typeface designed by James Todd in 2012. Inspired by early twentieth-century neoclassical forms and Dutch Fleischmann Type, Garvis succeeds in bringing the character of those typefaces into modern times by increasing the sturdyness of the forms without losing their character. Displaying subtle irregularities commonly found in traditional metal type, Garvis conveys a warm, human quality while maintaining an orderly solidity.

Printed & bound by RR Donnelley in Harrisonburg, Virginia